THE RHETORIC OF ROMANTIC PROPHECY

Cultural Memory

in

the

Present

Mieke Bal and Hent de Vries, Editors

THE RHETORIC OF
ROMANTIC PROPHECY

Ian Balfour

STANFORD UNIVERSITY PRESS

STANFORD, CALIFORNIA

2002

Stanford University Press
Stanford, California

Printed in the United States of America
on acid-free, archival-quality paper.

Library of Congress Cataloging-in-Publication Data

Balfour, Ian.
   The rhetoric of Romantic prophecy / Ian Balfour.
      p.   cm. — (Cultural memory in the present)
   Includes bibliographical references and index.
   ISBN 0-8047-4231-6 (alk. paper) — ISBN 0-8047-4506-4 (pbk. : alk. paper)
   1. English poetry—19th century—History and criticism.   2. Prophecy
in literature.   3. Blake, William, 1757–1827—Views on prophecy.
4. Literature, Comparative—English and German.   5. Literature,
Comparative—German and English.   6. German literature—History
and criticism.   7. Romanticism—Great Britain.   8. Prophecies
in literature.   9. Romanticisim—Germany.   10. Prophets in literature.
I. Title.   II. Series.
PR585.P77 B35   2002
821'.70938—dc21   2002070690

Original Printing 2002
Last figure below indicates year of this printing:
11   10   09   08   07   06   05   04   03   02

Typeset by Heather Boone in 11/13.5 Garamond

0013009504

To my brother and my sister

Acknowledgments

This book has been an unduly long time in the making, the only good excuse being that I responded to a request to write a monograph on Northrop Frye while the first version of this book was taking shape. It has become, in the meantime, something of a companion piece to a book on the sublime now close to completion. I am very grateful to my teachers in graduate school at Toronto and at Yale: the late Northrop Frye and the late Paul de Man, Jacques Derrida, the late Hans Frei, Cyrus Hamlin, Geoffrey Hartman, and J. Hillis Miller. Harold Bloom and Leslie Brisman provided helpful criticisms of the first version of this work. Deborah Esch provided much intellectual and other support for me and this book, all beyond the call. The Coleridge chapter especially was helped by Julie Carlson's keen eye for argument and the whole thing benefited from her judgment.

A year spent in the company of the excellent Romanticists at Cornell, Cynthia Chase, Mary Jacobus, and Reeve Parker, helped enormously and the accidental presence of Jerome Christensen was a sheer bonus. Jonathan Culler, as Director of the Society for the Humanities, was the perfect intellectual host.

For the reading of a chapter or more typically for intellectual and other sorts of camaraderie that inflected this book, directly or indirectly, I thank Stephen Barber, David Bromwich, Catherine Bush, Eduardo Cadava, Cathy Caruth, Tess Chakkalakal, David Clark, Sarah Clift, Rebecca Comay, Patricia Dailey, Phil Derrington, Paul Downes, Debra Dudek, Susan Ehrlich, Grant Farred, Len Findlay, Peter Fitting, Denise Fulbrook, David Galbraith, Terry Goldie, Len Guenther, Werner Hamacher, David Hensley, Tom Keenan, John Knechtel, June Larkin, Kimberly Latta, Lily Lee, Tom Levin, Ulrike Löbs, Charles Mahoney, Clare Morgan, Heather Murray, Danny O'Quinn, Patricia Parker, Andy Payne, Constance Penley, Jason

Potts, Tres Pyle, Marc Redfield, Jill Robbins, Andrew Ross, Amresh Sinha, Joan Steigerwald, John Sweeney, Karen Valihora, and Heather Wright. And for company and bright ideas in the penultimate phase I thank Chris Pye, Anita Sokolsky, Karen Swann, Steve Tifft and John Limon.

York University provided a conducive environment for most of this work and I am grateful to my colleagues in the English Department and in Social and Political Thought, especially Maurice Elliot during his stint as the enlightened despot of the English department, and Kim Michasiw for considerations in lightening my load.

I also want to thank almost all my students at York, Cornell, Stanford, SUNY Buffalo, UC Santa Barbara, and Williams for their intelligence and unpredictability, and for their part in provoking my reading and thinking.

To my editor, Helen Tartar, I am grateful for much help and encouragement over the years and for the patience of a saint. Thanks also to Tim Roberts and Stacey Sawyer for expert help with the manuscript.

The Social Sciences and Humanities Research Council of Canada provided much timely and generous support, as did, at an early stage, the Charlotte Newcombe Foundation.

My thanks go as well to the staffs of the many libraries who provided venues for and assisted my research at Yale, Cornell, Princeton, Stanford, York, and the University of Toronto. Thanks particularly to the libraries at the Princeton Theological Seminary, the Huntington, Yale Divinity School, the New York Public Library, the library at Marbach (especially the Hölderlin Archives), the Union Theological Seminary, and the extremely helpful staff of the Staatsbibliothek in Berlin.

Finally, a huge debt of gratitude is owed to my family for encouragement, patience, and for more than once bailing me out financially in timely fashion.

Contents

Prefatory Note

A kind of précis of materials from Chapters 2, 3, 4 and 6 was published as "The Future of Citation: Blake, Wordsworth, and the Rhetoric of Romantic Prophecy" in *Writing the Future*, ed. David Wood (London: Routledge, 1990), 115–128. Some pages of the analysis of Benjamin are derived from my essay "Reversal, Quotation (Benjamin's History)," *MLN* 106 (1991) 622–47.

Chapter 7 on Hölderlin features a long excursus in mid-chapter, which can be read either there or separately as a kind of appendix or after the section on Herder and Eichhorn. It is conceived in good measure for the illumination of Hölderlin's poetry and thinking and so is placed there, in the middle of things.

Readers wishing to view or download a separate bibliography for this book can do so at: http://www.yorku.ca/ibalfour/bibliographies/prophecy.htm.

THE RHETORIC OF ROMANTIC PROPHECY

1

Introduction: The Call of Prophecy and the Future (After Benjamin)

> . . . if the prophetic word is bound up in history's fracas and the violence
> of its movement, if it makes of the prophet a historical character burdened
> with heavy temporal weight, it seems nonetheless tied essentially to a
> momentary interruption of history, to a history having become for a
> moment the impossibility of history, empty, where the catastrophe
> hesitates to reverse into salvation, or in the fall already beginning to
> rise again or return.
>
> —Maurice Blanchot

The objects of a study of the rhetoric of Romantic prophecy are as elusive as they are diverse. William Blake could call two of his early poems "prophecies," and many of his later, longer works are commonly referred to as "Prophetic Writings." Yet there is hardly such a thing as prophecy in the sense of a clearly codified genre with definite contours—neither in Blake nor in European Romanticism generally. It is usually more appropriate to speak of "the prophetic" than of prophecy, if the latter is a genre and the former a mode that can intersect with any number of genres from the ode to the epic, in either poetry or prose. There are even instances of drama that are as recognizably "prophetic" as anything else.[1] If one is on safer ground in shifting from prophecy to the prophetic, the latter forms an abyss of its own. The modalities of the prophetic are complex and varied: All are beset by claims of divine inspiration whose face value is impossible to ascertain, and most are marked by obscure figuration and an unpredictable temporality, even when the temporal parameters seem clearly set out by the prophecy itself.

Prophecy is, from its very beginnings, a marginal phenomenon. If the rhetoric of Judaic prophecy is characteristically paradoxical, it is partly because the prophetic message often runs literally *para doxa*—that is, counter to the dominant belief. Yet if prophets are marginal figures, their design is to envelop the text from which they are marginalized. "Would to God that all the Lord's people were Prophets," writes Blake in the motto for *Milton*, at a moment when he cites Moses, who would in turn be cited by Milton. Unlike the psalmist, whose praises can be sung *ad infinitum*, the prophet looks forward to a time when his or her own message will be superfluous, such that his voice need no longer cry in the wilderness or anywhere else.[2] But in tracking the peculiar temporality of prophecy, we shall see that the dream of prophecy tends not to be fulfilled in any definitive way, certainly not immediately, as the texts that appear to predict discrete historical events—although these do not constitute all of prophecy—can be quoted, reworked, and reconfigured in virtually endless ways. That very lack of fulfillment turns out to be a driving force behind the prophetic tradition.

Why *Romantic* prophecy? The presence of prophecy—Biblical, classical, or modern—is by no means a constant historical phenomenon. The period of Biblical prophecy arguably lasted only two centuries or so, and the oracles of classical antiquity were famously extinguished around the time of Plutarch. In post-Biblical and postclassical life, the prophetic tends to emerge, as does the apocalyptic, at times of great social and political turbulence. This study concentrates primarily on English and German writing of the late eighteenth and early nineteenth centuries, encompassing the moment when each nation witnessed the French Revolution unfold just beyond its borders: In each case, the revolution altered politics and culture immeasurably. In Western Europe the prophetic developed much more fully in the line of Protestantism than in Catholicism (where authority lies in the corporate church body and the chain of command rather than in the inspired or enlightened individual), and so it informed British and German culture in a way that had only a dim analogue in France, for example.[3] We shall see that prophecy could be so vigorously revived as a mode of writing in British and German Romanticism partly because of a new way of reading the Bible—mythologically and poetically—that developed gradually in the eighteenth century and flourished in the years of political and intellectual tumult around the turn of that century.

This study is an essay in "comparative" literature in that it juxtaposes

English and German texts in ways that are, ideally, mutually illuminating. But in the readings, especially of Blake, Hölderlin, and Coleridge, the emphasis is much less on comparing their texts with a view toward establishing what is similar as it is on outlining the different ways that prophetic discourse could take shape and function, as writing and as reading. Moreover, in the works singled out here as exemplary, their very singularity makes them counterexemplary at the same time; the example is never fully exemplary. And so the texts discussed in what follows are, even if they have resonance beyond themselves, not simply representative in the sense of standing in for so many other texts that could occupy the same place. But, for all that, they still have a markedly historical character and are still bound up in the problematic we call "Romanticism." However eccentric or idiosyncratic the texts of Hölderlin and Blake may be—both authors were considered mad at one time or another, and their main works were hardly known by the public in their lifetimes—they were written at one time only and in a certain way. If there is a historical force to the analysis here, it lies not in the attempt to show how representative these texts were of some larger, pervasive phenomenon—although they sometimes are—but rather to mark what was possible to be thought and done at a given moment. More than that, the analysis implicitly and sometimes explicitly confronts what it means to read these texts at a date far removed from the moment of their production. And so the point of the readings will not be simply to determine the sense of these Romantic texts in and for their own time; the logic of prophetic discourse itself may help us glimpse the poverty of such historicism. The prophetic text, perhaps more than any other, resists being confined to one and only one moment, and in that respect too it may tell us—in extreme fashion—something about textuality as such. The prophetic moment has momentum. Even if a text, prophetic or otherwise, were *produced* in a single historical moment, the text, as text, resists ascription to that single moment.[4] To acknowledge this fact is not to deny the text's historicity but to recognize its complexity.

Beginning with a brief consideration of some passages on prophecy and history in Walter Benjamin, this book moves backward in time, first to Wordsworth, Novalis, and others to get a sense of the scope of Romantic prophecy in its practice and theory, with an eye to where and how the prophetic surfaces or erupts. Partly to qualify the sense of historical specificity and partly to confirm it, I then look schematically at some of the Ro-

mantics' poetic precursors. From there I turn to a group of Biblical and literary critics of the middle and late eighteenth century—mainly Lowth,
Hurd, Herder, and Eichhorn—to get a sense of the mechanics of prophetic interpretation, to register some of the ideological pressures bearing
on such interpretation, and to see what conceptual groundwork was being
laid for the Romantic readings of prophecy that would follow in their
wake. Finally, I turn to a series of extended readings of three exemplary
texts by Blake, Hölderlin, and Coleridge. In Blake, the interest is primarily in the dynamics of prophetic tradition and the mythology of inspired
writing; in Hölderlin, the focus is on the truth claim of prophetic poetry,
the problem of figuration, and the idea of a German nation and national
poetry; in Coleridge, the celebrated theory of allegory and symbol is read
alongside his political program in *The Statesman's Manual,* with attention
to the way prophetic quotation and posture inform both.

Something of a break occurs between the Biblical critics and Blake: It
is not as if there is a seamless transition from Biblical hermeneutics of the
middle and late eighteenth century to the poetics of the Romantic writers.
Nor are the three readings of Blake, Hölderlin, and Coleridge intended to
assemble a composite portrait of what Blake calls the "prophetic character."
Prophecy is not a single thing, and one has to attend to the differences that
are sometimes tenuously grouped together under a single word.

But let me risk a provisional attempt at defining "prophet" and
"prophecy," even if this book as a whole also works at destabilizing some
of the traditional senses of those terms. In Max Weber's somewhat clinical
definition, a prophet is "a purely individual bearer of charisma, who by
virtue of his mission proclaims a religious doctrine or divine commandment."[5] What distinguishes the prophet from other religious figures, for
Weber, is the nature of his calling. The priest lays claim to authority
through service in a sacred tradition, but "the prophet's claim is based on
personal revelation and charisma."[6] Yet the single and singular prophet undergoes an institutionalization of sorts, if only after the fact, as prophetic
sayings come first to be written down and then in time to be more or less
canonized as scripture. One could go further than Weber and specify that
the decisive factor in the prophet's relation to the divine word is its immediacy. Virtually all the prophetic books and sequences of prophetic sayings
in the Hebrew scriptures are introduced by a formula attesting that the
word of the Lord is coming to the prophet, who in turn delivers God's

message to the people. Often the divine words appear to be repeated verbatim, with the prophet acting as a mouthpiece for God and having his discourse wholly subsumed by God's own. This is also to say that the prophet's "personal" revelation can never be merely personal, if it is still to be a revelation.

At times, the prophetic encounter with God is staged as a dialogue, although in a sense it bears only a formal similarity to an interpersonal conversation. As Maurice Blanchot writes:

> The prophetic word is originally a dialogue. It is so in a spectacular manner when the prophet discusses with God and when the latter "does not only confide in him his message, but also his concern." "Am I going to hide from Abraham," God says, "what I am going to do?" But it is so [a dialogue] in a more essential way, to the extent that he only repeats the word entrusted to him, an affirmation in which an originary word finds expression, one which has nonetheless already been said. That is its originality. It is primary, but before it there is always a word to which it responds in repeating it."[7]

In the beginning, then, is the repetition of the word. Even if the prophet's word seems originary, it is always already a repetition of the divine one, a quotation with or without quotation marks. In general the Romantics demonstrate an implicit and sometimes explicit awareness of this predicament, which is at the same time a potential resource for poetry.

repetition

Gerhard von Rad laments that scholars have not paid sufficient attention to the "enormous variety in the idea of what a prophet was."[8] Behind each discussion of putatively prophetic texts, he contends, lies a well-defined concept of the prophet that is often unnecessarily reductive. It is unfortunately not enough of a commonplace that prophecy cannot be reduced to prediction. As Blanchot, following Andre Néher, writes: "The term of prophet—borrowed from the Greek to designate a condition foreign to Greek culture—deceives us if it invites us to make of the *nabi* he in whom the future speaks. The prophetic word is not only a word of the future."[9] Even a cursory survey of the Hebrew prophets, of all those referred to as *nabi*, reveals that prediction is but one among many of the rhetorical forms and functions of prophecy. Claus Westermann has shown how the lament, the prayer, and the threat are as characteristic of prophetic discourse as are the prediction and the oracle.[10] The model of prediction cannot be held up as exemplary without considerable, reductive violence. And the problems only multiply when, as Blanchot implies, one tries to yoke the Hebrew *nabi* (נָבִיא) and the Greek *prophetes* (προφητης) under a single term, as if they were simply identical.

The precise origins of the word *nabi* may well be as obscure today as they were when the first translators of the Hebrew scriptures into Greek were forced to find an equivalent.[11] Many believe the word *nabi* derives from a root verb meaning "to call" or "to announce," but it has proved difficult to decide definitively on its etymology. The Hebrew *nabi* can be seen equally as one who calls forth *to* his people or who is called *by* God. The former sense is carried over in the Greek *prophetes*, if the prefix *pro* is understood spatially rather than temporally. Thus the prophet, Greek or Hebrew, is in one sense rather like an orator, someone who speaks "in front of" an assembly or who speaks "for" someone else, much as when Moses delegates Aaron to speak on his behalf.

The reductive violence that von Rad laments in recent scholarly readings marks as well most Christian discourse on prophecy throughout the eighteenth century. For Samuel Johnson, charting the character of the English language in the middle of the century, the "pro" in prophet was understood almost exclusively in temporal terms. The only two listings under the entry for "prophet" in Johnson's *Dictionary of the English Language* read:

> PROPHET. *n.s.* (*prophète*), Fr., (προφήτης)
> 1. One who tells future events; a predicter; a foreteller.
> 2. One of the sacred writers empowered by God to display futurity.[12]

The limits of such dictionary definitions are severe, but even when one turns to one of the subtlest theological minds of the century, Bishop Butler, one can read this summary statement in his *Analogy of Religion*: " . . . prophecy is nothing but the history of events before they come to pass."[13] In reviewing and offering a critique of some major Biblical critics of the mid- and late eighteenth century, I will have occasion to assess the precise forms such violence takes and to register some sense of its far-reaching consequences.

~

A clearer profile of the prophet and prophecy should emerge in the course of the readings to follow, especially in the third chapter, devoted to Biblical hermeneutics of the eighteenth century. But we can begin to approach what is at stake in the corpus of Romantic prophecy and the prophetic in oblique fashion, by tracking the itinerary of the work of Walter

Benjamin, who began his sustained philosophical and literary work primarily through an engagement with the Romantic tradition.

The category of the prophetic emerges in striking fashion in a letter Benjamin wrote to Martin Buber in which he outlines the principles that led to him declining the offer to contribute to Buber's journal, *Der Jude*. In the constricted form of a letter Benjamin nonetheless undertakes a wide-ranging meditation on the relation of language and act in the context of politics "in its broadest sense" ("in seinem weitesten Sinne").[14] Parallel to his pioneering essay of the same year "On Language as Such and the Language of Man" ("Über Sprache überhaupt und die Sprache des Menschen"), Benjamin contests the widespread opinion that writing can influence the ethical world and the actions of people, insofar as it presents motives for actions. "In this sense," Benjamin contends,

language is only a means of a more or less suggestive *laying of groundwork* for motives, which determine the agent in the interior of the soul. It is characteristic of this view that, with regard to the relation between language and action, it does not draw any relation between them in which the former is not the means to the latter. (127)

In his essay mostly resolutely devoted to language, Benjamin denounces as bourgeois any conception that pictures language as essentially the communication of information, although it becomes clear that the category of "bourgeois" is not particularly circumscribed in historical terms. To the extent that the seducing serpent in the Garden of Eden promises Adam and Eve the *knowledge* of good and evil, even the serpent emerges as a kind of bourgeois *avant la lettre*. Whatever its provenance or historical site, such a concept also reduces action to the result of a process of calculation and, in doing so, involves an impoverishment of both language and action.

In the letter to Buber, as Benjamin tries to sketch a more adequate conception of language, knowledge, action, and their interrelations, the category of the prophetic appears unexpectedly and in a telling sequence: "I can only understand writing, as far as it effects matter, poetically, prophetically, objectively but in any event only *magically*, that is to say, immediately" (127). Benjamin continues " . . . only where this sphere of the world opens into the unutterably pure power can the magical spark spring between word and motivating [*bewegende*] action, where the unity of these two equally real entities resides [*ist*]" (127). Is there some way to construe these exorbitant sayings so that Benjamin's insights do not remain encrypted in a mystical or mystified philosophy of language? What place can a term like "magic" have in thinking about language? If the word "magic" simply conjures visions of illusion, optical or otherwise, those connotations have to be suspended in approaching Benjamin's usage. Moreover, the terms "poetic" and "prophetic" are perhaps only slightly less problematic than is "magic" for thinking of language in general. For Benjamin, the poetic, the prophetic, and the objective are all allied in their uniting of word and deed. Even if these terms tend to entail very different relations between word and world, in each of these spheres language is a magic act. Moreover, for Benjamin the extraordinary discourses of poetry and prophecy somehow harbor a secret (*Geheimnis*), a secret truth about all language.

To call language magic might seem itself a kind of magic trick, a verbal sleight of hand that tries to make all potential problems vanish. But in the essay on language, Benjamin terms magic a "problem," a name for a difficulty to be resolved rather than a solution.[15] As he says:

All language communicates itself *in* itself; it is in the purest sense the "medium" of communication. Mediation, which is the immediacy of all mental communication, is the fundamental problem for linguistic theory, and if one chooses to call this immediacy magic, then the primary problem of language is its magic."[16]

One can glimpse at least part of the problem in that this magic language— language as magic—is structured as a mediation characterized by its immediacy. This goes to the core of the character of prophecy and partly explains why Benjamin could invoke the prophetic in his letter to Buber. As a human vehicle of the divine word, the prophet is precisely a mediator.[17] But in relation to all other human discourse, prophetic language is marked by its immediacy. In principle, nothing gets lost in the translation from the divine to the human discourse that is prophecy. And thus the prophetic, as mediated immediacy or immediate mediation, comes to emblematize the highest and perhaps most definitive language, thus standing as the model according to which Benjamin tries to rethink—during the tumultuous years of the First World War—the relations of word and deed.[18]

That language, for Benjamin, communicates "itself," the linguistic being of things, and does not primarily communicate something else *through* language is one instance of a pervasive tendency in his thought to suspend thinking through the categories of means and ends. To imagine language as the means for communicating information is, for him, to succumb to the bourgeois debasement of it: The challenge is to conceive—and perhaps also to perform—language as a *medium* rather than as a means to an end. The very word "medium" seems to imply a structure of mediation, not unlike that entailed in the notion of "means." But the medium of language, for Benjamin, is so all encompassing as to contain not only the linguistic being of things but their mental essence as well. This "medium" does not stand in the middle of a trajectory on the way to some nonlinguistic goal outside language: It just is what it is. But what is that?

To think of language as communicating itself might appear the sheerest formalism and the most extreme type of logocentrism, an idealization or even fetishism of the word. After all, Benjamin has a very dim view of the importance of transmitting content, which is what so often is thought of as that which guarantees language's relation to the real. The suspension of language's function in transmitting content might seem a prelude to a decidedly mystical, even apolitical conception of language. Indeed, Benjamin expressly says in the same letter that "every salutary effect, indeed every effect not inherently devastating, that writing may have resides in its (the word's, language's) mystery [*Geheimnis*]."[19] If language is to be effective, Benjamin claims, it is not by transmitting content but "through the purest disclosure of its dignity and its nature [*Wesens*]."[20] The letter seems to teeter on the brink of invoking the ineffable as the essence of language, but when the ineffable or the unsayable is finally invoked it is entirely in a negative mode:

And if I disregard other effective forms—aside from poetry and prophecy—it repeatedly seems to me that the crystal-pure elimination of the ineffable [*Unsagbaren*] in language is the most obvious form given to us to be effective within language and, to that extent, through it. The elimination of the ineffable seems to me to coincide precisely with what is actually the objective and dispassionate manner of writing, and to intimate the relationship between knowledge and action precisely within linguistic magic. My concept of objective and, at the same time, highly political style and writing is this: to awaken interest in what was denied to the word; only where this magic sphere of speechlessness [*Wortlosen*] reveals itself in unutterably pure power can the magic spark leap between the word and the motivating deed, where the unity of these two equally real entities resides [*ist*]. Only the intensive direction of words into the core of intrinsic muting [*Verstummens*] is truly effective. I do not believe that there is any place where the word would be more distant from the divine than in "real" action. Thus, too, it is incapable of leading into the divine in any way other than through itself and its own purity. Understood as an instrument, it proliferates. (127)

So language here, far from paradoxically uttering the ineffable or even pointing to it, can only say what it can say.[21] And, Benjamin seems to imply in a moralizing way, that it should only say what it can say and not attempt anything else. Yet even here as he is circumscribing the pretensions of language—it can only say what it can say—to something prosaic, Benjamin can still invoke the models of prophecy and poetry. This move corresponds to an argument he would make emphatically in his dissertation on German Romanticism, namely, that according to the theory of Friedrich Schlegel and company, prose is "the idea of poetry." This counterintuitive proposition was put forward partly to demystify poetry even as it absolutized it.[22] By making any act of prose potentially "poetic" the Romantics, one might say, ascribed a weak Messianic power to any utterance.[23]

But we still need to be clear about the not-so-self-evident claim Benjamin is making about the relations between language and action. Benjamin makes plain in this letter and elsewhere that writing is a kind of action but that it does not encompass anything like the whole of action. Yet he is suspicious of writing that aims to be effective, to be related to action as cause to effect and so claims, paradoxically, that the only effective writing is that which suspends its design to be effective.[24] Such writing is truer to the demands of the word—but here "word" has something of its Hebraic sense of *davar* (דָּבָר)—where word cannot be separated from deed. Still, Benjamin can posit a "poor" kind of writing that is "action" (*Handeln*); this again is the "bourgeois" discourse of content communicated but one that has no real relation to the word and thus also no relation to the divine. This last is not a matter of indifference, since Benjamin rarely thinks of the political outside the horizon of the divine.[25] For all the dismissal of the ineffable or what is literally "unutterable" or "unspeakable" (*Unsagbaren*), Benjamin's letter can still sound implausibly mystical. Whereas the resistance to a certain instrumentalization of language is understandable—all the more so as various state powers had just mobilized for the First World War—it is harder to see what exactly language entails when the transmission of content is suspended or relegated to a matter of indifference. And it is not an easy paradox that the most highly political writing is effected by abandoning all attempts to effect anything in the world. Of course, the claim for the political "effectivity" of such language is just that: a claim. Whether Benjamin's strange hypothesis holds weight can be determined only in the performance of such language/action, as his own texts, and not only texts, went on to elaborate.

Given the simultaneous conception of language as action and action as language, Benjamin not only avoids the pitfalls of a certain formalism but he also opens up his thought to a new, if problematic, thinking of politics.[26] Yet before turning to matters of political theory and practice, Benjamin, in the 1916 "Language" essay, first establishes the character of language as action. He does so via a reading of the opening chapters of Genesis, not, he insists, as a vehicle of divinely revealed truth but for what "emerges of itself . . . with regard to the nature of language" (322). Here the analysis of the two creation stories issues in the delineation of a threefold rhythm of creation as "Let there be—He made—He named."[27] Benjamin implies that the structure of framing creation "proper" by the positing of being by God and naming by man underlines the creative force of those two acts. "Language," for Benjamin, "is . . . both creative and the finished creation, it is word and name" (323). If language is itself "creative," that is not quite to say that it always entails performative speech acts in the sense of J. L. Austin. But it is nonetheless clear that the essence of language, for Benjamin, does not lie in its function as representation, of verbal transcription of what is external to language. That function of language is more closely allied to the (bourgeois) transmission of information against which Benjamin is mounting resistance. One might think that Benjamin's insistence on the primacy of the name (which can well be derived from the opening chapters of Genesis) would link his conception of language precisely with categories of representation. So how does Benjamin disentangle the name from the discourse of content transmission of which he is so suspicious? Even more than as name, human language is determined as *naming* (*Nennen*), perhaps to distinguish it from the Aristotelian or Lockean heritage that would see in the name—Aristotle's *onoma*—the exemplary unit for the communication of knowledge or information. For Benjamin, naming has little or nothing to do with knowledge. Naming figures in knowledge but surpasses it as act.[28] Indeed, naming as knowledge/action is the language of language— that without which language would be nothing and that through which language communicates itself absolutely. Naming, in Benjamin's understanding, does not simply register what is outside language: It posits. As such, this language of positing is not subject to the constraints of truth and

falsity in the same way as representation (as Austin has shown for performative speech acts in general), and it opens up onto questions of power
even more directly and inexorably than does the language of representation.
Moreover, the positing movement of language, the *Setzen*, constitutes an essential link with what might appear to be an epiphenomenon of language
but that nonetheless leads Benjamin to its innermost character: translation.

One arrives at or produces knowledge in the first place only through
a process of translation. It soon becomes clear that translation, for Benjamin, is not a special case of language but its very structure. Human language is the site of the translation—literally the *Übersetzung*, the "positing
or setting above"—from things to names and from names to a shadowy
higher language Benjamin sometimes calls "pure."[29] But language not only
moves to a higher realm through translation, it also falls. And it falls into
something else, disfiguring itself, insofar as language, after the Fall, "communicate[s] *something* (other than itself)" (327). The Fall ushers in knowledge, especially, the story goes, the knowledge of good and evil. But Benjamin then offers a rather heterodox reading of the scene of seduction in
Genesis: "The tree of knowledge did not stand in the garden of God in order to dispense information on good and evil but as an emblem of judgment over the questioner. This immense irony marks the mythical origin
of law" (328). With this turn to "the judging word" and the law (*Gesetz*),
the models of language in Benjamin's theoretical program are complete,
since the transition has been made to ethics, the general sphere in which,
among other things, politics is played out. Here too it is a question of language as act, a language with consequences. A judgment may be based on
knowledge, but it is not of the order of knowledge: It "does not dispense
information," as Benjamin says. The tree of knowledge, in Benjamin's
reading, does not provide the knowledge that it is supposed to embody but
presents the permanent possibility of a judgment on the questioner. This
structure marks the origin of the law, an origin—Benjamin seems to imply—that is not merely a thing of the law but which informs it continually.
The Last Judgment, as Kafka observed, is a court that is always in session.

To articulate knowledge and ethics via the mediation of representation is to repeat a trajectory set out most cogently and influentially by Kant
in the itinerary of his critical philosophy. Beginning in the *Critique of Pure
Reason* with searching into the possibilities of our knowing nature (the external world had been previously thought to be constituted according to the

objective characteristics of space and time but then found to be determined by space and time as *a priori* subjective intuitions), Kant then turned in the second critique, the *Critique of Practical Reason*, to the domain of action and freedom, the realm of morals and ethics. Yet, as Kant was the first to admit, there was a gulf or abyss (*Abgrund*) between these two realms—or "jurisdictions" as he sometimes termed them—over which a "bridge" would have to be thrown. The bridge was the aesthetic or, in terms of faculties of the mind, judgment, which had to operate in part according to the potentially unruly dictates of the imagination, or *Einbildungskraft*, which Kant calls the "faculty of representation," the *Darstellungsvermögen*—a rather precarious if unavoidable path, according to some readings of Kant.[30] To think through representation was a prerequisite to thinking about action—moral, ethical, political—and the farthest thing from an aestheticist evasion of the demands of history, even for Kant, much less for Benjamin.

While Benjamin was first articulating his views on politics, language, and aesthetics, official philosophy in German was much preoccupied with a rethinking of Kant. The period in general can be termed neo-Kantian, and Benjamin seemed on the verge of coming to terms with the legacy of Kant in as direct a way as anyone. His programmatic essay of 1917–18, "On the Program of the Coming Philosophy," took virtually all its cues from Kant, even though Benjamin could also take Kant to task especially for one immense lacuna: the failure to acknowledge the centrality of language in addressing the problems of critical philosophy, whether the emphasis was on knowledge or action.[31] For a time Kant's writings on history—the philosophy of history—seemed a perfect focus for Benjamin's theoretical and political interests. But after months of hesitation Benjamin abandoned the plan to work on Kant and turned instead to the less directly "historical" matter of Friedrich Schlegel's theory of critique. The result was his doctoral dissertation *The Concept of Aesthetic Critique in German Romanticism* (*Der Begriff der Kunstkritik in der deutschen Romantik*). There he elaborated a theory of critique as fulfillment (*Ergänzung*) and completion (*Vollendung*). For Benjamin, following Schlegel, critique was not an external supplement that either could or could not be addressed to the work of art. Rather, critique was already immanent to the work of art, the paradigm for Schlegel being Goethe's highly self-reflexive novel, *Wilhelm Meister*. But the critique proper to the work of art is not definitive: The artwork calls for critique. "The task of critique [is] the completion of the work," Benjamin says baldly.[32] It fulfills a lack already internal to the work, although, paradoxically, only the good work of art has this "lack."[33] And this necessity of fulfillment—a word with a prophetic aura—comes to be the master schema that structures virtually all of Benjamin's thinking on language, translation, and history. Benjamin is echoing the extravagance of some of the Romantics when he speaks of critique in terms of a certain Messianism.[34] We will have to return momentarily to consider what the Messianic, for Benjamin, might and might not mean.

In his far-reaching essay from the early 1920s, "Critique of Violence" ("Kritik der Gewalt"), Benjamin sought, much as in his earlier, then unpublished essay on language, to reconceive law and justice outside the traditional economy of means and ends. This is, on the face of it, an even harder task than was the case with language: For what is justice when it does not entail just ends or justifiable means? Benjamin's essay was drafted partly in response to the perceived failure of parliamentary democracy, lamented alike by forces on the left and the right. One failing of that kind of democracy, Benjamin contended, was an obliviousness to the violence (Gewalt) of its own origins. Benjamin proceeds to consider a wide spectrum of social acts and institutions (parliament, the penal system, education, the police) but finds the most suggestive instance for the rethinking of violence in general to be arguably its most extreme: the general strike. Even more than war, Benjamin seems to claim, the strike is the most violent violence—which he sometimes calls "pure" violence—in that it can bring society utterly to a halt. And that is precisely its utopian and revolutionary potential. Conducted outside the parameters of means and ends, the general strike, according to Benjamin, could not strictly speaking be part of a political program, because that would always imply inscribing the strike action as a means to a future end. The truly revolutionary moment suspends the future without sacrificing the present to it. In the end (and at the end of his essay), Benjamin associates this most radical historical moment with nothing less than "divine violence."[35] The pointed example of divine violence is God's destruction of the company of Korah, recounted in Numbers 16, a story of the earth opening up to swallow a group Benjamin describes as "privileged Levites." This violence strikes, strikes without warning, "and does not stop short of annihilation."[36] The invocation of "divine violence" is in many ways no less a solution than is "magic," since according to Benjamin we can never be sure that we would recognize divine violence for what it is whenever it struck. One can readily see how this sort of power or violence cannot be recuperated for any political program, and yet it marks the horizon for political action. Such an "example" of violence would be of little or no theoretical interest if it were confined to the realm of the inscrutably divine. But this extreme act of violence is metonymically related, even in its purity, to the general strike, the nonviolently violent cessation of labor and, by extension, of social life. So the question can still linger as to why Benjamin repeatedly appeals to the divine and the Messianic in the thinking of politics, especially when he explicitly denounces theocracy as a politically viable option. One needs to inquire a little more into what he now and then calls the Messianic.

It is in Benjamin's celebrated, enigmatic "Theses on the Philosophy of History" that the Messianic emerges most prominently in the thinking of history and politics. If the general strike and divine violence were such singular models for action and history that they risked having little or no exemplary value, in the "Theses" Benjamin proposes only slightly less extravagant models. We shall turn to those in a moment, but first it will help to see how the prophetic surfaces in this nexus of Benjamin's thought at this time. In the drafts to the "Theses," Benjamin took as a point of departure Friedrich Schlegel's much-cited dictum: "The historian is a prophet turned backward" ("Der Historiker ist ein rückwärts gekehrter Prophet").[37] He begins by explicating the received or commonsensical reading of Schlegel's aphorism:

The saying, the historian is a prophet turned backward, can be understood in two different ways. The traditional reading holds that, displacing himself back into a past, the historian prophesies what would have counted as the future but which has in the meantime become the past. This vision corresponds exactly to the theory of historical empathy that Fustel de Coulanges cast in these terms: "If you want to revive an epoch, forget what you know of what has happened since then."[38]

Such "prophecy," in Benjamin's view, partakes of the suspect historicism that dictates that empathy with individuals of the past is the best method for understanding texts and artifacts of bygone eras. The inadequacy of this historicism lies first in the political tendencies usually associated with it—the empathy of official historiography is almost always on the side of the victors, as Nietzsche had argued in "We Philologists"—and second in that its task is an infinite one, with the goal of history assured as an ideal but indefinitely postponed—the worst of both worlds.[39] Benjamin goes on to suggest an alternate reading of Schlegel's aphorism, one that entails a radically different relation of past, present, and future:

But one can interpret the saying completely differently and understand it this way: The historian turns his back to his own time, and his seer's gaze ignites on the peaks of the peoples of mankind always receding deeper into the past. This seer's gaze is precisely directed toward that which for one's own time is far more clearly present than it is to the contemporaries who "keep pace with it." Not for nothing did Turgot define the concept of a present that presents the intentional object of a prophecy as essentially and fundamentally a political one. "Before we can inform ourselves about a given state of affairs," Turgot says, "it has already changed many times. So we always experience too late what has taken place. And thus one can say of politics that it is directed, as it were, at foretelling the present." It is precisely this concept on which the relevance (*Aktualität*) of genuine historiography is based. Whoever stumbles around in the past as in a rummage room of exempla and analogies has no idea of how much in a given moment depends on its being made present.[40]

The paradoxical task of politics, then, as of history generally, is to prophesy the present. And to make matters more complex, one achieves this visionary perspective on the present by turning one's back from one's own time to the past, not unlike the stance of Klee's *Angelus Novus*, whose back is to the future. To prophesy the present is, typically, to cite the past. Here, as elsewhere, Benjamin's schema for the understanding of history (*Geschichte*) in its multiple senses of the events and the recording of events always involves two and only two moments:

Historical articulation of the past means: to recognize in the past that which comes together in the constellation of one and the same moment. Historical knowledge is uniquely and solely possible in the historical moment. Cognition in the historical moment, however, is always a cognition of a moment.[41]

Partly because of this dual structure of the moment of knowing and the moment of the known, history lends itself to being understood in textual terms, according to the paradigms of writing and reading. Benjamin can even say baldly that "the historical method is a philological one."[42] This is to domesticate neither history nor historiography but just to call attention to the dialectical character of encounter, a rather different model from that presumed especially by bourgeois or official historiography of the nineteenth and early twentieth centuries, which conceived of history as a grand, continuous story—and often a history of inexorable progress, at that.

But Benjamin is even more specific about the textual character of history. In this he follows Marx in *The Eighteenth Brumaire* in his understanding of revolutionary moments of history as citations:

History is the object of a construction, whose site is not the homogeneous and empty time but time filled by the now (*Jetztzeit*). Thus, to Robespierre ancient Rome was a past charged with the time of the now which he blasted out of the continuum of history. The French Revolution viewed itself as Rome returned again. It cited ancient Rome the way fashion cites costumes of the past.[43]

For Marx, not all revolutionary citations are created equal, but, for Benjamin, the citation remains the model for the revolutionary moment of history, insofar as it interrupts and even brings to a halt the—illusory—linear movement of history as conceived variously by fascism, historicism, and varieties of vulgar Marxism. Benjamin goes on to link this revolutionary consciousness with a prophetic cessation of movement:

In the July revolution an incident occurred which showed this consciousness still alive. On the first evening of fighting it turned out that the clocks in towers were being fired on simultaneously and independently from several places in Paris. An eyewitness, who may have owed his insight to the rhyme, wrote as follows:

> Qui le croirait! on dit, qu'irrités contre l'heure
> De nouveaux Josués, au pied de chaque tour,
> Tiraient sur les cadrans pour arrêter le jour.[44]

> [Who would have believed it! We are told that new Joshuas
> at the foot of every tower, as though irritated with
> time itself, fired at the dials in order to stop the day.]

Elsewhere in the "Theses," Benjamin figures the movement of history as heliotropic, and thus the arresting of the sun—that is to say, time and history—by Joshua and his antitypes in France's July revolution (1830) constitutes the paradigmatic historical, revolutionary act. Similarly, the historical materialist must effect something of a cessation in thinking as usual, such that history crystallizes into an image or a figure like a monad. In this, Benjamin claims, the historical materialist recognizes "the sign of a Messianic cessation of happening, or, put differently, a revolutionary chance in the fight for the oppressed past" (263). That Benjamin can almost effortlessly shift in midsentence from the Messianic to the materialist implies that the one domain is a figural realm for the other and vice versa.[45]

The Messianic cannot simply be limited to or identified with the Messiah. The fact that Benjamin can speak of the "Messianic" force of the work of art or the Messianic character of virtually any sort of profane happiness is enough to enlarge our ordinary conception of that term.[46] The Messianic, for Benjamin, is especially a figure for the end, or rather for *an* end, because there can be more than a first and a second coming. (Benjamin distinguishes between an end and a goal, the latter seeming to entail an inexorable progress toward some resolution.[47]) Every generation, he says in the "Theses," has been endowed with "a *weak* Messianic power, a power to which the past has a claim" (254). The claim of the past is prophetic but not necessarily insofar as it accurately predicts the future. The prophetic claim of the past is on the present: It is not for nothing that Benjamin notes, in the last of the "Theses," that "the Jews were prohibited from investigating the future" (264). Benjamin is not remotely advocating some historical stance that simply turns to the past (nostalgically or otherwise) and suspends any interest in the future. But he is deeply suspicious of any notion that one can somehow know the future and then guide one's actions accordingly. Hence the importance of the prophetic thought quite apart from any knowledge that it is supposed to provide of the future. Prophecy is a call and a claim much more than it is a prediction, a call oriented toward a present that is not present.

But what sort of claim can be made for such prophecy? That Benjamin conceives of language, history, translation, and critique all in terms of completion, fulfillment, redemption, and even the Messianic indicates the pivotal role the prophetic plays in virtually every sphere of his thought. Prophecy emerges as a model and not a special case for the historian and critic, because every text, every event that is cited attains, if only retroactively, a prophetic aura. That is why the otherwise anomalous text of prophecy may have something to teach us of an unexpected generality. In the end, all writing that matters may be prophetic.

2

The Scope and Texture of Romantic Prophecy: Wordsworth and Novalis Among Others

> . . . something like prophetic strain.
> —Milton, "Il Penseroso"

In Romantic literature taken as a whole the prophetic is at once marginal and pervasive. A good many writers, major and minor, have little or no relation to the prophetic mode. But in other writers' work, including that of many of the most canonical figures, the prophetic is explicit and pronounced, sometimes so prevalent as to be almost invisible. In this section I address a number of examples of Romantic writing, from Wordsworth's extended epic meditation on his own life to a pithy "monologue" by Novalis, to achieve some sense of the range of the ways the prophetic surfaces in the Romantics as well as in some of their most significant precursors.

In the poem that would retroactively emerge as the central text of the English Romantic canon, Wordsworth's *Prelude*, the prophetic has a rather odd status, profound and even pervasive in some readings and all but absent in others. Read alternately as autobiography, personal epic, a series of lyric and/or sublime moments encompassed in a narrative frame, *The Prelude*, to judge from its reception, hardly seems to lend itself to being considered as prophecy or as prophetic. And yet a number of the most programmatic passages of the poem combine to cast a prophetic aura over the entire text.[1]

In the opening verses, Wordsworth recounts to his silent interlocutor, Coleridge, the scene of the poem's genesis:

> Thus far, O Friend! did I, not used to make
> A present joy the matter of my song,
> Pour out that day my soul in measured strains
> Even in the very words which I have here
> Recorded. To the open fields I told
> A prophesy: poetic numbers came
> Spontaneously, and clothed in priestly robe
> My spirit, thus singled out, as it might seem,
> For holy services. Great hopes were mine:
> My own voice cheered me, and, far more, the mind's
> Internal echo of the imperfect sound—
> To both I listened, drawing from them both
> A cheerful confidence in things to come.[2]

Here Wordsworth describes, or mythologizes, the prophetic scene at the origin of the poem that is to record the growth of his mind. Like the opening of many prophetic books of the Old Testament, the text begins with an account or a staging of the prophet's calling, of his being singled out as a vehicle for the divine word, with or without his will. Wordsworth employs many of the props of Hebraic prophecy—complicated somewhat by his conflation of priest and prophet—but with a singular difference. Here there is only one voice. Whereas the Biblical prophet testifies to the word of Yahweh coming upon him, Wordsworth is witness only to his own voice—a single voice, initially. But it is soon doubled by the "mind's internal echo." That echo strangely comes to usurp the place of the thing of which it is the echo. Wordsworth is cheered "far more" by the mind's echo of the original sound now deemed "imperfect." It is odd that a poet who so consistently celebrates the power of sound and voice should term the original sound "imperfect" and then subsequently be cheered all the more by the mere echo of that imperfect sound. Something is gained precisely where one would expect a loss. "Imperfect" seems here to mean "incomplete" rather than "faulty," and given that sense the echo could be the completion of that original sound. The doubling of echo implies reiteration and perhaps even survival, the possibility not only of a future prophecy but perhaps also of a prophetic tradition. The recollection, in writing, of a past prophecy spontaneously spoken to the fields is what moves Wordsworth back to the future and allows him to draw confidence in things to come.

The scene Wordsworth describes is in another respect utterly unlike the characteristic settings of Biblical prophecy: There is no audience. Wordsworth merely speaks by himself to the open fields. (Perhaps this is a characteristically Wordsworthian touch, implying a nature that could respond to him, but that is not the path the passage follows.) Though the Hebrew prophets are sometimes figured as voices crying in the wilderness, the prophetic word is typically nothing, or at best "imperfect," without an audience to be forewarned, threatened, or consoled. Wordsworth records here a scene of prophetic calling, even if his own voice is the source and echo of that calling.[3] Its prophetic character lies less in its content—except perhaps insofar as it is its own content—than in its promise for the future of his poetry. Yet already in rehearsing this recorded announcement, Wordsworth has taken a step toward the constitution of his audience, without which there would only be imperfect sounds.

If this scene of prophetic calling were an isolated passage in the text of *The Prelude*, it could be written off as a mere modulation of the invocation of the muse proper to any epic undertaking, a scene virtually external to the poem proper. But the passage is hardly isolated. Indeed, the ending of this great, unfinished poem is just as emphatically inscribed in the prophetic tradition. The very last lines return us to the rhetoric of prophecy that marked the outset:

> . . . Though men return to servitude as fast
> As the tide ebbs, to ignominy and shame
> By nations sink together, we shall still
> Find solace in the knowledge which we have,
> Blest with true happiness if we may be
> United helpers forward of a day
> Of firmer trust, joint laborers in a work—
> Should Providence such grace to us vouchsafe—
> Of their redemption, surely yet to come.
> Prophets of Nature, we to them will speak
> A lasting inspiration, sanctified
> By reason and truth; what we have loved,
> Others will love, and we may teach them how;
> Instruct them how far the mind of man becomes
> A thousand times more beautiful than the earth
> On which he dwells, above this frame of things
> (Which, 'mid all revolutions in the hopes
> And fears of men, doth still remain unchanged)
> In beauty exalted, as it is itself
> Of substance and of fabric more divine.
>
> (1805, XIII, 433–52)

These ultimate lines of *The Prelude* present not so much the fulfillment of the inaugural "prophecy of prophecy" as its restatement. Wordsworth once again, but now together with Coleridge, invests himself with the mantle of prophecy, claiming both of them as "prophets of nature." That phrase suggests that the poet, with a foundation in what he has learned from nature, can now speak both of nature and on behalf of it. The poet can echo the voice of nature and from that vantage point address the other-than-natural anxieties of his day, the hopes and fears of his contemporaries, the present discontents of the nation. As the voice of nature, he speaks a lesson supposed to be doctrinal and exemplary to a nation, and yet what that paradoxical lesson teaches is the superiority of pupil over teacher. Nature here inspires the poet to say how superior, how much more beautiful, the mind of man is compared to the earth on which he dwells poetically. These closing lines present what one is tempted to call a "secularized" version of the Biblical prophet. Even if the ultimate word and referent of the passage is "divine," a prophet of Nature is fundamentally different from a prophet of God.

In the penultimate book of *The Prelude*, Wordsworth presents yet another scene of the prophetic office of the poet, not in the mode of metaphor or citation but in a calculated yet extravagant simile. He confides to Coleridge:

> Dearest Friend!
> Forgive me if I say that I, who long
> Had harbored reverentially a thought
> That poets, even as Prophets, each with each
> Connected in a mighty scheme of truth,
> Have each for his particular dower, a sense
> By which he is enabled to perceive
> Something unseen before—forgive me, friend,
> If I, the meanest of this band, had hope
> That unto me had also been vouchsafed
> An influx, that in some sort I possessed
> A privilege, and that a work of mine,
> Proceeding from the depth of untaught things,
> A power like one of Nature's.
> (1805, XII, 298–312)

Here the poet emerges as something like a prophet in the Biblical tradition, with visionary power to see what has never been seen. Wordsworth follows the diction of eighteenth-century theology by invoking the "scheme" of truth, a term often used to describe the providential system of prophecy, in which the words of one prophet were quoted or complemented by another to provide internal coherence to the totality of the Biblical message. If Wordsworth's analogies are taken seriously, the poet's work is then understood as both natural and supernatural, much like the prophetic word in Jeremiah, which proceeds from a divine origin but acts with a force like nature's own.

Wordsworth's stance in the preceding passage is a complicated one, marked as it is by gestures that are alternately self-aggrandizing and self-effacing. On the one hand, Wordsworth inscribes his poetic project in the most exalted of traditions, that of divinely inspired Biblical prophets, who for him and his interlocutor Coleridge were proverbially sublime. (Wordsworth would write in the Preface to his 1815 *Poems*: "The grand store-houses of enthusiastic and meditative imagination . . . in these unfavourable times are the prophetic and lyrical parts of the Holy Scriptures, and the works of Milton . . . "[4]) On the other hand, he describes himself as the meanest of the band, and it is difficult to tell if this is true or false modesty, for Wordsworth is at this point still on the verge of the poetic career he envisions. In any event, the passage still seemed extravagant enough for Wordsworth to rewrite it for the final version in this way:

> Dearest Friend!
> If thou partake the animating faith
> That Poets, even as Prophets, each with each
> Connected in a mighty scheme of truth,
> Have each his own peculiar faculty,
> Heaven's gift, a sense that fits him to perceive
> Objects unseen before, thou wilt not blame
> The humblest of this band who dares to hope
> That unto him hath also been vouchsafed
> An insight that in some sort he possesses,
> A privilege whereby a work of his,
> Proceeding from a source of untaught things,
> Creative and enduring, may become
> A power like one of Nature's.
>   (1850, XIII, 299–312)

Here the link between poetry and prophecy is posed only hypothetically. And the "belief" in their identity is no longer simply "harbored" by Wordsworth but he invites Coleridge to share in a faith represented as something of a cultural given. The hubris of the 1805 version is considerably less stark, rendered even less so in the lines immediately following in the 1850 text: "To a hope/Not less ambitious once among the wilds/Of Sarum's Plain, my youthful spirit was raised;" (1850, XIII, 312–14). The corresponding lines of the 1805 text make no mention of ambition or youthful spirit that qualify, in retrospect, the extravagance of the claim to prophetic vision, although much of that ethos still remains intact in the later revisions.

In *The Prelude* not only is poetry prophetic when it speaks in the voice of nature, it is equally so when it speaks in its own voice. When Wordsworth comes to offer an allegory of poetry, in Book V, the aptly named book of "Books," the text is both prophetic and metaprophetic, prophecy about prophecy. The Dream of the Arab has become a crux of Wordsworthian interpretation and has occasioned no end of critical debate.[5] The authority of the dream, in more than one sense, is difficult to ascertain. Indeed, it is impossible to decide who—or what—is the subject of the dream and thus who or what should be the subject of interpretation. The 1805 text presents the dream as that of Wordsworth's friend, whereas the 1850 version has Wordsworth himself as the dreamer. To make matters worse, the dream seems to be a version of ones dreamt first by Descartes.[6] The very indirection of the dream narrative gives it a different character, as it were, from that of most episodes recounted in Wordsworth's epic. The history of the scene's reception has accorded it a privileged place in the canon of passages quarried from *The Prelude*, as if the displacement of the pronouncement about poetry inside the dream granted it a certain oracular status, like knowledge gained from journeys to the underworld in classical epic. What, then, does the dream say about poetry and prophecy?

The Arab appears to Wordsworth, or his friend, bearing two inanimate objects that require some explanation: a stone and a shell. When questioned about them, the Arab replies that the stone:

> 'Was *Euclid's Elements*. And this,' said he,
> 'This other,' pointing to the shell, 'this book
> Is something of more worth.' And, at the word
> The stranger, said my friend continuing,
> Stretched forth the shell toward me, with command
> That I should hold it to my ear. I did so,
> And heard that instant in an unknown tongue,

Which yet I understood, articulate sounds,
A loud prophetic blast of harmony;
An Ode, in passion uttered, which foretold
Destruction to the children of the earth
By deluge now at hand. No sooner ceased
The song, but with calm look the Arab said
That all was true, that it was even so
As had been spoken, . . .   (1805, V, 88–102)

The poet awakes to find, unlike Milton's Adam, that not all the dream was true. This dream, however, casts a shadow over the rest of the poem by rendering an ordinary or pedestrian scene potentially apocalyptic. It becomes a crucial passage for the idea of prophetic poetry, because when poetry is permitted (or is it forced?) to speak its own allegorical message, it tells only of an imminent destruction, of a deluge now "at hand," in a phrase echoing apocalyptic moments in Isaiah, the Gospels, and Revelation.

The apocalyptic ode issues "a loud blast of prophetic harmony," an eminently Wordsworthian oxymoron that captures, among other things, the potential tension between the manner of the Biblical prophetic word and its ultimate effect.[7] The prophet cries out in the wilderness, or the Lord compares his word to a fire (Jeremiah 5.14) or a hammer capable of smashing rocks to pieces (Jeremiah 23.29). The prophetic word can act violently: It explodes, erupts, disrupts, and even destroys. And yet the vision of the apocalyptic writer can often be an irenic one, not unrelated to the oddly "calm look" of the Arab noted here. Wordsworth seems to conflate here the Hebrew prophet and the Christian writer of apocalypse and then to offer that hybrid discourse as a model for poetry. But if the one and only message from the shell of poetry is "deluge now at hand," why does the Arab wear such a "calm look"? Is it perhaps because he knows the difference between a literal and a figurative apocalypse or between an event and the text of an event? Why else might the Arab calmly go off to bury the books of geometry and poetry, the latter book glossed as "a god, yea many gods" who "Had voices more than all the winds, and was/A joy, a consolation, and a hope" (1805, V, 106–09)? The passage implicitly displays the possible discrepancies between the content and the effect of prophetic rhetoric. Poetry poses the threat of a literal apocalypse but in a figural mode, and the knowledge of such a discrepancy may well be cause for consolation—but not necessarily forever, and perhaps not for long. The dreamer notes that the Arab "looked often backward with wild look." And when questioned as to the meaning of the glittering light glimpsed in the dreamer's backward glance, the Arab replies that it is "the waters of the deep/Gathering upon us." They are the waters of the apocalypse.

The interruption of the dream narrative within Wordsworth's itinerary alters not only the course of his life but also the way Wordsworth and his critics read. Any water, any light, any blast in Wordsworth's hands becomes potentially apocalyptic, whether natural or spiritual, literal or figurative, "neither" or "both at once." Readers of Wordsworth from Hazlitt to Bradley to Hartman have drawn attention to this as his virtual signature, the power peculiar to his poetry. Even though many of the episodes and descriptions in *The Prelude* have little to do with an explicit rhetoric of poetry or apocalypse, the message of the prophetic ode casts an arc over the entire poem. That this bleak pronouncement should be a cause for consolation, joy, and hope is perhaps less paradoxical if we understand that whatever literal destruction the ode foretells, it also implicitly constitutes a promise of meaning. The book will survive, because the book has been buried.[8] This book, the book of poetry as such, will survive the threat from destruction of and by Nature.[9] Natural destruction, for many of the Romantics, sometimes stands as a mere literalization of the more daunting, figurative apocalypse set out in Revelations.

A rather different scene of prophecy informs a passage allotted a paradigmatic status by Wordsworth in the "Prospectus" to *The Excursion*, a passage that has been no less crucial for many of Wordsworth's critics.[10] In presenting *The Excursion* to the public without the preliminary text of *The Prelude*, Wordsworth nonetheless wanted to convey a sense of the entire massive project and chose as "a kind of *Prospectus*" for the whole poem these verses from the end of the first book of *The Recluse*, including this invocation:

> Come thou prophetic Spirit, that inspir'st
> The human soul of universal earth.
> Dreaming on things to come; and dost possess
> A metropolitan Temple in the hearts
> Of mighty Poets; upon me bestow
> A gift of genuine insight; that my Song
> With star-like virtue in its place may shine;
> Shedding benignant influence, . . . [11]

These lines seem to hark back to the opening of *The Prelude*, to the scene of Wordsworth being singled out as a prophetic poet, and yet the difference is crucial. Here Wordsworth invokes the prophetic Spirit, very much in the tradition of Milton's calling and his "Hebraicized Muse," as Harold Bloom terms it. At the opening of *The Prelude*, by contrast, the prophetic spirit comes, so to speak, unannounced. Wordsworth bears witness to his inspiration, but it has come unbidden and, in this respect, the scene is much closer to the line of the Hebrew prophets than that of the Continental or English epic poets. Prophets of the Old Testament do not, as a rule, entreat God for the spirit of prophecy: When the word of the Lord comes, it comes regardless of the will of the prophet. Thus the formulation in the Prospectus to *The Excursion* is less "prophetic," less emphatically so, than the earlier scene in the *The Prelude*. The testimony to the descent of the prophetic spirit constitutes a far stronger claim to authority than does the invocation of a muse, however Hebraicized, however divine. The invocation of a prophetic muse, moreover, is far more formulaic and conventional in poetic discourse than is the testimony to being overtaken by it. This latter stance appears in the Romantics—by contrast to the major "pre-Romantic" poets—as a more radical return to the line of Hebrew prophecy, often more radical even than Milton's. But Wordsworth's poetry and that of his contemporaries did owe something to those poets of the mid-eighteenth century who, after the death of Pope, seized an opportunity to regain at least a muted version of the Miltonic line of prophecy.

～

In William Collins's "Ode on the Poetical Character," the most programmatic text in his corpus, the poet invokes the tradition of British bards and prophets so as to situate himself in the distinguished line of Spenser and Milton. The opening of the poem is less a traditional invocation of the muse than a recollection of a reading:

> As once, if not with light regard,
>   I read aright that gifted bard,
>   (Him whose school above the rest
>   His loveliest Elfin Queen has blessed)
>   One, only one, unrivalled fair
>   Might hope the magic girdle wear,

> At solemn tourney hung on high,
> The wish of each love-darting eye;
> Lo! to each other nymph in turn applied,
> As if, in air unseen, some hovering hand,
> Some chaste and angel-friend to virgin-fame,
>   With whispered spell had burst the starting band,
> It left unblest her loathed, dishonored side;
>   Happier hopeless fair, if never
>   Her baffled hand with vain endeavor
> Had touched that fatal zone to her denied!
> Young Fancy, thus, to me divinest name,
>   To whom, prepared and bathed in heaven,
>   The crest of amplest power is given,
>   To few the godlike gift assigns
>   To gird their blest prophetic loins,
> And gaze her visions wild, and feel unmixed her flame![12]

Collins rereads and reconfigures Spenser's narrative of the competition for Florimel's girdle in Book IV of *The Faerie Queene* as an allegory of poetic "election." The prophetic power of poetic imagination is given only to a few, and this gift is given not according to a preordained decision of a divinity but as the result of an agon of pretenders to the exalted office of poet. The closing lines propose a poetic fable—later to be reversed by Blake—that locates the source of the prophetic gift in the loins, such that chastity is the precondition of poetry, with sublimation of sexual energy as the motive for metaphor.[13] Much of the poem seems enlisted in the self-legitimation of Collins's poetic career, as if he is inscribing himself in a history of literature that might better be left to future arbitration. He appears to align himself with Milton when he says:

> I view that oak, the fancied glades among,
> By which as Milton lay, his evening ear,
> From many a cloud that dropped ethereal dew,
> Nigh sphered in heaven its native strains could hear.[14]

Yet the final lines foreclose the future that Collins had seemed to be promising himself:

> With many a vow from hope's aspiring tongue,
>   My trembling feet his guiding steps pursue:
>   In vain—such bliss to one alone

Of all the sons of soul was known,
And Heaven and Fancy, kindred powers,
Have now o'erturned the inspiring bowers,
Or curtained close such scene from every future view.[15]

Collins's vision of the future is, in the end, unexpectedly pedestrian. He hesitates, rather like Keats's Hyperion, to step into the temple of prophetic poetry, and instead of presenting an apocalyptic revelation of the divine, he restricts himself to a gloomy forecast of literary history. Milton had recorded in his Nativity Ode the silencing of the pagan oracles, but here Collins records the silencing of inspired, prophetic poetry. Even if the ending of Collins's ode fails to negate the self-aggrandizement implicit in its opening, it is clear that the poet declines the office of prophet, even as he covets it. As crucial a metapoetic document as the "Ode on the Poetical Character" is, one should not lose sight of its place in the spectrum of Collins's work, in which the prophetic persona is only occasionally adopted as one among others. The revival of the Pindaric ode in the mid-eighteenth century owed much to Collins's impetus, and his ancient model Pindar had referred to himself as a prophet in his paean "To the Delpians at Pytho." Yet the stance of the prophet in no way pervades his poetic production in the way it does for a William Blake or a Christopher Smart. In Collins one senses a certain distance from the prophetic, and when the problematic surfaces the poetry tends to be about the prophetic rather than to be itself prophetic.

In the discontinuous line of prophetic poetry that runs between Milton and Blake, the corpus of Thomas Gray stands as another key point. In Gray's "Progress of Poesy," a spirited *vade mecum* through literary history, the poet omits any mention of Hebrew prophecy, though he does record the following:

Woods that wave o'er Delphi's steep,
Isles that crown the Aegean deep,
Fields that cool Ilissus laves,
Or where Maeander's amber waves
In lingering lab'rinths creep,
How do your tuneful echoes languish,
Mute but to the voice of anguish?
Where each old poetic mountain
Inspiration breathed around:

Every shade and hallowed fountain
Murmured deep a solemn sound:
Till the sad Nine in Greece's evil hour
Left their Parnassus for the Latian plains.
Alike they scorn the pomp of tyrant-power,
And coward Vice that revels in her chains.
When Latium had her lofty spirit lost,
They sought, oh Albion! next thy sea-encircled coast.[16]

The word "progress" in Gray's title is a relatively neutral term, not nearly so positively marked as it is when it functions as a master category in the lexicon of Enlightenment philosophy of history. Gray does not really address the question of the progress of the arts, as, say, Rousseau and Hazlitt later would, but he describes rather the trajectory of poetry from Greece to Italy to England, the movement Geoffrey Hartman has termed "westering." Gray's charting of the itinerary of poetry, however, is not neutral in every respect: His Pindaric ode, at the moment when addressing the poetry of ancient Greece, reads much like an *ubi sunt* elegy, laments the lost era when poetry was truth and truth poetry. Is it all downhill from Delphi's steep? For Gray, as for Collins, the model and the myth of (pagan) prophetic poetry haunt poetic production in the present. Both poets opt to invoke the spirits—against whose poems theirs pale in comparison—rather than to have those ghosts appear unsummoned. Both rely on a certain metonymic power of great names to conjure with.

In the poetry of Thomas Gray, the figure of the bard emerges in full force. The bard is by no means identical with the Biblical prophet, though the similarities are numerous. Both claim to be inspired by a higher, divine authority. Both act as the voice and often the conscience of the people. (*Vox populi vox dei*, the saying goes, a saying that Blake would inscribe in the margins of Milton and that would find its echo in Hölderlin.) The major difference between prophet and bard lies in the way history functions for each of them. The British and Druidic figure of the bard is much like the epic poet, an individual repository of a people's histories, legends, and myths, whereas the Biblical prophet—as distinct from the writer of apocalypse—tends to be concerned above all with the people's impending crises, the demands of what Martin Buber called "the historical hour." However, in Gray's "The Bard," a poem that would deeply impress Blake, the titular hero does cut a prophetic figure:

On a rock, whose haughty brow
Frowns o'er old Conway's foaming flood,
Robed in the sable garb of woe,
With haggard eyes the poet stood;
(Loose his beard and hoary hair
Streamed, like a meteor, to the troubled air)
And, with a master's hand and prophet's fire,
Struck the deep sorrows of his lyre.
'Hark, how each giant-oak and desert cave
'Sighs to the torrent's awful voice beneath!
O'er thee, oh king! their hundred arms they wave,
Revenge on thee in hoarser murmurs breathe;
'Vocal no more, since Cambria's fatal day,
'To high-born Hoel's harp or soft Llewellyn's lay.[17]

Gray's Pindaric ode rests on the tradition that Edward I ordered the execution of Welsh bards thought to be a crucial force in the resistance to his reign. In Gray's version, one bard who escapes death is somehow able to confront Edward and his army from a crag that cannot be reached by the enemy. Although a poet like Blake could not share in the sentiment proclaiming a joyful prophecy of the coming Tudor dynasty, Gray's bard is very much a voice of the people and a figure of political opposition; it is in part this legacy that survives from the "Age of Sensibility" for the later generations of Romantic writers.[18] But as in Collins there is a certain distance from the prophetic, so in Gray the bardic figure is displaced as a persona from a hoary past. Suvir Kaul has demonstrated the nearly systematic ambivalence about authority legible throughout Gray's work.[19] Whether for ideological or psychological reasons—having to do with Bate's "burden of the past" or Bloom's "anxiety of influence"—Gray seemed reluctant to adopt the mantle of authority in the manner of a Milton or even a Pope. And in this, Collins, Gray, and company did not quite resemble the Romantics who would follow in their wake. But for one eminent poet of their generation, things were somewhat different.

Edward Young is one of the few poets of what is still provocatively called "Preromanticism"[20] whose work might generally be characterized as prophetic, and his line too descends directly to Blake, for whom poetry and prophecy were virtually identical. Blake came to know Young's poetry intimately from his work on the massive project of illustrating Young's masterpiece, *The Complaint; or Night Thoughts*, the poem that secured

Young's fame in Britain and on the Continent. The similarities with the later poetry of Blake, especially *Vala, or The Four Zoas*, are many, from its organization and nexus of themes to its diction and sublime style. Some sense of the likeness between Young and Blake can be gleaned in relatively economic fashion by considering not the unwieldy *Night Thoughts* but a lesser-known work by the former: "The Last Day." Young begins by contrasting his concerns, in the first decades of the eighteenth century, with those of his contemporaries:

> While others sing the fortune of the great;
> Empire and arms, and all the pomp of state;
> With Britain's hero set their souls on fire,
> And grow immortal as his deeds inspire;
> I draw a deeper scene, a scene that yields
> A louder trumpet, and more dreadful fields;
> The world alarm'd, both heaven and earth o'erthrown,
> And gasping nature's last tremendous groan;
> Death's ancient sceptre broke, the teeming tomb,
> The righteous Judge, and man's eternal doom.[21]

At first, Young seems to draw a stark opposition between history and myth, as his gaze penetrates beyond the props of everyday history to the theater of the world under the aspect of eternity. This appeal beyond history is only apparently ahistorical, because Young will soon return to address the present, and in a very specific way.

Near the outset of "The Last Day," Young invokes a traditional, neoclassical muse, but not before he has called on a much more powerful deity:

> But chiefly thou, great Ruler! Lord of all!
> Before whose throne archangels prostrate fall;
> If at thy nod, from discord, and from night,
> Sprang beauty, and yon sparkling worlds of light,
> Exalt e'en me; all inward tumults quell;
> The clouds and darkness of my mind dispel;
> To my great subject thou my breast inspire,
> And raise my lab'ring soul with equal fire.[22]

While it may be a humble gesture to entreat God's inspiration in writing poetry, it is much less so to compare oneself, as Young does, with the great Hebrew prophets, among whom Jonah is alluded to and Elijah named. The attitude most characteristic of both prophet and apocalyptist is the sense of

urgency prompted by a vision of a world and words being overwhelmed.
After recounting an event of recent history, Young interrupts himself to say:

> But why this idle toil to paint that day?
> This time elaborately thrown away?
> Words all in vain pant after the distress,
> The height of eloquence would make it less.
> Heavens! how the good man trembles!—
> And is there a Last Day? and must there come
> A sure fix'd, inexorable doom?[23]

The panic is all the more acute at the moment when the vision of the Last
Judgment and the act of recording it in writing coalesce:

> Such is the scene; and one short moment's space
> Concludes the hopes and fears of human race.
> Proceed who dares!—I tremble as I write,
> The whole creation swims before my sight;
> I see, I see, the Judge's frowning brow;
> Say not, 'tis distant; I behold it now
> I faint, my tardy blood forgets to flow,
> My soul recoils at the stupendous woe;
> That woe, whose pangs, which from the guilty breast,
> In these, or words like these shall be expresst.[24]

Like Jeremiah and Ezekiel before him, Young finds the prophetic vision literally painful to behold. The testimony of its effect accords with Kant's determination of the sublime force as a blocking of the vital forces (*Hemmung
der Lebenskräfte*), and that testimony is enlisted to persuade listeners of the
truth of his vision.[25] Yet for all Young's talk of shifting to a deeper scene and
seeming to leave the sphere of quotidian life for the spectacle of the Last
Judgment, the poem remains rooted in the political drama of its age. In the
prayer ending the second book of "The Last Day," Young addresses a divine
ruler, but his eye is equally on a human one closer to home:

> Thine is the vintage, and the conquest thine:
> Thy pleasure points the shaft, and bends the bow;
> The cluster blasts, or bids it brightly glow:
> 'Tis thou that lead'st our powerful armies forth,
> And giv'st Great Anne Thy sceptre o'er the north.[26]

In this passage, which has counterparts in a good many prophetic poets of
the eighteenth and early nineteenth centuries, God appears as the displaced

figure for a temporal, political leader. "The Last Day" was originally to be prefaced by a hyperbolic paean to Queen Anne, which the author, as the editors of his works agree, wisely chose to omit. Yet vestiges of it and the sentiment behind it remain in the body of the poem, and they are typical of the way in which politics, explicitly or allegorically, tends to surface in the representation of a realm supposed to be so utterly different.

If the poetry of Young is not so widely read now, except a bit grudgingly as a document of eighteenth-century taste or as a precursor to Blake, his work in criticism has better survived the test of time, especially his *Conjectures on Original Composition* of 1759. There, too, Young appeals to a mythic divine source of poetic inspiration, but some of his formulations are the more circumspect and prosaic ones of the critic, not the poet. He speaks, for example, of the "fable of inspiration" and recalls that genius "has always been supposed to partake of something divine." Even when his phrasing is less qualified, he pictures the desire for divine inspiration as a hallmark of great poetry, whether or not the claim is justified: "True poesy, like true religion, abhors idolatry, and though it honours the memory of the exemplary, and takes them willingly (yet cautiously) as guides in the way to glory, real, though unexampled, excellence is its only aim; nor looks it for any inspiration less than divine."[27] One senses something of a discrepancy between Young the poet and Young the critic, since the former blithely indulges in the fable of which the latter is suspicious. But in his own time, it was Young the poet who carried the day.

No such discrepancy obtains in the work of the eighteenth-century poet with perhaps the most patent claim to the prophetic mantle: Christopher Smart. In his poetry and his prose—although the distinction is not always pertinent in his writing—Smart consistently displays a deference to and a participation in the divine word: "For I have adventured myself in the name of the Lord, and he hath mark'd me as his own."[28] As Karina Williamson has observed in her edition of *Jubilate Agno*, Smart adopts the stance of prophet and writer of apocalypse, addressing his nation on any number of issues of the day as well as on the ultimate future of humanity. Institutionalized for insanity—although Samuel Johnson, for one, thought that unreasonable—Smart fit all too easily the figure of the voice crying in the wilderness, even if the wilderness was the streets of London.[29]

Smart's writing is exceptionally uneven: Moments of extraordinary power sit side by side with the most unintelligible or trivial pronouncements. He was perhaps too summarily dismissed in his own time and has been perhaps too readily lionized in ours. But for our purposes the interest is less in the variable quality of his poetic production than in the ways Smart rewrites and reworks Biblical material and for the prophetic figure his persona cuts. In the fragmentary, posthumous extravaganza of *Jubilate Agno* Smart could write: "*For Newton nevertheless is more of error than of the truth, but I am the WORD of GOD.*"[30] This is a proposition admirers of Smart rarely cite, preferring to invoke the more humble and even charming proclamation: "*I am the Lord's News-Writer—the scribe-evangelist Widow Mitchel, Gun and Grange bless the Lord Jesus.*"[31] Smart indeed alternates between the supplicant stance of the psalmist and the fiercely polemical one of the prophet. Not everyone is of the Word of God, and so to write on behalf of the always-embattled word requires that it—the word—be "a sword at my side."[32] Clement Hawes has helpfully drawn attention to the double-edged character of Smart's persona as "scribe-evangelist": the scribe, as the more or less passive transcriber of the words of the Lord; the evangelist, as the active proselytizer, the disseminator of the "good news."[33]

One trait that emerges emphatically in Smart—and to a degree unusual in other Christian poets of his time—is an insistence on the letter, the letter of the Hebraic Bible and even just of the Hebrew alphabet. Knowledge of Hebrew was not very widespread among Christian scholars, to say nothing of poets, but Smart attends closely to the Hebraic letter, even if it is sometimes to depart from a literal understanding of the text.[34] Witness Smart's extended extrapolation-cum-speculation on the Hebrew letter *lamed* (ל), corresponding to the English "l":

For the letter ל which signifies GOD by himself is on the fibre of some leaf in every tree.

> For ל is the grain of the human heart on the networks of the skin.
> For ל is upon every hair both of man and beast. . . .[35]

Hawes has rightly remarked of the first of Smart's observations here that Smart has translated from the Hebrew *lamed* to the English "l" then from "l" to "el," a transliteration of the Hebrew "ל," namely, a short form of one of the names for God.[36] Thus Smart makes a connection between two Hebrew terms via an English one, where no non-English speaker of Hebrew would possibly have done the same. This eccentric midrashic spirit is responsible for some of Smart's most characteristic writing. Smart's authority in this traffic with letters is none other than God: *"For I bless God for the Postmaster general and all conveyancers of letters under his care especially Allen and Shevlock."*[37] Such an insistence on the letter may be somewhat shocking to Christian readers raised on the primacy of the spirit. But there is a way in which this endless fascination with the letter turns into something of the order of the spirit through its very inventiveness, its proliferation of readings, its well-nigh infinite translations. *"For I have translated in the charity, which makes things better and I shall be translated myself at the last."*[38] Invoking the Augustinian principle of charity as the rubric under which all interpretation (of the Bible) is to take place, Smart, not unlike Benjamin, sees "translation" in more senses than one as a ubiquitous phenomenon.[39] In this Smart senses something of what Kristeva calls "a Single yet Infinite Meaning that supports human desire in the face of God."[40]

As ubiquitous as the predicaments and possibilities of language are, not everyone relates to the Word in the same way. "All good words are from God," Smart insists, but human beings who are "gifted in the word" have a special obligation, a vocation really, to speak, write, and act "in the name of the Lord."[41]

All these claims are made with the utmost certainty, prompted by an absolute faith and supported even by a patriotic or national(ist) sense that Smart is serving God and country—and that those two causes are one. For all of Smart's hermeticism and his periodic confinement, the desire is clearly for a public proclamation of the divine, reinvented and rearticulated for an England that strangely overlaps with Israel:

> Let Aziza rejoice with the Day Lily.
> *For I prophecy that the praise of God will*
> *be in every man's mouth in the Publick streets.*
>
> Let Zabbai rejoice with Buckshorn Plaintain
> Coronopus.
> *For I prophecy that there will be Publick worship*
> *in the cross ways and fields.*[42]

Although Smart had learned a good deal about parallelism in Hebrew verse from Robert Lowth's *Lectures on the Sacred Poetry of the Hebrews*, Smart's language is more given over to a rhetoric of addition and accumulation. It is Smart's small way of addressing the problem but also the possibility of a discourse that would be adequate to the infinity of God. The multiplication of phrases and verses—which Geoffrey Hartman has wittily termed "add-oration"—is one way to intimate that infinity even as one recognizes the impossibility of actually representing it. But "innumerable ciphers will amount to something," Smart says.[43]

In tracking backward from Wordsworth to the poets of the "Age of Sensibility," as Northrop Frye called it, we have always been encountering Christian, Protestant poets of various stripes. But, as we will see in more detail in the subsequent chapter, the eighteenth century was preparing the way for a reading of the Bible as myth, and so for virtually the first time in Western history, the Bible could be taken up, cited, learned from, and more without any particular doctrinal attachment to its content. One result of "historicism"'s approach to the Bible as one text among others was that the Bible became precisely that. And so in the era of Romanticism we can witness the emergence of a substantially new poetic stance toward the Bible, exemplified, for one, in the work of Percy Shelley.

If one were to look simply at Shelley's writings and comments on religion, "prophecy" would emerge an epistemologically suspect and politically dubious phenomenon. But something "like prophetic strain," to borrow Milton's phrase, riddles Shelley's poetic production and some of his prose. Milton Wilson does not hesitate to characterize Shelley's imagination in general as "prophetic."[44] Similarly, Harold Bloom discusses Shelley in *The Visionary Company* under the heading of "Urbanity and Apocalypse," beginning his analysis with the recognition of this paradox: "Shelley is a prophetic and religious poet whose passionate convictions are agnostic."[45]

Shelley often presents his poems, especially the explicitly political ones, as (or as if) proceeding from another voice, although not necessarily a divine one. The opening of "The Mask of Anarchy," for example, reads:

> As I lay asleep in Italy
> There came a voice from over the Sea
> And with great power it forth led me
> To walk in the visions of Poesy.[46]

Translated back into the details of Shelley's daily life, these verses seem to indicate little more than that he received a letter from his friend Peacock with news of the Peterloo riot and massacre, which prompted him to write the poem. But the phrasing of the poem suggests a more prophetic scenario, which gives way, in the body of the poem and especially its ending, to a sense that some prophetic spirit is arising from the events themselves:

> 'And that slaughter to the Nation
> Shall steam up like inspiration,
> Eloquent, oracular,
> A volcano heard afar.

> 'And these words shall then become
> Like Oppression's thundered doom
> Ringing through each heart and brain,
> Heard again-again-again-

> 'Rise like Lions after slumber
> In unvanquishable number—
> Shake your chains to earth like dew
> Which in sleep had fallen on you—
> Ye are many—they are few."[47]

The poet seems to act merely as the medium for words that are only incidentally his: The event itself is oracular and appears to transform itself into words, future words that the poet anticipates. The ambiguity of the phrase "these words," however, includes those of Shelley's poem and thus marks itself as something of a self-fulfilling prophecy, eloquent and oracular.[48]

Mary Shelley relates that Percy read the Bible daily, which to some seems incompatible with the behavior of an avowed atheist. Shelley could refer in "A Defence of Poetry" to the "astonishing poetry of Moses, Job, Solomon, and Isaiah" at the same time that, in a draft of his "Letter to Lord Ellenbrough," he could expose the prophecies of Moses as false and obscure. Shelley is careful not simply to identify poetry and prophecy and is also concerned to disentangle his notion of the prophet from a certain reductive but commonly held view of what a Biblical prophet is:

Poets, according to the circumstances of the age and nation in which they appeared, were called in earlier epochs of the world legislators or prophets; a poet essentially comprises and unites both these characters. For he not only beholds intensely the present as it is and discovers those laws according to which present things ought to be ordered but he beholds the future in the present, and his thoughts are the germs of the flower and the fruit of the latest time. Not that I assert poets to be prophets in the gross sense of the word, or that they can foretell the form as surely as they foreknow the spirit of events; such is the pretence of superstition which would make poetry an attribute of prophecy rather than prophecy an attribute of poetry.[49]

It is clear from this passage and the rest of the "Defence" that poetry is the primary category, partly because Shelley restores to the word "poetry" its original Greek sense of "making," and so it applies to the production not just of compositions in verse and, more important, not just of texts. But Shelley is concerned to garner for poetry something of the aura specific to prophecy. Poets as prophets may not know the form of events—even future events—but they do know their *spirit*, which is surely the most essential thing. And more than this, the prophetic poets, insofar as their thoughts are the germs of the flowers and fruit "of latest time," help produce the very future that they might otherwise seem merely to know in advance. This is possible because not only were the original poets prophets or legislators (and the *or* is not necessarily the sign of an either/or relation), but all poets are, famously, the "unacknowledged legislators of the world."[50] It is some small irony that the radical Shelley, admirer of William Godwin's *Enquiry Concerning Political Justice*, the foundational text of anarchism, should find in legislation a paradigm for poetry.

~

In German writing of the Romantic period, the theory and practice of prophecy assumes quite a different shape. For prophecy is much more an object of theory than it is a mode of poetic practice. A reading of the major Romantic theorists will reveal how prophecy is at once a marginal and privileged category: marginal, insofar as "the prophetic" is hardly an omnipresent concern among the theorists, yet privileged when the aphoristic speculations of a Novalis and a Schlegel on the topic of prophecy are read "in themselves." If read in an isolated sequence, the pronouncements by Friedrich Schlegel would make the most extravagant claims for prophecy as the model for both poetry and philosophy. But the illusion that prophecy is a master category in Schlegel's discourse should be dispelled in advance, even as we emphasize the importance of some of his insights.

The aphorisms and fragments of Schlegel are more playful and *hypothetical* than has been granted by many of his interpreters. They are less the distilled, carefully weighed judgments of a lifetime than they are verbal experiments, rather in the manner of Wittgenstein's *Philosophical Investiga-*

tions, though with fewer question marks. This aspect of Schlegel's thought can be glimpsed, for example, in a collection of fragments such as the posthumously published "Philosophy of Philology," in which a small lexicon of concepts ("art," "poetry," "philosophy," "philology," and "science") are yoked together in any number of copulative and genitive constructions (X is Y, the X of Y, the Y of X), almost as if to see what linguistic *bricolage* might produce. Not that Schlegel is simply arbitrary or random in his thoughts. But one has to attend to the hypothetical character of the pronouncements even when they come in the form of the most apodictic or self-assured statements. This holds, too, for those assertions couched in mathematic or scientific formulae, especially when applied to domains that lend themselves more to interpretive debates than to airtight equations. Yet for all the qualifications, the fragments of Schlegel do constitute a powerful collective statement on the insistence of the prophetic in the discourses of poetry and philosophy.

With characteristic aplomb Friedrich Schlegel proclaims in his *Literary Notebooks*: "Poetry is theosophy; no one is a poet except the prophet."[51] So lapidary a statement necessarily leaves the sense of "prophet" indeterminate, yet at the very least it seems clear that Schlegel does not have in mind some merely secularized version of the divine prophet. By "theosophy" Schlegel means not the modern mystical movement associated with that name but simply "wisdom of (or about) God." Elsewhere in the notebooks Schlegel glosses the notion of the prophetic in this way: "Enthusiastic is better than Allegorical. PROPHETIC is at once Enthus(iastic) and Allegorical. Thus, the highest."[52] The predicates Schlegel links to the prophetic are traditional ones: Prophecy is literally "enthusiastic" in the etymological sense that the god enters the prophet to speak in his or her voice. And prophecy is so highly figurative as to be thoroughly allegorical, where the meaning is typically something different from the manifest sense (as commentators from Augustine to Lowth agree). But why is it allotted the lofty designation of "the highest"? A fragment from the *Athenaeum* may point toward an answer: "The poeticizing philosopher, the philosophizing poet is a prophet. The didactic poem should be prophetic and certainly has the capability to be so."[53] In a period when and in a nation where the leading intellectuals were intensely interested in the traffic between literature and philosophy— even Hegel and Schelling tried their hands at poems!—it is no small matter to make prophecy the mediating category permitting their union and the passage from one to another. In its mediating and synthesizing functions, prophecy stands as "the highest." For Schlegel, the prophet seems to be a figure who unites the literary and rhetorical art of the poet with the truth-telling discourse of the philosopher. "Every poetic philos[opher] and every philos[ophical] poet," Schlegel says, "is a prophet."[54]

Was there anything or anyone to correspond to Schlegel's ideal of the prophet, the prophet who was also a poet and philosopher? Dante is the author most frequently invoked by Schlegel as a prophet, but the latter seemed to look in vain for an equally sublime figure in his own time. He did claim rather caustically that "Schiller and Klopstock are two halves of a whole, together they would make one good prop[hetic] poet."[55] Schlegel was probably not very well acquainted with the work of the one great contemporary poet who could arguably, if reductively, be thought of as half Schiller, half Klopstock: namely, Friedrich Hölderlin. But the absence of actual instances of the prophetic ideal made it only all the more beguiling as an idea.[56]

Schlegel's allusion to Klopstock as a "semiprophetic," good poet prompts us to turn our attention for the moment to the principal precursor to the Romantics as a model for inspired poetry. His fame rests primarily on the strength of *Der Messias*, the epic poem based on the Gospels that prompted poets and critics alike to compare him to Milton. When some of the dust stirred up by literati in Germany and England settled, Klopstock seemed to pale in comparison, and the slogan "the German Milton" prompted a good many sneers, including a famous one from Blake. When Wordsworth and Coleridge visited the aging poet, his lack of physical energy seemed to be a material emblem indicating that his poetry, too, was not as forceful as one had once thought.[57] But the tag of "the German Milton" was more appropriate in his own culture where the power of his verse was felt by virtually every major writer of the succeeding generation. Klopstock plays in Germany much the same role that Young did in England, and the former felt a great affinity with the latter. Young's *Night Thoughts* was translated by Klopstock's friend Ebert, and Klopstock addressed an ode to his celebrated English rival. "To Young" is a semiserious document in and about the anxiety of influence. Klopstock begins by enjoining Young, "a prophetic old man" ("prophetischer Greis") to die.[58] According to Klopstock's logic, Young has already left behind his monument (the *Night Thoughts*), earned his laurels as well as a place in heaven. And besides, what is someone who has seen the Last Judgment waiting for? The poem closes with Klopstock repeating the command to die, so that Young can become his *Genius* or tutelary spirit. Rarely has an Oedipal death wish been so baldly expressed in a poetic context, and the effect is not completely mitigated by the humorous tone. Even in this form, Klopstock's display of the anxiety of influence has a particular aptness for the prophetic tradition; the belated prophet requires the death of the precursor to be able to revise and repeat the prophetic word already prophesied. As time goes on, prophecy comes to depend increasingly on a tradition of prior prophecy, something with which Blake will come to terms as directly as possible in writing *Milton*.

Klopstock's more typical productions—the flippant ode "To Young" is uncharacteristic—were modeled on several strands of Biblical prophecy and are easily legible in poems such as "The Future" ("Die Zukunft"), "Prophecy" ("Weissagung"), and "The Redeemer" ("Der Erlöser"), as well as in his magnum opus, *Der Messias*, based in part on apocalyptic material from the New Testament. Especially since the former poems pose few interpretive difficulties, considerations of real complexity can be deferred until the chapter on Hölderlin. But we can also note for the moment another important aspect of the prophetic persona elaborated by Klopstock and in such a way as to provide a model for the generation to follow: in conjuring his semiexistent nation "Germany," which he termed his "second fatherland." In a poem such as "My Fatherland" ("Mein Vaterland"), Klopstock presents the poetic speaker as bursting forth with word and sounds he is incapable of containing. It is in these poems especially that Klopstock pulls out all the stops: The poetic sentences feature as many exclamation points as they do periods. At turns impassioned and bombastic, Klopstock's verses strain, by graphic illustration, to make every utterance of moment for the reader. At their best, the lines have the resonance and verbal force of a good Hölderlin poem.

Klopstock's achievement provided German poets of the late eighteenth and early nineteenth centuries with an important precedent: a vatic persona free to reread and rewrite the sacred text of the Bible. As Klopstock writes in his essay "On Sacred Poetry" ("Von der Heiligen Poesie"): " . . . I believe I may assume permission to write poetry in [the bounds of] religion [*in der Religion zu dichten*]; or in other words, . . . I consider it permissible as well to develop further, in a poetic mode, that which Revelation teaches."[59] Poetry, for Klopstock, is not remotely opposed in principle to revelation, as the fictional might be opposed to the true: It can not only imitate but *develop* the teaching of revelation. One can glimpse here something of the stance that Novalis would adopt in a saying of some years later: "Who has declared the Bible closed? Shouldn't the Bible be considered as still growing?"[60]

Among the various kinds of sacred poetry that can, according to Klopstock, be imitated and elaborated by latter-day poets is prophecy. In general, Klopstock believes that the imitation of sacred writing should not consist in miming the "style of revelation" ("die Schreibart der Offenbarung"); rather it should entail attention to the tone of presentation and to the grand design of religion. Having said this, however, Klopstock remarks somewhat cryptically: "The imitation of the prophets, insofar as their masterpieces of eloquence aim at expression [in Absicht auf den Ausdruck sind], is something else."[61] It is regrettable for our purposes that Klopstock simply leaves this claim hanging, without any explanation. Like all "higher poetry," in Klopstock's phrase, prophetic imitation would have to partake of "moral beauty," the sine qua non of this mode of writing.[62] From among the great works of "moral beauty" produced by poets, Klopstock singles out Young's *Night Thoughts* as exemplary, even above Homer. Klopstock saw in his own time the prospects for a significant revival of religious, inspired, and specifically prophetic poetry. Moreover, his own circumscribed achievement in this domain would "inspire" the succeeding generation of poets to imitate and even surpass it.

In turning back to the Romantics proper, indeed to Novalis as one of the arch-Romantics, we find that his fragments feature a concern with the shifting identities of poetry and prophecy similar to that of Schlegel, although the former is more prolix and, if possible, even more paradoxical. Novalis writes, for example:

Der Sinn für P[oesie] hat nahe Verwandschaft mit dem Sinn der Weissagung und dem religiösen, den Seher-sinn überhaupt. Der Dichter ordnet, vereinigt, wählt, erfindet—und es ist ihm selbst unbegreiflich, warum gerade so und nicht anders.[63]

[The sense for P[oetry] has a close kinship with the sense of prophecy and for the religious, oracular sense in general. The poet orders, unites, chooses, discovers— and it is incomprehensible even to himself why exactly it is in that way and not otherwise.]

Novalis's characterization of the poet-prophet heightens the sense of a divided subject: The verbs "order," "unite," "combine," and especially "choose" all suggest conscious action and volition, and yet the entire process seems at the same time beyond the control and comprehension of the prophetic character. Again, it is a double-edged gesture to compare the poet to the prophet, especially if one emphasizes the *mania* of the poet, that which the poet cannot control, that which Plato feared so much as a force not subservient to the demands of reason.

The figure of the prophet emerges most profoundly in Novalis's brief meditation entitled "Monolog," a text now singled out as a crux for the understanding of his work and for German Romanticism in general.[64] The text demands a reading in its entirety, for at least as important as its assertions about prophecy and language is the place the prophetic occupies in the text's itinerary. "Monolog" begins:

Es ist eigentlich um das Sprechen eine närrische Sache; das reiche Gespräch ist ein bloßes Wortspiel. Der lächerliche Irrtum ist nur zu bewundern, daß die Leute meinen—sie sprächen um die Dinge willen. Gerade das Eigentümliche der Sprache, daß sie sich bloß um sich selbst bekümmert, weiß keiner. Darum ist sie ein so wunderbares und fruchtbares Geheimnis,—daß wenn einer bloß spricht, um zu sprechen, er gerade die herrlichsten, originellsten Wahrheiten ausspricht. Will er aber von etwas Bestimmten sprechen, so lässt ihn die launige Sprache das lächerliste und verkehrteste Zeug sagen. Daraus ensteht auch der Haß, den so manche ernsthafte Leute gegen die Sprache haben. Sie merken ihren Mutwillen, merken aber nicht, daß das verächtliche Schwatzen die unendliche ernsthafte Seite der Sprache ist. Wenn man den Leuten nur begreiflich machen könnte, daß es mit der Sprache wie mit den mathematischen Formeln sei—Sie machen eine Welt für sich aus—Sie spielen nur mit sich selbst, drücken nichts als ihre wunderbare Natur aus, und eben darum sind sie so ausdrucksvoll—eben darum spiegelt sich in ihnen das seltsame Verhältnispiel der Dinge. Nur durch ihre Freiheit sind sie Glieder der Natur, und nur in ihren freien Bewegungen äußert sich die Weltseele und macht sie zu einem zarten Maßstab und Grundriß der Dinge.[65]

[Actually, there's a peculiar thing about speaking: Real discourse or conversation is mere wordplay. One can't help but be astonished at the absurd, wholly erroneous assumption people make—that their talk is about things. No one knows what is most distinctive about language, namely, that it is concerned solely with itself. This is why it is such a marvelous and fertile mystery—that when someone speaks just in order to speak, he pronounces the most magnificent and original truths. But if he wants to speak about something specific, the capricious nature of language will cause him to say the most ridiculous and mistaken things. This is also why a number of serious people hate language. They note its mischievousness but don't perceive that worthless chatter constitutes the infinitely serious aspect of language. If one could only make clear to them that it is with language as with mathematical formulae—they constitute a world by themselves, they play only among themselves, express nothing but their own marvelous nature, and for that very reason are so expressive and mirror the singular interplay of things. It is only through their freedom that they are parts of nature, and only in their free movement does the world soul express itself and make them into a delicate measure and abstract plan of things.]

From the outset, Novalis's claims are decidedly paradoxical: They fly in the face of common sense, which holds that language refers to things and that when one speaks about things, one can, in principle, tell the truth. By contrast, Novalis proposes that the only true conversation is wordplay, mere wordplay: "ein bloßes Wortspiel." The "play" or "Spiel" of Novalis's wordplay has little to do with the *Spieltrieb* or instinct for play that stands as the grand reconciling category between form and matter in the architectonics of Schiller's aesthetics as set out in his *Letters on Aesthetic Education*: It has no such teleological function in Novalis. Novalis's sense is much closer to what has been called recently "the play of the signifier," although Novalis stops short of some of the axioms attendant to that phrase in structuralist and poststructuralist discourse. The play of language, for Novalis, is concerned only with itself. The scandalous thought that language is only "about" itself—an idea to be echoed in the young Benjamin's meditations on language—seems to cut off language from the realm of truth, a function seemingly suspended in Novalis's "Monolog" from the outset. And yet the text circles round to try to recuperate for language the possibility of expressing truths, even in the mode of a certain mimesis. The mimetic or mirroring function of language also appears to have been jettisoned early on in the monologue, yet it too surfaces again in an oblique way. This occurs through the specter of mathematical formulae, for mathematics emerges as a self-contained discursive world which, far from being a special case of language, comes to stand as a paradigm of it.[66] Paradoxically, the very autonomy of mathematics is what constitutes its similarity to "ordinary" language, and so the "autonomous" is not at all singular. In language, as in mathematics, discursive play has only itself for its object and so expresses only its own nature. This very self-referentiality is then said to mirror that of the play of relations between things, not insofar as each word mimes the thing it is supposed to represent but to the extent that the structure of relations that constitute things and language respectively is strictly analogous. The figure of mathematics teaches an important lesson, but that analogue soon gives way to another:

So ist es mit der Sprache—wer ein feines Gefühle ihrere Applikatur, ihres Takts, ihres muskalischen Geistes hat, wer in sich das zarte Wirken ihrer innern Natur vernimmt, und danach seine Zunge oder seine Hand bewegt, der wird ein Prophet seinem dagegen wer es wohl weiß, aber nicht Ohr und Sinn genug für sie hat, Wahrheiten wie diese zu schreiben, aber von der Sprache selbst zum besten gehalten und von den Menschen, wie Kassandra von den Trojanern, verspottet werden wird. Wenn ich damit das Wesen und Amt der Poesie auf das deutlichste angegeben zu haben glauben, so weiß ich doch, daß es kein Mensch verstehen kann, und ich ganz was Albernes gesagt habe, weil ich es habe sagen wollen, und so keine Poesie zustandekommt.

[So it is, too, with language—whoever is sensitive to its touch, its tempo, its musical spirit, whoever hearkens to the gentle workings of its inner nature and moves his tongue or hand accordingly, will be a prophet; however, whoever knows it well enough but possesses neither ear nor language nor understanding for it will write truths like these but be taken in by and mocked by men, like Cassandra by the Trojans. If I have thought here to have explained the essence and function of poetry as clearly as possible, I know well that no one can understand it and that I have spoken nonsense; for I have wanted to say this and no poetry has come into being.]

The language of the world-soul, in the freedom and naturalness of its movements, is likened to the language of the prophet, who does not so much speak as moves his tongue or hand according to the machinations of language itself, rather like a marionette. The prophet is a "wordplayer" par excellence, a player with and of words, who speaks for the sake of speaking. Cassandra was a failed prophetess, not because her prophecies "failed" but because she attempted to speak of something determinate. And so, against all odds, Novalis is arguing for an ideal of utterly indeterminate prophecy —prophecy that is not about anything.

A remarkable feature of the "Monolog," in structural terms, is its abrupt transition from the analogue of the prophet to the topic of the "essence and function of poetry" ("Wesen und Amt der Poesie"). Without a single prior mention of poetry proper, Novalis believes that, through his reflections on the self-referential play of language, mathematical formulae, and prophetic speech, he has already pointed to the very essence of poetry. It is at this juncture that Novalis claims that no one is capable of understanding his discourse on discourse. It is also at this point that the text begins to reflect, self-consciously, on itself, literally to question itself:

Wie, wenn ich aber reden müsste? und dieser Sprachtrieb zu sprechen das Kennzeichen der Eingebung der Sprache in mir wäre? und mein Wille nur auch alles wollte, was ich müsste, so könnte dies ja am Ende ohne mein Wissen und Glauben Poesie sein und ein Geheimnis der Sprache verständlich machen? und so wär ich ein berufener Schriftsteller, denn ein Schriftsteller ist wohl nur ein Sprachbegeisteter?

[But what if I had to speak and this compulsion to speak were the sign of the inspiration of language, of a vitality of language within me? And what if my will also wished only what I were compelled to do? Then might not this, after all, without my knowledge and conviction, be poetry and elucidate a mystery of language? And might I not then be called to be a writer for what is a writer but one who is inspired by language?]

If Novalis's monologue is the embodiment of a certain intention or *vouloir-dire*, then given the logic of the text's initial assertions, it has disqualified itself from being able to speak the truth: The very attempt to tell the truth undermines in advance the possibility of doing so. But who is to say that the "Monolog" is the transcription of what Novalis wanted to say? He himself asks: "But what if I had to speak?" If Novalis were forced to say what he has to say, then he is like the prophet who speaks the divine word, regardless of his volition or intention. Novalis, or the text, or the voice who forces "Novalis" to speak, can decide neither its own authority nor its status as a discursive or a poetical text. What begins as a seemingly prosaic disquisition on language turns into a potentially poetic performance: The categorical assertions of the monologue's beginning give way increasingly to hypothetical and interrogative modes, such that the reader is at a loss to tell the rhetorical questions from the real.

Whatever the undecidable status of its "authority," one thing is clear: The text is as much a performance of wordplay as it is a reflection on it. If the self-reflective play of language is prophetic, then the "Monolog" is a self-fulfilling prophecy. In speaking about itself, only about itself, the text is indeed a mono-logue, a monologue that ultimately has only one thing to say, namely, that it is about itself. But if the text is truly prophetic, should it not then also be a dialogue or quasidialogue, even if we can no longer conceive of it simply as an interpersonal exchange? (The dialogic character of prophecy was taken by Blanchot, following the pioneering analysis by André Néher, to be definitive of prophetic discourse.) Novalis's monologue is a discourse divided between the two I's of the prophet, and its singular topic is its own self-division constituted by the prophetic, poetic play of language. What is most remarkable about Novalis's text for an understanding of Romantic prophecy is the strategic place the prophetic occupies in a text that is simultaneously a philosophy of language and a philosophy of poetry. The figure of the prophet makes possible the passage from language as everyday speech to language in its highest form, that is, as poetry. The play of language, of wordplay, suspends the referential function of language that common sense deems primary but also occasions the reintroduction of mimesis at a different, if not necessarily higher, level.

Our next example now in this schematic view of prophetic discourse in the Romantic period entails an overtly political text: Fichte's famous *Addresses to the German Nation*. But before turning to it a few general considerations are in order. Prophecy, as Max Weber has argued, is one of the earliest forms of political literature, the ancient ancestor of the modern-day broadside or pamphlet.[67] Hebrew prophecy arose at a time when Jerusalem was being consolidated as a city-state, the period when the monarchy was forming, even as it was severely threatened by a number of its imperial neighbors, such as Assyria. Indeed, prophetic discourse generally emerges most conspicuously in times of great political upheaval. In the modern period, the moment of the French Revolution occasioned a steady outburst of prophetic rhetoric, outside France even more than within. The classical Hebrew prophets were, in Gerhard von Rad's view, a radical wing operating independently of the more official cult, and thus prophetic politics are primarily oppositional or even revolutionary in character.[68] In its Romantic reincarnations, however, prophetic discourse ranges across the entire political spectrum from revolutionary to reactionary.[69] The prophetic reemerges in a number of ways in political writing of the Romantic period, as a topic certainly, but more often than not through strategic allusion, citation, or even the adoption of a prophetic persona. Coleridge's *The Statesman's Manual* will later provide the occasion for a detailed reading of the function of prophetic rhetoric in a political program. But for the moment a brief consideration of Fichte's *Addresses to the German Nation* will indicate some of the parameters of the problematic.

One of the most conspicuous and codified of prophetic forms is the oracle to the nation. As the birth of nations was especially at stake in Germany and France in the Romantic period, it is no wonder that a good many writers had recourse to a certain oracular rhetoric when addressing their nations. That is certainly the case with the most notorious such undertaking of the time: Fichte's *Addresses to the German Nation* (*Reden an die deutsche Nation*) of 1808. It is sometimes hard to disentangle completely Fichte's text from its afterlife in German history, since it became a touchstone of German patriotism, sometimes of the most reprehensible sort. Fichte's series of speeches can be thought prophetic in the narrow sense that they adumbrated doctrines of national and racial superiority that would later take hold with a vengeance. One could show that the later, conservative, and fascistic reception of Fichte is in part a reductive reading, since Fichte's pro-German patriotism coexisted—somewhat uneasily—with a strong republican and universalist streak characteristic of the most progressive forces of the Enlightenment.[70] Our focus, however, will be for the most part on the relatively circumscribed matter of how Fichte, with apparent ease, can liken his own predicament with that of a Biblical prophet.

Fichte's most immediate topic in his *Addresses* is education and its reform. As such, his text is pervasively oriented toward the future and yet, paradoxically, the goal of the movement of the German nation is identical with its origin. As Fichte summarizes, recalling the argument of his *The Fundamental Characteristic of the Present Age* (*Die Grundzüge des gegenwärtigen Zeitalters*), the work to which the *Addresses* are the sequel: "The real destiny of the human race on earth, I said in the lectures of which this is the continuation, is in the freedom to make itself what it really is originally."[71] Fichte's tenses have not got lost in translation here. The final phrase reads "daß es sich zu dem mache, was es eigentlich ursprünglich ist." The goal is the origin, to reverse a famous saying by Karl Kraus: Germany is to be in the future what it originally *is* not just what it originally *was*. The origin haunts and informs the present even as the present is also not commensurate with it, since it must be projected as a goal to be realized in the future.

Like so many of his contemporaries in the revolutionary period, Fichte sees his own time as a time of transition, poised between two great epochs of world history. He proceeds to say:

Now this making of itself deliberately, and according to rule, must have a beginning somewhere, and at some moment in space and time. Thereby a second great period, one of free and deliberate development of the human race, would appear in place of the first period, one of development that is not free. We are of the opinion that, in regard to time, this is the very time, and that now the race is exactly midway between the two great epochs of its life on earth. But in regard to space, we believe that it is first of all the Germans who are called on to begin the new era as pioneers and models for the rest of mankind. (40, 306)

Fichte hears a call, a call addressed to Germans in the first instance, a call he is now, as it were, transferring to his audience.[72] It is in the transformation of education (*Bildung*) that Fichte sees the institution of a new order and even a new "creation" ("eine ganz neue Ordnung der Dinge und eine neue Schöpfung"). He acknowledges his "prophecy" ("Weissagung") will sound strange to most people but claims that the very resistance to its reception will be one sign of its truth—a handy argument for any would-be prophet. In contrast to others who address the nation and merely "preach" ("predigen") to them, Fichte is more prophet than priest. His third address to the nation culminates in the following extraordinary comparison of himself with Ezekiel, together with a lengthy quotation from his Biblical precursor:

Let this generation hearken to the vision of an ancient prophet in a situation no less lamentable. Thus says the prophet by the river of Chebar, the comforter of those in captivity, not in their own, but in a foreign land. "The hand of the Lord was upon me, and carried me out in the spirit of the Lord, and set me down in the midst of the valley which was full of bones, and caused me to pass by them round about: and, behold, there were very many in the open valley; and, lo, they were very dry. And He said unto me, Son of man, can these bones live? And I answered, O Lord God, thou knowest. Again He said unto me, Prophesy upon these bones, and say unto them, O ye dry bones, hear the word of the Lord. Thus saith the Lord God unto these bones, Behold, I will cause breath to enter into you, and ye shall live: and I will lay sinews upon you, and will bring up flesh upon you, and cover you with skin, and put breath in you, and ye shall live; and ye shall know that I am the Lord. So I prophesied as I was commanded: and as I prophesied, there was a noise, and behold a shaking, and the bones came together, bone to his bone. And when I beheld, lo, the sinews and the flesh came up upon them, and the skin covered them above; but there was no breath in them. Then said He unto me, Prophesy, unto the wind, prophesy, son of man, and say to the wind, Thus saith the lord God, Come from the four winds, O breath, and breathe upon the slain, that they may live. So I prophesied as He commanded me, and the breath came into them, and they lived, and stood up upon their feet, an exceeding great army." (43–4, 310)

When read in the sequence of *Addresses*, this astonishing passage hardly sounds as extravagant as when cited out of context. A good deal of the imagery of Ezekiel's vision had been anticipated already in Fichte's text.

Hardly a page or two goes by without some reference to the opposition between the vital and the deadly, as for example in the repeated references to the differences between living languages and dead. Still, the passage is remarkable in several respects. Fichte compares himself to Ezekiel in a scene of direct dialogue with God and one of an unmediated vision, with Ezekiel being singled out to deliver God's message to his people. Moreover, Ezekiel is a prophet in captivity, as if somehow to suggest that Fichte is an exile in his country. It is, of course, proverbial in the Bible for a prophet to be without honor in his own country. Still, Fichte seems to be trying to garner the aura of a prophet by casting himself in advance as a solitary voice crying in the wilderness, even as he proclaims that the resistance to his message is the very sign of its truth.

The main function of Fichte's quotation of Ezekiel is to legitimate his own undertaking as divinely authorized, at least figuratively if not literally. Fichte seems to pass effortlessly from the citation of Ezekiel with its vision of scattered, fleshless bones receiving the breath of life from God through his prophet to his own vision of the dismembered body politic of Germany being put back together, now with the spirit of Fichte's lectures to inspire them:

Though the elements of our higher spiritual life may be just as dried up, and though the bonds of our national unity may lie just as torn asunder and as scattered in wild disorder as the bones of the slain in the prophecy, although they may have been whitened and dried for centuries in tempests, rainstorms, and burning sunshine, the quickening breath of the spiritual world has not ceased to blow. It will take hold too, of the dead bones of our national body and join them together that they may stand glorious in new and radiant life. (44, 310–11)

It is perhaps no wonder that a discourse so preoccupied with the shape of a nation to come would turn to Biblical prophecy that was formed in a period of intense nation building. As will be discussed in greater detail in the chapter on Hölderlin, the "Germany" of the last decades of the eighteenth century and the first of the nineteenth was much preoccupied with imagining just what a German nation might be, since there really was no such thing. And so prophetic discourse, with its orientation to the future, its air of authority, and its unverifiability, lent itself perfectly to the national(ist) projects of Fichte and a good many of his contemporaries.

PART I

PROPHETIC FIGURES IN
EIGHTEENTH-CENTURY INTERPRETATION

3

Robert Lowth and the Temporality of Prophetic Rhetoric

> Isaiah chose the way of metaphor.
> —Anne Carson, "Book of Isaiah"

I

The topic of Robert Lowth's lectures as Oxford's Praelector of Poetry in the 1740s was at once reverential and revolutionary: the sacred poetry of the Hebrews. Lecturing at a Christian university, Lowth could not likely have met with any opposition regarding the value of such a project. But there was little precedent for Biblical study under the rubric of the poetic or the aesthetic.[1] Lowth's predecessors at Oxford, Joseph Trapp and Joseph Spence, had made reference to Biblical passages in their lectures on poetry but did not come close to giving a full-blown treatment of the poetical character of the Bible.[2] That some passages and even whole books of the Bible, like the Song of Songs, were poetic in the strict sense was, in the mid-eighteenth century, neither a new nor a provocative thesis. Discussions of the topic, however, almost always arose as excurses in some overarching theological framework, within which aesthetic considerations were clearly circumscribed. Lowth broke sharply with that tradition. For that reason, a recognition of the character of Lowth's epoch-making lectures has to attend to where the emphasis is placed in the phrase "sacred poetry." In any event, the compatibility of the sacred and the aesthetic cannot simply be taken for granted.

Despite his efforts to respect what he calls "the sacred boundaries of theology," Lowth risks, simply by provisionally treating the Biblical text as one among others, a trespass of those boundaries.[3] The very undertaking seems to demand a comparison between the Hebrew poets and their Classical counterparts, a procedure that from the start places the psalmist, the prophet, and the pagan poet all on the same level. In addressing a Christian audience, Lowth need not belabor the doctrinal superiority of Isaiah and Ezekiel over Homer and Sophocles. But the complexity of the task and the considerable stakes involved in treating the Bible as a poetic text combine to give the lectures the character of an apology, a defense of sacred poetry.

In the Renaissance, the defense of poetry had become a productive and sometimes exalted genre in English and Continental letters, a vehicle for many and various critical insights of the period.[4] Yet for all the energy and acumen devoted to the task, poetry still seemed, from the mid-eighteenth to the early nineteenth century, to need no end of defenders. Lowth's lectures on Hebrew poetry share many of the commonplaces and strategies codified in the Renaissance defenses; what makes his project virtually unparalleled is its status as an apology for *sacred* poetry, which might seem to need no apology. The necessity of Lowth's defense, however, is in part dictated by the very tradition that produced so many defenses of poetry in general.

In laying the foundation for a kind of study later to emerge under the rubric "The Bible as Literature," Lowth is anxious to dispel certain myths circulating in poetry's name. The most urgent task is to do away with notions of poetry as mere ornament, diversion, or entertainment. At the outset, Lowth objects to the Horatian dictum, echoed in Sidney's *An Apology for Poetry* and elsewhere, that poetry's twin functions are "to instruct and to delight," Horace's *prodesse* and *delectare*. "I wish," Lowth writes, "those who have furnished us with this definition, had rather proposed utility as its ultimate object, and pleasure as the means by which that end may be effectually accomplished" (I,7,1). Rejecting a formulation in which instruction and delight merely coexist, he recasts the two functions in a hierarchical scheme in which the useful is ultimately more useful than the pleasurable. The subordinate place of pleasure, however, does not prevent "Poetry," as personified by Lowth, from being a "preceptor" to rival "Philosophy": "The one makes his appeal to reason only, independent of the passions; the other addresses the reason in such a manner, as even to engage the passions on his side. The one proceeds to Virtue and Truth by the nearest and most compendious ways; the other leads to the same point through certain deflections and deviations, by a winding but a pleasanter path" (I,7–8,1). While philosophy may be superior to poetry for avoiding the error of its ways, that seeming advantage turns out to be precisely philosophy's shortcoming. Both reach the same desired goal of virtue and truth, yet poetry has the added "utility" of being pleasurable, an argument that recalls Augustine's defense of figurative language in *On Christian Doctrine*.[5] By virtue of its very "deviations," poetry ultimately emerges as more virtuous still than philosophy.

If poetry, when juxtaposed first with philosophy, can be saved for the ends of virtue and truth, it is no wonder that it can later be paired with religion itself. Its position in this second configuration, however, is less exalted: "But after all, we shall think more humbly of Poetry than it deserves, unless we direct our attention to that quarter, where it is most eminently conspicuous; unless we contemplate it as employed on sacred subjects, and in subservience to Religion. This indeed appears to have been the original office and destination of Poetry; and this it still so happily performs, that in all other cases it seems out of character, as if intended for this purpose alone" (I,36,1). There is hardly a more characteristic critical gesture in eighteenth-century thought than to return to the "origins" of a given word or concept, as Lowth does here with poetry. Not all such returns, however, need determine the origin as the essence, as that which will govern or authorize the whole of a subsequent history or genealogy. Yet the origin of poetry, in Lowth, is also its destination. The two forces Nietzsche claimed could not be put together—origin and tendency—are here united to dominate the essence and the history of poetry. Lowth not only claims poetry for the province of religion, he also characterizes it as originally and essentially religious. In these terms, all poetry not partaking of this religious essence merely appears to be poetic: The farther removed from an origin and destination in religion, the less poetic it is. Thus Lowth, in a striking reversal of tradition, not only claims sacred poetry as a valid object for poetic analysis, he also implicitly dismisses all other poetry as not worthy of the name.[6]

If modern secular literature can, in effect, be dismissed so summarily, the case of Classical literature is less simple. Many of the monuments of Greek and Roman poetry engage the divine in a serious and sustained fashion, both as a topic and, at least in name, as a source of inspiration. In addressing a Christian audience, Lowth hardly has to prove that not all gods are created equal. A belief in the inherent superiority of the Judaic and Christian religions over their pagan rivals underwrites a whole range of his apodictic pronouncements, shading, as they do, into aesthetic judgments. Of the Biblical poets, he writes that:

the human mind can conceive nothing more elevated, more beautiful, or more elegant; . . . the almost ineffable sublimity of the subject is fully equaled by the energy of the language, and the dignity of the style. And it is worthy observation, that as some of these writings exceed in antiquity the fabulous ages of Greece, in sublimity they are superior to the most finished productions of that polished people."[7] (I,37,1)

In the beginning, then, was Hebrew poetry. Its sublimity—still to be proverbial in Coleridge's *Biographia Literaria*—is guaranteed in three ways: its noble topic, its lofty language, and its great antiquity.[8] Even though Hebrew poetry is more ancient, more "original" than its Greek counterpart (and hence, one might suppose, cruder or more natural), it turns out to be more sophisticated than even the masterworks of a refined culture. And the language of the sublime—usually defined by an incommensurability between a discourse and its object—is here posited as entirely consonant with its referent, even if in the mode of incommensurability. At this juncture in the lectures, the claim that the language of the Hebrew poets is commensurate with its sublime topic is simply asserted; a demonstration of its truth will be one of the central burdens of Lowth's project.

In the mid-eighteenth century, the technical terminology of literary analysis was still largely derived from Classical poetic and rhetorical manuals.[9] Though the various taxonomies and typologies of those treatises are by no means applicable only to Greek and Latin literature, the historicist in Lowth senses their inadequacy for an understanding of the unique features of Hebrew poetry. Here too the language of analysis is to be consonant with its object: "We must," Lowth writes, "endeavor as much as possible to read Hebrew as the Hebrews would have read it" (I,113,5). This hermeneutical stance, this "old" historicism that acknowledges historical difference but has faith in the bridging of gaps, prepares the way for insights into the characteristic form of Hebrew poetry.[10] The search for what distinguishes Hebrew poetry from its Classical counterparts leads Lowth to the "discovery" of parallelism, the achievement for which he is best remembered to this day. The category of parallelism still informs a good deal of poetic analysis in our time, even as Lowth's specific proposals for Biblical verse come under increasingly close scrutiny.[11] Lowth is justly praised for his originality; his extended analyses of the poetic and aesthetic features of the Bible were almost without precedent.[12] Several of the most eminent authorities before Lowth's time claimed to find Hebrew songs and psalms conforming to Latin metrical sequences.[13] Even when those texts failed to accord with the rules of Classical prosody, and when the laws of their composition could not be codified with any rigor, a persistent claim to their "poetic" character remained. Lowth saw it as his mission to set out a theoretical framework and practical examples to replace the observations of his many predecessors who had never quite done argumentative justice to their subject.

Before Lowth's time, there did exist a considerable tradition in English letters that, especially in the Renaissance and in the age of Milton, associated prophecy with poetry. Sidney recalls in *An Apology for Poetry*: "Among the Romans a Poet was called *Vates*, which is as much as Diuner, Fore-seer, or Prophet, as by his conioyned words is manifest."[14] He proceeds to associate David the Psalmist with the figure of the *vates* and specifically praises his handling of prophecy, which is "merely poetical," that is to say, nothing but poetical.[15] The word "poetical" is used here in the strict sense, though Sidney concedes that the rules governing the composition of the Psalms are "not yet fully found."[16] Sidney's contemporary Puttenham wrote in *The Arte of English Poesie*, in phrases to be echoed in Shelley's *A Defence of Poetry*, how poets were "the first priests, the first prophets, the first legislators and politicians in the world."[17] Puttenham further remarks of the poets: "So also were they the first Prophetes or seears, *Videntes*, for so the Scripture tearmeth them in Latine after the Hebrue word, and all the oracles and answers of the gods were giuen in meeter or verse, and published to the people by their direction."[18] That prophets are poets in the sense of visionaries was something of a critical commonplace in Sidney's time, and it would be revived again in Shelley's, but the thesis that prophecy was poetry in the strict sense retained for the time being the status of an intuition, a suspicion still to be confirmed.

Lowth's most succinct formulation of the nature of parallelism in Hebrew poetry owes nothing to the strictures of Greek and Latin prosody. He writes, in the first of his lectures on prophetic poetry: "The poetical conformation of the sentences which has been so often alluded to as characteristic of Hebrew poetry, consists chiefly in a certain equality, resemblance, or parallelism between the members of each period; so that in two lines (or members of the same period) things for the most part shall answer to things, and words to words, as if fitted to each other by a kind of rule or measure" (II,34,20).[19] Even without the phrase "as if fitted to each other by a kind of rule or measure," which was omitted in later editions of the text, Lowth's claim is a modest, almost minimal one. Parallelism, he contends, is of many varieties and gradations, the only essential component being a certain "equality" or "resemblance" between members (clauses) and periods (sentences).[20] Lowth outlines, in a typology some consider deleterious for the subsequent poetic analysis of the Bible, three kinds of parallelism: synonymous, antithetical, and synthetic or constructive.[21] Parallelism is synonymous when the same "sentiment" (*sententia*) is expressed in similar or equivalent terms. Lowth's initial example is drawn from the Psalms, but he hastens to add that "the Prophetic Muse is no less elegant and correct" (II,36,19), as evident in the following passage from Isaiah:

> Arise, be thou enlightened; for thy light is come;
> And the glory of JEHOVAH is risen upon thee.
> For, behold, darkness shall cover the earth;
> And a thick vapour the nations:
> But upon thee shall JEHOVAH arise;
> And his glory upon thee shall be conspicuous.
> And the nations shall walk in thy light;
> And kings in the brightness of thy rising.[22]
>
> (60.1–3)

The parallelisms in this passage are clear, but one should also note how the example typically serves more than one function: It stands here as an encapsulated statement of what Lowth will determine as the essential rhythm of prophetic discourse, namely, a period of obscurity followed by a period of enlightenment. The elements that need to be "balanced" here, clause to clause, are also constitutive of the rhetoric of prophecy generally. It may well be that some of the roots of Lowth's thinking about prophecy lie in the very syntactical structures of Hebrew poetry.

In antithetical parallelism, as the name suggests, words are opposed to words, sentiments to sentiments, clauses to clauses. Such structures are particularly well suited to the terse sayings of Proverbs and wisdom literature generally, but here again Isaiah is not without examples:

> In a little anger have I forsaken thee;
> But with great mercies will I receive thee again:

In a short wrath I hid my face for a moment from thee:
But with everlasting kindness will I have mercy on thee.

(52.7–8)

The gulf between the parallelism of Hebrew prophecy and the figure of antithesis in Classical literature and its legacy is not all that wide, and it seems
fitting that Lowth "discovered" parallelism at the end of the age of Pope.
But even in Pope, antithesis is rarely the dominant structuring principle
that it is in Biblical poetry: Parallelism among the prophets is so pervasive
as to form a structure of knowledge, whereas for the secular poets, antithesis remains one among many others in their array of figures.

By far the most problematic of Lowth's categories is the one he terms
synthetic or constructive parallelism, which is not so much defined as simply said, by default, to include "all such as do not come within the two
former classes" (II,49,19). He notes that this type features verses of longer
than average length, often with a single verse containing two "sentiments,"
but he is forced to conclude that "sometimes the scheme of parallelism is
very subtle and obscure, and must be developed by art and ability in distinguishing the different members of the sentences, and in distributing the
points, rather than by depending upon the obvious construction" (II,52–
3,19). The most insightful of contemporary critics writing on Biblical poetics has drawn attention to some of the limitations of Lowth's schema of
parallelism. For James Kugel, Lowth's shortcoming lies in a failure to acknowledge, in the parallelistic line A/B, the "afterwardness" of the B component.[23] In the present context, however, the accuracy of Lowth's account is less important than its effects. For many readers in the middle of
the eighteenth century, Lowth offered persuasive proof of the system of
Hebrew poetry, or at least of *a* system. Jerome's dictum that the prophetic writings were not metrical, together with similar judgments from
a variety of authorities, had done much to prevent the most rudimentary
investigations of prophetic poetry *as* poetry from being undertaken at
all.[24] A major contribution of Lowth's lectures was to enable the writings
of the prophets to be considered, virtually for the first time, poetic in the
strict sense.

Though parallelism is the formal feature Lowth singles out as most
characteristic of Biblical verse, the centrality of that category in Lowth's
work has been overstated in most recent accounts. Parallelism is not the
term he selects to capture what Herder would later call the "spirit" of He-

brew poetry. Lowth adopts the term *mashal* as the "word most properly expressive of the poetical style" (I,77–78,4). *Mashal,* for Lowth, is best translated as "parable," although he is quick to point out that term's inadequacy, since the Hebrew word comprehends three distinct, though compatible modes of discourse: the sententious, the figurative, and the sublime. Despite Lowth's attempt to account for the complexity of the term at this early juncture in the lectures, the word becomes increasingly problematic as he continues to "translate": "The word *Mashal,* in its most common acceptation, denotes resemblance (*similitudine*) and is therefore directly expressive of the figurative style, as far as the nature of the figures consists in the substitution of words, or rather of ideas, for those which they resemble" (I,104,5). Elsewhere Lowth glosses the word *mashal* as "expressive of power, or supreme authority," thus locating it in the sphere of the sublime. What Lowth calls "the most common acceptation," however, coincides with his own most frequent usage of *mashal* in the sense of the figurative or the parabolic, terms that more than any others characterize the essence of Hebrew poetry.

Lowth finds himself forced to speak of *mashal* in Latin terms, which he protests are inadequate to it. When he chooses to translate *mashal* as resemblance (*similitudine*), he expressly seeks to avoid importing with it all that the systems of Classical rhetoric entail. Lowth sees little use for "the almost innumerable forms of the Greek Rhetoricians" (I,105,5) and notes that he will ignore their primary distinctions between tropes and figures, as well as their many subdivisions. James Kugel takes Lowth's pronouncement as a sign of the rejection of a long-established procedure he calls the "tropes and figures approach."[25] But this apparent victory of Hebraism over Hellenism is not as decisive as Kugel suggests. The history of Lowth's reception has focused almost exclusively on his "discovery" of parallelism—also the main topic of Kugel's study—yet Lowth devotes only part of one of twenty-four lectures to the subject. By contrast, whole lectures take their titles and organizing principles from terms of Classical rhetoric, most notably "allegory" and "prosopopoeia." Lowth, in fact, proposes less a rejection of Classical rhetoric than a simplification. So streamlined is Lowth's schema—the whole of which is thought appropriate to the spirit of *mashal*—that it can all be subsumed under the single principle of resemblance:

By figurative language, I would be understood to mean that, in which one or more images or words are substituted in the room of others, or even introduced by way of illustration upon the principle of resemblance. That resemblance, if it be only intimated and confined to a few words, is called a *Metaphor*; if the figure be continued, it is called an *Allegory*; if it be directly expressed by comparing the ideas together, and by the insertion of any words expressive of likeness, it is called *Simile* or *Comparison*. On the same principle of resemblance, the *Prosopopoeia*, or Personification, is also founded, when a character or person is assigned even to things inanimate or fictitious (which is a bolder species of metaphor), or when a probable but fictitious speech is attributed to a real personage. (I,106–08,5)

The desire to avoid fitting the figurative language of the Hebrew poets into the procrustean frame of Classical rhetoric is understandable, yet it is hard to accept Lowth's revisionary system of figures at face value. Even his admiring translator, Gregory, does not let Lowth's enumeration of the principal figures stand uncorrected. Gregory "reminds" his author that the "associating principle is the true source of figurative language" (I,109n.,5), namely, the principle rhetoricians and linguists usually associate with the figure of metonymy, in opposing it to metaphor.[26] For Lowth's translator, the category of resemblance must be supplemented by those of "contiguity in time and space" and "cause and effect" to provide a fuller account of the figural system. While metaphor, especially in Lowth's system, depends on a natural or motivated resemblance, on an analogy already given in the order of things, metonymy can be "motivated" by so arbitrary a relation as mere contiguity, however random or unnatural. Hence the strategic value of making metaphor—as the figure of resemblance—the master trope of Biblical discourse and especially of Hebrew poetry and letting metonymy either fall by the wayside or be assimilated to metaphor altogether.

More suspect still than the omission of metonymy in Lowth's revisionary rhetoric is his attempt to assimilate the crucial figure of prosopopoeia to the principle of resemblance. Whereas metaphor may be founded upon analogies made possible by natural resemblance, prosopopoeia manifestly violates that principle, the very one Lowth claims unifies *all* figurative language. For prosopopoeia entails, quite literally, making a face (*prosopon*) or giving a face, and thus also a voice, to something that has neither.[27] The only kind of prosopopoeia conceivably based on resemblance would be the imitation of the speech of a dead person, if that discourse were known to correspond to the actual speech of the deceased. Yet even this special case of personification seems remote from the natural resemblance Lowth outlines. In most instances of prosopopoeia, the arbitrary imposition of a face and a voice by no means merely registers or takes note of a preexisting resemblance. The figure of prosopopoeia is indeed "metaphorical," insofar as it involves a transfer of properties from one entity to another, but resemblance is not the principle that authorizes such transfers. What is instituted through prosopopoeia resembles nothing, nothing other than itself.

At stake in Lowth's institution of a system of tropes and figures is more than a quibble about the "innumerable forms of Greek rhetoricians," more than a question of rival taxonomies. The text to which all these categories and classifications are applied is *the* sacred book in the Judeo-Christian tradition, the text that forms the basis of so much knowledge, belief, and action. Attendant problems of Biblical hermeneutics that seem confined to the "surface" of the text often have far-reaching consequences for religion and theology. The specter of prosopopoeia poses a particularly serious linguistic as well as a hermeneutic problem for the reader of the Bible, and Lowth points to the problem, even if he is unaware of the unpredictable lines of inquiry that would follow in his wake.

Lowth acknowledges that what are sometimes given in the Bible as the actual words of God may have been merely "attributed" (*attributa*) by a human author (I,358,16). A key passage in this regard occurs in Lowth's lecture on the "Sublimity of Sentiment," in which he offers numerous examples of the decidedly negative language required to give some idea of the "Divine Omnipotence." Introducing several verses from the Book of Job to demonstrate its sublime energy, Lowth describes the lines from Job as "that ironical kind of concession, which is sometimes put into the mouth of the Supreme Being" (I,358,16). Gregory's translation of "attributing" words to God as "putting words" into God's mouth is a bold one, and one that reverses what is supposed to be the relation of God's discourse to that of his prophets. The Lord says, in Deuteronomy 18.18: "I will raise them up a Prophet from among their brethren, like unto thee, and will put my words into his mouth; and he shall speak to them all that I shall command him." When Lowth cites these verses from the Book of Job, they appear, as they do in the Biblical text, to be the *ipsissima verba* of God, but Lowth makes explicit the possibility that they may be the words of a human author, and not merely a human recorder of divine speech.[28] (Significantly, these possibly "human" words quoted from Job are about the direct transmission of God's word to his prophets.) If one cannot in principle decide, from the evidence of the text's "surface," whether or not a given passage is of divine or human authorship, then it becomes difficult to establish a corpus of God's true words, to which poetic or fictional passages might be compared for their "resemblance."

The dilemma for the reader of divine personification is that "God" may be equally the subject or the object of prosopopoeia. As subject, "God" gives a face and a voice to all his human creations; as object, "God" is himself the creation of a linguistic device, which might in turn be said to enable creation itself. This latter position is neither believed nor voiced by Lowth, but something like it is articulated by his contemporary David Hume in his *Natural History of Religion*. "There is a universal tendency among mankind," Hume writes,

to conceive all beings like themselves, and to transfer to every object, those qualities, with which they are familiarly acquainted, and of which they are intimately conscious. We find human faces in the moon, armies in the clouds; and by a natural propensity, if not corrected by experience and reflection, ascribe malice or good-will to every thing, that hurts or pleases us. Hence the frequency and beauty of the *prosopopoeia* in poetry; where trees, mountains, and streams are personified, and the inanimate parts of nature acquire sentiment and passion. And though these poetical figures and expressions gain not on the belief, they may serve, at least, to prove a certain tendency in the imagination, without which they could be neither beautiful nor natural. Nor is a river-god or hamadryad always taken for a mere poetical or imaginary personage; but may sometimes enter into the real creed of the ignorant vulgar; while each grove or field is represented as possessed of a particular genius or invisible power, which inhabits and protects it. Nay, philosophers cannot entirely exempt themselves from this natural frailty; but have oft ascribed to inanimate matter the horror of a *vacuum*, sympathies, antipathies, and other affections of human nature.[29]

Thus far, Hume's analysis of prosopopoeia might seem to corroborate Lowth's view, since the figure is said to be both natural and beautiful and Hume explicitly appeals to the principle of resemblance, which for Lowth is the paradigm for all figures. But what Hume understands by the naturalness of the figure is not compatible with the demands of truth as it is for Lowth, for whom the figurative constitutes a deviation or deflection on the path to truth. The tendency for mankind to conceive all beings like themselves is a natural one, but "natural" in the sense of a frailty, from which, Hume confesses, even philosophers are not exempt.[30] What is lost with respect to truth may be more than compensated for by the beauty that personification provides in poetry, a small price to pay, perhaps, when only the "aesthetic" is at stake. But Hume continues in this same passage to say:

The absurdity is not less, while we cast our eyes upwards; and transferring our eyes upwards; and transferring, as is too usual, human passions and infirmities to the deity, represent him as jealous and revengeful, capricious and partial, and, in short, a wicked and foolish man, in every respect but his superior power and authority. No wonder, then, that mankind, being placed in such an absolute ignorance of causes, and being at the same time so anxious concerning their future fortune, should immediately acknowledge a dependence on invisible powers, possessed of sentiment and intelligence. The *unknown causes* which continually employ their thought, appearing always in the same aspect, are all apprehended to be of the same kind or species. Nor is it long before we ascribe to them thought and reason and passion, and sometimes even the limbs and figures of men, in order to bring them nearer to a resemblance with ourselves.[31]

Hume's passage begins with the figure of prosopopoeia and ends with the principle of resemblance, but the difference from Lowth's text could hardly be more pronounced. For Hume, the resemblance ascribed to personification is always a resemblance with *ourselves*, the immediate, earthly authors of prosopopoeia. Hume's figure projects resemblance rather than registers what is already given in nature. There is a stark contrast as well, insofar as Lowth's figure is ultimately of the order of truth and Hume's of the order of error, an error that is acceptable in the realm of poetry but unconscionable in theology or science. Both figures are natural—Lowth will even claim that all his figures are "naturally allied" (I,115,5)—but of a very different nature. Hume seems to suggest that the rigors of philosophical and theological discourse require a more exacting rhetoric than the fictitious positing of human faces and voices where there are none.

It is tempting to see the marked opposition between Lowth and Hume on the status of personification as a local conflict in the larger struggle between "faith" and "reason." Hume's writings were at the center of many theological controversies, and he was widely regarded as an unbeliever, despite and perhaps also because of his acknowledgment of an "intelligent author" who oversaw the workings of the universe.[32] Yet on the specific issue of the resemblance of prosopopoeia, at least one minister, arguably the leading rhetorician of his day, clearly sided with Hume. In his *Lectures on Rhetoric and Belles Lettres* Hugh Blair writes:

Indeed, it is very remarkable, that there is a wonderful proneness in human nature to animate all objects. Whether this arises from a sort of assimilating principle, from a propension to spread a resemblance of ourselves over all other things, or from whatever other cause it arises, so it is, that almost every emotion, which in the least agitates the mind, bestows upon its object a momentary idea of life.[33]

Although Blair is uncertain about the causes of personification, its structure is unambiguous: What is "spread" over all things is a resemblance of *ourselves*. Again, such resemblances are posited rather than registered or simply presented, and the foundation of resemblance in positing is the reason for the decidedly negative knowledge prosopopoeia yields.[34] Blair's analysis coincides with Hume's, and their insight into the structure of prosopopoeia is decisive in shifting authority from the divine to the human. This local rhetorical analysis takes its place in the larger intellectual movement that finds itself forced to rethink the status of divine authority.

Strictly speaking, the God of the prophets is not often the object of prosopopoeia, given that, in the prophetic books as well as in the Psalter, God's face is present primarily in its absence, a feature not lost on the Romantic poets. A good deal of Hölderlin's poetry, for example, lies in the shadow cast by the turning away of God's face. In the Bible, the reasons for the absence of God's face and the modalities of that absence vary widely from passage to passage, as recent scholarship has demonstrated.[35] The consequences for prophetic discourse, however, are clear: that withdrawal of God's face virtually requires a personification of sorts, one that throws all the more emphasis on the voice of God, as a sensible but invisible presence. This in turn places an extraordinary burden on the voice of the prophet—written or spoken—as the chosen mouthpiece or vehicle for the divine word, the voice of the voice.

It is precisely the absence of the divine face (French *figure* or Italian *figura*) that necessitates the use of figurative language by the Biblical poets. In his commentary on the 104th Psalm (which Hegel will later single out as exemplary of the sublime), Lowth claims that in delineating divine majesty and power "it is absolutely necessary to employ figurative language" (I,177, 8). Thus in rendering the absolute, which as such is unrepresentable, the necessity for figuration is itself absolute. The psalm in question is an allegory of figuration, since light appears as the garment of God, a garment that gives shape to the divine "body" even as it covers it. Here again, figurative language does not register an empirical resemblance but rather marks itself, regardless of the splendid quality of its images, as negative knowledge. There is a difference between the mediating language of figuration as indirect representation of the divine—that which provides knowledge of the divine but in a way that must be deciphered—and the language of the sublime proper, which signals the failure of knowledge but so as to suggest something beyond the negative index that it is. Thus the category of representation can by no means fully account for the language of prophecy, which always exceeds the bounds of mere knowledge. As mediator between the divine word and the human, the prophet is both the vehicle of divine presence and the sign of its absence: The prophetic word is typically ambiguous in its very structure. This applies even to the moments of greatest "presence," those of the theophanies, since they are not, despite the occasional formal qualities of dialogue, intersubjective conversations or encounters. Even if one brackets the massive dissymmetry between the divine and the human, a voice without a face is more like a text than it is like a person.

If figurative language in the representation of the divine is acknowledged as a necessary evil, it can be lamented as an inexorable aspect of the fallen condition of mankind. But what of figurative language when no such necessity prevails? "It is the peculiar design of the figurative style," Lowth writes, " . . . to exhibit objects in a clearer or more striking, a sublimer or more forcible manner" (I,111,5). The parallel phrases of Lowth's sentence, "clearer or more striking" ("evidentius ac clarius") and "sublimer or more forcible" ("grandius etiam ac elatius") create the impression that these two aspects of figuration are perfectly compatible. The former pair functions within the cognitive dimension of language, as the figures illustrate objects for the understanding and thus provide something of a linguistic analogue to sense-certainty. The latter pair, by contrast, involves the persuasive force of language rather than its cognitive clarity. Gregory's translation of *elatius* as "more forcible" might itself seem forced; his diction nonetheless corresponds to the way Lowth, elsewhere in the lectures, describes the sublime as "that force of composition, whatever it be, which strikes and overpowers the mind, which excites the passions, and which expresses ideas at once with perspicuity and elevation" (I,307,14).

Though the effect of the sublime can, in part, be a function of tropes and figures, it is associated in Lowth rather with rhetoric as persuasion and force and thus not linked to the relative epistemological clarity of tropological systems. The ideal of prophetic language, perhaps of language as such, would be the cooperation of trope and persuasion, of constative and performative, cognition and action, but the history of interpretation reveals it as an elusive ideal in the actuality of reading and writing. Yet it is telling that in this passage, as in the text as a whole, Lowth sees perspicuity and force united in a single prophetic discourse.

When Lowth chooses *mashal* as the one term most expressive of the Hebrew poets' style, he acknowledges that the word comprehends three different modes: the sententious, the figurative, and the sublime. His stress on the principle of resemblance (*similitudine*), however, foregrounds the figurative with respect to the other two modes. Moreover, throughout his lectures Lowth most often translates *mashal* as "parable," which in principle is as compatible with the sententious as with the figurative but in fact is associated by Lowth with the latter. What then does Lowth understand by "parable"? "The parabolic," he writes, "may indeed be accounted a peculiar style, in which things moral, political, and divine, are marked and represented by comparisons implied or expressed and adopted from sensible objects" [I,124,6]. A more complex definition occurs in his lecture on allegory, where Lowth contrasts metaphor and parable: "The sole intention of the former is to embellish a subject, to represent it more magnificently, or at the most to illustrate it; that, by describing it in more elevated language, it may strike the mind more forcibly: but the intent of the latter is to withdraw the truth for a moment from our sight [*veritatem ab aspectu paulum retrahere*]." Gregory's rendition of *paulum* as "for a moment" decides on the temporal dimension of a term that might equally be understood spatially or visually, the latter in keeping with the implicit metaphor of sight in the phrase *ab aspectu* ("from the face, from the sight"). Yet Gregory's translation is faithful to Lowth's pervasive emphasis on the temporality of prophetic rhetoric, in which a "moment"—a word with a charged resonance in Blake's work—always intervenes between the time of utterance and the time of fulfillment. To achieve a fuller sense of what is at stake in this moment, one should turn now to Lowth's powerful but problematic notion of the prophet.

Lowth notes that "the word *Nabi* was used by the Hebrews in an ambiguous sense and that it equally denoted a Prophet, a Poet, or a Musician, under the influence of divine inspiration" (II,14,18). Although he acknowledges the ambiguity here, Lowth almost always chooses to translate *nabi* by *propheta*, as a Latin equivalent of the Greek *prophetes*, in turn rendered as "prophet" by Lowth's English translator. As noted above, the dominant sense of the word prophet in Lowth's time was reductive, privileging the function of prediction above all others. Some Biblical critics and commentators of the period do demonstrate an awareness of the variegated texture of prophetic discourse, beyond the strictures of the definitions by Samuel Johnson, Joseph Butler, and others rehearsed earlier. Yet when it comes to characterizing prophecy in general, the model of prediction comes to the fore, as when Lowth writes:

Poeseos propheticae ingenium ex ipsius prophetiae natura et fine investigandum est. Omnis prophetiae finus proximus spectat ad eorum utilitatem, qui eventum praesignificatum aetate antecederunt; estque vel teror, vel consolatio. . . . (II,65,20)

[The genius of prophetic poetry is to be explored by a due attention to the nature and design of prophecy itself. The immediate design of all prophecy is to inform or amend those generations that precede the events predicted, and it is usually calculated either to excite their fears and apprehensions, or to afford them consolation. . . .]

Gregory takes liberties here with Lowth's syntax and, more important, with his diction, for the phrase "inform or amend" is a bold rendition of *spectare ad*, since "amend" emphasizes the persuasive aspect of prophecy. Lowth's Latin phrase, however, stresses the representational, cognitive aspect as prediction (*eventum praesignificatum*). Yet Gregory's translation appears less forced in light of the latter half of Lowth's formulation, which shows clearly that the *function* of prediction is to move the prophet's listeners. (In Austin's terms, prophecy appears to be a constative locutionary act that, ideally, has perlocutionary and persuasive force, a situation complicated by the fact that most prophecies are simultaneously constative and performative.[36]) But how exactly does prophecy, in Lowth's view, accomplish its designated ends? He observes:

The means which it employs for the accomplishment of these effects, are a general amplification of the subject, whether it be of the menacing or consolatory kind, copious descriptions, diversified, pompous, and sublime; in this also it necessarily avoids too great a degree of exactness, and too formal a display of the minuter circumstances; rather employing a vague and general style of description, expressive only of the nature and magnitude of the subject: for prophecy in its very nature implies some degree of obscurity, and is always, as the Apostle elegantly expresses it, "like a light glimmering in a dark place, until the dawn of day, and the day-star arise." (II,65,20)

It is no doubt problematic that Lowth must characterize the language of prophecy as "vague and general," since the knowledge at stake is of the utmost importance; the very truth of Christianity and the coherence of the

Bible as a text may depend on the veracity and intelligibility of prophecy.[37] Just where one might expect the greatest precision and clarity—since the import is so enormous—one finds that prophecy "in its very nature implies some degree of obscurity." The need to avoid "too great a degree of exactness" accounts for the necessity, in a word, of figuration, of a language that may be representational and referential, though not directly so. The history of interpretation shows that the generality of figuration is at once the blessing and the curse of prophetic speech: a blessing in that it permits a wide range of applications to various particular "events," rarely relegating the prophetic text to be a mere thing of the past;[38] a curse, inasmuch as that same generality renders the application of the text to one and only one event impossible. The very mode of its representation as generalized or generalizable figuration unsettles the cognitive certainty that prophecy seems ultimately to promise.

The fact that a prophecy can refer to more than one event is not necessarily a cause for perplexity to interpreters of the sacred text, because, as Lowth writes: "Prophecy frequently takes in, at a single glance, a variety of events, distinct both in nature and time, and pursues the extreme and principal design through all its different gradations" (II,67,20). The polysemy of prophecy poses no problem for orthodox interpretation, as long as a unity of design can be traced to the divine author; the events may be double, triple, or more, but the "glance" of divine vision must remain single. Yet Lowth acknowledges in the very next paragraph that the prophetic style is "chiefly employed in describing only the exterior lineaments of events, and in depicting and embellishing general effects" (II,67,20). Again, the difficulty with the exteriority and generality of prophetic speech is that the mode of its formulation, in effect, leaves room for interpretation beyond the single or double events that seem to be intended by divine or human authors. The prophetic text is not only about "something ever more about to be": It may always be about something other than what it seems.

II

The indirection, generality, and obscurity of prophetic discourse have far-reaching consequences for its peculiar temporality. In Lowth's eleventh lecture, on "Mystical Allegory," the argument about the necessity of both the obscurity and the generality of figuration closely parallels that of the later lectures on "Prophetic Poetry." Yet in this earlier formulation on the "genius" of prophetic poetry, Lowth makes a stunning claim:

The prophetic, indeed, differs in one respect from every other species of the sacred poetry: when first divulged it is impenetrably obscure; and time, which darkens every other composition, elucidates it. That obscurity, therefore, in which at first this part of the sacred writings was involved, is now in a great measure removed; there are now many things which the course of events (the most certain interpreter of prophecy) has completely laid open; from many the Holy Spirit has itself condescended to remove the veil, with which they were at first concealed. (I,227–48,II)

Lowth had been arguing that a good measure of the obscurity of the Hebrew scriptures could be ascribed to modern readers' ignorance of what were once common idioms and customs. What was formerly intelligible at the time became enigmatic by virtue of its utter difference from "corresponding" aspects of the modern reader's culture. The passage of time obscures the passages of the text. Thus the claim on behalf of prophetic poetry is all the more extraordinary; prophecy is the one and only type of poetry that time illuminates rather than obscures. So miraculous is this process that the very act of interpretation is rendered superfluous, as far as individual readers or subjects are concerned. The text is not presented as an interpretation of history; rather, history emerges as the certain interpreter of the text. It is no wonder that Lowth here must appeal to the Holy Spirit as the divine power who oversees the interplay of text and history, so singular is this absolute dialectic of letter and spirit.

It is a relatively simple matter to locate the urge to determine prophecy as prediction in the framework of a Christian hermeneutic that values the Hebrew Scriptures as the "Old" Testament, as that body of texts whose main virtue was to anticipate the "New." Certainly the Christological emphasis dominates much of Protestant exegesis throughout the eighteenth century, Lowth being no exception to the rule. Yet the accent on the prophetic word as essentially predictive is not merely the phantasized product of a Christian allegorical or typological rereading of the Hebrew text. The following verses from Deuteronomy, crucial for the image of the prophet in many respects, spell out the difference between the false prophet and the true. The Lord says to Moses:

I will raise then up a Prophet from among their brethren, like unto thee, and will put my words in his mouth; and he shall speak unto them all that I shall command him. And it shall come to pass, *that* whosoever will not hearken unto my words which he shall speak in my name, I will require *it* of him. But the prophet, which shall presume to speak a word in my name, which I have not commanded him to speak, or that shall speak in the name of the gods, even that prophet shall die.

And if thou say in thine heart, How shall we know the word which the LORD hath not spoken? When a prophet speaketh in the name of the LORD, if the thing follow not, nor come to pass, that is the thing which the LORD hath not spoken, *but* the prophet hath spoken it presumptuously: thou shalt not be afraid of him. (18.18–22)

The true test of the prophetic word, the most immediate of mediations, is whether or not it comes true. And the passage from Deuteronomy is hardly an isolated one. Similar pronouncements are to be found in almost all the major prophets, such as this claim of Isaiah's, which will become a key text for Richard Hurd's sermons on prophecy: "Behold the former things are come to pass, and new things do I declare: Before they spring forth I tell you of them" (42.9).[39] The importance is retroactively heightened by virtue of the recurrent formula employed by the evangelists to confirm the identity of the Messiah and the truth of "Christianity": "as it is written in the prophets" (ὡς γέγραπται ἐν τοῖς προφήταις) (Mark 1.2). Thus despite all the complications of understanding the figurative language of prophecy, the test of prophetic rhetoric remains still whether or not a text comes true, whether or not it corresponds to some state of affairs outside the language of the text.

Despite the explicit determination of prophecy as prediction, in the Old and New Testaments alike, the temporal status of much prophetic discourse remains difficult to ascertain, posing problems as formidable as those of figural language. In his lecture on the "Sublimity of Expression," Lowth remarks on the difference of Hebrew poetry from common language with respect to the "much more frequent change or variation of the tenses," so as to render a subject "more striking, and even to embody and give it a visible existence" (I,330,15). He goes on to contend that:

In all languages, in prose as well as poetry, it is usual to speak of past as well as future events in the present tense, by which means whatever is described or expressed is in a manner brought immediately before our eyes [*ante oculos*]; by looking back to the past or forward to the future. But in this respect there is a great peculiarity in the Hebrew language. For the Hebrew verbs have no form for expressing the imperfect or indefinite of the present tense, or an action which now is performing; . . . for the sake of clearness and precision, they express future events by the past tense, or rather by the perfect present, as if [*quasi*] they had actually taken place: and, on the contrary, past events by the future, as if [*quasi*] immediately or speedily to happen . . . (I,331–32,15)

It is just at the moment when prophetic speech should be clear and precise—so runs the paradox of Lowth's argument—that it risks being most clearly fictional, as the *quasi* constructions indicate. That the past can refer to the future and the future to the past means that one cannot decide simply from the surface of a given text whether it is prediction or history. And history itself is the key agent in the developer of this textual negative, as we have seen from Lowth's earlier contentions about the cunning logic of spiritual interpretation. To render the future by a past tense is, Lowth maintains, a "very common mode of expression" (I,333,15). He adduces two examples, one from Isaiah, and the following verses from Joel:

> For a nation hath gone up upon my land,
> Who are strong and without number:
> They have destroyed my vine, and have made my
> fig-tree a broken branch.
> They have made it quite bare, cast it away:
> the branches thereof are made white.
> The field is laid waste: the ground, the ground
> mourneth.   (1.6,7,10,&c)

Lowth comments here without hesitation: "The Prophet is undoubtedly here speaking of a future event; for, the very devastation, which, to strike the more forcibly on the mind, he has thus depicted as an event already past, is threatened by him in the sequel under another image to be immediately inflicted, unless the people repent of their wickedness" (I,335,15). The verses that follow in this and the subsequent chapter do indeed present prophetic visions and exhortations of the most typical sort, yet it is hard to see how the sheer juxtaposition of past- and future-oriented statements renders the past ones future in meaning. Is it not rather the presence of so many images of an archetypal or quasitypological character that would become prominent in the New Testament—the vine and the branches, the fig tree—that combine to cast a shadow of futurity on these verses? This passage is one of many in which one can recognize how a theory of prophecy as a discourse predictive of the future influences the reading of a particular passage as typically prophetic in the strict sense.

Lowth is more persuasive and less categorical in his discussion of the opposite grammatical configuration, whereby past events are referred to by way of future tenses. He draws his example from Deuteronomy 32, the Song of Moses, a passage that contains, in extraordinarily circumscribed fashion, much of the seminal rhetoric and imagery of the prophetic tradition. From Moses's song, Lowth excerpts these lines:

He will find him in a desert land,
In the vast and howling wilderness:
He will lead him about, he will instruct him;
He will keep him as the pupil of his eye.

(I,339,15)

Lowth then puts his case to the audience: "You will readily judge whether this passage can admit of any other explanation, than that of Moses supposing himself present at the time when the Almighty selected the people of Israel for himself; and thence, as from an eminence, contemplating the consequences of that dispensation" (I,339,15). Here Lowth can rely on the Pentateuch's rich history of Israel as a "past" source for each of the images in Moses's "prophecy." He perhaps too hastily dismisses "any other explanation," since the verses could well be applied either to the prior life of Moses or maybe even to the life of Jesus. Yet he is doubtless correct in claiming they can be construed in a sense quite opposite to their apparent future reference.

What is true for this type of grammatical ambiguity in single propositions or passages from the prophets will hold, remarkably enough, for the modes of prophecy and history in general, in the view of some Romantic poets and critics. Coleridge, for example, could write in *The Statesman's Manual*, a text in which prophecy figures largely as topic and as rhetorical posture: "According . . . to our relative position on its banks the sacred history becomes prophetic, the Sacred Prophecies historical, while the power and substance of both inhere in its Laws, its Promises, and its Comminations."[40] Coleridge's position is shared, according to Elinor Shaffer, by a number of what she calls "new critics," that is, those who practiced a version of Biblical Higher Criticism in the late eighteenth and early nineteenth centuries. To them she ascribes the achievement of having "gradually eroded this distinction [between prophecy and event] until all history became prophecy."[41] It is in part this indeterminacy of historical reference—history as prophecy, prophecy as history—that accounts for the power and the citability of the prophetic text. At any moment, the apparent future reference of a text may appear to be a thing of the past and the apparent past reference a prediction of the future. Hence the necessity for a kind of permanent vigilance in the reading of the prophetic text and of any text that may suddenly turn out to be prophetic.

III

The history of the Bible's reception in England and Germany in the decades following the publication of Lowth's lectures bears witness to his powerful influence on scholarship, philosophical criticism, and poetry alike. When Hugh Blair lectured on Hebrew poetry, in the context of his *Lectures on Rhetoric and Belles Lettres,* he did little more than summarize what Lowth had done before him, as Blair himself acknowledged. When Herder set out to write *Vom Geiste der Ebräischen Poesie,* he began by expressing his considerable indebtedness to Lowth and felt called on to spell out his differences from his predecessor. The latter's influence on poetic practice is much more difficult to gauge, although Stephen Prickett is surely right in claiming that the publication of Lowth's lectures "was to do more than any other single work to make the biblical tradition, rather than the classical one, the central poetic tradition of the Romantics."[42] The most striking instance of a direct impact on poetic practice is found in the work of Christopher Smart, although a full discussion of his relationship to Lowth remains a desideratum. And Lowth's critical performance won the praise of some who had little or no professional or doctrinal investment in his project. In his autobiography Gibbon remarks during a lament of the decay of learning in British universities on the value of a great professor and Lowth is his exemplar for that role. "I note with pleasure," Gibbon says of the professor's twin duties to students and the public, that "in the University of Oxford Dr. Lowth, with equal eloquence and erudition, has executed this task in his incomparable *Praelectiones* on the Poetry of the Hebrews."[43] Scholars will continue to debate the precise details of Lowth's influence, but of greater importance is the recognition of Lowth's place in a movement that would change fundamentally the way the Bible is read.

Lowth made explicit his desire to respect "the sacred boundaries of theology" and, true to his word, he provided a work best classified as a poetics of Scripture. Yet his searching analyses of Biblical rhetoric and grammar had major consequences for hermeneutics as well.[44] By outlining the complexities of the aesthetic, and at times fictional, character of Biblical passages, Lowth posed a whole range of problems for the traditional or orthodox interpretation of Scripture.[45] At the same time that Lowth probed the fictional aspects of the sacred text, he stressed the importance of historical understanding, of learning to read the Hebrew scriptures as the Hebrews did. As we have seen, Lowth was unlike the Hebrews in one important regard: The Bible became, to a significant extent, one text among others. More specifically, it stood as an anthology of religious, mythological documents of "Oriental" culture.[46] For Lowth it was no contradiction to read the Bible simultaneously as the product of one of many similar Oriental peoples and as the one and only divinely inspired text. Yet Lowth's double emphasis on the historicity and the poetic character of the sacred text would lead, later in the century, to the discovery of the centrality of "myth" as a category for the interpretation of the Bible. The path Lowth charted led in two directions: his historical criticism helped unsettle the status of the literal sense of the Bible as an index of actual history, while his elucidation of the aesthetics of Scripture helped open the sacred text to the powerful revisionary readings undertaken by the Romantic poets. Lowth wrote as a Christian and a believer, but the very rigor of Lowth's Biblical studies left the text, more than ever, open for interpretation.

There is little doubt that one of Lowth's greatest achievements was the "proof" that the prophets were poets. In Lowth's 1788 translation of Isaiah, he would show that prophecy, when translated properly, "looked" like poetry,[47] but the theoretical claim, complemented by much practical analysis, had already been made emphatically in the lectures of the 1740s. Among the several kinds of sacred poetry, the prophetic, for Lowth, holds the most exalted position: "The first rank I assign to the Prophetic or that species of poetry which is found to pervade the predictions of the prophets, as well as those contained in the books properly called prophetical, as those which occasionally occur in other parts of the Scriptures. These, I apprehend, will be generally allowed to be written in a style truly poetical" (II,4,18). Lowth's analysis of the parallelistic structure and figurative texture of prophetic speech was in itself enough to establish the poetic character of prophecy. But Lowth went further to claim that the prophets were the greatest of poets, and he helped secure their status as the sacred writers most worth emulating. The progress of poetry from the middle of the eighteenth century to the beginning of the nineteenth shows a gradual displacement of the Psalms in favor of the prophetic writings as the dominant model for religious poetry, a movement for which Lowth's lectures were a catalyst.

Of all the poets, Lowth claimed, Isaiah was the first in "sublimity and elegance" (I,166,6). When Lowth adduces his paradigmatic example of prophetic poetry, the passage comes predictably from Isaiah, Chapters 34 and 35. The text chosen is so rich and suggestive that Lowth's commentary on it provides a fitting, if open-ended close to the present account, because it epitomizes the principal issues at stake in the reading and writing of prophecy and offers a glance forward to the prophetic readings of the Romantics.

Lowth reads Isaiah 34 and 35 not only as a "remarkable prophecy" but equally as "a simple, regular, and perfect poem" (II,70,20) in two parts: "The first part of the prophecy contains a denunciation of extraordinary punishment, indeed nothing short of total destruction against the enemies of the church of God; and afterward, in consequence of this event, a full and complete restoration is provided to the church itself." Already in this preliminary description of the text, Lowth goes considerably beyond reading the Hebrew Scriptures as the Hebrews would have. The emphasis on the church seems anachronistic when understood in the historical context of Isaiah, but Lowth sees it as crucial to both parts of the prophecy, even though neither the word nor the concept of the church appears in the passage. The structure of the two chapters mirrors, in Lowth's revisionary reading, the rhythm of the Christian Bible itself; the first part foregrounds God as a destructive, vengeful force, and the second part envisions a full restoration of the "church." Clearly the doctrinal content of Lowth's hermeneutic is already at work in the task of description.

Lowth draws attention to the "magnificent exordium" of Isaiah 34, in which "the whole world should seem to be interested":

> Draw near, O ye nations, and hearken;
> And attend unto me, O ye people!
> Let the earth hear, and the fullness thereof;
> The world, and all that spring from it.
> (II,71,20)

Although Lowth does not comment on the exemplarity of Isaiah's apostrophe, it is a hallmark of prophetic discourse and of a trait that will be imitated by many of the Romantics. In particular, the address to the earth has a formulaic quality: It echoes Moses, anticipates Jeremiah and a number of the minor prophets, and will reappear in a text like Blake's "Introduction" to the *Songs of Experience*. Isaiah's message is, despite the cosmic comprehensiveness of the apostrophe, more immediately addressed to his audience during the reign of Hezekiah in a period of great political upheaval. The exordium well illustrates the dual or multiple focus of the prophetic word and shows how this aspect of its rhetoric, just as much as its highly figurative style, permits a single text to be read and reread in a wide range of contexts. Even just the ambiguity of the plural "nations" seems to let the sense irradiate in many directions. The flexibility of the prophetic message is such that it can be of the most immediate urgency, as well as of virtually endless, even eternal concern. In predicting an event of great consequence, the prophet not only offers a vision for future generations, he also renders the present moment perpetually precarious.

Lowth follows his citation of the apostrophe with a reading of the subsequent verses that recalls several points made in his general characterization of prophetic poetry:

He then publishes the decree of Jehovah concerning the extirpation of all those nations against whom "his wrath is kindled": and he amplifies this act of vengeance and destruction by an admirable selection of splendid imagery, all of which is of the same kind with that which is made use of by the prophets upon similar occasions; the nature of which is to exaggerate the force, the magnitude, atrocity, and importance of the impending visitation; whilst nothing determinate is specified concerning the manner, the time, the place, or other minute circumstances. (II,71–2,20)

The passages from Isaiah are indeed spectacular and sublime, with their images of mountains melting with the blood of carcasses, and of the heavens "rolled up like a scroll." There may well be, however, a tension between what is sublime as poetry and what is intelligible as prophecy, understood as the prediction of a future event. Lowth underlines both the obliqueness and generality of the figuration, as he does in many other instances. But here one may recognize the prophet's rhetoric as hyperbolic because, one presumes, no historical event could ever quite match the spectacular verbal vision of Isaiah. To what, for example, in the external world could the figure of the heavens rolled up like a scroll correspond? The indeterminacy of the text's reference, Lowth acknowledges, extends to such basic elements as time, place, and manner. The very sublimity of Isaiah's vision resists the possibility of ascertaining its truth as reference, in accord with the criteria for distinguishing true and false prophecy outlined in Deuteronomy 18 and elsewhere.

A similar argument might be made with respect to the subsequent passage Lowth cites from Isaiah:

> The sword of JEHOVAH is satiated with blood;
> It is pampered with fat:
> With blood of lambs, and of goats;
> With the fat of the reins of rams;
> For JEHOVAH celebrateth a sacrifice in Botzra,
> And a great slaughter in Edom.

Lowth remarks of these verses:

The goats, the rams, the bulls, the flocks, and other animals, which are mentioned in this passage, and those which follow, are commonly used by the prophets to denote the haughty, ferocious, and insolent tyrants and chiefs of those nations, which were inimical to God. On the same principle we may explain the allusion to Botzra and Idumea, a city and nation in the highest degree obnoxious to the people of God. These, however, the prophecy seems only slightly or cursorily to glance at: The phraseology is indeed of that kind which expresses generals by particulars. (II,73–74,20)

Some of Isaiah's obscurity is clarified by Lowth's appeal to the conventional use of certain animals as tropes for kinds of political leaders, but even the place names are not sufficient to identify the targets of Jehovah's wrath with much specificity. Lowth appeals to the prophecies about "other animals" in the Isaiah text, yet he omits the command that follows their enumeration: "Seek ye out the book of the LORD, and read: no one of these shall fail, none shall want her mate: For my mouth it hath commanded, and his spirit it hath gathered them" (34.16). The same text that demands a reading that will confirm the truth of its prophecy resists, through its own "phraseology," any definitive reading in terms of reference. Lowth is forced to admit that, for much of the prophecy, "The circumstances and progress of the particular events are not yet unfolded; for, this prophecy is evidently one of those which are not yet completely fulfilled, and of which the greater part at least is yet deposited in the secret counsels of the Most High" (II,78–80,20).

According to Lowth, the text of Isaiah remains, and indeed *should* remain, for the audience of his Oxford lectures during the 1740s, a scroll rolled up. For reasons that remain to be seen, however, it became clear in 1793 to a London poet, who often claimed to be privy to the counsels of the Most High, that it was time again to unravel Isaiah's scroll. Thus William Blake could proclaim in *The Marriage of Heaven and Hell*:

As a new heaven is begun and it is now thirty-three years since its advent: The Eternal Hell revives. And lo! Swedenborg is the Angel sitting at the tomb; his writings are the linen clothes folded up. Now is the dominion of Edom, & the return of Adam into Paradise, see Isaiah xxxiv and XXXV Chap: . . . "[48]

4

The Speaking Hieroglyph: Hurd, Warburton, and the Matter of Style

> Theology is a great house, scored all over with hieroglyphics
> by perished hands.
> —Walter Pater

When Richard Hurd came to deliver in 1772 the first series of William Warburton lectures on prophecy, the general findings of his interpretations had been "predicted" for him in advance. The deed of the trust established for the series by the Bishop of Gloucester spelled out the hermeneutic and ideological conclusions for all future lecturers: "To prove the truth of Revealed Religion in general and of the Christian in particular, from the completion of the Prophecies in the Old and New Testament, which relate to the Christian church, especially to the apostacy of Papal Rome. . . . [1] Hurd's undertaking, published as *Twelve Sermons Introductory to the Study of the Prophecies,* was the first and most eminent in a sequence of sermons given at London's Lincoln's Inn Chapel, a series that lasted well into the twentieth century. If today a Protestant theologian were to attempt a "proof" of the apostasy of the Catholic church based on Biblical testimony, it would likely be dismissed as an example of sectarian fanaticism. Already in Hurd's time, the project seemed to many to be incommensurate with a certain tolerant spirit of the times. An anonymous "Letter to Dr. Hurd"—whose author was later disclosed as no less than Edward Gibbon—recounted the setting of the sermons' publication and reception:

Some months ago it was reported, that Dr. Hurd was preparing to expound the Apocalypse, and once more to prove the Pope to be Antichrist. The public were amazed. By the gay and by the busy world, the very attempt was treated as an object of ridicule. Polite scholars lamented, that you should be prevailed upon to give up your more solid and liberal studies, for such obscure and unprofitable researches. Your own brethren of the church hinted, that it would be far more prudent to observe a respectful silence with regard to those awful and invidious mysteries. (363–64)

Gibbon surely expresses the dismay that must have been registered by many Protestants, to say nothing of Roman Catholics. He does record that the sermons were well received, despite distaste for the subject matter, and he praises the "skill of the Architect," even as he reserves judgment about the "weakness in the foundations" (364). The skill Gibbon notes is, among other things, that of a literary critic, since Hurd was as much a man of letters as he was a man of the cloth. His first major publication was an edition of and commentary on Horace's *Ars Poetica* and the *Epistola ad Pisones* in 1749. He authored a number of important essays that now would be categorized as "literary theory," and in 1762 published his celebrated *Letters on Chivalry and Romance*, still read today by students of the genre.[2] Hurd also prepared an edition of Cowley and left nearly complete materials for what is still the standard edition of Addison. And he dutifully edited the complete works of his mentor, William Warburton. Hurd was one of the most prominent literary figures of his day, but after the dust of a century had settled, Leslie Stephen could write of him: "Hurd is man for whom . . . it is difficult to find a good word. He was a typical specimen of the offensive variety of university don; narrow-minded, formal, peevish, cold-blooded, and intolerably conceited."[3] Hurd's sermons, however, were evidently popular with a good many of his contemporaries; the text went through four editions in a scant five years, and a fifth was issued in the 1780s. With regard to their religious and doctrinal content, the lectures are all but forgotten by contemporary theology, and they hardly constitute a monument in the history of religious thought in the eighteenth century. Much of the text now appears, as it did to Gibbon and others, as ideological cant.[4] Yet Hurd offers a striking example of what it was possible to think about prophecy in the late eighteenth century, and his close attention to linguistic and literary aspects of prophecy lends the sermons much more than an antiquarian interest. Few authors of the eighteenth century demonstrate so clearly how prophetic discourse works and how much is at stake in its workings.

In an era that conceived of itself as increasingly scientific and rationalistic—although an epoch too hastily called "The Age of Reason"—the time-honored truths of Judeo-Christian revelation were more vulnerable to criticism and attack than ever before. Spinoza's *Theological-Political Treatise* of 1670 was only the first in a long line of philosophical questionings of a tradition whose sacred text had rarely been subjected to the type of inquiry considered more appropriate for the book of nature or the palimpsest of history. The Warburton trust set out to counter at least one strain of impending "rationalism," although it will be clear that Hurd does not simply oppose the principle of reason nor the canons of logical argument. Indeed, he will try to show that there is no necessary disjunction between the rational and the revealed: Rather, they partake of a single logic, a logic of the *Logos* governing a balanced, providential economy.

Hurd is called on to defend the truths of revealed religion, and the Warburton trust dictates that the demonstration must turn on the truth of Biblical prophecy. Hurd laments the "prejudices and preconceptions" that had marred most pronouncements on prophecy until his time and proposes that we should not for a moment forget that the prophecies "may be what they manifestly claim to be, of divine suggestion" (2).[5] But Hurd by no means advocates a blind acceptance of the prophet's word, since the "just reasoner," he reasons, will try to ascertain whether or not the prophetic claim to divine inspiration is well founded.

The history of prophetic interpretation, even when prophetic words are accepted as indubitably divine, does not, for Hurd, prove very reasonable. His first sermon reviews a number of "false" ideas about prophecy: for example, the Jewish notion that prophecy is given for the benefit of "one peculiar and chosen people" (9); that it is designed to preserve an "awful sense of Providence" (10); or that its purpose is to console and prepare people anxious about the future. In particular, Hurd expends much energy dismantling what he calls the "invidious comparison" between scriptural prophecies and pagan oracles.

Each of the positions Hurd attacks is staged as a fictitious opponent to the author, and in the following instance the personified polemic complains that whereas we would expect momentous prophecies to be delivered in the clearest of terms, we find, to the contrary, that:

these pretended prophecies are expressed so ambiguously or obscurely, are so involved in metaphor and darkened by hieroglyphics, that no clear and certain sense can be affixed to them, and the sagacity of a second prophet seems wanting to explain the meaning of the first. . . . there is always room for some degree of suspense and hesitation: either the accomplishment fails in some particulars, or other events might be pointed out, to which the prophecy equally corresponds. (13)

Hurd postpones a full response to this objection, the most demanding of all, since his own analysis will confirm how Biblical prophecies are thoroughly "involved in metaphor and darkened by hieroglyphics." The burden of Hurd's argument will be to ascribe that obscurity its appropriate place in the providential economy of history.[6]

Having dismissed in summary fashion several putatively false ideas of prophecy, Hurd turns in his second sermon to "true" ideas and bases his sermon on the saying from Revelation 19.10: "The testimony of Jesus is the Spirit of Prophecy." That Hurd takes as the paradigmatic Biblical statement on prophecy its ultimate scriptural reference point, rather than a passage from Deuteronomy or Kings, Isaiah or Jeremiah, is evidence of his Christocentric vision: The end of prophecy is the only raison d'etre for its beginning. One consequence of this strategy, common to many Christian theologians at least since Augustine and still hegemonic in the eighteenth century, of determining the nature of prophecy in general on the basis of a late Graeco-Christian text, is that it tends to collapse the distinction between Jew and Christian, between prophecy and apocalyptic, between Hebrew *nabi* and Greek *prophetes*. Presupposing the vast architectonic unity of the Bible, with Jesus as its alpha and omega, Hurd honors the indenture of the Warburton sermons by demonstrating that the unity in question turns on the truth of the prophetic system.

Hurd senses possible objections to his Christocentric vision of prophecy but counters them only by claiming that his interpretation will be justified "if we reflect, how exactly it agrees with all that the Jewish prophets were understood to intend, and what Jesus himself and his apostles assert was intended by their predictions" (28–29). His formulation, "all that the Jewish prophets were understood to intend," is deliberately cautious, since the Hebrew prophets can hardly be thought to have intended, in a phenomenological or psychological sense, all their prophecies to be a testimony to Jesus. Hurd seems to be sparing the reader a tedious, pedestrian demonstration when he claims:

It were endless to enumerate all the prophecies of the Old Testament, which have been supposed to point at Jesus: And the controversy concerning the application of *some* prophecies to him may be thought difficult. But it is very certain that the Jews, before the coming of Christ, gave this construction to their scriptures: They even looked beyond the letter of their sacred books, and conceived *the testimony* of the Messiah to be the soul and end of the commandment. *The spirit of prophecy* was so firmly believed to intend that *testimony* that the expectation was general of some such person, as Jesus, to appear among them, and at the very time in which he made his appearance. (29–30)

This argument, elaborated without a single quotation or allusion, departs from Hurd's initially guarded formulation regarding prophetic intention. Here he claims that the dichotomy of letter and spirit that would seem so decisively to separate the Old Testament from the New is false in that it already operates within the "Old" Testament and thus that the emphasis on spirit is not merely the product of a Christian fantasy. The potential violence of the Christian hermeneutic is dissipated if it can be shown to be already at work in the Hebrew Scriptures: If the Jews already read "beyond the letter," all the more reason to read even farther beyond.

But does Hurd succeed in showing that Jesus is the sole object of prophetic discourse? Does he even attempt a proof? His failure to enumerate even some of the "endless" prophecies is all the more suspect in view of his repeated claims for the totalized and systematic character of Biblical prophecy. When he speaks of prophecy in general, Hurd opens a parenthesis to specify "that is, *all* the prophecies of the Old and New Testament" (34), as if nothing falls outside that system. And the totalizing gesture is glaring when he exclaims: "A spirit of prophecy pervading *all* time—characterizing one person, of the highest dignity—and proclaiming the accomplishment of *one* purpose, the most beneficent, the most divine, that imagination itself can project—Such is the scriptural delineation, whether we will receive it or no, of that economy, which we call Prophetic" (37).[7]

Any empirical study of what Hurd calls the "vast and splendid economy" of prophecy could show that not all the sayings of the prophets—of all those referred to as *nabi*—can be construed as testimony to the sprit of Jesus. It is no accident that the Christocentric exegesis of the prophets relies on a relatively small corpus of passages, such as Micah's prophecy of the Messiah's birth in Bethlehem or the prophecy of Immanuel's birth as foretold in Isaiah 7 (the latter a highly disputed passage that by no means clearly refers to the miracle of a virgin birth). And a similar problem plagues even the understanding of the very term signifying the "unique" privilege attendant to the life of Christ: "Messiah" may well mean something like "legitimate ruler" and thus not refer to any single figure at all.

Hurd had begun his second sermon by asserting that to understand "divine conduct" in the prophetic economy, attention must be paid to "the intention of the author," which is to say, the divine author. He then makes an extraordinary leap by claiming that prophecy must: " . . . be its own interpreter. My meaning, is that, setting aside all presumptuous imaginations of our own, we are to take our ideas of what prophecy *should* be, from what, in fact, we find it to have been" (21–22). Much of what is problematic in Hurd's analysis can be glimpsed in the juxtapositions of that final phrase, of what prophecy should be with what has been the case. Prophecy, for Hurd, conforms to its own ideal and is therefore perfectly adequate as its own interpreter. Lowth had suggested that the interpretation of prophecy, understood as the activity of an individual subject, is ultimately superfluous because the course of history renders prophetic texts, in due time, transparent. Hurd proposes something similar in his appeal to the self-contained, rational economy of prophecy, but in such a way as to foreclose the possibility of historical investigation along the lines Gibbon would follow in his response to Hurd's sermons. Not only does Hurd reject a Catholic appeal to tradition and authority, he goes against the grain of the Protestant principle of individual interpretation. If Hurd is right, prophecy needs no interpretation.

Though Hurd can baldly proclaim as a "fact" that all prophecies have their accomplishment in Jesus Christ, he does concede, and even claims to deduce, that "a considerable degree of obscurity may be reasonably expected to attend the *delivery* of the divine predictions" (45–46). He refers favorably to the notion, found in Lowth and traceable to Augustinian and patristic exegesis, that by casting some aspects of predicted events "into shade," the "moral faculties of the agent have their proper play" (46). To acknowledge the obscurity of prophecies at the time of their deliverance does not imply that prophecy is by nature or in essence obscure. Since Jesus is said not to come finally until "what was called the *last age* of the world," Hurd reasons that the prophecies should be "proportionably dark and obscure" (47). The remoter the predicted event, the more obscure the prophecy. The prophets speak, or perhaps mouth, the words of God at a time between what Hurd calls the "first dawnings of revelation" and the "fuller light of the Gospel," thus relegating their discourse to a figurative twilight zone. It is only through the intervening, "improper" play of the figurative that the moral faculties can have their "proper" play. The chiaroscuro vision of the prophets guarantees the link that binds the two dispensations, because the prophecies are, from the very first, double. As for Lowth, so for Hurd: the prophecy can "intend"—with or without the conscious intent of the prophet—two events at once. Hence the possibility and the necessity for prophecy to be "simultaneously" clear and obscure.

Nothing could be more reasonable, in Hurd's view, than prophetic obscurity, because the temporal economy of the two dispensations demands it. He proposes to treat the peculiarities of figurative language proper to this economy in his ninth and tenth sermons, devoted to the prophetic style and apocalyptic method, respectively. But he cannot conclude the second of two sermons on the "True Idea of Prophecy" without some attention to the problem of language. For Hurd, it is primarily the delivery of prophecies that is clouded in obscurity, but the coming of the event itself is not sufficient to dissipate the clouds. In any event, it is to figurative language, above all, that prophetic obscurity can be traced: "*Figurative language* is the chief of those means, by which it pleased the inspirer to throw a shade on prophecies, unfulfilled; but figurative language, from the very nature of it, is not so precise and clear as *literal expression*, even when the event prefigured has lent its aid to illustrate and explain that language" (68). Whereas Lowth had argued that the course of events was itself the most certain interpreter of prophecy (a doctrine also found in one of Hurd's masters, Pascal), the occurrence of the event does not, in Hurd's view, necessarily render the prophetic text transparent. The dark figures of the prophecy do not in time become, as it were, literal. Hurd cites with approval two passages from Thomas Sherlock's widely read *Discourses on Prophecy*: (1) "A figurative and dark description of a future event will be figurative and dark still, when the event happens"; (2) "No event can make a figurative or metaphorical expression to be a plain or literal one" (68n–69n). In the economy of Hurd's own text, the importance of figurative language is here only adumbrated and asserted to be central, but the rigor of Hurd's analysis prevents his circumscribing of the problem of language only to the two sermons devoted explicitly to it.

In his opening sermons, Hurd suggests that his analysis of Biblical prophecy will be subject to the dictates of historical evidence and the principle of reason. The latter term is particularly protean in the lexicon of the eighteenth century, but it implies a preliminary or provisional suspension of belief in the inherited dogmas of tradition. The problem of the Bible's historical reference would become, in the decades following Hurd's sermons, one of the most vigorously debated topics among religious and literary intellectuals, but Hurd circumvents many potential difficulties by simply assuming the historical truth of the Gospels, which in turn will be enlisted to confirm the historical truth of the Bible as a whole. Moreover, the fact that the Gospels are the history of the Logos, of the Word but also of Reason, implies that reason and (historical) revelation are perfectly compatible. So utopian a faith is questioned by one of the most eminent of contemporary religious philosophers, Paul Ricoeur, a thinker hardly predisposed to what he himself has termed the "hermeneutics of suspicion."[8] If one thing may be unequivocally said about all analogical forms of revelation, writes Ricoeur, "it is that in none of its modalities may revelation be included in or dominated by knowledge. In this regard the idea of something secret is the limit-idea of revelation. The idea of a revelation is a two-fold idea. The God who reveals himself is a hidden God, and hidden things belong to him."[9] The "knowledge" afforded by revelation then is always, in principle, negative knowledge, knowledge of the revealed as both disclosed and hidden. Even the writer of the Apocalypse records that the Whore of Mystery will remain on the scene until the very end of time, the moment when there will be no more need for interpretation.

The "fact" that the Gospels are the story of the Logos is one reason why Hurd's appeal to reason as such can coincide with an argument from authority, the authority of Scripture. But in his fourth sermon, "The General Argument from Prophecy," Hurd takes pains to circumscribe the jurisdiction of that authority. When he examines the evidence in support of the proposition that the testimony of Jesus is the spirit of prophecy, he takes for granted "not the truth of the prophetic scheme itself, but the truth of the *representation* of it in scripture" (75). Hurd underscores the importance of the systematic character of Biblical prophecy; he concedes that pagan divination has occasionally produced some stunning results but always in unrelated instances, in which chance may have been at work rather than providence. Taken singly, many of the prophecies directly concerning Christ are themselves rather indirect in their expression, such as the prophecy that "the seed of woman should bruise the serpent's head," and thus could refer to an enormous variety of things. But, Hurd contends:

when, to this general prophecy, the theme of all succeeding ones, it is further added, That this seed of the woman, should be the seed of Abraham; of the tribe of Judah; of the family of David; that he should be born at Bethlehem; that he should appear in the world at a time, limited by certain events, and even precisely determined to a certain period: when, after a particular description of his life and office, it is said of him, that he should be betrayed by an intimate friend. . . . When all this, I say, is considered; the improbability, that these *specific* characters should meet in the same person by *chance*, is so great, that a reasonable man will scarce venture on so hazardous a position. (92–93)

Here Hurd provides his most exhaustive enumeration of the prophecies concerning Christ, all of which assume the faithful historical reference of the Gospels and their accord with Old Testament predictions. In addition to the authority of Scripture, Hurd refers to a number of his near-contemporaries, such as Samuel Clarke and Pascal, both of whom argued for the centrality of the prophecy in the proof of Christ's divinity. It seems one need not choose between reason and revelation; of the Scriptures Hurd writes that "no man can read without seeing, that the prophecies contained in them, are extremely numerous—that many of these prophecies are minutely circumstantial—and that one person, whoever he be, is the principal object of them all" (89–90). Again Hurd implies that interpretation is an affair of reason, and claims that "the reasonable man" will see the systematic coherence of the prophecies and their reference to a single object, the Logos, which is to say, reason made man. But reason here is hardly a gift shared by all men, since Hurd knows full well that Jews, deists, atheists, and even some Catholics dispute the findings of his Protestant Christianity. Yet against what is so clearly a conflict of interpretations, Hurd appeals to the universality of reason, and even of sense perception. The reasonable man will see, and seeing is believing. He leaves unexamined the possibility that correlations of prophecy in the Gospel accounts of the life of Jesus are not so much providential fulfillments of prophecies as citations of them, an argument that would be made most forcefully by David Friedrich Strauss in his monumental *The Life of Jesus Critically Examined* more than half a century later. By assuming the historical truth of the New Testament, Hurd has already gone half the way in "proving" the truth of Hebrew prophecy, the very phenomenon that permits the transition from Old to New Testament, thus giving the Bible its unity as a book. Hurd's proof of the truth of revealed religion is, if not circular, then semi-circular, for the assumed truth of one "half" of the Bible is enlisted in the demonstration of the truth of the whole. He emphasizes that what is at stake is no mere epistemological problem but rather faith itself, the faith that, as Pascal believed, depended on the truth of the prophecies.

The formal coherence of the Bible is so artfully elaborated that it might, to the unreasonable man, appear like nothing so much as a literary text. In an effort to distinguish the integrity of Biblical prophecy from the mere contrivances of literary fictions, Hurd summons the epics of Virgil and Spenser as counterexamples. Both poems are written from a historical vantage point well past the time of their express historical topic. Virgil often introduced his encomia for the Augustan regime in the form of prophecies and in allusive descriptions whose secondary sense referred to the government of Virgil's own day, as much as to the ostensible characters of the epic. Such literary prophecies belong to the genre of the *vaticinium ex eventu*, of prophecy after the fact, and for Hurd these bear only a structural similarity to Biblical prediction. Yet it is precisely in Hurd's own time that research into Biblical history begins to show that the *vaticinium ex eventu* is a recognizable genre of Hebrew prophecy, as Gibbon, among others, would argue in his response to Hurd's sermons with respect to the Book of Daniel. These investigations, which would receive a full-fledged philological treatment in the work of Eichhorn in Germany, necessitated a radical reassessment of the literal, historical reference of the Bible in general and of prophecy in particular.

Having stated the case for prophecy in general, Hurd turns finally to a detailed reading of prophecies concerning Christ's first coming. The text for the fifth sermon makes clear what has already been adumbrated, namely, that prophecy for Hurd is essentially prediction; the chosen verses come from Isaiah: "Behold, the former things are come to pass, and new things do I declare: before they spring forth, I tell you of them" (42.9). At the outset, Hurd makes the highly suspect assertion that all prophecies are of two kinds: They refer either to "the person and character and office of the Messiah, or to the fate and fortunes of that kingdom." Even if the last phrase is understood liberally, it suggests a serious misunderstanding of a whole range of prophetic utterances, even of prophecy conceived as prediction, since the Hebrew prophets addressed the most topical of political situations, ones which often could not be interpreted as adumbrations of events in the life of the Messiah or his kingdom. It is no accident that the prophetic texts of the Old Testament cited in the New are few in number and circumscribed in scope. Hurd is by no means obliged to limit so drastically the scope of prophecy to prove the divinity of Christ or the coherence of the prophetic "scheme," but here his radically Christocentric hermeneutic forces him into an untenable line of argument.

At the moment when Hurd seems called on to enumerate a series of successful prophecies of Christ's first coming, he restricts himself to the most celebrated of all, though not an unambiguous one, from the book of Isaiah: "—Hear ye now. O HOUSE OF DAVID—The Lord himself shall give you a sign; Behold, a virgin shall conceive, and bear a Son, and shall call him Emmanuel" (7.13–14). Much of the miraculous nature of this prediction, as applied to the life of Christ, is dissipated if the Hebrew word *almah* is understood, as is plausible and probable, to mean "young woman" and not "virgin." The vision still looks forward to the coming of a savior, and the allegorical name Emmanuel lends itself to application beyond persons literally bearing that name. But Hurd asks if the prediction is not "more reasonably understood of that other child" (108), that is, if the figurative sense is more "proper" than the literal or proper sense. The child promised is a "sign" to Ahaz of his deliverance, but it is also a "type" of another deliverance for the house of David. Hurd maintains there is nothing in his interpretations of signs that is not "easy or unforced," although modern Protestant theologians and translators have since agreed that the rendering of *almah* as virgin is indeed forced and have revised English versions accordingly. Hurd descends, in his words, "no farther into a detail on the scriptural prophecies concerning Christ's *first coming*" (118), again appealing to the immense task that a full investigation would entail and again chastizing the Jews for their prejudices and perversity in failing to see the light.

In contrast to the first coming of Christ, the second coming is not a single event but rather "gradual and successive" (103). The second coming commences with the resurrection and continues, according to Hurd, until the very end of the world. The New Testament, it must be conceded, contains many seemingly contradictory statements about the kingdom of God, alternately proclaiming it to have arrived or to be deferred until the Last Judgment.[10] Under the rubric of the Second Coming, Hurd curiously discusses, in his sixth sermon, only three prophecies, ones concerning the destruction of Jerusalem, the dispersion of the Jews, and the conversion of the Gentiles. Hurd is most persuasive in showing that the prediction of the Jews' dispersion is indeed remarkable, given the likelihood that they could have been obliterated in the power struggles of the early Christian era. His interest is not so much in the prophecy of "events," strictly speaking, as in the grand outlines of the history of the Jews and Gentiles forecast by the prophets. For Hurd, the Second Coming is essentially the dissemination of the Christian religion, excluding its aberrant mutation in the form of the Catholic Church of Rome. The prophecies of the Second Coming cannot be separated from those predicting the appearance of Antichrist, the subject that Hurd must address to fulfill the terms of the Warburton trust. There is no need to dwell on the largely embarrassing details of Hurd's argument about the Roman Catholic pope as Antichrist. It may be noted in passing, however, that there Hurd appeals more than at any other juncture to an argument from the history of interpretation and an appeal to the "great Protestant principle" that the Pope is Antichrist. He cites such diverse figures as Dante, Petrarch, and Wycliffe, all of whom accused specific popes of being the embodiment of Antichrist, and sees little difficulty in making the transition from judgments against a number of less than infallible popes to the time-honored, general axiom that the Pope *is* the Antichrist.

The ninth and tenth sermons are the focal points of Hurd's poetics of prophecy, the places where he addresses questions of language most explicitly and extensively. His Biblical text for both sermons comes from Ezekiel 20.49: "They say of me, Doth he not speak parables?"—a question to be echoed in the New Testament and among many subsequent readers of prophecy. Hurd objects that a sense of the prophecies as mysterious or cipherlike can be the result only of modesty, laziness, or presumption. He sets out to show (1) that "the prophetic style was of common and approved use, in the times when the prophecies were delivered, and among the people to whom they were addressed" and (2) that this style "is constructed on such principles, as make it the subject of just criticism and reasonable interpretation" (234–35). In tracing the origins of the prophetic style, Hurd follows in abbreviated fashion an itinerary already established, as he acknowledges, by his mentor William Warburton. In his elephantine magnum opus, *The Divine Legation of Moses Demonstrated*, Warburton devoted a long excursus on the antiquity of Egyptian learning available to Moses, focusing particularly on the subject of hieroglyphs. The section soon became known on the Continent as the "Essay on Hieroglyphs" and emerged as a standard point of reference in the vast philosophical and philological literature of the time on the origins of language. Condillac was only one of many who drew extensively on Warburton's analysis; Champollion, famous for having deciphered the Rosetta stone, thought Warburton's essay eminently sensible.[11] Warburton was an important writer on virtually every subject he touched; as Gibbon said: "The learning and the abilities of the author had raised him to a just eminence; but he reigned the dictator and tyrant of the world of literature."[12] Warburton's "Essay on Hieroglyphs" is important for an understanding of prophecy in two ways: It offers prophetic discourse as an exemplary model of original language, and it tells a complicated story that shows how much is at stake in the politics of hieroglyphics.[13] And so it warrants a momentary excursus from Hurd's sermons, which were so massively informed by Warburton.

The Divine Legation of Moses Demonstrated is, in Leslie Stephen's view, "an attempt to support one gigantic paradox by a whole system of affiliated paradoxes."[14] The Deists had argued against the divinity of the Old Testament because of the absence of reference to a future life, and Warburton counters the argument by a three-step proof that he thought fell little short of "mathematical certainty": (1) The doctrine of a future life is necessary for society's well-being; (2) the doctrine is acknowledged by virtually everyone, such that it must be a universal truth; (3) the doctrine is not found in the Mosaic dispensation; ergo, the doctrine of a future state must simply have been assumed. Warburton's proof, then, that the doctrine of a future state is essential to the Mosaic dispensation rests on the total absence of any reference to it.

The principal interest of Warburton for an understanding of prophetic rhetoric arises from one of the affiliated paradoxes to which Leslie Stephen refers; it concerns the hieroglyphic style of prophetic speech, a discourse that must be acknowledged as both clear and obscure, natural and arbitrary. The local issue that prompts Warburton's discussion is the necessity of proving "the high Antiquity of Egypt," which in turn requires that he "trace up *Hieroglyphic* Writing to its Original."[15] Warburton's main task is to dispel the myth that hieroglyphics were invented by Egyptian priests to keep their knowledge hidden from the people. To do so, Warburton offers a short history of writing, within a history of language, the two histories being for him, as for Vico, virtually coextensive.

Of the two ways of communicating ideas to others, by sounds or by figures, the latter "was, soon after that of *Sounds*, thought upon to make those Conceptions lasting and extensive" (67). Writing appears "soon after" the language of sounds, and its appearance seems entirely natural, a simple process of representation: "The first and most natural way of communicating our Conceptions by *Marks* or *Figures*, was by tracing out the *Images* of Things. To express, for Instance, the Idea of a Man or Horse, the Informer delineated the *Form* of each of those Animals. Thus the first Essay towards *Writing* was a *mere* PICTURE" (67). In time, however, the "Inconveniences" attendant on the great bulk and volume of compositions in figures prompted ingenious and civilized nations to "abridge" such texts, and the most celebrated invention in this regard was the Egyptian hieroglyphics, a writing that was "both a *Picture* and a *Character*" (70). The abridgement was conducted according to metonymic and metaphoric transformations, the latter substitutions occurring where *"any quaint Resemblance or Analogy, in the Representative, could be collected from their Observations of Nature, or their traditional Superstitions"* (72). One might think that substitutions founded on resemblance would be naturally or universally intelligible, and yet they include the figure of an eagle, supposed to represent a king estranged from his people, and a hawk, supposed to represent a man who exposes his children through poverty. Even after offering egregious examples from popular superstition, and examples of analogies that are hardly self-evident, Warburton continues his appeal to *"Analogy"* and *"the Nature of the Thing"* (73). In arguing that each change in the mode of writing was natural and necessary, Warburton believes he is dispelling the nefarious myth that the Egyptian hieroglyphs were "a Device of *Choice* for *Secrecy.*" He contends rather that they were, of necessity, for *"popular Use"* (75).

Warburton does admit that a certain obscurity attended the "scantiness" of the hieroglyphs, which in turn gave rise to another change, illustrated by the invention of Chinese ideograms. Unlike Mexican hieroglyphs, which joined characteristic marks to images, the Chinese notation did away with images and retained only "contracted *Marks*." Yet even those marks "do yet betray their Original from Picture and Images" (76).[16] The trace of the original remains through the various "revolutions" (Warburton's word), through the necessary transformations writing undergoes. The endpoint of this "gradual and easy Descent" from picture to letter is the alphabet, which is "only a compendious Abridgement of that troublesome Multiplicity" (78). Warburton pauses to note that the Greek verb *graphein* means both to paint and to write, another indication of his attempt to retain the concept of representation, in its narrow pictorial sense, even as writing departs radically from images.

In Warburton's history of hieroglyphics, within the history of writing, within the history of language, the Egyptian hieroglyphs occupy a middle ground between the Mexican and the Chinese. Neither of the latter two were, according to Warburton, "employed for *Mystery* or *Concealment*" (79). Thus Warburton reasons: "What therefore we find of this Practice in their *middle Stage* of Cultivation amongst the *Egyptians*, we may be assured had an extrinsic cause, and was foreign to their Nature" (79–80), because the concurrence in the method of recording thoughts offers proof of "the sole uniform Voice of Nature" (80). The one aberrant discourse of Nature's voice is the use of hieroglyphs for purposes of secrecy by Egyptian priests—their invention, indeed, can be traced to the "Secretary" of the king. At a certain juncture—which will turn out to be the juncture of the uncertain—it seemed necessary to invent a literary language to convey royal commands over long distances, and the letters of this artificial alphabet expressed "*Words*, not *Things*" (130). In time, this "political" alphabet became common and thus occasioned the invention of a "sacred" alphabet to preserve the hidden doctrines of the priests. The flagrant mistake of most students of the history of hieroglyphs, according to Warburton, is to take this secret, priestly language as the rule rather than the exception. Yet for Warburton, even this seemingly perverse, unnatural writing hardly constitutes a tremor in the voice of nature: Even the secret alliance of church and state that created those hieroglyphs was a matter of strategic necessity.[17]

The voice of nature dictates even methods of writing, and so in explaining the complex history of writing, Warburton can make a "natural" transition from writing to speech: "But for still further evidence that it was *Nature and Necessity*, not *Choice and Artifice*, that gave Birth and Continuance to these several Species of *Hieroglyphic Writing*, we shall now take a View of the Rise and Progress of its *Sister-Art*, the art of SPEECH; and *these* being set together and compared, will reflect mutual Lustre on one another" (81). As with writing, so with language, Warburton's first gesture is to trace it up to its original. In the beginning, for Warburton, was the imperfect word:

LANGUAGE, as appears both from the Records of Antiquity, and the Nature of the Thing, was at first extremely rude, narrow, and equivocal; so that Men would perpetually be at a loss, on any new Conception, or uncommon Adventure, to explain themselves intelligibly to one another: This would naturally set them upon supplying Deficiencies of Speech by apt and significant *Signs*. Accordingly, in the first Ages of the World, mutual Converse was upheld by a mixed Discourse of Words and Actions. (81–83)

The records of antiquity and the book of nature concur on what was often called in Warburton's time the "poverty" of original language, its necessary lack of "proper" terms. Nature and necessity enable man in time to overcome that lack, but in the process, something other than a necessary use of language emerges:

And Use and Custom, as in most other Circumstances of Life improving what arose out of *Necessity*, into *Ornament*, this Practice subsisted long after the Necessity had ceased; especially amongst the *Eastern* People, whose natural Temperature inclined them to a Mode of Conversation which so well exercised their Vivacity, by *Motion*; and so much gratified it, by a perpetual Representation of *material Images*. (83)

The exemplary instances of a mixed discourse of word and action, combining the traits of vitality of motion and graphic representation of inert, material images, are drawn from the prophetic books of the Bible:

Of this we have *innumerable* Instances in *Holy Scripture*: As where the false Prophet *pushed* with Horns of Iron, to denote the entire Overthrow of the *Syrians*; where *Jeremiah*, by God's direction, *hides* the Linen Girdle in a Hole of the Rock near *Euphrates*; where *he breaks* a Potter's Vessel in Sight of the People; *puts on* Bonds and Yokes, and *casts* a Book into *Euphrates*, where *Ezekiel*, by the same Appointment, *delineates* the Siege of *Jerusalem* on a Tile; *weighs* the Hair of his Beard in Balances; *carries* out his Household-stuff, and *joins together* the two Sticks for *Judah* and *Israel*. By these Actions the Prophets instructed the People in the Will of God, and conversed with them in Signs. (83)

Warburton will later call such instances examples of "speaking actions," a notion not be confused with J. L. Austin's "speech acts." Indeed, the former might well be designated as "act-speeches."[18] A speech act is irreducibly linguistic, although it is like a nonlinguistic action insofar as it "does" something even as it is enunciated. The prophetic action in the preceding instances is not verbal, although it seems to demand translation into a linguistic mode: The action is itself a sign that has to be *read*, has to be translated into language. Warburton suggests here that the prophet's actions speak for themselves, but that is hardly the case in general and not even so in the Biblical passages to which he alludes. When Jeremiah, for example, is told to break a potter's vessel before his people, the Lord also commands his prophet to say on his behalf:

"Even so will I break this people and this city, as *one* breaketh a potter's vessel, that cannot be made whole again" (19.11). Or when Jeremiah casts his book into the Euphrates, the passage as a whole reads: "And it shall be, when thou hast made an end of reading this book, *that* thou shalt bind a stone to it, and cast it into the midst of Euphrates: And thou shalt say, Thus shall Babylon sink, and shall not rise from the evil that I will bring upon her: and they shall be weary. Thus far *are* the words of Jeremiah." (51.63–64)

Warburton fails to recognize the way that prophetic words speak louder than actions, since the relation between the action and its allegorical referent must be spelled out by God's words to the prophet. The Hebrew term *davar* means equally word and event and thus suggests at virtually every turn an identity of word and action, corresponding to Warburton's determination of the originary language as a "mixed discourse of word and action." But the distinction between word and nonlinguistic action cannot simply be collapsed. God does not do so, and neither need Warburton.

Warburton continues the passage cited above with a transition to a different, but related, mode of prophetic discourse:

But where God teaches the Prophet, and, in Compliance to the Custom of that Time, condescends to the same Mode of Instruction, then the *significative Action* is generally changed into a *Vision*, either *natural* or *extraordinary*: As where the Prophet *Jeremiah* is bid *regard* the Rod of the Almond-Tree, and the Seething-Pot, the Work on the Potter's Wheel, and the Baskets of good and bad Figs; and the Prophet *Ezekiel*, and the Resurrection of the dry Bones. (83–4)

Vision does not speak for itself here, any more than action does in the previous passage. Consider the full context of Warburton's first example from Jeremiah:

Moreover the word of the LORD came to me saying, Jeremiah, what seest thou? And I said, I see a rod of an almond tree. / Then said the Lord unto me, Thou hast well seen: for I will hasten my word to perform it. / And the word of the Lord came unto me the second time, saying, What seest thou? And I said, I see a seething pot;

and the face thereof *is* toward the north. / Then the Lord said unto me, Out of the north an evil shall break forth upon all the inhabitants of the land. (1.11–14)

Seeing is not understanding. Jeremiah *sees* perfectly well the vision God presents to him but does not "see" its proper interpretation. Once again, God must provide the deciphering of the allegorical vision. Neither a pure action nor a pure image provides a prophetic message that does not have to be supplemented or complemented by words, without which a sound interpretation is scarcely possible.

Warburton argues that the prophetic discourse of "Information by Action" was by no means extraordinary, even if his initial examples were instances of divine intervention via language. He contends rather, as Hurd will, that such actions partook of *a very common and familiar Mode of Conversation*" (86) and offers further examples from classical antiquity to fill out his argument. Warburton makes a similar claim with respect to the highly figurative, intensely metaphorical style of the prophets. In a general argument to be echoed by Hurd, Warburton traces the necessity of metaphor in this way:

> The *Metaphor* arose as evidently from *Rusticity of Conception,* as the Pleonasm from the *Want of Words.* The first simple Ages, uncultivated and immerged in Sense, could express their rude Conceptions of abstract Ideas, and the reflex Operations of the Mind, only by material Images: which, so applied, became *Metaphors. This* and not the Warmth of Poetic Fancy, as is commonly supposed, was the true Original of figurative Expression. (147)

Parallel to the divide in Egyptian hieroglyphics between the popular and the sacerdotal, Warburton posits a distinction between two types of metaphor, one "*open* and *intelligible,*" the other "*hidden* and *mysterious.*" Prophetic discourse is again held up as exemplary, and in a striking way; the first instance features a metaphor that unites the two types Warburton had distinguished in his preliminary remark. The text in question is the famous prediction of Balaam from Numbers 24.17: "There shall come a STAR out of Jacob, and a Sceptre shall rise out of Israel." Warburton observes that the prophecy may relate to David, since the metaphor of a scepter commonly denoted a ruler. But the figure of the star has a "secret and hidden Meaning" as well in the Egyptian hieroglyphics, namely, God. Warburton cites the phrase "the star of your God" from Amos 5.26 as proof that the star is a "material image" of God. Thus the passage from Numbers is best interpreted by taking "star" as a metaphor of the abstruse, mysterious kind to refer to Christ. The strategic value of the hieroglyphic metaphor should be clear: It permits a division within metaphor such that it is at once common and secret, transparent and obscure. The complicated history of the hieroglyph can be compressed into a simultaneous structural relation, and in turn reordered onto the temporal axis of Biblical history with an emphasis on one aspect or another as the given moment demands. It is no wonder that in his most abridged formulation of the idea of prophetic discourse, Warburton has recourse to a striking oxymoron: "In a Word, the Prophetic Style seems to be a speaking Hieroglyphic" (152).

Much of what has been presented here in this rather Warburtonian digression on Warburton appears in abbreviated form in Hurd's discussion of prophetic style. Like his mentor, Hurd claims that the style of the prophets "was only the poetical, and highly figurative style of the Eastern nations" (235).[19] That discourse is typical of what he calls the original language of all nations, but Hurd cannot be accused of a simple nostalgia for some lost golden age when all was poetry, passion, and imagination. Like Warburton, Hurd maintains that the original language is "extremely imperfect," and he continues:

Their stock of words being small, they explain themselves very much by *signs*, or representative actions: and their conceptions, in that early state of society, being gross and rude, the few words they have, are replete with material images, and so are what we call highly metaphorical; and this, not from choice or design, or even from any extraordinary warmth of fancy, but of necessity, and from the very nature of things. (237)

In abridging Warburton's history of language, Hurd gives a less differentiated account, one that emphasizes even more strongly the representational character of writing, the way metaphor is writing "in picture," and the way picture-writing was succeeded by symbols or "representative marks" grounded on resemblances to particular objects. Though Warburton addresses the notorious "secrecy" of Egyptian hieroglyphs, it is only to circumscribe and domesticate it within an encompassing narrative. Even as he acknowledges the authority of Moses's interdiction of graven images, Hurd has to stress the pictorial or representational quality of prophetic language.

Ezekiel's question, "They say of me, Doth he not speak parables?" serves as the text for both the sermon on prophetic style and the one on apocalyptic method. To the question posed to Ezekiel, Hurd replies, as he must, with a resolute "Yes." Why was the parable so appropriate a form? Because the hieroglyphic style had "a degree of obscurity in it, so far at least to furnish the Jews, who had no mind to listen to their Prophets, with a pretence of not understanding them" (243–44). The objection of Ezekiel's audience to their prophet's obscurity is Hurd's "proof" of their lack of understanding. And yet Hurd maintains in the very same paragraph *"[t]hat this mode of writing was of common and approved use in the ages, when the prophecies were delivered, and among the people, to whom they were addressed"* (244, italics in original). How can Hurd make both these claims at once? He must argue implicitly that the Jews did not understand their own language, a language of common and approved use. Moreover, the lexicon of that language was derived not only from convention (with which they must have been utterly familiar); it was also grounded on the symbolic principles of the hieroglyphs, "on fixed and constant analogies" given in God's book of nature. Hurd exceeds the common Christian strategy of simply claiming that while the Jews understood their prophets in a narrow and literal fashion, the Christians were privy to the more proper, ultimate meaning of the prophetic texts that the Jews were simply not in a historical position to understand. He claims, in effect, that the Jews were illiterate in their own language and in a language that, in some sense, ought to have been universal. They were somehow oblivious to the resemblances set out by God in nature itself. So violent and arrogant a position seems to partake precisely of the sort of prejudice Hurd lamented at the outset of his sermons.

Hurd's position on the language of prophecy is curiously equivocal. On the one hand, he describes the hieroglyphic learning of the Egyptians that the Israelites inherited as a "treasure" brought along into the land of Canaan. On the other hand, he comments that "[t]he East was wholly infected" (240) by the hieroglyphic spirit. His ambivalence may be linked to the ambiguity and arbitrariness of hieroglyphic discourse, even though he protests that it is entirely natural and ultimately intelligible. At times, the examples Hurd offers hardly seem capable of persuading even a receptive audience. As an instance of intelligible hieroglyphics, he blithely cites the figure of a horse whose head was found buried in the foundations of Carthage and interpreted as a symbol of prosperity, as if a decapitated horse could signify nothing else.

Determined to demonstrate that the seemingly mysterious language of prophecy is, no less than "any other language or technical phraseology"

(250) subject to "just criticism and rational interpretation," Hurd nonetheless offers as examples hieroglyphs much less precise than the terms drawn from most technical phraseologies:

When the prophecy is of remote events, the *subject* is frequently not announced, or announced only in general terms. Thus, an *earthquake* is described—a *mountain* is said to be thrown down—a *star*, to fall from heaven; and so in numberless other instances. Now, an earthquake, in hieroglyphic language, denotes a *revolution in government*; a mountain is the symbol of a *kingdom*, or *capital city*; a star, of *a prince* or *great man*: but of *what* government, of *what kingdom*, of *what* prince, the prophet speaks, we are not told, and are frequently unable to find out, till a full coincidence of all circumstances, in the event, discloses the secret. (252)

Like Lowth, Hurd locates the "genius" of prophecy in the enigmatic generality of its figuration, though the prophetic figures are far less determinate than is suggested by the nearly one-to-one correspondences Hurd outlines. Can one really limit the sense of a mountain, even within the corpus of the prophets, so that it only figures a kingdom or a capital city? Here Hurd follows the lead of Isaac Newton's commentaries on prophecy in reducing the manifold possibilities of prophetic figures to a single sense, a formal parallel to his circumscription of all prophecies to refer to the spirit of Jesus Christ.

Hurd is much more perspicacious when he argues that a chief difficulty in the interpretation of prophecy lies in the prophet's "*mixed use of the plain and figured style*" (253–54). The prophetic descriptions, he notes, "are sometimes *literal*, even when they appear most figurative; and sometimes, again, they are highly *figurative* when they appear most plain" (254). The difficulty, ideally, is dissipated by the event prophesied. Thus when Jesus warned that if the temple were destroyed, he would raise it up in three days, it became clear only "after the fact" that what appeared to designate the literal temple in fact referred to the temple of his body. One corollary of this principle, not explicitly stated by Hurd, is that in a reading of a prophetic text before the event prophesied, one cannot tell the difference between the literal and the figural, for the one could always turn out to be the other. Pascal, one of Hurd's great teachers in matters of prophecy, had written in the *Pensées*: "On n'entend les prophéties que quand on voit les choses arrivées . . . ," which implies that a prophecy cannot truly be understood simply as a text: To understand the words of a prophecy is not necessarily to understand its meaning.[20] One can inquire into the sense of prophetic words prior to a predicted event, but there is no possibility, according to Pascal, of correlating a text and its meaning until the event has occurred. And it should be recalled that Hurd earlier notes that sometimes even the actual occurrence of a prophesied event is not enough to clarify the figural obscurity of the text.

Speaking in parables is the common theme that links the sermon on prophetic style with that on the "style and method of the Apocalypse." Hurd argues that the intricate symbolism of the Book of Revelation owes much to the language of the prophets, with the minor difference that in the Apocalypse the symbols are "much thicker sown" than throughout the many books of the prophets.[21] That the scene of the apocalyptic vision is in Jerusalem and not Judea accounts for some differences in imagery, but the main distinction of the Apocalypse lies in the continuity of its symbolism, its character as a single, rigorous symbolic system. Hurd's analysis of the Apocalypse is deeply indebted to Joseph Mede's *A Key to the Revelations*, an influential treatise of the early seventeenth century well known to Milton and his contemporaries. Mede's method was "intrinsic argument," a formalist analysis that gave priority to the internal structure of the text. By considering the text as "a naked recital of facts, literally expressed," Mede came to the conclusion that the parts of what appears to be a history, a chronological unfolding of events, are in fact "homogeneous" and "contemporary," related to the same subject in the same period.[22] He divided the Apocalypse into two parts, both consisting of "synchronical" sets of prophecies: The former, concerning the affairs of the empire, are contained in the "sealed book," and the latter, the affairs of the church, are contained in the "open book." This structure, determining the prophecies as both historical and, to a limited extent, synchronic, allows great latitude in the interpretation of the Apocalypse, room enough for the peculiarities of Hurd's own.

Hurd's treatment of the style and method of Revelations in his tenth sermon is far more perfunctory than the corresponding analysis of prophetic rhetoric. Its chief service, it seems, is to lay a dispassionate, theoretical groundwork for what we have already seen as the more purely ideological conclusions of the final sermons on the Antichrist. Though Hurd recognizes that the "season" may be "unfavorable" for any attempt to fulfill the demand of the Warburton trust, he does not shrink from the task. To prove that the prophecies of Antichrist refer to the apostasy of Papal Rome, Hurd relies on the Bible as a single, vast unity whose singular author transcends the diverse texts of Daniel, St. Paul, and St. John the Divine. To the Christians addressed by the author of Revelations, the fact that Rome was the locus of the Antichrist only confirmed what they already knew by providing a single, proper name for a complex of evils. For them, "Rome" was the Rome of secular Caesars who persecuted the Christians. How then can Hurd go against what seems to be the grain of the text to locate the Antichrist in the Roman Catholic Church? Primarily by his appeal to Paul's doctrine, in 2 Thessalonians, that the man of sin, whom Hurd understands as Antichrist, will "sit in the temple of God."[23] That is to say, the forces of Antichrist are not simply the opponents of Christ; they pretend, in both senses of the word, to be true inheritors of Christ's legacy. Hurd also finds support for the determination of the Antichrist as a religious as opposed to secular power in Daniel's prophecy (7.24) that the kingdom of the Antichrist will be "diverse" with respect to the ten kingdoms. But Hurd's manipulation of the circumscribed Biblical passages, conducted at times with an almost Midrashic ingenuity, is hardly enough to sway any reader not already converted. The Edward Gibbons of his time still had reason to be amazed that the attempt to prove the Pope was Antichrist had been taken up again.

To trace the argument from prophecy in the writings of Hurd and Warburton is to confront, at virtually every turn, paradox, prejudice, or both. Their perspicacity as literary critics—and this is especially true of Hurd—leads them often to the crux of philosophical, philological, and theological issues, but their solutions to the problems posed are just as often fraught with contradictions. The texts of both writers are dominated by dogma: That Hurd's conclusions were given in the Warburton indenture in advance of his sermons is only the most conspicuous instance of a pervasive disposition. But beyond all the ideological cant of Hurd's performance, there remain genuine insights into the paradoxical nature of prophetic discourse, best characterized in Warburton's impossible formula: the "speaking hieroglyph."

In his essay on Coleridge from which the epigraph to this chapter comes, after noting how the house of theology is scored by the hieroglyphics of perished hands, Pater goes on say: "When we decypher one of those hieroglyphics, we find in it the statement of a mistaken opinion; but knowledge has crept onward since the hand dropped from the wall; we no longer entertain the opinion, and we can trace the origin of the mistake."

In the analysis of Hurd and Warburton, we have no doubt tried to trace the origin of a certain mistake. But this risks being the same sort of story that Hurd and Warburton told themselves, a story tracing the origin of mistakes about hieroglyphics, a story of obscurity and error overcome in the end by knowledge. There may be no criticism without such a story implied. But with regard to the story of the hieroglyph, and its exemplary expression in the prophetic word, perhaps what is called for is precisely a resistance to narrative, a resistance to inscribing the prophetic performative into a narrative that would resolve all difficulties into a coherent story. The power of the prophetic word *is* this resistance.

5

Herder and Eichhorn: Word, Deed, and Fiction in Prophetic Discourse

"Did you ever read the Bible?"
—Vladimir to Estragon, *Waiting for Godot*

In the musty corridors of German theology of the eighteenth century—much of it written in the wake of the scholasticism of Christian Wolff—Herder's writings emerge as a breath of fresh air. He created, in Karl Barth's phrase, "room" for theology.[1] Like many leading German intellectuals of his day, he was trained to be a minister, but he rebelled against the confines of that profession without abandoning many of the concomitant values and habits of thought. He was expansive and flexible in his embrace of ideas, not all of them compatible with one another, as he moved in his itinerary from an early pietism to what Rudolf Haym terms "the borders of deism."[2] Although he kept his distance from many aspects of the profession, his reading of the Bible was far from amateurish. Herder could profess that he wrote as a theologian, and in the opinion of Emmanuel Hirsch, the great historian of Protestant theology, Herder's was the most important theological voice in the period between Semler and Schleiermacher.[3]

Herder's studies of the Bible form part of a vast project of cultural and anthropological hermeneutics, much of it marked by a deep concern with the origins and development of societies.[4] His prize-winning *Abhandlung über den Ursprung der Sprache* (*Essay on the Origin of Language*) and his work in the collection and transmission of folk culture are but two examples of a strong interest in the language of origins, the beginning, as

it were, of the word(s). With respect to Hebrew poetry, Herder's valoriza-
tion of its originary character springs much less from a dogmatic or doctrinal predisposition than from an enthusiastic embrace of the "Oriental"
origins of Judeo-Christian culture.[5] For him, as for his associate and correspondent of two decades, Johann Gottfried Eichhorn, the study of the
Bible held a prominent place in the burgeoning field of Oriental studies.
In this context, the Bible's status as a *sacred* text was by no means of paramount importance. Herder prefers to speak of "the Bible" rather than of
"Scripture," a term more redolent of belief, and his *Briefe, das Studium der
Theologie betreffend* (*Letters Concerning the Study of Theology*), written as a
guide for theological candidates in his diocese, opens with this credo:

> One must read the Bible in a human [*menschlich*] way: For it is a book written
> through human agency for human beings; human is the language; human were
> the external means whereby it was written and preserved; human, finally, is the
> sense with which it must be grasped and every aid that elucidates it, as well as the
> entire purpose and use to which it should be applied. You can, therefore, safely be-
> lieve that the more humanly (in the best sense of the word) you read the word of
> God, the closer you will come to the purpose of its originator, who created man
> in His image and acts humanly for us in all works and benefices in which He
> shows Himself to us as God.[6] (X,7)

Coleridge, for one, took exception to these lines and retorted in the margins
of his copy: "In other words the Bible or Word of God is not the Word of
God. Truth is Truth—Falsehood is Falsehood—the only medium is fable.
But this is *kindisch* [childish], not *menschlich* [human]."[7] For Herder, there
is no problem in recognizing the Bible as simultaneously the word of God
and the work of human hands. Yet there is something tendentious in the
phrasing that so often stresses the human character of the text while only
once acknowledging it as the word of God. Moreover, Herder moves almost silently from the neutral term *menschlich* to the value-laden *humaner,*
connoting the highest sense of humanity. But what troubles Coleridge most
is the more scandalous displacement from the divine to the human, a movement, to his mind, from an indisputable position to a highly dubious one.

   A good many German theologians, philologists, and literati of the
late eighteenth century were informed readers of important developments
in British Biblical criticism. Lowth's *Lectures on the Sacred Poetry of the Hebrews* in particular were celebrated by Moses Mendelssohn, Herder, and
others as a pioneering achievement.[8] Thus when Herder set out to write

his *Briefe, das Studium der Theologie betreffend,* as well as his later *Vom Geiste der Ebräischen Poesie* (*On the Spirit of Hebrew Poetry*), he defined his project substantially in relation to Lowth's. Herder's praise for Lowth is not effusive, perhaps because Lowth had anticipated so much of Herder's response to reading the Bible, including considering it as an Oriental and literary text. But Herder, with some justification, felt Lowth had focussed too narrowly on technical aspects of Hebrew poetry. And Lowth's formalistic analysis, in his view, was coupled with an attitude that at times reduced poetry to a rather minor matter, to the neglect of what Herder called its "spirit."

One small but significant sign of Herder's indebtedness to Lowth is that in the discussion of prophecy in *Vom Geiste der Ebräischen Poesie,* Herder feels no need to prove that Hebrew prophecy *is* poetry. He can take it for granted—Lowth had made the case definitively—and simply begin to outline the characteristics of the prophet and prophetic speech. What, then, is the prophet, in Herder's view? He cautions against looking to the etymology of the word *nabi* as being authoritative or even as providing much of a clue. One should consult rather the use (*Gebrauch*) of the term throughout the Bible. And an inductive investigation shows the prophet to be the "mouth of God," the one who reveals what would otherwise remain secret, "der Verkündiger seiner Geheimnisse" (XII, 48). The prophet is not necessarily a poet; the earliest "seers," whose careers are recorded in the "historical" books of the Bible, are not necessarily poets in the strict sense. Poetry as a discourse, however, is well suited to the communication of God's word; all languages, Herder claims, identify poets as seers. The Hebrew prophets were inspired and their effect—a major concern for Herder—was literally to "enthuse" their audience. Herder has no patience for the Platonic characterization of the poet/prophet as crazed ecstatic, as a simply unconscious vehicle of God's word. It would be a serious error, in his view, to mistake the "sublime, political spirit" of Isaiah for that of a merely entranced visionary.

That is not to say, however, that prophetic discourse emerges as a paradigm of clear and distinct communication. The prophets deliver God's *secrets* and are themselves enigmatic in their turn. Their status prompts a singular acknowledgment from Herder that his normally exalted hermeneutic mode of sympathy or empathy (*Einfühlung*) comes up against its limits in trying to understand the inner state of the prophet: "Moreover it is a wasted effort to want to whirl or brood oneself into the inner disposition of the prophet, after the times have changed so much. With the prophets themselves, the mode of divine inspiration was different according to times and sensibilities" (53). Instead of a divination, as one aspect of the hermeneutic of *Einfühlung* or empathy later codified by Schleiermacher, Herder proposes attention to the "individual mode of imagination and style" as the most fruitful and practical interpretive strategy. He leaves the question of inspiration up in the air, as it were. The effects of inspiration are undeniably powerful, but its source and character remain largely inscrutable.

In the section of *The Spirit of Hebrew Poetry* devoted to "The Calling and the Office of the Prophets," prophetic poetry emerges as the most immediate—although not absolutely so—of divine discourses. For Herder, Moses is the archetypal prophet, the standard by whom all others are to be measured. God appears to Moses to give a series of "signs" that are to dispel the doubts of the despairing Israelites. When God manifests himself to Moses, he does so in the form of fire, a mediating "symbol," since God cannot properly be seen: "Moses Jehovah ist unanschaubar; sobald er im Symbol irgend einer Natursache erscheint: so ist diese sein Engel, d.i. sein sichtbarer Bote, oder nach Moses schönen Ausdruck: Gottes Name ist in ihm, . . . das Antlitz Gottes könne niemand schauen oder nachbilden" (34–5). ("Moses' Jehovah is invisible; as soon as he appears in the symbol of any thing of nature, so this thing is his angel, that is, his visible messenger, or in Moses' beautiful expression: God's name is in it, . . . no one can see nor imitate the face of God.") Remarkable here is the presence of the name that guarantees the identity of the deity and his messenger and that allows for the passage between the visible and the invisible. So unmediated is this mediation of the messenger—but is a name not already a mediation?—that Herder can say: "The God who reveals himself here names himself Jehovah and is also called the angel of Jehovah" (34).

The visions of Moses—these visions of the invisible—are for Herder the foundation of the whole "economy" of prophecy in the Old Testament; the earliest post-Mosaic prophets cite and revise the "writings" of their great predecessor. But the prophets retain individual visions commensurate with their historical situations and not only that: Each has a distinctive mode of writing, a characteristic style. Isaiah is a "royal" prophet, and therefore his vision of God is colored by the splendor of the earthly king he sees before him. God becomes what the prophet beholds, because God himself cannot be seen. The later prophets had no access to the relatively unambiguous symbolic appearances of God as Moses did. One sign of the decline of the prophetic office is the passage from the symbols of Moses to the images or figures (*Bilder*), to which David, for one, was privy. For the later prophets, these night visions (*Nachtgesichte*) of dubious clarity were no longer an integral part of the prophetic experience; most prophets, says Herder, were exposed to the *word* of God without any phenomenal appearance, in however attenuated a form. Yet the loss of sensible appearance was a gain in terms of God's gradual revelation to mankind. "More than the appearance," writes Herder, "was the word" (40). ("Mehr als die Erscheinung war das Wort.") The advantages of verbal revelation are manifold: The word is recoverable, citable, and transmissible in a way that a theophany is not. It is only with the arrival of the word(s) that history can begin.

To this point, Herder's exposition of the prophetic vocation is much like that of his forerunners. What sets Herder's apart from the rest is the passage he singles out as paradigmatic of prophecy. One reason Moses stands out as the greatest prophet is by virtue of the identity of word and action that characterizes not just his speech but his very being, as if he embodied the synthesis of the two senses of vocation. "His whole life was the word of God, the act." ("Sein ganzes Leben war Wort Gottes, Handlung") (40). That identity is to some extent built into the Hebrew term *davar*, both word and act, and indeed it is the word *as* action that Herder privileges as the epitome of prophecy. The principal proof-text for Herder's vision of prophecy comes from Isaiah 55:

> Ich denke nicht, wie ihr gedenkt,
> ich handle nicht, wie ihr wohl handelt.
> Wie hoch der Himmel über der Erde ist,
> so handle ich, so denk ich höher als ihr.
> Denn wie der Regen und Schnee vom Himmel niedersteigt,
> und kehrt nicht wieder zurück, bis er getränkt die Erde,
> und hat sie Sprossen gemacht Laub und Kraut,
> das sie dem Säenden Samen giebt und Brot:
> So ist mein Wort, das je aus meinem Munde ging,
> es kehrt zu mir nie leer zurück,
> es thut was ich gewollt,
> es richtet aus, wozu ichs ausgesandt.
> So sollt auch ihr in Freude von mir gehn u.f. (41)

[For my thoughts *are* not your thoughts, neither *are* your ways my ways, saith the LORD./For *as* the heavens are higher than your ways, and my thoughts than your thoughts./For as the rain cometh down, and the snow from heaven, and returneth not thither, but watereth the earth, and maketh it bring forth and bud, that it may give seed to the sower, and bread to the eater:/So shall my word be that goeth forth out of my mouth: it shall not return unto me void, but it shall accomplish that which I please, and it shall prosper *in the thing* whereto I sent it./For ye shall go out with joy . . .]

God's word, spoken through the prophet and constituting the ideal model for his discourse, is likened to a natural process that cannot but accomplish its goal. It extends in time and reaches fruition in the inexorable activity of its unfolding. The metaphor of the seed sown adumbrates its exemplary use in the New Testament parables of the Sower that identify the Lord with his word and his word with the seed. The prophetic word works like nature—but the most important thing is that it *works*. It acts or performs, and it is in that restricted sense a performative speech-act that is always and eternally felicitous. Elaine Scarry argues that the prophetic word is "never self-substantiating," that "it seeks its confirmation in a visible change in the world of matter."[9] This is certainly true of a good many of the prophets' utterances. Either the sayings themselves or the subsequent actions recorded make that clear. Nonetheless, as became evident in the analysis of the prophetic word in Warburton, the event in the "material world" tends to be supplemented in its turn by further speech in order to interpret the matter, so to speak. As if the act itself resisted having meaning ascribed to it or could have any number of meanings assigned—hence the need for a verbal supplement.

For all its power, the prophetic word pales in comparison with the divine word proper, with the latter nonetheless remaining the absolute model against which the former is measured. When Goethe's Faust translates the opening axiom of the Gospel of John as "Im Anfang war die Tat" ("In the beginning was the act"), he is entirely consonant with Herder's notion of the originary, prophetic word.[10] Given the exalted status of "das thatvolle Wort"—literally, "the deedful word"—for Herder, it comes as no surprise that he shares little of the widespread Christian exegetical tendency to see prediction as the dominant paradigm for prophecy. Nor is it any wonder that he could come to characterize prophecy in general as "political art" ("politische Kunst"), even if the specific character of prophetic politics is by and large left indeterminate by Herder. His view of the plan of revelation is still decidedly Christocentric, but he by no means reduces Hebrew prophecy to Messianism, neither explicitly nor by example. In his *Briefe, das Studium der Theologie betreffend* Herder complains about the exegetical habit of searching through passages from the Old Testament—without regard for their proper, historical context—to find whatever anticipations of Christ might be legible.[11] Prophecy offers "a vista into the future" ("eine Aussicht in die Zukunft"), but precise prediction of any particular historical event is entirely contrary to the prophetic spirit (X, 202). In this, Herder very much anticipates the Romantic poets, German and British, in their widening sense of a future-oriented prophecy not confined to prediction.

The spirit of Herder's historicism demands a preliminary investigation into the specificity of the texts in question, of the style and even idiosyncrasies of each Biblical author. But as a student of what Goethe would later call "world literature," Herder permits himself some comparative speculation on the character of prophecy across cultures. Herder is most particularly interested in adducing parallels between the Hebrew poets and the Greek, occasionally supplemented by references to Ossian, still thought then to be an authentically ancient poet. He claims, in a sentiment that will resonate later in the work of Hölderlin:

If in Greece the poetry of the sages and poets had been preserved more purely with more authentic remains, then we would see more similarity (with prophets of other cultures) such as now in the mouth of Calchas, Aeschylus' Cassandra, and those who prophesy in appearances or while dying: It would be impossible not to recognize it. (43)

It is difficult to see on what grounds Herder can make so categorical an assertion about texts that no modern person has ever read or could read. His stance seems to proceed from a faith in an underlying humanity across cultural differences or perhaps, more specifically, from a conceptual and rhetorical tendency to identify the singular object under study as in some sense representative of the universal, much as the Hebrew nation—rather strangely for a German of his time—will be seen to be exemplary to and for all nations.

When scrutinizing Herder's writings on Hebrew poetry and Judeo-Christian theology, one is not surprised to find him according such preeminent status to them: The subject matter virtually demands it. Yet one can glimpse the paradigmatic importance of the Hebrews for Herder especially when he is not writing primarily on the above-mentioned topics. So, for example, in his reflections on the nature of the public and the fatherland in the various versions that go under the name of "Haben wir noch das Publikum und Vaterland der Alten?" ("Do We Still Have the Public and the Fatherland of Old?"), not only does the Hebrew people instantiate something like the ideal social formation, the Hebrew prophet has a key mediating role in achieving that ideal.[12] From its origins, the Hebrew people was considered as a "genetic Individual," as "one people." And this unity was established partly through the relation to the future established by "the dying patriarch" ("der sterbende Stammvater"), who speaks to his sons "for the whole series of future times" (303). Even before the son of the tribe was born, "the prophecy had already taken place for the whole of the future people" (303). Herder underscores the ability of Moses to *address* his people as "one person," as if they were a single moral being. Moreover, all subsequent prophets are said to speak in the same way for "the whole people." No matter that the actual "circle" of listeners may have been small, the idea was correspondingly great. Even in the occasionally still, small voice of the prophet and of the psalmist, Herder always hears the "lofty, widely resounding tone of patriotism" (303–04). It is through this resonant voice that the public becomes "vital" ("lebendig") and constitutes a single collection in which "one stands for all and all for one" (304). As singular as this relation sounds, Herder continues to hear the echoes of the "prophetic tone" ("Prophetenton") in any truly national public. And so far from thinking of the Hebrew people as an ideal now lost to ancient history, Herder contends that every people still has something like the public of the Hebrews through "its language" ("Sprache") (304). One could even say its tongue, because, as in his famous treatise on the origin of language, Herder conceives of language as essentially oral and aural.[13]

The shift from the Hebrews to every people on earth permits a further turn—in this short section entitled "The Public of the Hebrews"—to the German people, which comes to occupy almost half the section. Even the general pronouncements about the nation, such as "a nation is formed and educated through its language" (304), are made with a view to the history and the calling of the *German* nation. But, in the end, Herder must acknowledge that far from being a unified nation, whole lands (something like "provinces") of "Germany" are torn apart from one another, whole provinces hardly understand one another. So divided are Germans from one another that many seem to have lost a "reliable common organ of their innermost feelings" ("zutrauliche gemeinschaftliches Organ ihrer innigsten Gefühle") (306). So the unified nation of the Hebrews stands as an exemplary model of what Germany should become. "If," Herder argues, "the voice of the fatherland is the voice of God, then it can only resound for the common, all-encompassing, and deepest goals in the *language of the fatherland*" (306). One nation, one voice, under one God, who seems in his infinite wisdom to have chosen to express himself in the voices of finite nations, the Hebrew's first and foremost.[14]

Though Herder rightly and importantly calls prophecy "political art," there is not much that is identifiably political in the texture of his readings of the Hebrew prophets and poets. But there is at least something vaguely democratic in his particular emphasis on the people and on folk culture. (And Herder saw Biblical culture and folk culture as continuous— he worked on the Song of Songs at the same time as he was anthologizing nonreligious folk songs.) The appeal to folk culture implicitly runs up against the canons of courtly culture still dominant then in the lands we loosely call "Germany."[15] If the nostalgia for a primeval poetry is a return to a time *before* politics, that gesture is not in itself apolitical. In particular, Herder's return to the poetry and culture of the Hebrews expresses not a longing for a theocratic regime but rather a desire for a unified public whose one language can be translated, almost insensibly, from God to the prophets to the people. The Hebrews, for Herder, are not a thing of the past but a model for an elusive future.

∼

The work of Johann Gottfried Eichhorn constitutes one of the earliest full-scale attempts to study the Bible from a relatively "disinterested" position of scholarship. Eichhorn was trained as a philologist and became in 1775, at the age of twenty-three, a Professor of Oriental Languages at Jena.[16] Among his teachers were Michaelis, whom Herder called "our philological prophet," and Heyne, the classical philologist whose work extended into what now would be regarded as comparative mythology. Johann David Michaelis, who had annotated and "corrected" Lowth, was a dedicated scholar who shared a Lutheran disdain for modern Jewish mores, but his desire to read through—or around—the thicket of rabbinic commentary and legends to get to the truth of the Bible meant that Michaelis became a zealous philologue of the "true" Mosaic dispensation. Michaelis's attention to the myriad details of languages and dialects, together with a consideration of larger issues of philosophy of language, offered Eichhorn a model for scholarly procedure.[17] Later on in his career, as a fully estab- lished professor and commanding intellectual presence in Germany, Eich- horn worked in close contact with Herder, after the latter had sent him in September of 1780 the first two parts of his *Briefe, das Studium der Theolo- gie betreffend.* Indeed, after that point, it is difficult to separate who was teaching whom as their studies of the Bible progressed in lockstep.[18]

Eichhorn quickly became one of the most prolific and prominent Biblical scholars of his time, and his influence was not confined to Ger- many. In outlining a course of education for his son Derwent, Coleridge could recommend the reading of

Eichhorn's introductions to the O. and N. Testament, and to the Apocrypha, and his Comment on the Apoc al ypse [*sic*] (to which all my Notes and your own pre- vious studies will supply whatever antidote is wanting)—these will suffice for your *Biblical* learning, and teach you to attach no more than supportable weight to these and such like outward evidences of our holy and spiritual Religion.[19]

Coleridge scholars who argue the case for Eichhorn's crucial influence of- ten create a somewhat misleading impression by breaking off this passage after the phrase *"Biblical* learning."[20] But Coleridge's emphasis on the word "Biblical" means that Eichhorn's work has to do with the Bible as a book (*biblos*). And he underscores that such learning involves external mat- ters of the text rather than the inner truth of Christian religion. Nonethe- less, if God "hides in the details," then a scrupulous attention to the word of God will be indispensable, and in these matters Eichhorn may well be the best guide available.[21]

Eichhorn's most influential work, the *Einleitung in das alte Testament* (*Introduction to the Old Testament*), is important for its advocacy of what is now called the "older documentary hypothesis," the notion that the Book of Genesis, especially, was not the work of a single hand but a compilation primarily of two quite divergent groups of writings.[22] Eichhorn terms his project "Higher Criticism": It entails investigations of the date, authentic- ity, coherence, and origin of the various Biblical texts. As such, the Higher Criticism has as little as possible to do with exegesis, but the consequences of the findings of Higher Criticism can be far-reaching for any understanding of the Bible.

In the *Introduction* Eichhorn repeatedly refers to his undertaking as "literary history" ("Literär-Geschichte"), hardly a common term at the time. Under that rubric Eichhorn understands a kind of formalist philology inherited from the study of classical antiquity, but a formalism not at all at odds with the emergence of what could then have been called a "new historicism."[23] For Eichhorn, the Bible has to first be thought of as one Oriental text among others and understood in the light of the historical moments of its "human" production, to use Herder's term that Eichhorn will echo. Eichhorn's researches led him to conclude that Hebrew prophecy was much like the oracular discourses of other cultures, although he would not hesitate to exalt it above, for example, the Greek oracle in terms of its philosophical truth. But what exactly does Eichhorn understand by Hebrew prophecy?

Like Herder, Eichhorn finds that inquiring into the term *nabi* is of little help; the word is used for so broad a range of characters and types that its definition is necessarily protean. In the wake of Lowth, Eichhorn often speaks of poets and prophets in the same breath, though his analyses of the texts share little of Lowth's concerns with rhythm and meter, much less anything like parallelism. As far as literary analysis proper goes, his work is somewhat closer to what James Kugel calls the "tropes and figures approach," as befits a student of classical philology, although in the main the texture of Eichhorn's work is that of textual criticism and literary history.

Eichhorn rather unexpectedly groups both poet and prophet under the one rubric of "writer," *Schriftsteller.* Yet he usually—with some notable exceptions—stops short of simply identifying prophet and poet, maintaining that the former cannot be termed a poet "in the most proper sense" ("im eigentlichsten Verstande") (214).[24] Rather than primarily as a poet, the prophet is cast as a "counselor," a "lawgiver," a "statesman," a "leader of the people ("Volksführer")," even as a "demagogue." The prophets are collectively "the general voice of the nation" ("die allgemeine Stimme der Nation"). In Eichhorn's view, prediction is only one of many prophetic functions, certainly not the paradigmatic one. He speaks of the prophet's warning and threatening as much as he does his prophesying. Moreover, a glance at his enumeration of the varied roles of the prophet shows that prophecy has little to do with providing knowledge to those addressed.

What matters in prophecy is not so much whether it is true or false but what it *does*. And what it ideally does is, like Herder's *thatvolle Wort*, accomplish something, preeminently to persuade a recalcitrant people to change its ways and to reorient that people to its new future.

Yet Eichhorn's *Introduction* is not a seamless and not even a particularly consistent text. If Eichhorn can at one point distinguish the prophet from the poet "in the true sense" he can elsewhere simply assert that the prophets "spoke as [or like] poets" ("sprachen wie Dichter") (6). Moreover, the prophets spoke as inspired beings ("Begeisterte") (5), which impelled them to the use of figures and comparisons ("Bildern und Vergleichungen"). Somewhat in the manner of Lowth, when Eichhorn turns to general formulations about the prophet and prophecy, he tends to go against his own empirical insights and reverts to commonplaces about prophecy as prediction. But with a difference.

In his painstaking philological labors Eichhorn is sensitive to the individual styles of the various Biblical authors, but some of his lapidary formulae for prophetic discourse in general go decidedly against the grain of mainstream Christian commentary. A good many Christian commentators could subscribe to Eichorn's pronouncement that "most speeches of the Hebrew prophets are predictions" (19) ("so sind die meisten Reden der Hebräischen Propheten Weissagungen"). The following, however, is one conclusion that more pious commentators would find impossible to draw: "The divine oracles are elaborated according to a single form. In a time of fortune they end with a fearful premonition of misery, and in a time of misery with joyful prospects toward the future" (9). No matter how bad or good things may be, the prophet "foretells" the inverse of the current situation. But what is the status of this foretelling? The world is consistently turned upside down according to the chiastic model that insists on translating from misery to good fortune and good fortune to misery. The future is "dictated" by the present, and always as its opposite. Given this judgment, it is difficult to maintain a notion of prophecy as the authoritative, divinely inspired prediction of the future. Nowhere is it clearer in Eichhorn that prophecy has nothing to do with a *knowledge* of the future.

Like that of his contemporary Herder, Eichhorn's understanding of the language of prophecy is informed by an articulated philosophy of language and a philosophy of history. He draws attention to the "entirely general expressions" ("ganz allgemeinen Ausdrücken") of the prophets that arise more from a "presentiment" ("Vorgefühl") than from a certain knowledge of the future. Indeed, ignorance is one of the driving forces behind the language of the prophetic oracles: The tendency of the prophet when faced with an incomprehensible situation is to think of it in terms of a providential design. "When in doubt, ascribe it to God's plan," is the unwritten motto of the prophets. In this respect, prophecy is the product of a "primitive" mentality, whose traits are sketched at length in Eichhorn's path-breaking *Urgeschichte* (*Primeval History*), a commentary on the opening chapters of Genesis.[25]

The first book of the Bible at once requires and forbids the exacting sort of historical analysis envisioned as necessary by Eichhorn. He suspends the implausible belief that Moses was the author of the entire Pentateuch, while conceding that the original author must have been "a man like Moses" (271), which is to say, among other things, learned in the Egyptian culture of hieroglyphics and writing. This man like Moses was not, of course, a witness to the origins of man but rather "created his history of the world from the reports of the temple archives of his nation, that is, out of documents far beyond the reach of Moses's time" (238).[26] Anticipating Herder's pronouncement in his *Briefe*, Eichhorn maintains that Genesis is a human document and "should be read and analyzed in a human way" (275) ("selbst will menschlich gelesen und geprüft sei").

The modern historicist spirit of Eichhorn turns to the opening book of the Bible to find that that text is antithetical to it, in that it possesses "no historical art" (278), and thus it would be folly to read it as an historically referential document. To do so would be to confuse two radically different kinds of language, for as Eichhorn observes:

In the time in which man related the sagas of primeval history and repeated the genealogies of races, there was not yet any prose, rather speech itself was still wholly poetic and lacking in expressions, especially in the proper (*eigentlich*) designations of things. Language was still based entirely on the physical and necessarily had a carnal husk (*eine körperliche Hülle*) for a common concept (*gemeinen Begriff*); it had to be aided by a multitude of comparisons, images, and metaphors, and thanks to this character it often approached allegory. A presentation of traditions in proper words was thus impossible; it always had to be tropical and symbolic. (282–83)

Rather like Vico, for whom the first phase of language was also poetic, Eichhorn is neither nostalgic nor sentimental about this primary language of poetry. (This is opposed to, say, Herder and even Hamann, who positively celebrated poetry as, in Hamann's words, "the mother tongue of the human race.") It simply was the case, for these theorists, that all language was poetic and in reading texts from this first age of language one had to take this "fact" into account. We shall see in a moment, however, that the language of the prophets partakes of this necessary figuration, although at a stage intermediate between the hoariest myths of primeval times and the enlightened narratives of historiography and philological science.

For all his minute attention to the specificity of the "J" (Jahweh) and "E" (Elohim) strands of the Genesis text, Eichhorn sees them as "two fragments of a single monument" (330): The contradictions are largely superficial.[27] In any event, Eichhorn's ultimate goal is to disentangle the mythical truth of the text from its merely surface meanings. And to do so, he proposes, in the closing section of the *Urgeschichte* entitled "How One Must Read Genesis," a mode of historicist interpretation of the sort that Benjamin would condemn, for it advocates forgetting the present and yet at the same time translating the past into the present:

Read it as two historical works of prehistory (*Vorwelt*) and breathe the air of its age and its fatherland. Forget the century in which you live and the knowledge that it offers you—if you cannot do that, do not delude yourself that you enjoy the book in the spirit of its origin. The youth of the world that it describes demands a spirit (*Geist*) toned down to its depth; the first rays of a twilight of reason (*Vernunft*) do not carry the clear light of day; the shepherd speaks only to a shepherd and the original Oriental only to the soul of another Oriental. Without a good acquaintance with the habits of pastoral life, without exact knowledge of the Orient and its customs, without an earnest familiarity with the modes of thought and representation of the uncultivated world, especially of most ancient Greece and the uneducated nations of more recent times, one would easily become a betrayer of the book whenever one desired to be not a savior but an exegete. (383–84)

Here Eichhorn emerges as an Hegelian *avant la lettre*, since the primitive mythical world of uncultivated peoples is not set up simply as other than or inferior to the enlightened age of reason. Rather, this early religious discourse of myth is constituted as what is *not yet* of the order of reason and "philosophical truth," a notion explicitly invoked by Eichhorn (377).[28] The language of the prophets—Eichhorn makes clear in his *Introduction*—is expressed in figures (*Bilder*), not, and not yet, in the language of concepts proper to philosophy, theology, or philology. Or, as Eichhorn phrases a similar point in the *Urgeschichte*: "All concepts had to be concealed in a lofty figurative language" (289). As in Hegel, religion participates in the *representation* (*Vorstellung*) of the absolute, but not yet in a form adequate to its object. The solar trajectory of history that leads from the Orient—or "land of the morning" ("Morgenland")—to the evening of history in the West, the *Abendland,* informs Eichhorn's narrative of progress from myth to truth, no less than Hegel's.[29] Thus it is not only the prophets who are prophetic: All the mythical "truths" of the Scriptures prefigure their future truth to be realized in the rational language of philosophy. It is here that one can glimpse Eichhorn's difference from the later Herder, who gradually came to recognize the epistemological claims of poetry in a way that did not demand their translation into a higher language of criticism. As Herder would say in *On the Spirit of Hebrew Poetry*: "One can see that I am not . . . using the word poetry to mean falsehood; for in the realm of the understanding the significance of the poetically composed symbol is truth" (XII, 15–16).

Eichhorn's inquiries into the oldest texts of the Bible led him to discover the category of myth that would come to be so crucial for Biblical study from David Friedrich Strauss to Northrop Frye. To call a Biblical text "mythical" does not necessarily cast any doubts on its truth, only on its truth understood in slavishly literal or referential fashion. Yet such an invocation of myth would often, against the will of its author, be taken as a strong challenge to the hegemonic and traditional notion of the Bible as the true word of God. And certainly the question of truth would be raised in a challenging way in Eichhorn's readings of the prophets. He uses categories like "originality" and "invention" ("Erfindung"), thus throwing the emphasis on human rather than divine production. He can even invoke the category of "fictions" ("Fiktionen") (73) to describe the character of prophetic speech. By suspending the notion of a divine author informing each and every word, Eichhorn allows himself the possibility of making discriminating literary judgments of the sort appropriate to secular poetry. Isaiah can be praised as the first poet in elegance and sublimity, but some aspects of Ezekiel's writings can be dismissed as mere "Kopie." How many Biblical scholars before Eichhorn's time could have spoken of the prophet's visions as "blosse Einkleidung, blosse poetische Dichtungen" ["mere adornment, merely poetic productions"] (249)? For Eichhorn, the presence of poetic accoutrements is often a suspicious sign, a sign of the displacement of truth by fiction. For Herder, there is no necessary tension between the two. Why, Herder asks, deny God or his messengers the virtues of the aesthetic that one would otherwise praise in a secular context? In Eichhorn, the imbrication of poet and prophet retains a very different force: The prophet is somewhat diminished, pulled down from the pedestal of a divinely inspired author, and the poet, who can use figures of speech and fictions with invention and originality, is raised to the heights of what was once a prophet. In the end, Eichhorn's view of the prophet/poets is not as demystifying or dismissive as his earlier contemporary Reimarus, who, as filtered at least through Lessing, cast prophetic discourse as an already fictional corpus that could be and was distorted by New Testament authors.[30] Eichhorn had no very visible axe to grind, and the persuasiveness of his critique lay largely in his even-handed treatment of his subject. The very dispassionate character of his work, however, helped reopen a text for the impassioned readings of the poets, and not just poets, of his day.

It is common to think that the somewhat arcane researches of an Eichhorn filtered through to England only through the usual suspect, Samuel Taylor Coleridge, who was the clearinghouse especially for so much German speculation in philosophy and religion. But the findings and speculations of Eichhorn and company reached England earlier and in a more effective, public way than in the marginalia or letters of Coleridge. The force of the rationalist, philological criticism of the Bible was felt in Britain through the work of Alexander Geddes, a heterodox Scottish Catholic who ended up finding favor in the radical Protestant circles around the publisher Joseph Johnson.[31] Raised in Scotland in the heyday of its Enlightenment, Geddes made his way to London after a detour of, among other things, studying "Rhetoric" at the College de Navarre in Paris. Not unlike Hurd and Warburton, Geddes was also a man of letters, a translator of Homer and Horace, Virgil and Theocritus. Yet it was as a commentator on and translator of the Bible that Geddes had his biggest impact. Geddes went against Catholic tradition by not foregrounding the Vulgate version of the Bible, which necessitated a very different kind of philological work. And Geddes became persuaded that a philologically authoritative translation would have to take account of the recent path-breaking criticism originating in Germany. When he first started to circulate his *Prospectus for a New Translation of the Bible* well in advance of its publication, Geddes sought and won the approval for the project from none other than Bishop Lowth, by that time a powerful political figure as well as the author of the most distinguished literary criticism of the Bible the century had seen. Before his death in 1802 (when he was still under ecclesiastical censure), Geddes produced a large, if unfinished, body of translations of and commentaries on parts of the Bible that made their mark in British letters and may even have directly influenced literary production.[32]

What Geddes found resonant and instructive in the work of Eichhorn was the sense of the Bible as a work of literature. Geddes could speak of the Bible's creation story in the same breath as Ovid's *Metamorphoses*, calling the former "a most beautiful mythos, or philosophical fiction."[33] Geddes meant no disrespect to Christianity or to the Hebrew Scriptures by invoking these terms. Indeed, he thought the creation story perfectly well calculated for the purposes of establishing belief in the one supreme God of Christianity. Like Vico, he thought the language of myth to be, necessarily, the original discourse of uncultivated nations. If beauty took priority over historical truth, it was nonetheless not irreconcilable with a certain kind of truth. The creation story is a *philosophical* fiction, that is to say, a myth translatable into the more rational, logical truth of philosophy. Geddes saw no contradiction between a faith in God founded in reason and a critical examination of the text. The Bible may indeed be in a definitive sense the word of God, but that did not mean that Geddes had to accept "every scrap of prophecy, poetry, minstrelsy, history, biography, as the infallible communications of heaven, oracles of divine truth."[34]

∼

Taken together, the works of Lowth, Hurd, Warburton, Herder, and Eichhorn demonstrate the power and complexity of the language of prophecy and how much is at stake in its function within the Bible and within the history of the future projected in it. The perspicacity of these scholars and readers as literary critics did much to illuminate the character of prophecy as poetry in the strict and extended senses of the term. Lowth, Hurd, Warburton, and Herder all had a theological investment in their "literary" endeavors; Eichhorn adopted the somewhat more disinterested stance of a mere philologist of a sacred text. All of them contributed, sometimes against their express intentions, to disturbing the certainty of prophetic discourse as a vehicle of divine knowledge of the future. The highly figured, oracular discourse of the prophets—the "speaking hieroglyphs," in Warburton's phrase —was only tenuously able to bear the burden placed on it. The stakes could not have been much higher, for the very truth and coherence of the Bible depended on the truth of the prophetic word. But if these scholar/critics unsettled the status of prophecy as authoritative knowledge of the future, they were able to illustrate the power of prophetic speech as a performative rhetoric beyond the constraints of truth and falsity. Prophecy emerges as "political art," and the dominant paradigm for this art is the word as deed.

Literary and historical criticism of the Bible from the mid-eighteenth to the early nineteenth century effected a revolution in the way the sacred text was read. One of the most palpable products of this revolution in reading came in the poetry of the British and German poets of the Romantic period who were now taking up the task of rereading and rewriting what was already a new Bible. In all this, the corpus of the prophets offered the most powerful impetus for the idea and actuality of a new kind of poetry.

PART II

READINGS IN PROPHETIC WRITING

The Mediated Vision: Blake, *Milton*, and the Lines of Prophetic Tradition

> . . . I am not ashamed afraid or averse to tell You what Ought to be Told. That I am under the direction of Messengers Daily & Nightly but the nature of such things is not as some suppose.
> —Blake, letter to Thomas Butts, January 10, 1802

> He that comes second must needs quote him that comes first.
> —Emerson

> The closer we are to 1650, the closer we seem to be to Blake.
> —E. P. Thompson

> Down for you is up.
> —Lou Reed

I

It is common to speak of William Blake's poems as prophecies and to consider their author a prophet, a peculiarly visionary and "modern" poet. Blake's reputation as a major poet and artist now seems secure, although he was scarcely so highly regarded by his contemporaries. At the extreme, he was simply considered mad, although in hindsight, it looks as if any madness that possessed him was mainly the madness of metaphor.[1] The postponed reception of his work, much as in Hölderlin's case, helped construct the aura of the prophet that continues to envelop him. To write of Blake as a prophet conforms to a mythology and a tradition that he himself set in motion. One extravagant example of a latter-day understanding of Blake as seer comes from one of his first editors, W. B. Yeats:

There have been men who loved the future like a mistress, and the future mixed her breath into their breath and shook her hair about them, and hid from them the understanding of their times. William Blake was one of those men, and if he spoke confusedly or obscurely it was because he spoke things for whose speaking he could find no models in the world.[2]

Lurid phrasing aside, two important things emerge in this passage: first, the idea that latter-day readers are now in a better position to understand Blake than were his immediate contemporaries; second, the notion that Blake's writing was *sui generis*, that he was an artist working virtually without worldly or even textual models.

Some straightforward reasons explain why it might be easier to understand Blake at a later date than in his own time: the greater availability and circulation of his texts, and the critical and scholarly efforts of a large community of readers who have elucidated literary and historical contexts framing Blake's works. When one groups Blake with the major Romantic poets, his poetry may seem decidedly eccentric. Even just at the level of proper names, for example, the reader may puzzle over characters called Elynittria or Theotormon, Bromion or Leutha, whereas names from the *Lyrical Ballads* such as Lucy, Michael, Susan, or Simon are familiar enough to come complete with an air of intelligibility. The baroque verbal texture and speculative extravagance of Blake's poetic visions can appear arcane and forbidding, a homespun hieroglyphics. But if one aligns Blake with precursors such as Young and Smart, Collins and Gray, he begins to emerge as a less shadowy figure, more like the last in a poetic line than the first. Moreover, if one follows Northrop Frye's path-breaking *Fearful Symmetry* in seeing Blake as a reader and rewriter of a Bible hitherto read all too complacently and reductively, then a good deal more of Blake's eccentricity disappears. Further still, a vigorous and often subtle historical scholarship, pioneered by David Erdman's *Prophet Against Empire*, has situated Blake in a political milieu in which he surfaces as not so isolated a figure. As E. P. Thompson notes: "Against the background of London Dissent, with its fringe of deists and earnest mystics, William Blake seems no longer the cranky untutored genius that he must seem to those who know only the genteel culture of the time."[3] To recognize all this is to address and challenge Yeats's second point: Blake may have had a few models in his artist's studio after all.

The growing recognition that Blake's work appears deeply embedded in certain traditions rather than falling outside tradition generally is at odds with some conceptions of Blake's status as prophet and visionary. In those views, the prophet, in virtual isolation, dwells in the immediacy of his revelations, engaged in his present and facing toward the future—all of which seems to accord well with Blake's conception of originality.[4] But if prophecy is always oriented toward a future—even when it does not take the form of prediction—it is also profoundly a thing of the past, an echo, a citation. Even the most idiosyncratic of poetic prophets can hardly work outside tradition altogether. And, as it happens, Blake engages the Hebraic, Christian, and English prophetic traditions in a spectacular and highly self-conscious way.

The resonance of the words "prophet" and "prophecy" in Blake's work are many and various, and not all of them coincide with the current or contemporary senses of those words. In his most direct gloss on the subject, in his annotations to Bishop Watson's *An Apology for the Bible*, Blake sneers, much as Shelley did in his "Defence of Poetry," at the "modern sense" of the word "prophet":

Prophets in the modern sense of the word have never existed Jonah was no prophet in the modern sense for his prophecy of Nineveh failed Every honest man is a Prophet he utters his opinion both of private & public matters/Thus/If you go on So/the result is So/He never says such a thing shall happen let you do what you will. a Prophet is a Seer not an Arbitrary Dictator.[5]

Blake offers a sharp corrective to the reductive "modern" notion that the prophet is a predictor of future events to occur inexorably in the course of a providential history. By invoking the example of Jonah, Blake focuses on a moment that makes clear that God has more pressing concerns than the literal fulfillment of his prophet's predictions. Following the Lord's directions, Jonah went to Nineveh and prophesied the fall of the city in forty days time. Threatened with imminent destruction, the king dutifully covered himself in sackcloth and ashes, and his people followed suit by repenting their misdeeds, with this result: "And God saw their works, that they turned from their evil way; and God repented of the evil, that he had said that he would do unto them; and he did <u>it</u> not" (3.10).[6] Instead of rejoicing at Nineveh's change of heart, Jonah becomes angry with his God. Jonah, one could say, fails to recognize the conditional character of the prophetic word ("If you go on So/the result is So"), even when it is phrased in not so conditional a way. That the prophecy here takes the explicit form of a prediction does not make it any less conditional. The prophecy is a promise but not necessarily a promise of the fulfillment of its declared content: It does not necessarily mean what it says. In J. L. Austin's terms, Jonah is preoccupied with the constative content of the prophetic word, whereas God is ultimately more concerned with its perlocutionary force, its power to persuade.[7] Compared to God's concern with the spiritual health of Nineveh's people (despite being the enemy of the Israelites), Jonah's stubborn insistence on the literality of the prediction seems perverse and trifling. In the eyes of the Lord, saving lives is a much higher priority than saving face for Jonah. Jonah's predicament is quite unlike that of a good many other prophets, and to that extent his case is as counterexemplary as it is exemplary but in such a way as to cast an oblique light on the whole phenomenon of prophecy, its language and its effects. That Blake singles out Jonah as the paradigmatic prophet here is instructive, because Jonah's case forces one to rethink the nature of prophecy as prediction, to rethink prophecy in its "modern" sense.[8]

In his polemic against the modern, reductive view of prophecy as prediction, Blake calls the prophet a "seer," a term that harks back to a Biblical tradition that claims the seer (*roeh*) as the forerunner to the prophet (*nabi*). In 1 Samuel 9.9 it is written: "Formerly in Israel, when a man went to inquire of God, he said, 'Come, let us go to the seer'; for he who is now called a prophet was formerly called a seer." It makes sense that Blake, as much a visual artist as a poet, would gravitate to the earlier term. Yet his literary work is far more indebted to the later, classical prophets than to the sketchy corpus of the early, legendary seers. Still, the term harbors a special significance for Blake, partly for its implications for the visual arts and the more general sense of the visionary. The much less "visionary" Hazlitt could write in his *Lectures on the English Poets*: "The province of the imagination is principally visionary, the unknown and undefined."[9] Only the first part of Hazlitt's dictum is consonant with Blake's thought, since for the latter there is nothing indefinite about the imagination or its products.[10] And the imagination, for Blake, provides *knowledge* of a different and more valuable kind than the natural sciences. The imagination may be visionary, but its vision is as verbal as it is visual, and even in the illuminated works, more the former than the latter.[11] Blake rails against the notion of the prophet as "Arbitrary Dictator," although he has no qualms about taking "dictation" from spirits whenever they present themselves to offer lines of poetry.

When Blake claims the prophet is one who "utters his opinion both of private & public matters," he employs a sense of prophecy recalling its usage in Protestant discourse of the seventeenth century and much farther back to a Pauline sense of "prophesying." In Jeremy Taylor's important treatise *The Liberty of Prophesying* (1647), for example, to "prophesy" is synonymous with to "speak forth" or to "speak out" and thus has more to do with freedom of expression or sheer speaking on behalf of God than with prediction of the future.[12] In line with this tradition, every man can indeed be a prophet, and, in Blake's view, every honest person is. So capacious an understanding of the term accords with the Mosaic motto forming the epigraph for *Milton,* which now—following Blake—sounds less utopian than it otherwise might: "Would to God that all the Lord's people were Prophets."

Blake's notion of the prophet was formulated over against Bishop Watson's *An Apology for the Bible,* a text drafted in response to Tom Paine's *The Age Of Reason.* Paine's treatise was a widely circulated tract with many affinities with Blake's thought. For Blake, as for Paine, the task of reading the Bible was urgent and political—although Paine was infinitely more critical of it as a *source* of political wisdom and practice. "To defend the Bible in this year 1798 would cost a man his life," Blake wrote on the back of Watson's title page, implying that the Bishop's apology was for something other than the Bible. Something other, that is, than the text understood by Blake as the "Bible of Hell," as he sometimes called it.

Paine's *Age of Reason* is intent on discrediting the idea of the prophet as a providentially inspired predictor of history. And so, for reasons very different from Blake's, Paine is anxious to remark on the identification of prophet and poet:

There is not, throughout the whole Book called the Bible, any word that describes to us what we call a poet, nor any word which describes what we call poetry. The case is that the word *prophet,* to which latter times have affixed a new idea, was the Bible word for poet, and the word *prophesying* meant the art of making poetry to a tune upon any instrument of music.[13]

Paine is fanciful and reductive on this last point, but the accuracy of his statement is less important than the fact of his making it. For Paine, these senses of "prophet" and "prophesy" are stripped "of all religious meaning," without in any way constituting a judgment on the morality or immorality of the prophet. He values the writings of the "Jewish poets" but regrets they are mistakenly thought to be mouthpieces for the word of God. The text of the Bible, he argues, is so beset with difficulties of translation, transcription, and transmission that no such book could be the adequate vehicle for the Word of God. That word, Paine maintains, "exists in something else," namely, in creation, the book of nature whose pages are open for all to read. Creation, the only unambiguous divine word, "publishes" itself, and is not subject to the vicissitudes of ordinary texts; more important still, the book of nature cannot be enlisted in any program of political domination.

By contrast to Paine, Blake had a much higher, if not absolute, regard for the text and the principles of the Christian Bible and a much dimmer view of what Paine terms "creation." Blake tends to call Paine's creation "Nature" and thinks almost nothing of it when considered in itself: "Where man is not[,] nature is barren," say the Proverbs of Hell (E, 38). Humanity, for Blake, is a creation of the Word, and its highest office is the re-creation of that Word. This by no means entails a servile adoration or mimicry of the sacred text, nor a strict adherence to the letter of its laws. Paine spoke of prophecy as one of the three religious phenomena that "impose upon mankind" and thus as something that "ought always to be suspected."[14] If Blake found something questionable about the prophets, he would simply summon them for a face-to-face confrontation:

The Prophets Isaiah and Ezekiel dined with me and I asked them how they dared so roundly to assert. that God spake to them; and whether they did not think at the time, that they would be misunderstood, & so be the cause of imposition.

Isaiah answer'd. I saw no God, nor heard any, in a finite organical perception; but my senses discover'd the infinite in every thing, and as I was then perswaded. & remain confirm'd; that the voice of honest indignation is the voice of God, I cared not for consequences but wrote.

Then I asked: does a firm perswasion that a thing is so, make it so?

He replied. All poets believe that it does, & in ages of imagination this firm perswasion removed mountains; but many are not capable of a firm perswasion of any thing. (E, 38–9)

Blake's fanciful encounter with the great prophets confirms their authority, but their "own" testimony expands the notion of prophecy so widely as to include any honest utterance spoken from conviction. Isaiah's words anticipate Blake's own in the marginalia to Watson noted above: "Every honest man is a Prophet/he utters his opinion both of public and private matters."

Blake's revisionary scenario clearly overturns the notion that the prophets simply recorded God's exact words, the *ipsissima verba*. And yet the authority of prophetic rhetoric normally derives in large measure from its representation as coming from a divine source outside the human mind.[15] The only authority required by Blake is a "firm perswasion" of truth. Like the "inner light" of the radical Protestant tradition, "firm perswasion" is its own proof. By summoning up Isaiah and Ezekiel from the dead and having them speak again—but who is speaking?—Blake calls on the authority of the prophets to rebut the arguments of Locke and his followers.[16]

In the later editions of *An Essay Concerning Human Understanding* Locke appended a section on "Enthusiasm" as the penultimate one of the *Essay*, following immediately on the section on "Faith and Reason." Reason, Locke contends, "is natural *Revelation*, whereby the eternal Father of Light, and Fountain of all Knowledge communicates to Mankind that portion of Truth, which he has laid within the reach of their natural Faculties."[17] Diametrically opposed to reason and revelation is what Locke calls *enthusiasm*, a condition in which men "have often flatter'd themselves with a *perswasion* of an immediate intercourse with the Deity, and frequent communications from the divine Spirit."[18] Locke criticizes the circularity of enthusiastic "logic," which maintains that visions are revelations because they are firmly believed, and firmly believed because they are revelations. Directly counter to Blake's Isaiah and Ezekiel, Locke argues that "the strength of our Perswasions are no Evidence at all of their own rectitude."[19] When one examines the language of those so sure of themselves because their "perswasions" are strong, one finds a rhetoric of internal light, the "Light of bright Sunshine," which is felt but not literally seen. If all this "cant is strip'd of the Metaphor of seeing and feeling," the residue is the result of a persuasion not of a demonstration.[20] To this pseudolight Locke opposes the "true Light of the Mind," which is nothing but the "Evidence of the Truth of any Proposition," very much like the natural light, the *lumen naturalis* of Descartes's epistemology. Where then might Biblical prophecy fall in the spectrum that stretches from the illusory illumination of the enthusiasts to the true light of the rational philosopher?

Although the prophets are firmly persuaded of the truth of their "inward" visions, these are, Locke says, supplemented by "outward signs" to convince others of the "Author" of the revelations and the "visible signs" to assert the divine authority of the message. Thus the burning bush offered to Moses, in Locke's view, stands as unambiguous, empirical proof of divine revelation, such that he can conclude:

These and several the like Instances to be found among the Prophets of old, are enough to shew, that they thought not an inward seeing or perswasion of their own Minds without any other Proof a sufficient Evidence, that it was from GOD, though the Scripture does not every where mention their demanding or having such Proofs.[21]

Locke's example is carefully chosen: It helps his case that it is a visual more than a verbal revelation. Although a good many prophetic revelations are supplemented by such external signs, as we saw in rehearsing Warburton's and Hurd's claims, most are not. Locke implies, however, that there was simply a failure to mention the signs that would have been there in any event.

Empirical signs are one thing: But what is the status of the *text* of empirical signs in Locke's epistemological hierarchy? Is a sacred text an empirical proof or only the record (or even the fiction) of something that may or may not have been empirically proved or empirically verifiable? What is the difference, to put it somewhat differently, between the experience of the burning bush and the story of its experience? Locke, as a professed Christian, seems in the preceding passages and throughout the *Essay* to assume the veracity of the Bible as history, even if elsewhere he troubles that assumption. A text is arguably nothing but "external signs," yet what matters in a text is not usually in any important way what is visible in it.[22] This may partly explain Locke's reluctance to ascribe prophetic authority to the word as such. Even if one is assured that a certain text is of the order of a revelation, that is still less, according to Locke, than the assurance of the "Senses."[23]

Locke often writes as if Reason and Revelation, Reason and "Holy Writ," were coterminous and of complementary authority. Yet there tends, ultimately, to be no question that "*Reason* must be our last Judge and Guide in every Thing."[24] It is no wonder that a philosopher who can value scientific reason over the (not necessarily reasonable) express word of God, who distrusts all "enthusiasm" and who is deeply suspicious of figurative language, should come to be the object of William Blake's scorn. Locke certainly professed to live and write as a Christian, when he took the trouble to write commentaries on the Pauline epistles, for example, or to argue for *The Reasonableness of Christianity* in the treatise by that name. Yet Blake considered him nothing less than a hypocrite. As he wrote in his annotations to Watson: "Conscience in those that have it is unequivocal, it is the voice of God Our judgment of right and wrong is Reason . . . I believe that the Bishop laught at the Bible in his slieve & so did Locke" (E, 613). And so all Locke's Christianity was mere lip service, not an attention to the word of God read in the full light of imagination.[25]

When in *The Marriage of Heaven and Hell* Blake asks Isaiah and Ezekiel to favor the world with their lost works, they both reply that none are of value equal to the extant collections, implying that the published works are more than sufficient, if properly understood. Blake seems content to let the prophets speak for themselves, as it were, and yet their responses betray a radical process of translation at work: "I then asked Ezekiel. why he ate dung, & lay so long on his right side & left side? he answerd. the desire of raising other men into a perception of the infinite" (E, 39). A phrase like "perception of the infinite" is recognizably Blake's idiom, however faithful it might be to the spirit of Ezekiel.[26] The Blakean commentary is insinuated into the very mouths of the prophets and thus presents an instance of prosopopoeia in the restricted sense of summoning the dead from the grave to speak once again. Thus can Blake's words be made to appear, retroactively, original and divinely inspired.

One can see the advantage of having Isaiah and Ezekiel come back from the dead—but were they ever really dead?—to offer versions of Blake's program for spiritual enlightenment. Strict views of Hebraic prophecy confine God's direct communication with prophets to a very circumscribed period, roughly from the eighth to the sixth century B.C.E. After that, in the Christian view, God communicated, after a long hiatus, primarily through his Son, the Word of God, and indirectly though the texts recording his teachings. Blake sees no need for such a narrow and historically discontinuous view of inspiration. In *An Apology for the Bible* Bishop Watson confesses it was strange for God to have made an "immediate manifestation" of himself. Blake retorts: "It is strange that God should speak to man formerly & not now. because it is not true . . . " (E, 615). Somewhat along the lines of Novalis's protest that the Bible is not a "closed," that is to say, finished book, Blake argues for the possibility of a permanent and generalized condition of prophecy. (In this he followed his main precursor Milton, and, had he wanted, he could have traced his authority back to the epistles of Paul.[27]) For a number of reasons, then, it would also be mistaken to think that where there once was prophecy, there now is poetry, as if the latter had just displaced the former. In his very first published work, bearing a motto, the "Voice of one crying in the Wilderness," drawn from Isaiah and John the Baptist, Blake could write: "The Religions of all Nations are derived from each Nations different reception of the Poetic Genius which is every where call'd the Spirit of Prophecy" (E,1). As comparative religion this is dubious, but it stands as all the clearer a statement of Blake's conviction of the strict identity between poetry and prophecy.

II

Blake called only two of his poems prophecies: *America* and *Europe*. But a great many of his works are more or less loosely thought of as prophetic or even published as "Prophetic Writings." To approach what Blake called the "prophetic character" I propose proceeding via *America* and *Europe* to see what in those works might suggest the term "prophecy" as the best name for those (kinds of) poems. This should help prepare the way for discussing other texts not expressly designated as prophecies.

Written in 1793, *America* is a highly mythologized account of the American Revolution, and, on the face of it, it would be difficult to see how such a poem, written well after the revolution it recounts, could be termed a prophecy in any straightforward sense. What could it mean to write a prophecy of an event already in the past and now receding farther into it? In what does the prophetic character of the poem lie?

America is one of the earliest of Blake's poems to address explicitly and in detail a recognizable historical event. Names are named, and one can even make out a few precise dates. Among the names are the famous ones of recorded history: Washington, Franklin, Paine, and Hancock, even if they exist side by side with some not set down in any history book: Enitharmon, Urthona, and Orc. The names themselves are a good index of the peculiar texture of the work that will come to be characteristic for Blake: the intertwining of the historical with the mythological. The machinery of myth is largely derived from the Bible, and it serves as the frame in which historical events are to be read: Indeed, it is the very medium in which they occur.

The whole of *America* is termed a prophecy, yet the text is then subdivided into a "praeludium" and a "prophecy" proper. A praeludium prefaces the prophecy of *Europe*, too, and both poems anticipate in their structure the later *Milton*, prefaced, as it is, with its remarkable Bard's song.[28] Blake himself distinguishes between praeludium and prophecy, and yet these pieces preparatory to prophecy that are, in one sense, external to it come to be significant and, in effect, integral parts of the poems called prophecies. These preludes function as supplements in the Derridean sense: seemingly contingent things that nonetheless emerge, if only retroactively, as necessary or irreducible parts of the whole. Outside the prophecy proper and yet rendering what follows possible, the praeludium is usually in Blake a scene of inspiration or prophetic calling. But in *America* it takes more the form of a coming of age for Orc, perhaps the sensual equivalent of a calling as a rite of passage to a higher realm.

The opening lines of America mark the first appearance in Blake of Orc, "red Orc," whose name derives from a Latin term for hell. Orc quickly comes to embody the idea and the act of revolution in Blake's mythology, although revolution has to be understood in its two, potentially opposed, senses: an upheaval or immense change, as well as an incessant, mechanical turning, as of a planet revolving around the sun. The main action of the bard's song is the highly charged sexual encounter between Orc and the unnamed shadowy daughter of Urthona as the former reaches puberty ("When fourteen suns had faintly journey'd o'er his dark abode . . . "). The brief song closes with the shadowy daughter's apostrophe to Orc: "This is eternal death; and this the torment long foretold." As one gradually becomes familiar with Blake's lexicon, one learns that "eternal death" often means something very much like "life," as commonly understood. The shadowy daughter had just rehearsed to Orc that he had "fall'n to give me life in regions of dark death," which implies that the fall is really a descent, not a fall in the loaded Christian sense.[29] Blake took vehement exception to the orthodox doctrine of creation as predicated on the strict separation of God and man. Since Blake preferred to think in terms of the "human face divine"—identifying the divine with the human as much as syntax would allow—the idea of creation as usually handed down was spurious in that it presupposed a division between two entities that were in fact one. So the "creation" was a fall, and the "Fall" not really the fall it was made out to be.[30] In Blake the word "fall'n" is disencumbered of much of its Christian and Miltonic weight. It tends to be associated with a voluntary movement from a higher realm to a lower, often in the mode of sacrifice, as will repeatedly be the case in *Milton*. Orc's "fall" is not unlike that of Christ's descent to life, that is, "eternal death," and so Orc's revolutionary act is, among other things, an imitation of Christ. It is no accident that Orc is called "the image of God" precisely at the moment he is falling.

In the prophecy proper, Orc, whose genealogy links him with Prometheus and Adam as well as Jesus, is the mythical form of America and its revolutionary energy. One cannot quite say Orc is the embodiment of America, because he moves above as much as through the more properly historical action: He resembles a comet or a planet as much as a nation or a revolution. *America* is the first of Blake's poems to feature Orc, and in it the outlines of a soon-to-be-familiar story become clear. The young bundle of revolutionary and sexual energy that is Orc is pitted against an aging tyrant and an enforcer of "moral law" (read "immoral") named Urizen. Their encounters unfold in a political romance of liberation for the Orc figure—that is Blake's most insistent focus—and yet Blake will eventually chart the tendency for Orc to become in time the very Urizen figure he had so adamantly opposed. *America* concentrates on the early part of what Frye calls the Orc "cycle" and does not explore the repetitions or reversals built into that cyclical movement. Instead, when history repeats itself, it does so as the translation of the Orc principle from one revolutionary moment to another. In the final plate it is said of Urizen:

> His stored snows he poured forth, and his icy magazines
> He open'd on the deep, and on the Atlantic sea white shiv'ring.
> Leprous his limbs all over white, and hoary was his visage.
> Weeping in dismal howlings before the stern Americans
> Hiding the Demon red with clouds & cold mists from the earth;
> Till Angels & weak men twelve years should govern o'er the strong:
> And then their end should come, when France receiv'd the
> > Demons light.   (E, 57, Plate 16)

That is to say: The French Revolution is a repetition of the American Revolution. This is a rather remarkable notion, since the two revolutions were markedly different in character, the one a struggle for independence from a colonial oppressor, the other a class-motivated revolt from within a sovereign nation.[31] By abstracting their differences, Blake composes a single amalgam of the revolutionary spirit. The difference in time between the two revolutions allows for the American revolution to function as the prefiguration of the French and thus it is prophetic in the most common sense of the word. The American Revolution, for Blake writing in 1793, is of more than "historical" interest because it becomes the paradigm of revolution, the model for future revolutions.[32] Hegel, in his lectures on the philosophy of history, could later speak of America as "the country of the future" ("das Land der Zukunft"),[33] and Blake, too, sees in America an open future no longer bound to and by a past of unfreedom. Blake could write a "prophecy" of a past event, partly because that event in the past had a certain futurity built into it or, at the least, could be read retroactively as a prefiguration, the text of a repetition to come.

In the opening speech that Blake gives to George Washington, the latter records the effects of Albion's oppression in terms that recall certain patterns in Biblical history:

> A bended bow is lifted in heaven, & a heavy iron chain
> Descends link by link from Albions cliffs across the sea to bind
> Brothers & sons of America, til our faces pale and yellow;
> Heads deprest, voices weak, eyes downcast, hands work—bruis'd,
> Feet bleeding on the sultry sands, and the furrows of the whip
> Descend to generations that in future times forget.   (E, 52, Plate 3)

In addition to the proliferation of parallelisms that give this passage a Biblical resonance, the reference to "sultry sands" sounds more like Egypt than America of the New England colonies. And in general the imagery is shadowy enough to apply to the American instance but not be limited to it. Washington's speech recalls all those Biblical moments of Israel's enslavement and exile, all the while conscious of the possibility that "future times" will "forget." He rehearses the repetitive history of oppression in order that *that* history not be repeated: The recognition or remembering is posited as a key moment in the trajectory of liberation. It is not Washington but Orc who announces a break from the cycle of oppression, even if his own imagery—much of it derived from nature—has something cyclical to it:

> The times are ended; shadows pass the morning gins to break;
> The fiery joy, that Urizen perverted to ten commands,
> What night he led the starry hosts thro' the wide wilderness:
> That stony law I stamp to dust: and scatter religion abroad
> To the four winds as a torn book, & none shall gather the leaves;
> But they shall rot on desart sands, & consume in bottomless deeps;
> To make the desarts blossom, & the deeps shrink to their fountains.
>   (E, 54, Plate 8)

How does one talk about a time when "times are ended"? Even more than in Washington's speech, it is figures from the Bible, and notably from the prophets, that serve as a matrix for the description of unprecedented things. The sultry sands of enslavement that Washington sees give way to Orc's vision of a blossoming desert in the starkly paradoxical terms set out in Isaiah 35: " . . . and the desert shall rejoice, and blossom as the rose." Blake's passage certainly owes something to the cyclical character of so much natural imagery: Morning breaking implies the whole cyclical trajectory from morning to evening to night, back to morning and so on endlessly. But if deserts and blossoms are natural, their conjunction, as in Isaiah and again in Orc's speech, is decidedly not. One could call these impossible scenes of nature mythical, but for Blake such impossibilities are the very stuff of history. He would later write in the "Descriptive Catalogue" of 1809 of giving "the historical fact in its poetical vigour," which is to say, "as it always happens" and not as

some Historians pretend, who being weakly organized themselves, cannot see either miracle or prodigy; all is to them a dull round of probabilities and possibilities; but the history of all times and places, is nothing else but improbabilities and impossibilities; what we should say, was impossible if we did not see it always before our eyes. (E, 543)[34]

The mythical revolutionary moment, then, does not hover somewhere above or beyond history but stands as a paradigm for the historical act. And "acts themselves alone are history," Blake insists in the very same text. That these acts are impossible does not prevent them from happening. It makes sense, then, that Blake would so often have recourse to the writings of the prophets, whose texts are riddled with the records—prophecies? histories? dreams?—of impossible acts. And it may be that all of *Milton* can be thought of as the allegory of one such impossible act.

America closes with Orc storming the bastions of the Urizenic Albion, whose guards struggle in vain to close the "five gates of their law-built heaven." The gates are the five senses of the literal body that have to be transcended, that have to be articulated with spirit, although the body is not simply negated or abandoned as some versions of Christianity would have it. Blake's second poem termed a prophecy opens, in two of its versions, precisely where *America* leaves off, with a reflection on the "five windows" that "light the cavern'd Man." Like its predecessor, *Europe* too embeds a pointed reflection on a historical, geopolitical conjuncture in an elaborate mythical framework that is nothing less than cosmic. Its cyclical and panoramic vision of history adumbrates the grand epics *Milton* and *Jerusalem* in its preoccupation with the architecture and architectonics of this world and the next. In this it is indebted to Ezekiel more than most, the most visually detailed and diagrammatic of the prophets.[35]

America is a poem about a revolution and perhaps revolutions. It is by now a familiar paradox that the revolutionary moment—which has a claim to being radically new—turns out, typically, to be a repetition or even a citation of an earlier revolution. We have seen how a good deal of Benjamin's theory of history—although it was not simply a "theory"—turned on a notion of citational repetition derived from the seminal opening pages of Marx's *The Eighteenth Brumaire of Louis Bonaparte*. (One of the instances Marx invokes is Locke's and the Glorious Revolution's citing of the Hebrew prophet Habbakuk, and it is in principle no different from the French Revolution's quoting of the Roman, perhaps the most prominent paradigm for the historical and revolutionary act, in Marx as in Benjamin.) Benjamin seems unambiguously an advocate of the revolutionary moments he invokes, and Blake, too, as one of the most radical poets of his or any other day, is usually read as an unequivocal supporter of the American and French revolutions. *America* especially is normally understood as an "optimistic" poem. But some critics, Robert Maniquis among them, have pointed to a more divided stance legible in the poems.[36] Given Blake's abhorrence of war, it is hard for him to be entirely unequivocal in support of a revolution that is also what he calls "a strife of blood." For that matter, the Biblical Apocalypse is not exactly a pretty sight, a war of sorts in and out of heaven, even when one is grouped with the sheep rather than the goats.

Europe, like *America*, is in part a prophecy in the narrow sense, and it implies that the announcement of the Last Judgment is no easy matter:

> Between the clouds of Urizen the flames of Orc roll heavy
> Around the limbs of Albions Guardian, his flesh consuming.
> Howlings & hissings, shrieks & groans, & voices of despair
> Arise around him in the cloudy
> Heavens of Albion. Furious
> The red limb'd Angel siez'd, in horror and torment;
> The Trump of the last doom; but he could not blow the iron tube!
> Thrice he assay'd presumptuous to awake the dead to Judgment.

> A mighty Spirit leap'd from the land of Albion,
> Nam'd Newton; he seiz'd the Trump, & blow'd the enormous blast!
> Yellow as leaves of Autumn the myriads of Angelic hosts,
> Fell thro' the wintry skies seeking their graves;
> Rattling their hollow bones in howling and lamentation.   (E, 64, Plate 12)

The spectacle of Newton and the red angel fighting over the trumpet of the Last Judgment is unexpectedly comic, even though a good deal of Blake's early work, from *The Marriage of Heaven and Hell* on, is conducted in the mode of satire.[37] Not only is the mock-heroic diction indecorous—but then the Hebrew prophets were hardly models of decorum—Newton is systematically reviled in Blake's work as a proponent of mathematical reason, one who views God as the overseer of a machinelike universe devoid of living form. The invocation of Newton in this passage is appropriate in another way, because he was, in a less well-known guise, a theologian and a Biblical critic, author of commentaries on the book of Daniel and Revelation. There is no proof that Blake was familiar with Newton's Biblical writings—although they were well known throughout Britain and Europe —but it is hard to believe they would have met with his approval. Consider this passage from Newton on the Books of Daniel and Revelation:

For understanding the Prophecies, we are, in the first place, to acquaint ourselves with the figurative language of the Prophets. This language is taken from the analogy between the world natural, and an empire or kingdom considered as a world politic. Accordingly, the whole natural world politic, consisting of thrones and people, or so much of it as is considered in the Prophecy: and the things in that world signify the analogous things in this. For the heavens, and the things therein, signify thrones and dignities, and those who enjoy them, and the earth, with the things thereon, the inferior people. . . . [38]

Neither this system of one-to-one correspondences—elaborated in great detail in Newton's account—nor the recognition of such a hierarchy of dignities and inferiors could have met with a positive reception by Blake. And so it is doubly ironic that so misguided a reader of the Book of Revelation should be struggling to blow the trumpet of the Last Judgment. But the arrival of Newton is a blessing in disguise, because he plays a major role in the consolidation of error that Blake calls "opacity." And it is this congealing of error that marks the appearance of the force of Antichrist, thus setting the stage for the long-awaited scene of the Last Judgment. It is as if error has to be confronted fully or even embraced before truth can appear in its plenitude.

In many ways, *Europe* is very much like *America*: a highly condensed, mythical extravaganza framing contemporary history. But rather than rehearse the similarities, one can use the example of *Europe* to discuss some rather different things Blake does in that poem and some things that fill out our picture of Blake's notions of the language of prophecy. *Europe's* opening, in at least two of its copies, offers a scene of inspiration quite unlike the majority of Blake's prophetic poems, because it derives less from the Bible than from the unlikely world of Shakespearean romance. A fairy reminiscent of Ariel sings a song about the pleasure of liberated senses and is first surprised and then seized by the poet. The fairy acknowledges the poet as his "master" and, in response to questioning about the nature of the material world, the fairy promises "to write a book on leaves of flowers." The flowers are soon gathered together and magically transformed:

> They hover'd around me like a cloud of incense: when I came
> Into my parlour and sat down, and took my pen to write:
> My Fairy sat upon the table, and dictated EUROPE.   (E, 60, Plate iii)

The literal flowers undergo a metamorphosis into "the language of flowers," the rhetoric of Blake's poem, and the fairy "slave" has now become the master, not an "arbitrary dictator" perhaps, but nonetheless someone who dictates.[39] What is typical of Blake's beginning—the emphasis on the activity of writing—is relatively uncharacteristic of the prophetic tradition. The prophetic, more than almost any other poetic or rhetorical mode, relies, according to its own self-presentation, on the power of voice and sound. And it does so in a way that is potentially antithetical to writing.[40] But there is much in Blake—and in some of the Hebrew prophets—that runs counter to this configuration of writing and speech. Just as the singing of the fairy's song gives way to the writing of *Europe*, so in the "Introduction" to the *Songs of Innocence*, the song of the piper is followed by an inscription:

> Piper sit thee down and write
> In a book that all may read—
> So he vanish'd from my sight.
> And I pluck'd a hollow reed.

> And I made a rural pen,
> And I stain'd the water clear,
> And I wrote my happy songs
> Every child may joy to hear. (E, 7)

Writing here is an instrument of dissemination and democratization, producing books "that all may read." The lyric seems to present an unambiguous vision of writing as pure and purifying: "And I stain'd the water clear." But is the water paradoxically stained clear, that is, clarified by the act of writing? Or, is it rather that the water is clear before being stained by the poet's pen? The grammar allows for the two diametrically opposed readings. If all the *Songs of Innocence* were expressive of their titular state, then the former possibility would be the more tenable interpretation, but the juxtaposition of the earlier lyrics with the *Songs of Experience* casts—retroactively—the shadow of experience back onto the poems of innocence. The former interpretation—that of the water being clarified—recalls an incident from 2 Kings 2.19–22 where Elisha, the prophetic successor to Elijah, miraculously renders the water of a spring no longer toxic. But what is perhaps unclear in the "Introduction" to the *Songs* becomes unequivocal in the address "To the Public" at the beginning of *Jerusalem*:

> Reader! [*lover*] of books! [*lover*] of heaven,
> And of that God from whom [*all books are given,*]
> Who in mysterious Sinais awful cave
> To Man the wond'rous art of writing gave,
> Again he speaks in thunder and in fire!
> Thunder of Thought, & flames of fierce desire:
> Even from the depths of Hell his voice I hear,
> Within the unfathomd caverns of my Ear.
> Therefore I print; nor vain my types shall be:
> Heaven, Earth & Hell, henceforth shall live in harmony
>
> (E, 145, Plate 3)

The passage establishes two things for the character of the prophetic word: first, it legitimates writing as such by returning it to its legendary origins on Mount Sinai and pronouncing it wondrous [41]; second, it moves so effortlessly from writing to voice, from voice back to writing, that the opposition between the two modes no longer seems pertinent.[42] In doing so, Blake recapitulates a process already at work within the canonical prophetic tradition of the Bible. There the emphasis on the *voice* of the Lord, however mediated by the prophet, is pervasive, from the "still, small voice" [literally, "the voice of thin silence"] (I Kings 19.12) to the voice compared to the "noise of many waters" (Ezekiel 43.2), a phrasing that would leave its impression on Wordsworth. Stressing the vocal is consonant with the urgency and immediacy of the prophetic word, of the call to judgment or the provocation to action. Yet it is not so long into the tradition before an entire group comes to be known as the "writing prophets," in contrast to the more legendary figures like Elijah and Elisha, whose sayings do not appear to have been written down in their lifetimes. When the Lord prophesies woe for the rebellious people of Judah and Israel who go down into Egypt and trust Pharaoh, he directs Isaiah: "Now go, write it before them in a table, and note it in a book, that it may for the time to come for ever and ever (30.8)."[43] The text even becomes for Isaiah a conspicuous metaphor for prophetic vision:

For the Lord hath poured out upon you the spirit of deep sleep, and hath closed your eyes: the prophets and your rulers, the seers he hath covered. And the vision of all is become as the words of a book that is sealed, which *men* deliver to one that is learned, saying, Read this, I pray thee: and he saith, I am not learned. (29.10–2)

Here the prophetic text, as metaphor, appears negatively marked: hermeneutically sealed or illegible, decipherable only to a few. But the possibility of such a comparison is more important than its negative valence in this instance, and indeed the sealed book can, in principle, be opened up and read again, as it will be in the Revelation of St. John. If the two passages from Isaiah suggest permanence and (temporary) obscurity, the prophets offer other, markedly different models for the prophetic word. Take, for example, these verses from Habbakuk:

I will stand upon my watch, and set me upon the tower, and will watch to see what he will say unto me, and what I shall answer when I am reproved./And the Lord answered me, and said Write the vision, and make *it* plain upon tables, that he may run that readeth it./For the vision *is* yet for an appointed time, but at the end it shall speak, and not lie: though it tarry, wait for it; because it will surely come, it will not tarry. (2. 1–3)

This model, too, has its resonance in Blake, in the interplay of vision and word, and in the desire for the prophetic word to be available for all to read. And it seems to straddle the very different states of present and future: The word tarries but will not tarry. Yet here the understanding of the vision seems deferred ultimately until the occurrence of the events prophesied, a state of affairs that, to Pascal's mind, was a defining characteristic of Biblical prophecy. Thus a certain obscurity still obtains even in the face of the most visible and most legible of visions. It is partly a historical irony and partly something built into the production of Blake's texts that these contrasting models of the prophetic word shape the discursive force field for a poet and artist who addressed his texts to the public in a mode—almost "individualized" copies—that all but prevented their having much of an audience.[44]

III

In moving from the brief, early prophetic texts to the epic undertaking of *Milton* one experiences a quantum leap in difficulty. For all their strangeness, the early illuminated poems like *Europe* and *America* do not tax interpretation unduly: The political thrust, for one thing, is clear in each case, and at least the schematic outlines of Blake's developing myths are readily intelligible. But with *Milton* and *Jerusalem*, to say nothing of *The Four Zoas*, one confronts extreme versions of Blake's heterodox myth-making in all its complexities. *Milton* will be the focal text in what follows, and an initial difficulty it presents is simply to determine what kind of poem it is.[45] Blake did not apply to it the designation of "prophecy" as he did with *Europe* and *America*, and, as we have seen, it is not clear that there is such a thing as a *genre* of prophecy in the first place. For all of Blake's disdain of classical culture—including the blistering attack on Plato, Ovid, and company that prefaces two copies of *Milton*—"epic" seems a plausible designation. Blake had planned, it seems, twelve books, which were perhaps reduced to the two books of the finished poem (conveniently requiring him only to efface the "1" before the "2" in the number "12" already engraved). Certainly the scope is vast enough for an epic. What is more, the poem features an invocation of muses, numerous catalogues, an elaborate "machinery" of deities and other creatures, and a hero who descends from one world to the next, much like Odysseus or Aeneas.

Yet how could Blake rail against classical literature and at the same time be heavily indebted to the traditions of epic literature? *Milton*'s mediation is crucial here. The epic—and epic culture—Blake despised was principally the war epic of Homer and his imitators: the line of *The Iliad* much more than *The Odyssey*. In Book VI of *The Aeneid* Anchises prophesies (after the fact) the future history of Rome for Aeneas, and Blake singles out as representative and reprehensible Anchises' exhortation to the Romans to practice the arts of war, implicitly opposed, in Blake's view, to the practice of art.[46] For all of *Milton*'s indebtedness to the examples of Homer and Virgil, *Paradise Lost* broke with tradition as much as it followed it. Not only did it adopt a Biblical theme and a corresponding lexicon of imagery and allusion, it set its only war in heaven and took an utterly different course in depicting the domestic world of Adam and Eve.[47] On the surface, this can appear like a shift from the public to the private, figured most vividly in the "solitary way" that Adam and Eve take in the poem's closing lines.[48] And yet it is no surprise that for a radical Protestant poet of the seventeenth century a focus on the individuality and individualism of the protagonists by no means forecloses the political: Indeed, their story can be read even as a politically engaged work.[49] Although from Blake's viewpoint, Milton was too given over to classical models, he did maintain a clear hierarchy of Biblical over classical culture, most explicitly in *Paradise Regained*, where Jesus rejects Satan's supposedly seductive offers, among them, some of the glories that were Greece and Rome.[50]

But *Milton* is hardly a regular epic, not least because of its length. The "reduced" or condensed character of the finished poem suggests its affinities with the so-called brief epic, or epyllion, a minor and less codified genre but one featuring some influential examples, *Paradise Regained* foremost among them.[51] The major structural feature of the brief epic is its singularity of focus. (And indeed, we shall see that for all the bewildering complexity of the poem, *Milton* can be said to have one and only one action, a single moment that is repeated, witnessed, contested, or avoided by every character in the text.) It is not clear how widely Blake read in the genre of epyllion. But the example of *Paradise Regained*, with its sharp focus and its sustained, repetitive agon between Jesus and Satan would have provided a major precedent for Blake's poem bearing Milton's name. Milton's own paradigm for the brief epic had been the Book of Job, and so Blake's precedent had a doubly Biblical heritage, not a nefarious Classical one.[52] Job's trials are episodic but are really all versions of the same thing: the test of his faith in God in the face of adversity. Blake's *Milton* has something of this character: The oxymoronic structure of a single, repeated action allows for it to considered a brief epic in the tradition of Job.[53] This repetitive, recursive structure brings us to yet another way to think about the character and the difficulty of *Milton*.

One possible name for the difficulty proper to the poem is "allegory." Swinburne once claimed that "of allegory pure and simple there is scarcely a trace in Blake."[54] And famously, Blake rarely had a good word to say about allegory. In *A Vision of the Last Judgment* he writes dismissively of "Fable and Allegory" as "a totally distinct and inferior kind of Poetry," distinct, that is, from "Vision or Imagination" (E, 554). He is explicit about "the Hebrew Bible & the Gospel of Jesus" not being "Allegory but Eternal Vision or Imagination of All that Exists" (554), apparently discounting Paul's express appeal to the concept of allegory in the interpretation of the Hebrew scriptures, as well as centuries of allegorizing commentary.[55] But in at least one spectacular instance, Blake reverses his prevalent judgement.[56] What Foster Damon calls "a slip of the pen" nonetheless stands as Blake's most categorical definition of sublime poetry. In a letter to Thomas Butts of July 1803—the probable period of *Milton*'s composition—Blake writes: "Allegory addressed to the Intellectual powers while it is altogether hidden from the Corporeal Understanding is My Definition of the Most Sublime Poetry" (E, 730). Critics have struggled with these seemingly incompatible possibilities—allegory or not allegory—and usually have chosen to promote one or the other in their readings of Blake.[57] But the debate need not be fought out at the level of Blake's extrapoetical pronouncements: The texts themselves provide ample material. Moreover, allegory is not simply something one chooses to write or not to write. Allegory is not only, or not even, a genre but is also a mode of signification that can inform or pervade any kind of text, regardless of intention. At its limit, allegory is simply a characteristic of language as such, insofar as language can always mean something other than what it says. In the world of allegory, Walter Benjamin maintains, "[a]ny person, any object, any relationship can mean absolutely anything else."[58] At times, Blake's textual world does seem to partake of such vertiginous possibilities of signification. But there is a difference between the conditions of allegory's possibility—where anything can mean anything else—and the actual forms allegory assumes, which, once in place, are no longer purely arbitrary in the way that linguistic signs, in principle, are. Allegories are always allegories of *something (or other)*, if only sometimes of themselves, and certainly Blake's texts are often concerned with marking the specificity of their allegorical characters.[59]

One does not have to read far in Blake's major poems to see how they spell themselves out as allegorical. *Milton* is notable for the way the narrator often pauses to explain how a certain character—if entities like the four Zoas can be termed characters—is called by mortals: Los, we are told, "is nam'd Time Enitharmon is nam'd Space" (Pl. 23). Similarly "Bowlahoola is namd Law, by mortals" and Golgonooza "namd Art & Manufacture by mortal men" (Pl. 23). This is a double-edged gesture in Blake because it acknowledges both the necessity and the undesirability of such allegorizing translations. To identify Los with time tells the reader something crucial about Los, but to qualify the name "Time" as one bestowed by mortals is to mark the term as inadequate, since "mortal" designates a state of perception decidedly below that of "human" in Blake's lexicon.[60] Typically, Blake, in almost Spenserian fashion, defers divulging such translations, such that one first has to encounter the unallegorized, untranslated characters and understand them by their actions and words, by their functions in the narrative or even "system" of the text. So at many turns in Blake's works the reader is caught in the double bind of the simultaneous necessity and impossibility of allegorical translation. And if that is the case with the explicit allegorical character of the poem, the difficulties only multiply in the exceedingly gray area where it is difficult to decide what is allegorical and what is not, a problem that Plato thought plagued children especially. But it is not only a problem for the young.

In "The Rhetoric of Temporality" Paul de Man made the case for allegory being fundamentally a matter of temporality. And he later argued that temporality is still constitutive of allegory, even if the allegorical referent has nothing to do with time.[61] The allegorical text itself can operate in terms of sequence and duration, but its referent need not, as such, be subject to the laws of temporality. This can be illustrated by the textbook example from the English tradition, Spenser's *The Faerie Queene*. The virtues that are the referents of Spenser's allegory are not themselves necessarily subject to time—chastity, say, or holiness—but representations of them emphatically do take time. This temporal gap pertains even to visual art, whose spatial character seems so resistant to time. But at the very least temporality enters visual allegory as the time interpretation takes, the time necessary to move from the visual surface to the more or less clearly encoded meaning. Even if the visual object or field could be present to perception in an instant—a virtual impossibility—allegorical meaning, and meaning as such, does not present itself all at once.

But of what then might *Milton* be an allegory? To anticipate an answer that will need to be demonstrated: a moment, or perhaps *the* moment. The "moment" in Blake, and not only in Blake, has something of the paradoxical character of allegory in general: It is decidedly of the order of time and yet can be abstracted from time, marking an interruption in its "flow," if that is what time does.

It may seem odd to say that *Milton* is about a moment, when one of the chief hallmarks of the poem is its discontinuity, complete with bewildering alterations of substance and style, as well as dizzying shifts in perspective. *Milton* is not all that long a poem, and yet it virtually defies being read without the reader being arrested at many turns. In this, it is much like the books of Isaiah, Ezekiel, and Jeremiah. The verses of each of their "books" do not add up to many pages either; yet they are so dense and disjunctive that they repeatedly bring the course of reading to a standstill.[62] Eighteenth-century commentators remarked on the discontinuities of the prophets enough to provoke a backlash among certain critics: Thomas Howes, in his *Critical Observations on Books Antient and Modern*, argued the prophetic books were disorderly only in chronological terms. If one sought in them, rather, "historic order" (in which the prophecies were accomplished) or, more plausibly "oratorical order," then the problem of discontinuity disappeared.[63] Although ingenious, this subtler appeal to the aesthetic unity and formal coherence of the prophets could not quite resolve all the problems along those lines, and so the defense was often accompanied by appeals to vague notions like "spirit." An earlier critic such as Herder could appeal precisely to "spirit" as a unifying principle for Hebrew poetry, but he felt no need to argue that the books of the prophets had the formal coherence of, say, Virgil's eclogues. Howes seemed obligated to compare Hebrew poetry to its classical counterparts—if there really were any—rather than to assess it in its own terms, as Herder and others had argued should be done.

If there was something of a formal unity to the books of the major prophets, it was principally one conferred after the fact by redaction. The books are by and large divided into groups of similar verses: oracles against foreign nations in one place, oracles for and against Israel or Judah in another, and so on.[64] Even so, there is a kind of absolute character to the individual prophetic utterance that makes it discontinuous, no matter what the sequence is in which it is inscribed. (This is not unrelated to the eminent "quotability" of prophetic sayings.) Something of this discontinuity is replayed in Blake's epics, one index of which is the sometimes arbitrary sequencing of plates. Not all copies of *Milton* are set in the same order, which suggests that narrative sequence is not the highest priority in the poetic program.[65] This has a good deal to do with the poem's highly repetitive, recursive structure. And this will return us, momentarily, to the matter of the moment.

We saw how Blake's early prophecies featured a "praeludium" to the poem proper, and *Milton* offers the most elaborate instance of this structure. Most books of the Biblical prophets begin with a superscription and situating of the prophet, closely followed by a scene of the calling, the vocation to a vocation. The invocation in classical epic, as in *The Iliad*, tends to recede into the background of the poem, but in *Milton* it becomes bound up in the action of the poem that it is said to cause in the first place.[66] Following a formulaic apostrophe to the Daughters of Beulah—who are Muses, but emphatically not the Muses of Greek and Roman mythology— Blake implores them to:

> Say first! what mov'd Milton, who walked about in Eternity
> One hundred years, pondring the intricate mazes of Providence
> Unhappy tho' in heav'n, he obey'd, he murmur'd not. he was silent
> Viewing his Sixfold Emanation scatter'd thro' the deep
> In torment! To go into the deep her to redeem & himself perish?
> What cause at length mov'd Milton to this unexampled deed [?]
> A Bards prophetic Song! for sitting at eternal tables,
> Terrific among the Sons of Albion in chorus solemn & loud
> A Bard broke forth! all sat attentive to the awful man.
>
> Mark well my words! they are of your eternal salvation: (M, 2)

This stands as the prelude to the larger prelude that is the Bard's song, the song that will move Milton to descend back to life, and so it functions as a second invocation. The phrase "Mark well my words! they are of your eternal salvation" is set off both from the preceding and the following lines by a slender blue line that extends part way out into the plate. Even if the semicolon that follows suggests the phrase is connected more to the subsequent lines than the preceding, it is not clear, at least for the moment, who is speaking. It could equally be the bard or the poet who writes *Milton*.[67] As it happens, the pertinence of such a distinction lessens in the course of the poem because all the inspired characters are allied and even united with one another, which is one way that what seems to be only a prelude folds into the subsequent action. And much as there is confusion about who is speaking—often, Neil Hertz contends, a situation characteristic of the sublime— it is also not clear who exactly is being addressed.[68] Who is to mark well the words? The characters internal to Blake's text or the reader or both?

The Bard's song opens with a creation myth abridged from the huge quarry of *The Four Zoas*. The story of the Urizenic creation of man as a sensorily deprived, unimaginative being is rather perfunctory in this context, although it helps establish something of the epic scope. The myth of origins quickly gives way to the account of the *agon* between Satan and Palamabron. Like the long and brief epics by Milton himself, the Bard's song stages a stark contrast between conflicting characters faced with an immense ethical decision, a struggle between nothing less than good and evil.[69] Even critics reluctant to stoop to—even theoretically opposed to—biographical criticism have read *Milton* as an allegory of Blake's particular situation as an artist. After all, Blake calls himself, his brother, and other characters by name, and he proffers details as pedestrian as the street on which he lives.[70] Virtually everyone agrees that one can "identify" Satan in the poem with Blake's patron William Hayley, a well-meaning poet and supporter of the arts but someone who either misunderstood or abused his position. In some ways the historical Hayley was an excellent match for Blake: author of a sympathetic, if somewhat flat-footed life of Milton and a patron, too, of another outcast visionary, William Cowper. He was also the author of a considerable work on epic poetry, in which he championed especially the homegrown English strain. Hayley seemed far from the stereotypical profile of the merely polite aristocratic patron, and yet his proximity turned out be more vexing to Blake than if the two had been worlds apart. And so Hayley looms a key figure behind the Bard's pronouncement that "Corporeal Friends are Spiritual Enemies" [Pl. 4].[71] Moreover, it is clear that Blake thought of himself as a prophet in relation to Hayley. As he wrote baldly to his patron, in a letter replete with echoes of Milton:

Receiving a Prophet As a Prophet is a Duty which If omitted is more Severely Avenged than Every Sin & Wickedness beside It is the Greatest of Crimes to Depress True Art & Science. . . . Let us go on Dear Sir following his Cross let us take it up daily Persisting in Spiritual Labours & the Use of that Talent which it is Death to Bury. & of that Spirit to which we are called—(E, 767)

But if in *Milton* Hayley served as a model for Satan, the latter can hardly be reduced to the former, and the force of the poem scarcely depends on our knowledge of the biographical facts of Blake's life. The mythical extravagance of the conflict between Satan and Palamabron vaults above the outwardly mundane circumstances of Blake's daily life.

That Milton's legacy was now in the hands of someone called Satan was perhaps reason enough for Milton to be moved to return from the afterlife.[72] But what had happened, poetically speaking, in the hundred or so years intervening between the death of the historical Milton and Blake's coming of age? Certainly the texture of the Bard's song and the poem in general suggests that Blake could acknowledge certain precursors in the eighteenth century: Gray, Blair, and Collins, for example, some of whose works he illustrated. But the main period in Milton's wake has with some reason been termed neoclassical or Augustan.[73] Blake's "preface" to *Milton* makes plain what the author thinks of the Augustans' classical models:

The Stolen and Perverted Writings of Homer & Ovid: of Plato and Cicero. which all men ought to contemn: are set up by artifice against the Sublime of the Bible. but when the New Age is at leisure to Pronounce: all will be set right: & those Grand Works of the more ancient & consciously & professedly Inspired Men, will hold their proper rank, & the Daughters of Memory shall become the Daughters of Inspiration. . . . We do not want either Greek or Roman Models if we are just & true to our own Imaginations, those Worlds of Eternity in which we shall live for ever; in Jesus our Lord. (E, 95)

If the writings of Homer and Ovid were stolen and perverted from the start, how much more perverse would the literature of England's belated Augustan age appear? Then the reigning ethos of literary production dictated that to imitate or even translate the great writers of Greece and Rome was as lofty an act as that of original creation. Think of the status of Pope's *Iliad*, for example, or the numerous highly touted imitations of Horace and Juvenal. For Blake, Milton again stands as a more exemplary mediator between the Biblical and the classical traditions. Witness his formulation on the matter of memory and inspiration in *The Reason of Church Government* where he speaks of a work

not to be raised from the heat of youth, or the vapors of wine, like that which flows at waste from the pen of some vulgar amorist, or the trencher fury of a riming parasite, nor to be obtained by the invocation of Dame Memory and her Siren daughters, but by devout prayer to that Eternal Spirit who can enrich all utterance and knowledge, and sends out his seraphim with the hallowed fire of his altar, to touch and purify the lips of whom he pleases.[74]

The closing phrase alludes to the purification of Isaiah, the singeing of his tongue by fire at the moment of his calling to prophesy. Prayer to the Holy

Spirit, not servile imitation of Classical precedents, is the prelude to prophecy. If this is the Miltonic and Blakean model of poetic inspiration, what then would Blake have made of the Augustan era's exemplary poet, Alexander Pope, who, when writing a poem called "The Messiah" could, even as he acknowledges that "the images and descriptions" of Isaiah are superior to those of Virgil, nonetheless profess to write his sacred eclogue "[i]n Imitation of Virgil's Pollio."[75] One might say that for Blake, Pope is the Antichrist. Writing about Jesus Christ in imitation of Virgil is the world of imagination turned upside down. And so in a decade in which even Wordsworth was still lamenting the nefarious legacy of Pope and company, Blake felt compelled to summon back Milton, a poet for whom prophecy and poetry were virtually identical.[76]

If memory and inspiration were opposed in Milton's *The Reason of Church Government*, Blake rehearses just those terms when the hero of his poem announces his momentous descent:

> I come in Self-annihilation & the grandeur of Inspiration
> To cast off Rational Demonstration by Faith in the Savior
> To cast off the rotten rags of Memory by Inspiration. . . .
>
>   (Pl. 41)

Blake has his Milton make an even starker distinction between memory and inspiration, casting them as utterly antithetical. But one of the central paradoxes of Blake's poem is that it performs so much of its inspirational rhetoric in the mode of "memory"—that is to say, in the mode of citation, allusion, and repetition.

The process begins already with the epigraph to *Milton*: "To Justify the Ways of God to Men," an exact citation of the programmatic opening lines from *Paradise Lost*. Who speaks these words, and why? The exactness of the citation masks the difference in the repetition, because the pivotal terms "God" and "Men" mean something radically different in Milton and Blake. "GOD is Jesus," Blake proclaims in his *Laocoon*, whereas Milton would more likely have written the not-so-symmetrical reverse.[77] Blake's whole theology—or is it an anthropo-theology?—is predicated on the identity of the divine and the human, the in-difference of God and man. Blake's poem, moreover, is not interested in justifying to men the ways of Milton's God, the God of *Paradise Lost*.[78] So Blake overturns the program of his predecessor, performing a certain disruptive kind of quotation, a "Miltonic inversion," so to speak, and a prime example of the revisionary mechanism Harold Bloom calls

Tessera, which is completion and antithesis; I take this word not from mosaic-making, where it is still used, but from the ancient mystery cults, where it meant a token of recognition, the fragment say of a small pot which with the other fragments would reconstitute the vessel. A poet antithetically "completes" his precursor, by so reading the parent-poem as to retain its terms but to mean them in another sense, as though the precursor had failed to go far enough.[79]

Walter Benjamin saw "completion" as the task and the definitive mode of critique, a necessary response to the call of the work of art. Blake's *Milton* is certainly a critique in more senses than one. His completion and critique of Milton, a decidedly double-edged maneuver, partakes of the logic of pleroma or fulfillment that characterizes Jesus' relation to his Judaic precursors, the relentless recasting of the letter into spirit.[80]

The prefatory plates of *Milton* feature another instance of citation that illuminates Blake's position in a certain line of prophecy.[81] As a closing epigraph to the plate that features the rant against classical culture as well as the national hymn "Did those feet in ancient time . . . " Blake cites the following exclamation from Moses: "Would to God that all the Lords people were Prophets" (Numbers 11.29). The quotation of this particular verse is apt for its universalizing gesture and its accord with Blake's notion that every honest man is a prophet, that prophecy is in principle possible for all. It is apt, too, in that Blake's quotation embeds within it Milton's own citation of the same passage at the most apocalyptic moment of the latter's treatise on freedom of the press and more. As Milton announces in *Areopagitica*: "For the time seems come, wherein Moses, the great prophet, may sit in heaven rejoicing to see that memorable and glorious wish of his fulfilled, when not only our seventy elders, but all the Lord's people, are become prophets."[82] Is Milton's thinking here merely wishful? Christopher Hill observes that "[i]n England the revolutionary decades gave wide publicity to what was almost a new profession—the prophet, whether as interpreter of the stars, or of traditional popular myths, or of the Bible."[83] Still, Milton's proclamation seems to be restating Moses's wish in the form of a fact, even if that too is something of a wish. Blake's echo of Milton in the quotation from Moses implicitly recognizes the wish not to have been fulfilled. The very comprehensiveness of the wish seems to allow in advance for its being endlessly citable:

In this case, Blake's quotation of Milton quoting Moses hardly constitutes a critique, much less as an antithesis to Milton's inherited terms.

Contemporary criticism has posed rather stark alternatives when it comes to formulating Blake's relation to Milton. Harold Bloom has grounded a whole theory of modern poetry on the notion of the anxiety of influence, and in many ways he takes the Milton-Blake axis as paradigmatic of the agon between a belated poet and his precursor. The extreme version of Bloom's theory dictates that the very example of the strong precursor strangles the imagination of the later poet in his cradle. If this is supposed to be the case for Blake vis-à-vis Milton, one can understand the vehement reaction of a critic such as Joseph Wittreich Jr. who protests: "Blake, his own words testify, was not psychologically crippled by Milton; rather, he had both the joy of seeing divine countenance in Milton more distinctly than in any prince or hero and the capacity to forget his greatest qualities in Milton's greater ones."[84] But are Blake's own words a straightforward testimony, to be taken simply at face value? What relation does Blake's claim that the face of Milton smiled on him as a child bear to the actual character of his texts?

On the face of it, Blake hardly seems "anxious" about Milton's influence. No other Romantic poet confronts Milton so directly and emerges so apparently unscathed.[85] If he was strangled in his cradle, Blake died an unusually slow and pleasant death. But with respect to genre, it seems clear that Milton did have a largely debilitating effect on the Romantics. All the major male Romantic poets, with the possible exception of Shelley, seriously aspired to write an epic: None really succeeded, despite the "failures" of enormous poetic merit like *The Prelude* and Keats's Hyperion poems. Blake's *Milton* and *Jerusalem* feature spectacular moments of poetry and are grand in their conception, but it is not so evident that they are very successful as poems, and certainly not as regular epics.

Bloom has rightly argued that the study of influence cannot be limited to a tracking of allusions and direct references to prior texts and authors. He shares Coleridge's disdain for those who fixate on mere "verbal parallelisms." One example of a resonance not limited to direct statement has to do simply with *where* certain words occur in the spectrum of a poetic line. A passage from *Milton* can illustrate this point:

> But as a wintry globe descends precipitant thro' Beulah bursting,
> With thunders loud, and terrible: so Miltons shadow fell,

Precipitant loud thundring into the Sea of Time & Space.
Then first I saw him in the Zenith as a falling star,
Descending perpendicular, swift as the swallow or swift;
And on my left foot falling on the tarsus, enterd there;

But from my left foot a black cloud redounding spread over Europe.

(Plate 15)

One of the spectacular features of Blake's poem is the striking series of incorporations that occur when one figure after another—Milton, Blake, the Bard, Los—are folded into one another, such that the singularity of the proper name becomes, at best, a convenient fiction. We shall return in a moment to explore especially the prophetic character of such incorporations and their relation to the performance of Blake's text. But first let us look at this typical instance of Blake's repetition and reconfiguration of Milton's poetry. (The phenomenon is pervasive, even if one cannot always translate echoes and allusions into some coherent "meaning.") Three times in the space of seven lines Blake employs variants of the word "fall": "fell," "falling star," and "falling." The word "fall" sometimes comes replete with weighty Christian denotations and connotations. But I think Blake is drawn especially to the cumulative force of its Miltonic usage, his special foregrounding of the word in the syntax of his verse. In Blake's passage, two of the three variants of the word "fall" occur at the end of the line. I suggest this is itself eminently Miltonic.

It is no wonder that versions of the word "fall" would be pervasive in *Paradise Lost*, given its chief story is the Fall of mankind. Yet Milton goes out of his way to see that a preponderance of the usages of "fall" or its variants occurs at the ends of lines. Witness these words of Satan:

> Down they fell
> Driven headlong from the pitch of heaven, down
> Into this deep, and in this general fall
> I also; . . .   (P.L. II, 771–73)

By highlighting this example I do not want to suggest that the fall is always as "general" as it literally is here. But something important is at stake in Milton so insistently placing words like "fall" at the end of the line, as the verse descends, line by line, down the page. One cannot help being caught up in this falling. As the line "descends," so descends (the eye of) the reader. It has long been established, most notably in Stanley Fish's *Sur-*

prised By Sin, that a good deal of the drama of Milton's poem involves the implication of the reader, especially as concerns his or her education through the progress of the poem. I would suggest that some such implication (etymologically, a "folding in") of the reader takes place in the encounter with the lines. Words like "fall" or "falling" hang for a moment suspended at the end of the line before the reader moves on to the next. (This is much like the way the word "hang" works in Wordsworth's poetry and in the poetry of his precursors analyzed in Wordsworth's "Essays Upon Epitaphs." Indeed, one of Wordsworth's chief examples is the way the word "hang" functions in Milton.) The poem falls, the reader falls.[86] As it happens, Blake repeats precisely the Miltonic placement of falling words.

Vincent De Luca has called our attention to the most extreme example of this rhetoric of falling in Blake's corpus. Here are the relevant lines from *The Book of Los*:

> Falling! Falling! Los fell & fell
> Sunk precipitant heavy down down
> Time on times, night on night, day on day
> Truth has bounds. Error none: falling, falling:
> Years on years, and ages on ages
> Still he fell thro' the void, still a void
> Found for falling day & night without end.
>   (BL 4.27–33; E, 92)

This could almost amount to a parody of Milton's language of falling: there is bathos here in more than one sense.[87] De Luca emphasizes the physical or phenomenological sense of falling but these are not just any accidental falls: They have a spiritual resonance, even if Blake does have a decidedly heterodox conception of the fall.

Yet it is easier to note the massive presence of Milton in such Blakean passages than to say what precisely these textual effects mean. They do not seem to fit neatly into the summary positions of Bloom or Wittreich on the nature of the Blake-Milton relation. But if we turn back to the passage from *Milton* foregrounding Milton's "fall" we find another key trait, one germane to the character of a prophetic tradition. To recall the lines in question:

> Then first I saw him in the Zenith as a falling star
> Descending perpendicular, swift as the swallow or swift;
> And on my left foot falling on the tarsus, enterd there;
> But from my left foot a black cloud redounding spread over Europe.

It may seem indecorous—literally pedestrian—for Milton to be incorporated into Blake's foot. But that is hardly a bad sign in a work that places so much emphasis on poetic "stance," visually as well as in an implicit play on the poetic notion of feet. (And what is a poem composed of, if not of feet?) Blake's anatomy lesson here is precise: Milton enters Blake's foot at the tarsus, an odd word that must recall St. Paul, who before his conversion was known as Saul of Tarsus. In Blake's poem, it is not so clear who is converting whom. Milton is both the Covering Cherub[88] and the Redeemer. It is his task to return to "Eternal Death"—which is to say, life as we know it—and to redeem, among others, William Blake. But even to achieve this, he must be "converted" by Blake into a "Milton" only adumbrated by John Milton in his own lifetime. The redemptive conversion by a poetic alter ego ideally works both ways.

It may also be germane that Paul is the author of the principles of Christian allegory, of the doctrine of spiritual interpretation, so tellingly formulated in the King James Version as "the letter killeth, and the spirit giveth life." The allusion to Paul at the moment of Blake's incorporation of Milton may signal how that gesture depends on allegorical reading. Blake reads Milton much as Jesus (from Blake's viewpoint) read the Hebrew Scriptures, to cast off what was merely legal and historical and to concentrate the force of what is imaginative and thus, in Blake's eyes, "eternal." This dialectic of letter and spirit, rather violently simplified in some versions of Christian doctrine, is modeled on the notion of *pleroma*, or fulfillment. Christ proclaims that he has come not to destroy but to fulfill the law. But does the process simply stop (is fulfilled) when the letter is translated into spirit? One problem, of which Blake is acutely aware, is that the "spirit" tends to come in letters of its own. The spirit, especially as rendered in a text, such as the Gospels or Blake's *Milton*, cannot simply be divorced from its representation. Blake is especially cognizant of the tendency of a new, liberatory religious figure or movement (such as Luther, say) to turn eventually into the legalistic, institutionalized thing that he opposed in the first place—a version of the mythical struggle between Orc and Urizen. Thus spiritual or allegorical understanding must perform a kind of permanent revolution, rather than rest content with some spiritual meaning that will harden, one day, into the stoniest of letters.

But why does this dialectic of conversion and spiritual understanding assume the strange form of incorporation, of the folding of one body into another? No doubt it has something to do with the doctrine of the Word becoming flesh, of the Word taking on bodily shape. Especially given that the sacrament of communion entails an ingesting of that Word, a taking of the Word into the body. But I would suggest that the Blakean phenomenon of incorporation has some of its roots in a specifically prophetic tradition. For one of the most striking representations of the immediacy of the prophet's relation to the divine is the scene, often repeated, of the prophet literally eating the words of God. Jeremiah, for example, says to his God: "The words were found, and I did eat them; and thy word was unto me joy and rejoicing of my heart: for I am called by thy name, O LORD God of hosts" (15.16). So complete is the internalization of the divine word here that the prophet even comes to be called by the name of God.

Though Ezekiel does not achieve precisely this sort of linguistic identification with his God, he too internalizes the divine word, because with reference to the "roll of a book" (2.10) the text reads:

Moreover, he said unto me, Son of man, eat that thou findest; eat this roll, and go speak unto the house of Israel. So I opened my mouth, and he caused me to eat that roll. And he said unto me, Son of man, cause thy belly to eat, and fill thy bowels with this roll that I give three. Then did I eat it; and it was sweet in my mouth as honey for sweetness. (3.1–3)

The same vision, modulated slightly, returns in the Book of Revelation, the text that is the highly allusive and citational *summa* prophecy and apocalypse:

And I went unto the angel, and said unto him, Give me the little book. And he said to me, Take it, and eat it up; and it shall make thy belly bitter, but it shall be in thy mouth sweet as honey. (10.9)

Such literal incorporations of the word are, I suggest, part of what is behind the odd dynamic in *Milton* whereby each of the visionary figures merges with another: the Bard with Milton, Milton with Blake, and Blake with Los. Each of these figures is already identified with their *words*; thus to become one with the other is very much like the prophet's internalization of the divine word, especially given Blake's notion of the identity of the divine and the human. The prophets, of all authors in the Bible, have the most immediate relation to the word of God. Blake's imaginative identification of all the visionary figures with one another is one way to (re)present some such immediacy of the inspired word.

The graphic eating of words by the prophets depicts a striking giving over of oneself to the words of the (divine) other. We saw before how so much of the poetic program and protocols of *Milton* depended on the practice of quotation. And what is it that happens when one quotes? The text speaks or writes in the voice of another. One voice gives way or is even momentarily sacrificed to another, more or less violently. In the case of the prophet, it is clear that what matters most are not his (or, rarely, her) own words, but the words of the Lord. Despite the distinctively personal styles of the major prophets—it would be hard to confuse an extended passage from Ezekiel with one from Jeremiah—their own voices are, in principle, strictly subordinated to the (other) word for which they are the vehicle. (Los, Blake's "spirit of Prophecy," is called "the vehicular Terror.") This giving over of one's voice seems related, in its structure, to Blake's notion that "to set another before you" is "the most sublime act." The only sacrifice worth making, in Blake, is self-sacrifice, a sacrifice of self or selfhood. The supreme example of this—and Blake, we recall, termed the Bible "a book of examples" (E, 618)—is Christ's sacrifice of his (divine) self for the sake of all humanity. Though Milton's return from the afterlife in Blake's poem is called an "unexampled deed," it is unprecedented only for a human being. Milton's descent is, in part, an *imitatio Christi*, a passage from a higher realm of actual eternity to the mundane life Blake calls "Eternal Death."

I do not mean to suggest that each time one quotes another, one performs an imitation of Christ, or even that it is necessarily an ethical act. But Blake, despite his fierce claims for originality and individuality, sees something paradigmatic in the prophetic sacrifice of one to another and of one's own words to those of another. But within this general paradigm, it will matter a great deal whom or what one quotes.

The moment of self-sacrifice in *Milton* is a moment of descent: Book One is preoccupied with the descent of Milton (to redeem Ololon, his female emanation) and Book Two with the descent of Ololon, both of which are versions of the descent of Jesus Christ to take on humanity. That this takes the form of a descent implies not only movement within a spatial scheme but a temporal one as well. A fall takes time. Yet the poem conspires in a number of ways to represent these descents as if they take no time at all. One strategy is to present what initially look like discrete events only then to have them revealed as the same event witnessed from different perspectives. (Readers of the twentieth-century novelists, such as Faulkner, may be familiar with such procedures, but they are uncommon in Blake's period.) Thus, Milton's descent is viewed from multiple vantage points, such that what seems at first to be different moments turn out to be the same one. Blake even provides a general account of what he calls "every Moment," each of which does the same thing:

> . . . others of the Sons of Los build Moments & Minutes & Hours
> And Days & Months & Years & Ages & Periods: wondrous buildings
> And every Moment has a Couch of gold for soft repose,
> (A Moment equals a pulsation of the artery)
> And between every two Moments stands a Daughter of Beulah
> To feed the Sleepers on their Couches with maternal care
>   . . .
> Every Time less than a pulsation of the artery
> Is equal in its period & value to Six Thousand Years
> For in this Period the Poets Work is Done: and all the Great
> Events of Time start forth & are conceived in such a Period
> Within a Moment: a Pulsation of the Artery.   (M, 28 & 29)

This passage outlines the work of the sons of Los, the Spirit of Prophecy who is the allegorical figure called "Time" by mortals. The claims for the poet's work are immense: It includes nothing less than all of what Christians think of as history, from creation to the millennium. The double figuration of this moment is paradoxical: On the one hand, it is identified with the pulsation of an artery, an entirely instinctual and natural action; on the other hand, poetic labor is imaged as the construction of building blocks, as if involved, say, in reconstructing some version of the temple of Jerusalem. The seemingly contradictory strands of figuration can perhaps be seen as the elaboration of a single Biblical metaphor: The body of the Lord *is* the temple. In any event, the figuration constructs the poetic moment as both temporal and timeless, organic and inorganic, narrative and architectonic. The paradoxical status of this moment, a moment with and without "momentum," is reflected in a corresponding passage from Book Two:

> There is a Moment in each Day that Satan cannot find
> Nor can his Watch Fiends find it, but the Industrious find
> This Moment & it multiply. & when it once is found
> It renovates every Moment of the Day if rightly placed [.]
> In this Moment Ololon descended to Los & Enitharmon
> Unseen beyond the Mundane Shell Southward in Miltons track
>   (M, 35)

Both passages address the same instant of poetic inspiration, a moment that can redeem the whole of history or any given day, each of which can be a figure for the other in the visionary calculus by which a thousand years is but a day in the eyes of God. This unlikely conflation of the vast duration of all of history with the seemingly ephemeral character of the moment happens to correspond strikingly to Blake's testimony of the scene of writing the poem that may well be *Milton*:

I have written this Poem from immediate Dictation twelve or sometimes twenty or thirty lines at a time without Premeditation & even against my Will. the Time it has taken in writing was thus renderd Non Existent. & an immense Poem Exists which seems to the Labour of a long Life all produced without Labour or Study. (E, 728–29)

This moment of unalienated labor that is the genesis of the poem is very much like the moment repeatedly referred to and enacted within the poem, the paradigmatic moment of descent and self-sacrifice. And the giving over of one's words to those of the other marks this metapoetic moment as much as it does the scene of inspiration internal to the poem, each being "immediate" in more ways than one.

But if this poetic moment of descent and self-sacrifice is in some sense the only real action of the poem, that does not mean that the moment in question is always perceived in the same way. And indeed, the noncomprehension of the moment is one of the principal reasons that there is any sense of time conveyed at all. This has partly to do with Blake's complicated cosmology and ontology, whereby one and the same being exists in different modes and strata of existence at the same time. Let us look again at the moment of Milton's descent already cited above in its version from Plate 15. A few plates later we read:

> . . . the Spectrous body of Milton:
> Redounding from my left foot into Los's Mundane space,
> Brooded over his Body in Horeb against the Resurrection
> Preparing it for the Great Consummation; red the Cherub on Sinai
> Glow'd; but in terrors folded round his clouds of blood.
>
> Now Albions sleeping Humanity began to turn upon his Couch;
> Feeling the electric flame of Miltons precipitate descent.   (M, 20)

Still another version of Milton's descent occurs one plate later, although it could be construed simply as a continuation of the previous passage. More striking is the fact that the same descent (not its repetition by Ololon) appears again toward the end of Book Two:

> . . . and condensing all his Fibres
> Into a strength impregnable of majesty & beauty infinite
> I saw he was the Covering Cherub & within him Satan . . .
>
> Descending down into my Garden, a Human Wonder of God
> Reaching from heaven to earth a Cloud & Human Form
> I beheld Milton with astonishment . . .   (M, 37)

And then the very next plate features the last but not the least version of this same moment:

> And Milton collecting all his fibres into
>   impregnable strength
> Descended down a Paved work of all kinds of precious stones
> Out from the eastern sky; descending down into my Cottage
> Garden: clothed in black, severe, & silent he descended.
> The Spectre of Satan stood upon the roaring sea & beheld
> Milton within his sleeping Humanity . . .   (M, 38)

Taken together these not-quite-thirteen ways of looking at Milton demonstrate the overwhelming importance of perspective in the poem. In Plate 15, the emphasis is on Milton's relation to Albion, as certain historical "errors" of Milton are sketched, such as his succumbing to the "female will." In Plate 20 Milton's descent sparks the arousal of Albion and gives way to a lyrical excursus on the renovation of the senses. And in the subsequent plate, this same descent of Milton serves to define the hero's position in relation to Satan. There is, however, a key difference between the visions of Book One and Book Two, one that turns on Blake's recognition (or not) of who and what Milton is. In Book One, Blake had written:

> But I knew not that it was Milton, for man cannot know
> What passes in his members till periods of Space & Time
> Reveal the secrets of Eternity: for more extensive
> Than any other earthly things, are Mans earthly lineaments.
>   (M, 21)

The descent of Milton in Book Two appears to be the same event, but it is perceived in a radically different way. What can account for the change? The "original" descent of Milton enables Blake to pass from the world of

Generation, the quotidian world of fallen nature, to that of Eternity. The passage from Plate 21 continues:

> And all this Vegetable World appeared on my left Foot,
> As a bright sandal formd immortal of precious stones & gold:
> I stooped down & bound it on to walk forward thro' Eternity.

In a gesture resembling what Warburton identified in the prophets as a "representative action," Los had earlier (Plate 8) placed a sandal on his head as a sign of mourning, which Robert Essick has traced to Ezekiel 24.17,23, although it may also allude to Isaiah's barefoot journey in the desert as "a sign and wonder upon Egypt and upon Ethiopia" (20.3). That Blake can don the sandal here indicates a redemptive moment, making possible the step from experience to Eternity.

Blake's inability to recognize Milton for who he is "until periods of Space & Time reveal the secrets of Eternity" is one crucial instance of a pervasive deferral of knowledge or at least of a pervasive uncertainty about whether or not (something like) the Apocalypse has arrived. Another occurs when the narrator recollects the "old prophecy" that Milton should arise from Felpham's vale (that is, Blake's real-life abode). Los addresses his sons as follows:

> . . . the Seven Eyes of God may have space for Redemption.
> But how this is as yet we know not, and we cannot know
> Till Albion is arisen, then patient wait a while,
> Six Thousand years are passd away the end approaches fast;
> This mighty one is come from Eden, he is of the Elect,
> Who died from Earth & he is returnd before the Judgment.
> This thing
> Was never known that one of the holy dead should willing return
> Then patient wait a little while till the Last Vintage is over.
>
> (M, 23)

The status of Los's knowledge here is doubly paradoxical. Not only does he speak authoritatively of something that "as yet we know not, and we cannot know," that knowledge is supposed to be possible only when Albion is risen. The problem is that there is little or no indication that Albion really rises within the bounds of the poem. The arrival of Milton "the Awakener" does stir Albion's sleeping body with the electric flame of his descent. But Albion rises (in Plate 39) only to have his strength fail a few lines later. Thus unlike the instance of deferred understanding discussed previously—when Milton is not recognized by Blake as Milton—this latter inability to know is not at all resolved within the action of the poem. And yet much of what is bound up in this unknowable event concerns the possibility and actuality of redemption. One way Blake establishes the authority of a prophetic voice even here is through the fiction of speaking, as it were, from beyond the grave, from the vantage of Eternity.

An uncertainty similar to that concerning the rise of Albion marks, too, the representation of the Last Vintage, for which the sons of Los are advised to wait patiently. Toward the end of the first book, in what looks very much like the later phases of the French revolutionary wars, Blake writes:

> The Wine-press on the Rhine groans loud, but all its central beams
> Act more terrific in the central Cities of the Nations
> Where Human Thought is crushd beneath the iron hand of Power.
> There Los puts all into the Press, the Oppressor & the Oppressed.
> Together, ripe for the Harvest & Vintage & ready for the Loom.
>
> They sang at the Vintage. This is the Last Vintage!
> & Seed
> Shall no more be sown upon Earth, till all the Vintage is over
> And all gatherd in, till the Plow has passed over the Nations
> And the Harrow & heavy thundering Roller over the mountains . . .
>
> (M, 25)

This Last Vintage is announced by the sons of Luvah, the Zoa associated with love, and thus these lines might be construed more as the expression of a desire than an actuality. But Los soon confirms their proclamation:

> Fellow Laborers! The Great Vintage & Harvest is now upon Earth
> The whole extent of the Globe is explored: Every scatterd Atom
> Of Human Intellect now is flocking to the sound of the Trumpet
>
> (M, 25)

Yet this "Last" Vintage is not the last; the closing lines of the poem look forward to yet another:

> Rintrah & Palamabron view the Human Harvest beneath
> Their Wine-presses & Barns stand open; the Ovens are prepar'd
> The Waggons ready: terrific Lions & Tygers sport & play
> All Animals upon the Earth, are prepard in all their strength
>
> To go forth to the Great Harvest & Vintage of the Nations
>
> (M, 42–43)

One way to explain the apparent discrepancy between the two distinct "last" vintages is to recall Robert Lowth's observations on the ambiguity of tenses in prophetic discourse, whereby a future event will be denoted by a "past" tense and a past event by a "future" tense.[89] The tense of a prophetic proposition, according to Lowth's persuasive analysis, does not always correspond to the temporality of its referent. (Something of this same confusion—although without the same grammatical configurations—pervades New Testament texts concerning the Kingdom of God, with some claiming it as having already arrived and others [but contemporaneously!] proclaiming it still to come.) Thus the announcement of the arrival of the Last Vintage need not be taken literally, and perhaps not only for grammatical reasons.

In addition to these grammatical matters, the dynamics of figuration also come to complicate the representation of the Last Vintage, Harvest, and Judgment. The vintage and harvest are plausible as figures for the end because they mark the end of a given cycle of nature—and yet it is precisely the cyclical character of the seasons that prevents any harvest or vintage from being the last. And as we shall see once again, even declaring a harvest or vintage as the "last" does not necessarily mean it is the last.

Blake's figuration of the end as a vintage or a harvest hardly seems to partake of Blake's ideal of "minute particulars" that grounds his aesthetic. His visions of the end in *Milton* scarcely designate the details of "time, place, or manner" catalogued by Lowth as characteristic of prophecy. Blake's choice of vintage and harvest—both of which have Biblical precedents—is significant in that those events have both natural and man-made aspects. And as dim a view as Blake sometimes has of nature, it is to his advantage that the prophetic word operate something like a natural organism:

The Nature of Visionary Fancy or Imagination is very little Known & the Eternal nature & permanence of its ever Existent Images is considerd as less permanent than the things of the Vegetative & Generative Nature yet the Oak dies as well as the Lettuce but its Eternal Image & Individuality never dies. but renews by its seed. just [*as*] <so> the Imaginative Image returns [*according to*] <by> the seed of Contemplative Thought the Writings of the Prophets illustrate these conceptions of the Visionary Fancy by their various sublime & Divine Images as seen in the Worlds of Vision (E, 555)

In this remarkably Platonic passage, Blake passes smoothly from literal seeds to the "seed of Contemplative Thought," from the natural to the human. His association of the seed with the prophetic word has a lofty precedent in the passage from Third Isaiah that Herder found paradigmatic for prophetic discourse:

For as the rain cometh down, and the snow from heaven, and returneth not thither, but watereth the earth, and maketh it bring forth and bud, that it may give seed to the sower, and bread to the eater: So shall my word be that goeth forth out of my mouth: it shall not return unto me void, but it shall accomplish that which I please, and it shall prosper *in the thing* whereto I sent it. (55.10–11)

The circulation of rain and the growth of the seed are appropriate figures for the prophetic word in that they require a certain duration to be enacted but they inevitably reach their goals. But perhaps not every seed reaches such a destination.

Isaiah's vision of the word as seed may be one of the pre-texts for the more spectacular identification of Word and seed that occurs in the Gospels.[90] In the parable of the sower that begins the "parable chapters" of Mark and Matthew, Jesus recounts the story of some seeds falling by the wayside, some falling on stony ground, some being scorched by the sun; only some seeds fall on good ground and bring forth fruit and multiply. When his disciples ask Jesus—in a version of a question posed by Ezekiel's audience—why he addresses (the) people in parables, Jesus responds:

Because it is given unto you to know the mysteries of the kingdom of heaven, but to them it is not given. For whosoever hath, to him it shall be given, and he shall have more abundance: but whoever hath not, from him shall be taken away even that he hath. Therefore speak I unto them in parables: because they seeing see not; and hearing they hear not, neither do they understand. And in them is fulfilled the prophecy of Esaias. (13.11–14)

The passage Jesus cites from Isaiah—Harold Bloom calls it a "terrifying injunction"—is the Lord's very first message to Isaiah following his election and purification for prophetic office. God's wish for the people to hear and not understand seems barely intelligible as anything other than ironic and yet Jesus seems to take it literally and understands it to have been duly fulfilled. The ironies are multiplied in the Gospels when Jesus has to explain the parable of the sower that was supposed to be understood by the "insiders," his disciples:

When any one heareth the word of the kingdom, and understandeth it not, then cometh the wicked one, and catcheth away that which was sown in his heart. . . . But he that received seed into the good ground is he that heareth the word, and understandeth *it*; which also beareth fruit, and bringeth forth fruit, and bringeth forth, some a hundredfold, some sixty, some thirty. (13.19 and 23)

The word is the seed, and Jesus, the Word made flesh, authorizes the identification of the two. Once again, the relation of the prophetic and parabolic entails both obscurity and deferral of understanding, if not utter lack of comprehension. Although the analogy between word and seed may seem like the very paradigm of the organic metaphor, the emphasis in the Biblical parables is often precisely on the discrepancy between a seed and its eventual product, as, for example, between the mustard seed and the full-blown tree that supports so many birds of the air, figuring the kingdom of heaven (Matthew 13.31–32).

That the "last" vintage or harvest is difficult for the reader—and for some of Blake's characters—to recognize as the definitively last poses little or no problem for Blake's understanding of things. In the elaborate commentary entitled *A Vision of the Last Judgment* Blake asserts: "What are all the Gifts of the Spirit but Mental Gifts whenever any Individual Rejects Error & Embraces Truth a Last Judgment passes upon that Individual" (E, 562). The simple use of the indefinite article here—"a" instead of "the"— is heresy for the commonsensical understanding of the Bible and Christian doctrine. Much of the paradoxical character of Blake's prophetic rhetoric is crystallized in this odd phrase "a Last Judgment"—a phrase repeated several times in this text. There should only be one Last Judgment, but Blake insists on the notion of "*a* Last Judgment," understanding it as an infinitely repeatable event, possible anytime anyone rejects error and embraces truth.

As *Milton* approaches its end—and the end now approaches fast—the text becomes increasingly figurative and citational (two principal hallmarks of prophetic speech) at precisely the moment when one might expect a dissipation of the clouds for a literal and unmediated revelation. Toward the end, some allusions to the Book of Revelation are, to say the least, thinly veiled, as the commentary on Ololon's speech to Milton makes plain:

> No sooner she had spoke but Rahab Babylon appeard
> Eastward upon the Paved work across Europe & Asia
> Glorious as the midday Sun in Satans bosom glowing:
> A Female hidden in a Male, Religion hidden in War
> Namd Moral Virtue; cruel two-fold Monster shining bright
> A Dragon red & hidden Harlot which John in Patmos saw
>
> (M, 40)

It would be reductive to call this an "allusion" to Revelation: Blake explicitly lays claim to the same vision as John the Divine, at the same time as he echoes a Miltonic formulation.[91] Other invocations of the prophetic and apocalyptic traditions are more compact and complex. The "scene of writing" from the poem's penultimate plate offers the most spectacular instance:

> Then as a Moony Ark Ololon descended to Felphams Vale
> In clouds of blood, in streams of gore, with dreadful thunderings
> Into the Fires of Intellect that rejoic'd in Felphams Vale
> Around the Starry Eight: with one accord the Starry Eight became
> One Man Jesus the Savior. wonderful! round his limbs
> The Clouds of Ololon folded as a Garment dipped in blood
> Written within & without in woven letters: & the Writing
> Is the Divine Revelation in the Litteral expression:
> A Garment of War, I heard it namd the Woof of Six Thousand Years
>
> (M, 42)

Northrop Frye has written of the imaginative recreation of the Old Testament vision in the New, which reaches "its climax in the dense mosaic of allusions and quotations in the Apocalypse."[92] This apocalyptic vision at the end of *Milton* partakes of such citational density: The text "written within and without in woven letters" alludes to Revelation's "book written within and on the backside, sealed within seven seals" (5.1), although Blake prefers the phrasing of Ezekiel (as rendered in the King James version):

But thou, son of man, hear what I say unto thee: Be not thou rebellious like the rebellious house; open thy mouth, and eat what I give thee. And when I looked, behold a hand *was* sent unto me; and lo, a roll of a book *was* therein; And he spread it before me; and it was written within and without; and *there was* written therein lamentations, and mourning, and woe. (2.8–10)

Blake's text encapsulates the theme of the immediacy of the prophetic word as incorporated or internalized in God's spokesman, but it does so *in* the mode of allusion and citation. Indeed, virtually every phrase in Blake's passage echoes the Biblical Apocalypse: The image of the "Garment dipped in blood" refers to a crucial passage where it is said of the rider on a white horse: "And he *was* clothed with a vesture dipped in blood and his name is called the Word of God" (19.13).[93] And the reference to Jesus coming in the clouds of Ololon recalls a host of similar passages, such as Revelation 1.7 ("Behold, he cometh in clouds"). Thus the passage partakes eminently of the paradoxical character of prophecy: The most future oriented and "immediate" of discourses is pervasively citation of texts of the past. And to make matters more complex, the images that riddle these passages—the garments, the clouds—tend to underscore the figural quality of the visions.[94] The garment is a traditional figure for the figural, for what is detachable from the body but serves to veil it, and clouds mediate and perhaps even obscure the full appearance of Jesus as savior, precisely where one might expect a Blakean reveling in the splendor of the naked body, as in so many version of his engraving "Glad Day."

The greatest paradox of this climactic passage, however, lies in the appearance of "the Divine Revelation in its Litteral Expression." What can it mean for *Milton* and Blakean prophecy that at the climax of this poem the most highly figured text in the Biblical canon appears literally, that is to say: as a text. *Milton* is a highly self-conscious, self-reflexive poem, as much about what is entailed in the prophetic calling as it is a performance in the prophetic mode. It is particularly aware of its coming at so late a date in a long tradition of prophecy, underscoring the inevitability of mediation. Even so, it is striking that at the ultimate moment of the poem, this text of revelation reveals the text of Revelation. Revelation reveals revelation, as a text. The event toward which the poem seems to have been moving—the rise of Albion—never quite takes place in the poem. It might even be said that before it can, Albion must rise to the occasion of reading Revelation.

Milton's final triumphant speech in the poem seems to confirm the fulfillment of the program he prescribed for himself, one virtually identical to the ethos of the "Preface" celebrating the power of inspiration:

> I come in Self-annihilation & the grandeur of Inspiration
> To cast off Rational Demonstration by Faith in the Savior
> To cast off the rotten rags of Memory by Inspiration
> To cast off Bacon, Locke, & Newton from Albions covering
> To take off his filthy garments, & clothe him with Imagination
> To cast aside from Poetry, all that is not Inspiration.　(M, 41)

Milton's speech enlists the stark binary opposition that structures the apocalyptic discourse that categorically separates the sheep from the goats, the wheat from the chaff. Once again, the imagination is diametrically opposed to memory. Yet the rhetoric of inspiration, throughout the poem and especially in the final plates, is ubiquitously citational and allusive, which is to say, among other things, of the order of memory. Not that *Milton* is less powerful for this—it is just that the method of poem in some respects belies its manifesto. However, what emerges clearly at the end of the poem is the conjunction of the theme of self-annihilation with the practice of citation, a conjunction of thematic and formal elements: quotation—especially of the prophetic sort—is the discursive form of self-annihilation. In Blakean as well as Biblical prophecy, no "self" is understood to speak the prophetic word, however individual the style or idiosyncratic the formulation might be. In writing to the Reverend Trusler on the subject of some of his designs, Blake claimed:

And tho I call them Mine I know they are not Mine being of the same opinion with Milton when he says That the Muse visits his Slumbers & awakes & governs his Song when Morn purples the East. & being also in the predicament of that prophet who says I cannot go beyond the command of the Lord to speak good or bad. (E, 701)

Blake's works—like Milton's poems, like the prophet's words—are his and not his, with the emphasis on their author being more possessed than possessing. Once again, this giving up or over of one's voice is the paradigmatic poetic and prophetic act, a sacrifice that is the condition of redemption. This is the moment of moments in Blake, the moment of inspiration, the moment in the day that Satan cannot find.

It is in part the imbrication of figure and citation that freezes this moment and gives it its momentum. Insofar as this moment is "pictured," is rendered in a (usually visual) figure, the moment is arrested. But insofar as it is a figure and its reference is more or less uncertain, it leaves the text open for interpretation, open to an uncertain future.

Hölderlin's Moment of Truth: "Germanien" and the Oracle to the Nation

(WITH AN EXCURSUS ON REVELATION, REPRESENTATION, AND RELIGION IN THE AGE OF GERMAN IDEALISM)

> EIN DRÖHNEN: es ist
> die Wahrheit selbst
> unter die Menschen
> getreten,
> mitten ins
> Metapherngestöber.
>
> [A ROAR: it is
> truth itself
> appearing among
> mankind,
> in the midst of
> the metaphor-flurry.]
> —Paul Celan

In the spring of 1794, the young poet Hölderlin wrote to his mother of his longing for home and remarked almost casually: "Everywhere I find, that a prophet counts little in his fatherland, and abroad too much!" ["Ich finde überall, daß ein Prophet in seinem Vaterlande wenig gilt, und in der Ferne zuviel!"][1] Hölderlin's rewriting of the Biblical byword came to prove prophetic, though closer to terms contrary to his own. In his "fatherland" —but one will have to ask: What exactly is his fatherland?—Hölderlin now ranks as one of the most exalted poets, whereas abroad his name is either unknown or stands as a virtual cipher for an obscure poetic corpus that stubbornly resists translation. In Germany he can be hailed as "the poet's poet," as Heidegger not atypically calls him, but in other countries he is more like "the German poet," to invoke a phrase of Hölderlin's own, a poet who remains foreign, enigmatic. (This is not to say that he is not *also* an enigma, and even a foreigner, in what is now and then called "Germany.") The peculiar fate of Hölderlin's delayed reception marks him, even more dramatically than Blake, as a prophetic poet, little read or appreciated in his lifetime and for virtually a century after the period of his greatest creativity.[2] That alone might have been enough to create—retroactively—a prophetic aura, although once he began to be read widely, his early editors and commentators, such as Norbert von Hellingrath and the circle around Stefan George, were quick for any number of reasons to praise Hölderlin to the skies as a prophet and a seer. In a poetic tribute to his precursor, George could write:

Un heißt es ein greifbares wunder wenn durch menschenalter nicht beachtet oder nur als zarter erträumer von vergangenheiten plötzlich der große Seher für sein volk ins licht tritt.[3]

[And it can be called a palpable miracle if for generations he was not noticed or only as a gentle dreamer of the past and then suddenly the great seer of his people steps into the light.]

Long after the initial euphoria surrounding Hölderlin's "discovery" in the first decades of the twentieth century, attention to him as a peculiarly "modern" or prophetic poet continued to span a broad spectrum of commentary, from Gadamer to Foucault, from Kommerell to Adorno. The extraordinary delay in the reception of Hölderlin's work contributed much to the aura of a prophet who seems to belong as much to later times as to his own. Gadamer, for one, speaks of Hölderlin's "Gegenwärtigkeit," his "presentness," which he can even term "absolute."[4] And the common invocation of Hölderlin as an "early modern"—however empty a phrase that is—points to a widespread perception of the poet as a writer of "our" time.[5] Sometimes the reading of Hölderlin as prophet is celebratory, sometimes merely analytic, as in a certain remark by Adorno on the famous closing line of "Andenken": "Was bleibet aber, stiften die Dichter" ("But what remains, the poets institute"). Adorno comments: " . . . the 'what remains' . . . points, purely according to its grammatical form, toward an existence and a corresponding memory like that of the prophets; in no way toward a Being that would not exist in time, as if it were transcendent of time."[6] All such gestures take Hölderlin more or less at his word: Like Blake, he was the very first to invoke the myth of his own prophetic calling.

The darkest moment of Hölderlin's belated reception as poet and prophet occurred during the period of Nazi domination in Germany, when his works were, through selective citation and the crudest interpretive violence, pressed into ideological service for Hitler's regime.[7] Friedrich Beißner, the devoted editor of the monumental Stuttgart edition, may not have been simply a disinterested philologist when he prepared under the auspices of the Nazi's cultural wing an edition of Hölderlin's poems for the troops to carry into the trenches of World War II.[8] The popular Nazi understanding of Hölderlin, littered throughout the literary journalism of the 1930s, was demonstrably a misreading in the most straightforward sense. Although it is understandable how a celebratory poem called "Death for the Fatherland" ("Der Tod fürs Vaterland") might be enlisted in the Nazi cause, Hölderlin's poem addressed the possibility of such a sacrifice in opposition to an imperial power, not on behalf of one. Never has there been a more violent and sustained appeal to the idea of the German fatherland than under the Nazi regime, but what Nazi ideologue would have paused to consider that by "fatherland" Hölderlin often meant his native Swabia? "Schwaben über alles" could scarcely have been a rallying cry for many German or even Swabian people of the 1930s.[9] Even in its widest sense, that of a pan-Germanic nation, Hölderlin's conception of the fatherland had little (though not quite nothing) to do with what would later become the Third Reich.

If the run-of-the-mill Nazi appropriations of Hölderlin were manifestly massive errors in translation (and worse), the situation is far less clear-cut in the case of Heidegger's powerful readings of Hölderlin, most of them elaborated in the 1930s and early 1940s. Although not simply a spokesman here for his regime—he shared, for example, few of the Nazi's prevailing aesthetic values—Heidegger, in his commentary from 1934/35 on "Germanien" and "Der Rhein," could sometimes speak of "unser Vaterland Germanien" ("our fatherland Germania") as if there were no real discontinuity between Hölderlin's nation and his own.[10] Though Heidegger's own reading of Hölderlin is avowedly violent in its turn—as well as violent in ways it does not acknowledge—it does question forcefully the simple-minded historicism that would try to consign and confine Hölderlin's poetry to its own time, to hermetically seal it off, as it were, from any subsequent history. To recognize that there was nothing remotely fascistic or protofascistic about Hölderlin's politics is not to say there is an absolute break between his fatherland and Heidegger's. The fate of a word—and not just a word—cannot be confined to the sphere of intentionality.

Heidegger draws attention to Hölderlin's deferred reception but not simply to assert that the poet is therefore more of "our" time than his own. Heidegger claims in the series of lectures from 1934/35 devoted to "Germanien" and "Der Rhein":

We must come to terms with the fact that the Germans required a full hundred years before the work of Hölderlin came before us in this form, which forces us to concede that we are today still in no way mature enough for its greatness and its future power.[11]

Resisting the more complacent notion that we—whoever "we" are—are now in a position to "appreciate" the once obscure Hölderlin and to recognize his greatness, Heidegger protests that we are not yet even up to the challenge of reading him: His power still lies in the future. Although there is an implicit arrogance to Heidegger's claim, here and elsewhere, that no one else has been quite in a position to read Hölderlin, and Heidegger is alone in recognizing that, there is also a certain humility in acknowledging the limits of his and "our" understanding, however apodictic some of his pronouncements sound.

Heidegger does not posit a simple narrative of enlightenment, such that we will assuredly reach the point—although it would not really be a "point"—of understanding Hölderlin some day in the future. As he says in the same series of lectures:

Hölderlin's poems become from year to year more inexhaustible, greater, more foreign, in an ultimate sense they are not to be accommodated. There is still no real historico-intellectual space for them. It will not come to them from the outside, rather they themselves will have to create it. If we are not disposed in the future to dwell in the storms of this poetry, then this attempt remains, in fact, only an idle game.[12]

Heidegger postulates a narrative of non- or antienlightenment: The works become even more foreign as time passes, and they are not to be encompassed in any scheme of understanding—except perhaps one of their own creation. If there is a future to Hölderlin's poetry—and Heidegger hears its call even if that future, by definition, does not exist—it is in some sense the work's own future, a future instituted by the very texts in question. Heidegger never tires of citing Hölderlin's dictum "Was bleibet aber, stiften die Dichter." ("But what remains, the poets institute.") That this scenario differs radically from the traditional understanding of the prophetic, Heidegger wants to make abundantly clear:

Poets, if they are of their essence, are *prophetic.* They are, however, not at all "prophets" according to the Judeo-Christian meaning of this term. The "prophets" of these religions do not pronounce the founding word of the holy, they only prophesy or predict [*voraussagen*] it. They even prophesy the god, in whom the security of salvation is calculated in terms of otherworldly blessedness. One should not disfigure Hölderlin's poetry through "that which is religious in religion," which remains a matter of the Roman understanding of the relation between men and gods. One should not overburden the essence of this poetic office, insofar as one makes the poet into a "seer" in the sense of one who predicts the future. What is holy, what is poetically pronounced in advance, only opens the time-space [continuum] of an appearance of the gods and points to the place of the dwelling of historical man on this earth. The essence of this poet may not be thought according to its correspondence to these "prophets," rather what is "prophetic" in this poetry must be grasped from the essence of the poetic prophesying [*Voraussagens*].[13]

Heidegger's contention cannot really be proved or disproved, certainly not just by pointing to this or that isolated passage as evidence. The power of his claim lies in its not taking for granted the ability to understand Hölderlin, something that a wealth of philological research can seduce one into believing. In doing so, Heidegger almost of necessity speaks of understanding Hölderlin as an event displaced into the future, and not a future whose coming is guaranteed. This is why Heidegger both does and does not invoke the language of prophecy as traditionally understood. It must be noted, however, that in distinguishing Hölderlin's prophetic mode from the Judeo-Christian, Heidegger has to resort to a reductive view, a caricature really, of the Biblical prophet. If one attends to the plethora of prophetic functions in the Bible, as the earlier chapters tried to demonstrate, it is impossible to limit the prophet to a predictor or even to make prediction the paradigmatic function of the prophet. Marlene Zarader has persuasively demonstrated a virtually systematic denial of especially the Judaic heritage in Heidegger's readings and thinking: His conception of prophecy is a case in point.[14] We shall see how it is neither necessary nor possible to disentangle Hölderlin's prophetic posture from the Judaic or the Christian. But how is it then that Hölderlin's work presents itself as prophetic?

I shall return to take up the vexed question of the future and the nation or fatherland in Hölderlin's work—they are inextricably bound up with each other—but for the moment one could also note that simultaneously with his championing by a conservative and nationalist Right, Hölderlin was only somewhat less vigorously promoted by an internationalist Left.[15] Lukács, Benjamin, and Adorno were just some of Hölderlin's sympathetic readers, and Lukács especially was attentive to the republican character of his work. Not that Hölderlin's poetry was and is a cipher from which one could justifiably read off the most contradictory political messages. Yet there is something built into Hölderlin's abstract and mythologizing poetry that resists direct statement and opens itself up to divergent readings: Indeed, that openness is part of the ambiguously prophetic character of his work.[16] It is what helped make his work futural, what gave and gives a future for his texts.

∼

The opening stanzas of "Wie wenn am Feiertage" ("As on a Holiday") present one of the most striking scenes of inspiration riddling Hölderlin's poetry, one where the trees of a grove exposed to nature's thunder and lightning are likened to the poet's exposure to the gods[17]:

> So stehn sie unter günstiger Witterung
> Sie die kein Meister allein, die wunderbar
> Allgegenwärtig erzieht in leichtem Umfangen
> Die mächtige, die göttlichschöne Natur.
> Drum wenn zu schlafen sie scheint zu Zeiten des Jahrs
> Am Himmel oder unter den Pflanzen oder den Völkern
> So trauert der Dichter Angesicht auch,
> Sie scheinen allein zu seyn, doch ahnen sie immer.
> Denn ahnend ruhet sie selbst auch.
>
> Jetzt aber tagts! Ich harrt und sah es kommen,
> Und was ich sah, das Heilige, sei mein Wort.   (II, 118)

> [So now in favorable weather they stand
> Whom no mere master teaches, but in
> a light embrace, miraculously omnipresent,
> God-like in power and beauty, Nature brings up.

So when she seems to be sleeping at times of the year
Up in the sky or among plants or the peoples,
The poets' faces likewise are sad,
They seem to be alone, but are always divining,
For divining too she herself is at rest.

But now day breaks! I waited and saw it come,
And what I saw, the hallowed, shall be my word.]

Not only is the poet singled out as the one to receive the holy vision, his poetic activity is established, by analogy, as both natural and divine. Moreover, the curious phrase "among plants or the peoples" suggests that the poet moves equally in the spheres of nature and history. Strangest of all, the poet's prophetic consciousness, in the mode of *ahnen*, or divination, is said to characterize nature's own.[18] Nature is personified, endowed even with a consciousness of the future, in order then to have the poet's presentiments acquire an aura of the natural. But this presentiment is introduced in a puzzling formulation: "Sie scheinen allein zu sein, doch ahnen sie immer." (They seem to be alone, yet they are always divining.") What is at stake in the "doch," the "yet," that separates the two clauses of Hölderlin's statement? Divining, although an utterly singular activity, is precisely that which keeps the poets from truly being alone: Divination, as mediation between the gods and the people, is the opening to community. And community is preeminently, for Hölderlin, a thing of the future, temporarily, if not permanently, displaced from the present, especially in the era of the departed gods.[19]

The poet's vision in "Wie wenn am Feiertage" is literally that: He emphasizes what he *sees* but remarks in the same breath on the transformation, in the mode of the subjunctive, from vision to word: "Und was ich sah, das Heilige sei mein Wort." ("And what I saw, the holy would be my word" *or* "And let what I saw, the holy, be my word.")[20] This translation from the phenomenal to the linguistic—this becoming (of) language—is a key moment of mediation as the poet's song veils the divine message for the benefit of the people, the *Volk*:

Doch uns gebührt es, unter Gottes Gewittern,
Ihr Dichter! mit entblößtem Haupt zu stehen
Des Vaters Stral, ihn selbst, mit eigner Hand
Zu fassen und dem Volk ins Lied
Gehüllt die himmlische Gaabe zu reichen.

(II, 119–20)

[And hence it is that without danger now
The sons of earth drink heavenly fire.
Yet, fellow poets, us it behooves to stand
Bare-headed beneath God's thunderstorms,
To grasp the Father's ray, no less, with our own hands
And, veiling in song the heavenly gift,
To offer it to the people.]

The gift of the divine message is mediated by the prophet and thus already "veiled" ("gehüllt"), before it is perhaps further veiled in its translation for the people at large. The prophetic song that will institute the future community is not necessarily a prediction of a future inexorably to come about. All the closing verses make clear is that the song is one of warning:

Ich sei genaht, die Himmlischen zu schauen,
Sie selbst, sie werfen mich tief unter den Lebenden,
Den falschen Priester, ins Dunkel, daß ich
Das warnende Lied den Gelehrigen singe.
Dort   (II, 120)

[That I approached to see the Heavenly,
And they themselves cast me down, deep down
Below the living, into the dark cast down
The false priest that I am, to sing,
For those who are learned, the warning song.
There]

There is something paradigmatic here about the poem ending with the word "there," and not just because so much of what survives by Hölderlin is fragmentary. The poem insistently points to something beyond itself, yet it is in principle productive of whatever is beyond it, because it is itself the privileged site of mediation between the gods and the mortals.[21] References to the poet as mediator of the divine word are myriad throughout Hölderlin's writing, from the early poems to the late, where they are enveloped virtually in a theory of mediation. Many such invocations are simply conventional and unproblematic, as in the early ode "Buonaparte," in which poets are figured as "holy vessels" ("heilige Gefäße") or in the frequent metonymic identification of the poet with the lyre, or *Saitenspiel*: The poet's instrument works as a figure for the poet *as* instrument. Yet the relation between the poet and the gods can assume much more complex configurations, even in a modest poem such as *"Der Blinde Sänger"* ("The

Blind Singer"). The text is primarily elegiac in tone, lamenting a past of youth and light that has given way to a present of darkness and despair. The poem explores the familiar paradox of blind vision, inherited from the lore and the facts surrounding poets like Homer and Milton. The absence of literal vision throws all the more emphasis on sound and voice, placing the prophetic burden squarely on the poet's word and his responsiveness to the divine language that envelops it. The poet summons a certain strength from the memory of brighter days and then transforms this metalepsis into prolepsis, looking forward to the advent of a savior and liberator. Yet the figuration of the poet's relation to that god perplexes any simple notion of the poet as mere receptacle of the divine word:

> Ihm nach, ihr meine Saiten! es lebt mit ihm
> > Mein Lied und wie die Quelle dem Strome folgt,
> > > Wohin er denkt, so muß ich fort und
> > > > Folge dem Sicheren auf der Irrbahn.
>
> > > > > (II, 55)

> [My strings! With him, with him does my poem live,
> > And as the source must follow the river's course,
> > > Where his thought goes I'm drawn, impelled to
> > > > Follow the sure one through devious orbits.]

It is possible to translate *Quelle* as stream, as Michael Hamburger does, which would mark the poet as a small stream compared to the grand river of the god. But given the massive importance Hölderlin attaches elsewhere to the word *Quelle* as source or origin, it is difficult to avoid hearing some such resonance here. In this sense, Hölderlin's bold conceit would align the poet with the source of the river—so often for him the figure for the movement of history—and the god with its subsequent course. What could this mean for the poet to be, analogically, the "source" of the god? Such a configuration reverses the commonplace notion of the gods as "source" of the poet's inspiration and consequently places an even greater burden on the poem (and the poet) as a "conduit" of revelation, of the song that produces "the work of gods and humans," ("der Götter und Menschen Werk, der Gesang, damit er beiden zeuge"), as it is phrased in "Wie wenn am Feiertage." Hölderlin's figure moves both ways, positing, in its ambiguity, a dialectical relation between the poet and his god, where one might have expected something far more asymmetrical.[22]

One of the passages elided above in the brief discussion of "Wie

Wenn am Feiertage" invokes the mythical figure of Dionysus, a presiding deity for much of Hölderlin's prophetic poetry. It is Dionysus who dominates the mythological framework for Hölderlin's most explicit mediation on the poetic calling in his ode "Dichterberuf" ("The Poet's Vocation"):

> Des Ganges Ufer hörten des Freudengotts
>   Triumph, als allerobernd vom Indus her
>   Der junge Bacchus kam, mit heilgem
>   Weine vom Schlafe die Völker wekend.
>   (II, 46)

> [The banks of the Ganges heard the triumph
>   Of the God of Joy, when all-conquering
>   From Indus the young Bacchus came, rousing
>   The peoples from sleep with holy wine.]

Rather than staging a scene of inspiration, as in "Wie wenn am Feiertage," "Dichterberuf" tells a story of its unfolding, recalling the progress of poetry from its Oriental origins—and for Hölderlin Greece, strikingly, belongs to the "Orient" as much or more than to the "West"—to its present moment of crisis. In this itinerary of poetic genius, the prophets occupy a prominent position:

> Und darum hast du, Dichter! des Orients
>   Propheten und den Griechengesang und
>   Neulich die Donner gehört, damit du
>
> Den Geist zu Diensten brauchst und die Gegenwart
>   Des Guten übereilst, in Spott, und den Albernen
>   Verläugnest, herzlos, und zum Spiele
>   Feil, wie gefangenes Wild, ihn treibest?
>   (II, 47)

> [And poet, was it for that you heard the
>   Orient's prophets and Grecian song, and
>   lately the thunder, to make
>
> A trade of the Spirit and anticipate its
>   Beneficent presence, in mockery, and heartless,
>   deny the simple-minded and drive it about, like a captured
>   beast exhibited to the vulgar for a fee?]

The great exemplars of inspired "writing" from antiquity—Biblical prophets and Greek poets—are summoned as a reproach to the poets of the present. Hölderlin's invocation, in a single breath, of Classical and Biblical authors is representative of a pervasive habit of mind. Hölderlin and his friends and classmates at the Tübingen *Stift*, Hegel and Schelling, are famous for having more or less communally called for "a new mythology," a synthetic discourse that would resolve the tensions between the not necessarily compatible languages of philosophy, religion, poetry, and more.[23] In Hölderlin's case, one aspect of this new mythology was a syncretic rewriting of old mythologies, principally the Judeo-Christian and the Hellenic. The tendency to juxtapose the two traditions is visible from Hölderlin's earliest extended work, his master's dissertation at Tübingen, which literally "compared the literature" in the Proverbs of Solomon and in Hesiod's *Works and Days*. More significantly, the major elegies and hymns perform stunning rereadings of the two great rival mythologies, Hellenic and Judeo-Christian, and in the process radically transform the status of both. In "Brod und Wein" ("Bread and Wine"), the figures of Christ and Dionysus, through a deft disposition of common images as well as a strategic withholding of proper names, merge into a single unnamed deity: "der kommende Gott" ("the god who is coming"). This god—who is always a god to come—has no particular name. Hölderlin's paradoxical program is even more pointed in the hymn "Der Einzige" ("The Unique One"), where the subject of the poem, Jesus Christ, is called the brother of Herakles and Dionysus. This is to say: the unique one is not unique, the single one not simply singular. Hölderlin and a good many of his contemporaries—not just Schelling and Hegel but also Friedrich Schlegel—understood German literature and philosophy to be particularly well positioned, indeed called on, to draft this new mythology, even when its content was not markedly German. The new mythology was to be cosmopolitan and, at its limit, universal.

~

To this point in my study I have concentrated primarily on prophetic discourse in the Biblical tradition, but for Hölderlin and his generation of German writers, ancient Greek culture was often as much or more of a force for the imagination. Indeed, the phenomenon has even been described as "the tyranny of Greece over Germany," so pervasive was the impact of Greek culture on late eighteenth- and early nineteenth-century art and letters in the German-speaking world.[24] It would come as no surprise, then, if the prophetic strain of German poetry were decidedly indebted to, and engaged in reworking, the classical oracle.

A good deal of Hölderlin's poetry takes place under the sign of the oracle, or its absence. Like Milton, Hölderlin is haunted by the silencing of the ancient oracles. The poet laments in "Der Archipelagus" ("The Archipelago"):

> Daß ich spähe nach Rath, und lang schon reden
>   sie nimmer
> Trost den Bedürftigen zu, die prophetischen Haine
>   Dodonas,
> Stumm ist der delphische Gott . . .   (II, 110)

> [That I look for guidance, and long now they've
>   ceased to speak word of
> Comfort to men in such need, the prophetic groves
>   of Dodona
> Mute is the Delphian God . . .]

A similar concern is voiced in these insistent, anaphoric lines from "Brod und Wein":

> Aber wo die Thronen, wo? Die Tempel, und wo die Gefäße
>   Wo mit Nectar gefüllt, Göttern zu Lust der Gesang?
> Wo, wo leuchten sie denn, die fernhintreffenden Sprüche?
>   Delphi schlummert und wo tönet das große Geschick?
>   (II, 92)

> [But the thrones, where are they? Where are the temples, the vessels
>   Where, to delight the gods, brim-full with nectar, the songs?
>   Where, then, where do they shine. The oracles winged for far targets?
>   Delphi's asleep, and where now is the great fate to be heard?]

As often in Hölderlin, the repetitive questioning calls attention to an absence. It is in the void left by the silenced oracles that Hölderlin's poems resonate. Hölderlin is acutely aware of the chasm between his culture and that of ancient Greece: The oracle was formerly a powerful force, even a matter of life and death. In his "Remarks on *Oedipus*" Hölderlin analyzes the hero's error, which he specifies, surprisingly, as not so much having killed his father and married his mother but having "interpreted the oracle too infinitely" ("den Orakelspruch zu unendlich deutet")! Oedipus's fate is sealed by an error in oracular interpretation rather than, say, in any crime he committed, a failure of reading rather than an unethical act, conscious or unconscious. The hero who would eventually blind himself was guilty of having, in Hölderlin's memorable phrase, "one eye too many."

Hölderlin left no extended commentary on the status of the oracle but some sense of what his like-minded contemporaries would have thought can be gleaned from Hegel's rather straightforward discussion of the oracle in his *Aesthetics*. Hegel begins simply by recalling the bare outlines of what would have been more or less common knowledge:

> The signs through which the gods revealed themselves were for the most part quite simple: at Dodona the rustling and soughing of the sacred oak, the murmur of the spring, and the tone of the brazen vessel which resounded in the wind. So, too, at Delos the laurel rustled, and at Delphi, too, the wind on the brazen tripod was a decisive factor. But apart from the immediate natural sounds, man himself is also the voice of the oracle when he is stupefied and stimulated out of his alert and intelligent presence of mind into a natural state of enthusiasm . . . [25]

Though Hegel considers the oracle under the rubric of classical *art*, it speaks, initially, with the voice of nature, as it were: The simple signs of the oracle consist of nothing but natural sounds.[26] And even when a human being acts as a medium for the oracle, he or she is "naturalized," no longer in a sober state of reason—the faculty normally definitive of man in general—but overwhelmed in a state of natural inspiration (*Naturzustande der Besonnenheit*). Yet the natural signs are merely external: By themselves they could hardly account for the lofty status of the oracle:

> But there is still another aspect in the external signs [*Zeichen*]. For in the oracles the god is indeed apprehended as the one who *knows*, and to Apollo, therefore, the god of knowledge, the most famous oracle [that is, the one at Delphi] is dedicated; yet the form in which he declares his will remains something natural and completely vague, a natural voice or word-sounds without any connection. In this obscurity of form the spiritual content is itself dark and therefore needs *clarification* [*Erklärung*] and *explanation* [*Deutung*]. The pronouncement of the god is submitted at first purely in the form of something natural. But although the explanation makes the inquirer aware of it in a spiritualized form, it nevertheless remains obscure and ambiguous. (I, 457)

Though it is clear from Hegel's description how an oracle might partake of what Hölderlin calls "göttlichschöne Natur" ("divinely beautiful nature"), Apollo's knowledge appears here only in the mode of a natural voice, an unarticulated resounding of words. These words without connection render the spiritual content of the oracle obscure, thus necessitating that interpretation become an integral part of the oracle—a supplement in the strong sense. The oracular message demands clarification or explanation (*Erklärung*) but it too remains obscure, precisely what a "clarification" is not supposed to be. The paradoxical task the oracle sets can be formulated, following Hegel, as "Undeutlichkeit deuten"—which might be freely translated as "to interpret the uninterpretable." At any rate, it resists interpretation. The oracle, for Hegel, is typically *zweideutig* or *doppelsinning*, literally ambiguous in the strict sense of being capable of *two* interpretations, as was the case with some of the legendary oracles from Delphi.[27] Yet it would not surprise Hölderlin, for one, that the oracle could be more than simply ambiguous in Hegel's strict sense.

It is not only the modern interpreter who encounters such ambiguity, as if somehow it were just or mainly the product of the immense historical and the considerable linguistic distance between Hegel's Germany and ancient Greece. Plutarch, himself one of the very last oracular "officers," could write this summary statement from his vantage point in late antiquity:

. . . inasmuch as the god employs mortal men to assist him and declare his will, whom it is his duty to care for and protect, so that they shall not lose their lives at the hands of wicked men while ministering to a god, he is not willing to keep the truth unrevealed, but he causes the manifestation of it to be deflected, like a ray of light, in the medium of poetry, where it submits to many reflections and undergoes subdivisions, and thus he did away with its repellent harshness. There were naturally some things it was well that despots should fail to understand and enemies should not learn beforehand. About these, therefore, he put a cloak of intimations and ambiguities (*amphilogias*) which concealed the communication so far as others were concerned, but did not escape those that had no need to know and who gave their minds to the matter.[28]

At once clear and obscure, intelligible and illegible, the oracle, for Plutarch, finds its most appropriate medium in poetry—and partly for political reasons. It is not just the medium or form that conceals and reveals: The spiritual content remains obscure. Heraclitus was perhaps the first to speak of the oracle in terms of signs (*semainei*).[29] Hegel, too, would consider the oracle and classical art in general under the rubric of the sign, or *Zeichen*, rather than of the symbol, insofar as he distinguishes classical art from symbolic or romantic art. Yet many of the characteristics of the symbol, understood in the structural rather than the historical sense, overlap with those of the oracle. When in the *Aesthetics* Hegel describes the symbol in general, he claims that it remains "according to its own concept essentially *ambiguous* [*zweideutig*]." He continues:

In the first place, the look of a symbol as such raises at once the doubt whether a shape is to be taken as a symbol or not, even if we set aside the further ambiguity in respect of the *specific* meanings which a shape is supposed to signify amongst the *several* meanings for which it can often be used as a symbol through associations of a more remote kind. (I, 306)

Not only is a symbol ambiguous in its very essence, a certain degree of ambiguity persists for the reader, viewer, or listener as to whether what appears to be a symbol should be taken as such or not. Moreover, Hegel's determination of how the ambiguity can be dissipated is rather restricted: "Such dubiety disappears only when each of the two sides [of the symbol], the meaning and its shape, are expressly named and thereby their relation is enunciated at once" (I, 306). Explicit naming of the relation between meaning and form marks only such genres as the parable and so is hardly representative of artworks in general. Although all art, for Hegel, is symbolic in the sense that it is defined by the "concrete interpenetration of meaning and shape" ("das konkrete Ineinander von Bedeutung und Gestalt") (I, 304), most art is also haunted by its aspect as sign, and some arts more than others. No art stands under the sign of the sign more than poetry does. On the status of poetry in relation to the rest of the arts Hegel maintains:

Architecture cannot so subordinate the sensuous material to the spiritual content as to be able to form that material into an adequate shape of the spirit: Poetry, on the other hand, goes so far in its negative treatment of its sensuous material that it reduces the opposite of heavy spatial matter, namely sound, to a meaningless sign (*bedeutungloses Zeichen*) instead of making it, as architecture makes its material, into a meaningful symbol (*andeutender Symbol*). But in this way poetry destroys the fusion of spiritual inwardness with external existence to an extent that begins to be incompatible with the original conception of art, with the result that poetry runs the risk of losing itself in a transition from the region of sense into that of the spirit. (II, 968)

One is always taught that poetry loses something in translation. Hegel's point is more radical: Poetry risks losing *itself* in transition, the transition from sense to spirit. All poetry is poetry in motion, so to speak—but not necessarily in a fortuitous way. (Hölderlin, as we shall see, shares something of this sense of poetry as essentially an art of transition, of *Übergang*.) Poetry's instability as art is tied to its status as sign and not symbol; in the domain of the sign there is no necessary or motivated relation between signifier and signified. Poetry, as the art of the word, is thoroughly given over to the sign rather than the symbol. And so the oracle, as a preeminent discourse of the sign, may come to seem less a special case of (the ambiguity of) poetry in general than something like its (ancient) paradigm. For Hegel, no less than Plutarch, the ambiguity of the oracle is best suited to the structurally ambiguous discourse of poetry, a discourse of truth, to be sure, even of the absolute, but not yet in a form finally adequate to the truth.[30]

The legacy of the classical oracle is not merely a topic that appears now and again in Hölderlin's poetry, not just "background" material to be invoked to explain this or that passage. In the words of one of his shrewdest critics, Max Kommerell:

. . . the gods come or go, turn themselves toward or away from [mortals], they make signs or threaten, and the course of light, times of day, times of year, thunder and all those gestures in which Hölderlin perceives the total life revealed for him, all this becomes an oracle, an augury, a sign, whether an event that prefigures, brings to completion or reaches perfection, something whose deciphering falls to the poet. Thus the poem of the poet is, through and through, the second word, the response to the word spoken by god.[31]

The oracle, then, informs the very character of Hölderlin's verse: its rhythms, its tonalities, its axiomatic phrasing. But we shall see that Hölderlin's textual heritage is divided between the Hellenic and the Hebraic and that his invocation of the Delphic and other Greek oracles does not take place, strikingly, to the exclusion of the Biblical prophets.

In the records of the Hebrew prophets, two of the most prominent genres are the oracle to one's nation and the oracle to foreign nations: Often the "anthologies" that we know as the books of the prophets group these oracles together, regardless of the sequence of their composition or the sequence of the events to which they refer. In Hölderlin's late work especially, the nation or the people is the predominant social matrix within which and for whom his prophetic discourse is spelled out. It is not as if Hölderlin simply mimes the oracular utterances of the Biblical prophets, but he does often and conspicuously address his poems to the nation or the fatherland in ways that more than faintly echo his Biblical predecessors.

But what nation is this? Wieland had written in the *Teutsche Merkur* during the 1780s that, properly speaking, there was no such thing as the German nation, and certainly that was still the case as Hölderlin wrote around the turn of the century.[32] "Deutschland" had from the start something of a phantasmatic, fictional character, though the consequences attendant to these fictions were undeniably real. Even as late as Nietzsche's *Ecce Homo*, "Germany" is still pictured as an imaginary entity, well after its official founding as a nation-state. This means, among other things, that the nation is very much a thing of the future, as much something to come as something actual. Germany, for Hölderlin, is only and always on the verge of being Germany.

In Hölderlin's day the nonexistence of "Germany" could be ascribed primarily to the condition of *Kleinstaaterei*, the division of some phantom, unified Germany into a huge number of small states, each with distinct governmental apparatuses, social protocols, and often dialects not easily intelligible to other "Germans."[33] "Germany," then, could not really be represented or, paradoxically, could be so only as a "representation," a representation of something unrepresentable. In his magisterial study of *Nations and Nationalisms* Eric Hobsbawm invokes exactly this notion of representing the unrepresentable as a necessary but impossible predicament of the modern nation in general—and the nation is nothing if not modern.[34] What is more, this predicament seems even more, or more peculiarly, pertinent to Germany than to a good many other nations.

How then does the nation figure in Hölderlin's poetry and thought? We could begin by turning to the relatively simple ode "An die Deutschen" ("To the Germans"), which presents an oracle to such a nonexistent nation, a distant descendant of the Hebrew oracle now set out in classical metrical form. Its very status as a poetic address to the German nation is complicated, however, by the existence of a later companion poem entitled "Rousseau": The two call out to be read together and indeed can be understood as different versions of the same poem.

"An die Deutschen" begins with a (self-)reproach to the Germans, with their poverty in deeds imbalanced by an abundance of thoughts. But the poet looks forward, in the mode of a question, to a future articulation of thought and deed:

> Aber kommt, wie der Stral aus dem Gewölke kommt,
> Aus Gedanken vielleicht, geistig und reif die That?
>   Folgt die Frucht, wie des Haines
>   Dunklem Blatte, der stillen Schrift?   (II, 9)

> [But as lightning from clouds, out of mere thoughts perhaps
> Will the deed in the end, lucid, mature, leap out?
>   As from dark orchard leaves, from
>   Quiet scripts does the fruit ensue?]

The passage figures, albeit in the mode of a question, the movement from thought to deed as a natural process. The single word *Blatt,* meaning either *leaf* or *sheet of paper*—the ambiguity applies equally in German or English—prepares the way for the speculative translation from the organic to the linguistic. The event or act anticipated in the poem is the approach of the god, but the god is still absent: The act foregrounded is the "thought" of the poem itself. In this sense, the poem answers its own question about the relation of thought and deed in the affirmative. But the affirmation of the prophet is still the affirmation of an absence, underscored in the middle stanzas of the ode by the apostrophe to the "spirit of the people" ("Genius des Volks"). How does this spirit appear? The poet asks "Wann erscheinest du ganz, Seele des Vaterlands?" ("When will you appear completely, soul of the fatherland?"), and the question is never answered one way or another. The implication, here and elsewhere, is that such a spirit appears somehow, but never as such, never as a totality. The temporality of the people and the fatherland resists such representation because no figure or image could claim to gather together their essence. A few stanzas later, in a passage to be reworked in "Rousseau," we read:

> Wohl ist eng begränzt unsere Lebenszeit
> Unserer Jahre Zahl sehen und zählen wir,
>   Doch die Jahre der Völker,
>   Sah ein sterbliches Auge sie?   (II, 10)

> [True, the span of our life briefly extends; we can
> See and count the few years granted to us on earth,
>   But the years of the peoples,
>   These, what mortal man's eye has seen?]

Here, too, the emphasis is on how the history of a people surpasses representation: the nation as sublime "object." No mortal, the rhetorical question implies, has ever seen the "years of the peoples." Only the seer apostrophized in the final stanzas can possibly see over "his own time" to grasp the immense sweep of the people's history. But there is an emptiness, too, even in the prophet's vision:

> Und die Künftigen auch, sie die Verheißenen
>> Wo, wo siehest du sie, daß du an Freundeshand
>>> Einmal wieder erwarmest,
>>>> Einer Seele vernehmlich seist?
>
> Klanglos,   ists in der Halle längst,
>> Armer Seher! bei dir, sehnend verlischt dein Aug
>>> Und du schlummerst hinunter
>>>> Ohne Namen und unbeweint.   (II, 10–11)

> [And those others to come, those for whose advent we wait,
>> Where, o where can you see them, that once more you'll be
>>> Warmed by one hand that's friendly
>>>> Audible to one living soul?
>
> Without resonance,   long empty for you it's been
>> In your hall, poor seer, now; yearning your eye grows dim,
>>> And you drowse away, vanish
>>>> Never noticed, unnamed, unwept.]

Even for the seer, capable of perceiving the future and the promised ones, the total vision of the people is fleeting, and his message seems to find no audience. (Once again, the insistent, anaphoric questions signal a desire and an absence more than a prelude to an answer.) The shadowy seer addressed in "An die Deutschen" has no name, but he acquires one in the companion poem written in its wake. It is a very strange name for a German: Jean-Jacques Rousseau.

The opening strophes of "Rousseau" reconfigure passages from "An die Deutschen" with Rousseau now identified as the prophet who can see beyond his own time, the one who names the promised ones, even if his message too does not find its desired resonance. In the earlier poem, the seer was distinguished from the mortals by his ability to see the years of the peoples. Here, too, Rousseau is something other than mortal. In the great "Rhein" hymn, Rousseau is unexpectedly associated with the demigods, who are, technically, those born from a god and a mortal. In the ode bearing his name, Rousseau is more eerily cast among the unburied, *die Unbegrabenen*, living an afterlife as a ghost who will not go away. The fatherland is haunted by this voice from beyond the grave, a ghost of the past who is also, almost by definition, a ghost of the future.

Rousseau appears above all as a figure of historical totality and as a mediator between the gods and the mortals:

> Vernommen hast du sie, verstanden die Sprache der Fremdlinge,
>   Gedeutet ihre Seele! Dem Sehnenden war
>   Der Wink genug, und Winke sind
>   Von Alters her die Sprache der Götter.
>
> Und wunderbar, als hätte von Anbeginn
>   Des Menschen Geist das Werden und Wirken all,
>   Des Lebens Weise schon erfahren
>
> Kennt er im ersten Zeichen Volendetes schon,
>   Und fliegt, der kühne Geist, wie Adler den
>   Gewittern, weissagend seinen
>   Kommenden Göttern voraus.   (II, 15)
>
> [You've heard and comprehended the strangers' tongue,
>   Interpreted their soul! For the yearning man
>   The hint sufficed, because in hints from
>   Time immemorial the gods have spoken.
>
> And marvelous, as though from the very first
>   The human mind had known all that grows and moves,
>   Foreknown life's melody and rhythm,
>
> In the first signs he can measure the whole;
>   And flies, bold spirit, flies as the eagles do
>   Ahead of thunderstorms, preceding
>   Gods, his own gods, to announce their coming.]

Rousseau is cast here not as a foreigner but rather as the one who has understood the foreigners (including perhaps the Germans). Like the eagle that will appear so often in Hölderlin as the vehicle of superhuman sight, Rousseau is conspicuous for his view of the entire trajectory of humanity, especially as thought through the history of its peoples. But the oddest thing is that in this later ode Rousseau now occupies the position of the soul of the fatherland. This means, in effect, that Rousseau is something of a German, an ideal German even, one who has glimpsed and, in a way, embodies the proper destiny of Germany and Germans.

The later, complex poems of Hölderlin take up the question of the fatherland with a marked intensity. A whole group of poems typical of the late period is commonly referred to as the "Vaterländische Gesänge," songs of the fatherland. The term derives from Hölderlin's remarks on Sophocles and coincides also with a claim in a late letter where the poet refers to a new kind of text that will engage "the fatherland or time" (VI.1, 435). One of the many extraordinary things about these late poems is that these two terms, fatherland and time, will amount virtually to the same thing, or at least be inextricable, the one from the other. I now turn to an extended reading of one the poems where this imbrication is most spectacularly at work.

GERMANIEN

   Nicht sie, die Seeligen, die erschienen sind,
Die Götterbilder in dem alten Lande,
Sie darf ich ja nicht rufen mehr, wenn aber
Ihr heimatlichen Wasser! jetzt mit euch
Des Herzens Liebe klagt, was will es anders,
Das Heiligtrauernde? Denn voll Erwartung liegt
Das Land und als in heißen Tagen
Herabgesenkt, umschattet heut
Ihr Sehnenden! uns ahnungsvoll ein Himmel.
Voll ist er von Verheißungen und scheint
Mir drohend auch, doch will ich bei ihm bleiben,
Und rückwärts soll die Seele mir nicht fliehn
Zu euch, Vergangene! die zu lieb mir sind.
Denn euer schönes Angesicht zu sehn,
Als wärs, wie sonst, ich fürcht' es, tödlich ists,
Und kaum erlaubt, Gestorbene zu weken.

   Entflohene Götter! auch ihr, ihr gegenwärtigen, damals
Wahrhaftiger, ihr hattet eure Zeiten!
Nichts läugnen will ich hier und nichts erbitten.
Denn wenn es aus ist, und der Tag erloschen
Wohl trifft den Priester erst, doch liebend folgt
Der Tempel und das Bild ihn auch und seine Sitte
Zum dunkeln Land und keines mag noch scheinen.
Nur als von Grabesflammen, ziehet dann
Ein goldner Rauch, die Sage drob hinüber,
Und dämmert jezt uns Zweifelnden um das Haupt,
Und keiner weiß, wie ihm geschieht. Er fühlt
Die Schatten derer, so gewesen sind,
Die Alten, so die Erde neubesuchen.
Denn die da kommen sollen, drängen uns,

Und länger säumt von Göttermenschen
Die heilige Schaar micht mehr im blauen Himmel.

Schon grünet ja, im Vorspiel rauherer Zeit
Für sie erzogen das Feld, bereitet ist die Gaabe
Zum Opfermahl und Thal und Ströme sind
Weitoffen um prophetische Berge,
Daß schauen mag bis in den Orient
Der Mann und ihn von dort der Wandlungen viele bewegen.
Vom Aether aber fällt
Das treue Bild und Göttersprüche reegnen
Unzählbare vom ihm, und es tönt im innersten Haine.
Und der Adler, der vom Indus kömmt,
Und über des Parnassos
Beschneite Gipfel fliegt, hoch über den Opferhügeln
Italias, und frohe Beute sucht
Dem Vater auch, nicht wie sonst, geübter im Fluge
Der Alte, jauchzend überschwingt er
Zulezt die Alpen und sieht die vielgearteten Länder.

Die Priesterin, die stillste Tochter Gottes,
Sie, die zu gern in tiefer Einfalt schweigt,
Sie suchet er, die offnen Auges schaute,
Als wüßte sie es nicht, jüngst, da ein Sturm
Todtdrohend über ihrem Haupt ertönte;
Es ahnete das Kind ein Besseres,
Und endlich ward ein Staunen weit im Himmel
Weil Eines groß an Glauben, wie sie selbst,
Die seegnende, die Machte der Höhe sei;
Drum sandten sie den Boten, der, sie schnell erkennend,
Denkt lächelnd so: Dich, unzerbrechliche, muß
Ein ander Wort erprüfen und ruft es laut,
Der Jugendliche, nach Germania schauend:
"Du bist es, auserwählt,
Allliebend, und ein schweres Glük
Bist du zu tragen stark geworden,

Seit damals, da im Walde verstekt und blühendem Mohn
Voll süßen Schlummers, trunkene, meiner du
Nicht achtetest, lang, ehe noch auch geringere fühlten
Der Jungfrau Stolz und staunten weß du wärst und woher,
Doch du es selbst nicht wußtest. Ich miskannte dich nicht,
Und heimlich, da du träumtest, ließ ich
Am Mittag scheidend dir ein Freundeszeichen,

Die Blume des Mundes zurük und du redetest einsam.
Doch Fülle der goldenen Worte sandest du auch
Glükseelige! mit den Strömen und sie quillen unerschöpflich
In die Gegenden all. Denn fast, wie die heiligen,
Die Mutter ist von allem,
Die Verborgene sonst genannt von Menschen,
So ist von Lieben und Leiden
Und voll von Ahnungen dir
Und voll von Frieden der Busen.

   O trinke Morgenlüfte,
Biß das du offen bist,
Und nenne, was vor Augen dir ist,
Nicht länger darf Geheimnis mehr
Das Ungesprochene bleiben,
Nachdem es lange verhüllt ist;
Denn Sterblichen geziemet die Schaam,
Und so zu reden die meiste Zeit,
Ist weise auch von Göttern.
Wo aber überflüßiger, denn lautere Quellen
Das Gold und ernst geworden ist der Zorn an dem Himmel,
Muß zwischen Tag und Nacht
Einsmals ein Wahres erscheinen.
Dreifach umschreibe du es,
Doch ungesprochen auch, wie es da ist,
Unschuldige, muß es bleiben.

   O nenne Tochter du der heiligen Erd'
Einmal die Mutter. Es rauschen die Wasser am Fels
Und Wetter im Wald und bei dem Nahmen derselben
Tönt auf aus alter Zeit Vergangengöttliches wieder.
Wie anders ists! und rechthin glänzt und spricht
Zukünftiges auch erfreulich aus den Fernen.
Doch in der Mitte der Zeit
Lebt ruhig mit geweihter
Jungfräulicher Erde der Aether
Und gerne, zur Erinnerung, sind
Die unbedürftigen sie
Gastfreundlich bei den unbedürftigen
Bei deinen Feiertagen
Germania, wo du Priesterin bist
Und wehrlos Rath giebst rings
Den Königen und den Völkern.   (II, 149–52)

~

[Not them, the blessed, who once appeared
Those images of gods in the ancient land,
Them, it is true, I may not now invoke, but if,
You waters of my homeland, now with you
The love of my heart laments, what else does it want, in
Its hallowed sadness? For full of expectation lies
The country, and as though it had been lowered
In sultry dog-days, on us a heaven today,
You yearning rivers, casts prophetic shade.
With promises it is fraught, and to me
Seems threatening too, yet I will stay with it,
And backward now my soul shall not escape
To you, the vanished, whom I love too much.
To look upon your beautiful brows, as though
They were unchanged, I am afraid, for deadly
And scarcely permitted it is to awaken the dead.

    Gods who are fled! And you also, present still,
But once more real, you had your time, your ages!
No, nothing here I'll deny and ask no favors.
For when it's over, and day's light gone out,
The priest is the first to be struck, but lovingly
The temple and the image and the cult
Follow him down into darkness, and none of them may shine.
Only as from a funeral pyre henceforth
A golden smoke, the legend of it, drifts
And glimmers on around our doubting heads
And no one knows what's happening to him. He feels
The shadowy shapes of those who once were here,
The ancients, newly visiting the earth.
For those who are to come now jostle us,
Nor longer will that holy host of beings
Divinely human linger in azure Heaven.

    Already, in the prelude of a rougher age
Raised up for them, the field grows green, prepared
Are offerings for the votive feast and valley
And rivers lie wide open round prophetic mountains,
So that into the very Orient
A man may look and thence be moved by many transformations.
But down from Aether falls

The faithful image, and words of gods rain down
Innumerable from it, and the innermost grove resounds.
And the eagle that comes from the Indus
And flies over the snow-covered peaks of
Parnassus, high above the votive hills
Of Italy, and seeks glad booty for
The Father, not as he used to, more practiced in flight,
That ancient one, exultant, over the Alps
Wings on at last and sees the diverse countries.

   The priestess, her, the quietest daughter of God,
Too fond of keeping silent in deep ingenuousness,
Her now he seeks, who open-eyed looked up
As though she did not know it, lately when a storm,
Threatening death, rang out above her head;
A better destiny the child divined,
And in the end amazement spread in heaven
Because one being was as great in faith
As they themselves, the blessing powers on high;
Therefore they sent the messenger, who, quick to recognize her,
Smilingly thus reflects: you the unbreakable
A different word must try, and then proclaims,
The youthful, looking towards Germania:
"Yes, it is you, elected
All-loving and to bear
A burdensome good fortune have grown strong,

   Since, hidden in the woods and flowering poppies
Filled with sweet drowsiness, you, drunken, did not heed
Me for a long time, before lesser ones even felt
The virgin's pride, and marveled whose you are and where from,
But you yourself did not know. Yet I did not misjudge you
And secretly, while you dreamed, at noon,
Departing I left a token of friendship,
The flower of the mouth behind, and lonely you spoke.
Yet you, the greatly blessed, with the rivers too
Dispatched a wealth of golden words, and they well unceasing
Into all regions now. For almost as is the holy
The Mother of all things, upholder of the abyss,
Whom men at other times call the Concealed,
Now full of loves and sorrows
And full of presentiments
And full of peace is your bosom.

O drink the morning breezes
Until you are opened up
And name what you see before you;
No longer now the unspoken
May remain a mystery
Though long it has been veiled;
For shame behooves us mortals
And most of the time to speak thus
Of gods indeed is wise.
But where more superabundant than purest wellsprings
The gold has become and the anger in Heaven earnest,
For once between day and night must
A truth appear.
Now threefold circumscribe it,
Yet unuttered also, just as you found it,
Innocent virgin, must it remain.

Once only, daughter of holy Earth,
Pronounce your Mother's name. The waters roar on the rock
And thunderstorms in the wood, and at their name
Divine things past ring out from time immemorial.
How all is changed! And to the right there gleam
And speak things yet to come, joy-giving, from the distance.
Yet at the center of time
In peace with hallowed,
With virginal Earth lives Aether
And gladly, for remembrance, they
The never-needy dwell
Hospitably amid your holidays,
Germania, where you are priestess and
Defenseless proffer all round
Advice to the kings and the peoples.

The appearance of truth, the future of the nation, the character of
the gods, the task of the poet: The stakes in this poem could hardly be
greater. Yet the avoidance of this major hymn, "Germanien," has been almost total in Hölderlin criticism since World War II. By stark contrast,
the prestige of the poem was far greater in the first decades following the
"discovery" of Hölderlin by the George school and others. The reasons for
this subsequent neglect are remarkably simple. A cursory reading of the
poem—but only a cursory one—can yield the picture of Hölderlin prof-
fering a protofascist or aggressively nationalist vision of "Germania," a

chosen nation whose future preeminence is prophesied as something desirable. It is no wonder that an uneasy silence enveloped the poem in the post-World War II era.

Yet in the period before World War II, the status of "Germanien" within the Hölderlin canon was utterly different. A rousing 1914 address entitled "Hölderlin und die Deutschen" by his first great editor, Norbert von Hellingrath, culminated simply by citing the poem in full, almost as if its (patriotic) sense were self-evident. Heidegger devoted an entire lecture course to "Germanien" and "Der Rhein" in the winter semester of 1934–35, giving equal weight and more than a literal priority to "Germanien," a judgment that would seem perverse by the standards of postwar criticism. Finally, in Friedrich Beißner's selection of Hölderlin's work for the Nazi troops, the poetry section—which did not even include poems such as the masterpiece "Patmos"—closed with nothing other than "Germanien."[35] The sharp historical divide in the reception of the poem suggests how massively factors other than aesthetic judgment were at work in determining the place of "Germanien" in the Hölderlin canon. One way back into the poem can proceed via a reading of its prophetic character, to which I now turn.

As much as any of Hölderlin's works, "Germanien" is inscribed in the traditions of prophetic and oracular discourse, though the precise character of its relation to those traditions has eluded numerous commentators. Put briefly, it has been read primarily as a thoroughly "Greek" poem, whereas I would argue it evinces the syncretic mythopoeic strategies peculiar to Hölderlin's radical blending of Classical and Judeo-Christian tradition. The reference in the opening lines to "the old country" ("in dem alten Lande") is glossed by Friedrich Beißner and Jochen Schmidt as Greece, and yet the only Greek place mentioned in the poem is Parnassus and that as only a single place in the eagle's trajectory from India to Greece to Italy to Germany. In other poems, such as "Brod und Wein," refraining from explicitly naming a character or place is often part of a strategy that deliberately refuses specificity so as to suggest some more general, even universal, mythic entity. Neither Christ nor Dionysus needs to be named and the resistance to naming allows precisely for their identification. Yet a critic like Korff does not hesitate to identify the eagle in "Germanien" simply as Zeus's bird. The eagle is indeed associated with the supreme Greek deity, especially as a vehicle for auguries and oracles, as in *The Odyssey*. Eagles loomed large at the site of the Delphic oracle and in the Homeric epics:

Their movements could be read as auguries of human history. But no Greek eagle comes close to providing a precedent for the most remarkable feature of Hölderlin's eagle: its ability to speak. Speaking eagles do emerge, however, in the mainstream of Christian poetry, as in Dante's *Paradiso* and Chaucer's *House of Fame*. In post-Biblical tradition, the eagle is associated with John the Evangelist—who in Hölderlin's time was still considered identical with the author of Revelation and thus metonymically with the word of God. In Luther's Bible, on which Hölderlin was raised, the woodcut that prefaces the Gospel of John in some editions features an eagle at his side, with both perched on a mountain plateau looking up to God in the clouds of heaven. Neither simply Classical nor Christian, Hölderlin's eagle is both at once.

Still another instance of Hölderlin's mythical syncretism is legible in the scene of the poem's prophesying:

> . . . und Thal und Ströme sind
> Weitoffen um prophetische Berge,
> Daß schauen mag bis in den Orient
> Der Mann und ihn von dort der Wandlungen viele bewegen.

> [. . . and valley
> And rivers lie wide open round prophetic mountains,
> So that into the very Orient
> A man may look and thence be moved by many transformations.]

These mountains, too, could well be the oracular sites of Greece, such as the most famous at Delphi.[36] This identification would be doubly appropriate, since many of the temples are, in Vincent Scully's punning phrase, "oriented toward the east,"[37] to the source of light, always identified by Hegel with the divine. Yet in the Bible, no less than in Greek history or legend, mountains are a prominent locus of prophecy, a physical symbol of proximity to the divine. The historical books record gatherings of prophets at Mount Carmel (1 Kings 18.20), and mountains are often the scenes of prophetic vision, as for Moses or for St. John's vision of the New Jerusalem. Ezekiel is even instructed to prophesy *to* the mountains of Israel (36.1), because the addressees of the prophetic word encompass no less than nature itself. Moreover, the importance of looking to the Orient from Hölderlin's prophetic mountains accords well with the eschatological traditions that would locate the origin of the Second Coming in the East, as is intimated even in the Gospels. Like Herder's before him, Hölderlin's disposition is to foreground the identities between Hebrew prophecy and Greek oracle, not their differences. Hölderlin was about as far away as possible from seeing the Hebraic and the Hellenic as opposed principles, even if (and partly because) the Hebraic culture he knew was heavily filtered through the prism of Christianity and its Greek-inflected languages.

The most conspicuous hallmark of prophetic discourse, its sine qua non, is the representation of one's words as originating in a divine source, hence the importance in "Germanien" of the eagle as a messenger of the divine. The poem's opening stanzas set the scene for the extraordinary speech by the eagle, a speech that is not only a prophecy but simultaneously a virtual philosophy of prophecy or a prolegomenon to it: an allegory of prophecy, not unlike Wordsworth's dream of the Arab.[38] The eagle has been sent to educate Germania in the prophetic office for which she has been singled out. A radical change in her language is effected by the eagle's visitation:

> . . . Ich miskannte dich nicht
> Und heimlich, da du träumtest, ließ ich
> Am Mittag scheidend dir ein Freundeszeichen,
> Die Blume des Mundes zurük und du redetest einsam.
> Doch Fülle der goldenen Worte sandtest du auch
> Glükseelige! mit den Strömen und sie quillen unerschöpflich
> In die Gegenden all.
>
> [. . . Yet I did not misjudge you
> And secretly, while you dreamed, at noon,
> Departing I left a token of friendship,
> The flower of the mouth behind, and lonely you spoke.
> Yet you, the greatly blessed, with the rivers too
> Dispatched a wealth of golden words, and they well unceasing
> Into all regions now.]

The flower of language left by the eagle is not just a "language of flowers," no mere rhetoric of adornment. Germania's words are not simply her own; in the metaphoric logic of the passage, they are "implanted" by a messenger of the gods. The divine afflatus effects a spectacular transformation, readable in the transition from the individual to the universal, from the one to the all. The priestess's simplicity and solitude ("in tiefer *Ein*falt," "*ein*sam") give way to her being the source of a universal presence, flowing into every place ("in die Gegenden all"). What is simple—the one fold, the *Einfalt*—unfolds. And the vehicle of the transformation is "the golden word," gold still associated here with the divine word yet no longer in its shadowy, insubstantial form as the misty vapor of the divine sagas.

The hymn opens with the poet caught in the apparently paradigmatic Hölderlinian dilemma, suspended between past and future epochs of divine presence. All that remains of the former presence is a golden vapor, identified as the saga of the departed gods. The poet now classes himself among the doubting ones, "uns Zweifelnden," but he looks toward heaven for the true image or figure ("das treue Bild") that descends from the aether radiating sayings of the gods. The poet, already assuming a prophetic posture, comes to sacrifice his voice to that of the eagle, the messenger of the gods. The eagle's task is to awaken Germania to the enormity and difficulty of her calling. Within the speech of the eagle, the central, oracular injunction to Germania presents what can be called the moment of truth, for the poem certainly, and perhaps for poetry, period:

> O trinke Morgenlüfte
> Biss daß du offen bist,
> Und nenne, was vor Augen dir ist,
> Nicht länger darf Geheimniß mehr
> Das Ungesprochene bleiben,
> Nachdem es lange verhüllt ist;
> Denn Sterblichen geziemet die Schaam,
> Und so zu reden die meiste Zeit,
> Ist weise auch von Göttern.
> Wo aber überflüßiger, denn lautere Quellen
> Das Gold und ernst geworden ist der Zorn an dem Himmel
> Muß zwischen Tag und Nacht
> Einsmals ein Wahres erscheinen.
> Dreifach umschreibe du es,
> Doch ungesprochen auch, wie es da ist,
> Unschuldige, muß es bleiben.

> [O drink the morning breezes
> Until you are opened up
> And name what you see before you;
> No longer now the unspoken
> May remain a mystery
> Though long it has been veiled;
> For shame behooves us mortals

And most of the time to speak thus
Of gods indeed is wise.
But where more superabundant than purest wellsprings
The gold has become and the anger in Heaven earnest,
For once between day and night must
A truth appear.
Now threefold circumscribe it,
Yet unuttered also, just as you found it,
Innocent virgin, let it remain.]

The passage seems to move from a recognition of the concealment of truth as secret (*Geheimnis*) to the certain prediction of that truth's revelation. What was once a veiled discourse of mortals and/or gods seems about to be replaced by the language of Germania, who simply has to name what is before her eyes for truth to appear. The eagle's message to Germania appears to predict unequivocally the future revelation of "truth"—or what is perhaps not exactly the same thing, the one thing that is true, *ein Wahres*. Yet the very terms of the prophecy complicate the message profoundly.

Much of the interpretation of this "moment of truth" turns on the word *erscheinen* or its cognates and thus on the mode of truth's appearance *as* appearance. The first instance occurs in the poem's opening lines:

Nicht sie, die Seeligen, die erschienen sind,
Die Götterbilder in dem alten Lande,
Sie darf ich ja nicht rufen mehr . . .

[Not them, the blessed, who once appeared,
Those images of gods in the ancient land,
Them, it is true, I may not now invoke . . .]

The initial appearance of the gods is distinctly mediated: They appeared not as themselves but as figures, *Götterbilder*. The emphasis on the poet's former practice or ability of invoking (*rufen*) the images of the gods suggests that their presence was verbal rather than visual. But now they can no longer respond to the poet's call, as if in a dialogue.

The next instance of the word "scheint" follows closely on the use of "erscheinen":

Denn voll Erwartung liegt
Das Land und als in heißen Tagen
Herabgesenkt, umschattet heut
Ihr Sehnenden! uns ahnungsvoll ein Himmel.

Voll ist er von Verheißungen und scheint
Mir drohend auch, doch will ich bei ihm bleiben,
Und rückwärts soll die Seele mir nicht fliehn
Zu euch, Vergangene! die zu lieb mir sind.

[For full of expectation lies
The country, and as though it had been lowered
In sultry dog-days, on us a heaven today,
You yearning rivers, casts prophetic shade.
With promises it is fraught, and to me
Seems threatening too, yet I will stay with it,
And backward now my soul shall not escape
To you, the vanished, whom I love too much]

Heaven is said to "seem" or perhaps to "shine" in a threatening way, though this is precisely at a moment of marked plenitude: The country is full of expectation, and the sky is—or we are—full of presentiment ("ahnungsvoll" may refer equally to "Himmel" or to "uns").[39] The word "voll" (*full*) appears three times in the space of six lines, but what sort of plenitude is this? Presentiments and promises are signs of a certain absence: A heaven full of promises is not a heaven of promises fulfilled. It is no wonder that this vision of threefold plenitude, a linguistic more than a literal vision, is not entirely reassuring to the poet.

Still another instance of "scheinen" occurs in a related context:

Denn wenn es aus ist, und der Tag erloschen
Wohl trifts den Priester erst, doch liebend folgt
Der Tempel und das Bild ihm auch und seine Sitte
Zum dunklen Land und keines mag noch scheinen.

[For when it's over, and day's light gone out,
The priest is the first to be struck, but lovingly
The temple and the image and the cult
Follow him down into darkness, and none of them may shine.]

It may seem as if there is no antecedent for the "es" of the first clause since the passage is cited out of context. Yet even in its full context there is no clear antecedent for the pronoun, although it most likely refers to the now absent light of the day. The very obscurity of the formulation virtually reflects its own content, since it is precisely about the absence of "shining," of any luminous presence in the wake of the departed gods. The lines immediately following, however, do admit a certain light, or half–light:

Nur als von Grabesflammen, ziehet dann
Ein goldner Rauch, die Sage drob hinüber,
Und dämmert jezt uns Zweifelnden um das Haupt,
Und keiner weiß, wie ihm geschieht.

[Only as from a funeral pyre henceforth
A golden smoke, the legend of it, drifts
And glimmers on around our doubting heads
And no one knows what's happening to him.]

The saga of the absent gods is a sign of their former presence, but it appears only in the twilight, or *Dämmerung,* like the twilight (*Zwielicht*) in the opening stanzas of "Patmos." Its attribute of gold may function as a sign of its authenticity or truth; yet "golden" modifies only the mist, the *Rauch,* which figures the text of the departed gods as something shadowy and insubstantial. The poetic persona shifts here significantly from the singular "I" to the collective "we," to a community of readers characterized as doubting ones (*Zweifelnden*) as they—and perhaps we—are faced with the dubious task of reading the saga of the gods.

The semantic resonances of "scheinen" and "erscheinen" are rather ominous, then, by the time the poem reaches the spectacular moment of truth's appearance:

Wo aber überflüssiger, denn lautere Quellen
Das Gold und ernst geworden ist der Zorn an dem Himmel,
Muß zwischen Tag und Nacht
Einsmals ein Wahres erscheinen.

[But where more superabundant than purest wellsprings
The gold has become and the anger in Heaven earnest,
For once between day and night must
A truth appear.]

In contrast to the truth that had remained secret, the eagle's speech now looks forward to the necessary appearance of truth, a doubly singular truth ("einsmals ein Wahres") around which all is to be circumscribed. The importance in Hölderlin's poem of the one, apparently momentous, truth seems clear, but one must note that even this grammar of singularity is ambiguous. For the "one" of "ein Wahres" could refer to a unique appearance of the one (necessary) truth *or* to the appearance of one truth among others: *a* truth. One cannot, on the basis of the grammar of the passage, distinguish between "a" truth (one among others) or the "one" truth (one to the exclusion of others). Precisely at the moment of truth, when a decision is required, it is impossible to decide on the identity of the "truth" in question. One should note also the difficulty in translating "ein Wahres" as "one truth" or "a truth," because "Wahres" is not simply identical to "Wahrheit." "Wahres" could be glossed as "one thing that is true," whereas "eine Wahrheit" would be more likely rendered as "one truth" or "a truth." The difference is potentially crucial in terms of language, since "Wahres" need not be linguistic, whereas "Wahrheit" tends—but not necessarily—to be already of the order of language, as in the truth of a proposition. One could easily be tempted to translate or paraphrase "ein Wahres" as "das Wahre," which even Heidegger does in passing in his commentary, although the two phrases are not the same. In any event, the character of this truth remains to be seen.

Hölderlin's thematization in "Germanien" of the necessity of truth's appearance is virtually philosophical in formulation, much like the "abstract" pronouncement in "Mnemosyne": "Es ereignet sich aber das Wahre . . . " ("But the true emerges . . . "). The one, unique truth emerges as something like the Logos—if there can be anything "like" the Logos—and indeed Hölderlin's formulation anticipates Hegel's and Schelling's phrasings when they invoke the appearance of Christ.[40] Witness Hegel, for example: "[the unity of man with God] must also be present for the sensuous imagining consciousness, it must become an object for the world, it must appear [sie muß erscheinen], and indeed in the sensuous form of the spirit, which is the human. Christ appeared [Christus ist erschienen]."[41] When Hegel continues this line of thinking, his formulation is even closer to Hölderlin: "Proper to the appearance of the Christian God is the fact that it is singular [einzig] for its type: It can happen only once [einmal]."[42] The phrasing of the pronouncement of truth's appearance—"[Es] . . . muß zwischen Tag und Nacht/Einsmals ein Wahres erscheinen"—also has much in common with famous formulations of the essence of the aesthetic and the poetic among Hölderlin's Idealist contemporaries, many his friends and associates.[43] One thinks, for example, of Schiller's determination of art as "freedom in its appearance" ("Freiheit in der Erscheinung") or of Hegel's perhaps apocryphal but massively influential definition of the beautiful as "the sensuous appearance of the idea" ("das sinnliche Scheinen der Idee") or of Schelling's formula for the poetic, "the absolute viewed in its appearance" ("das Absolute angeschaut in der Erscheinung"). If these determinations of the aesthetic, which always includes the poetic that is sometimes its model, are indeed analogous to Hölderlin's statement, then "Germanien" not only participates in an aesthetic or poetic mode but is equally a reflection on it, in ways that remain to be read.

Hölderlin's formulation of the necessary appearance of truth thus appears proximate to various key Idealist dicta on the character of religion (at least in the guise of Christ, the Logos), art, and philosophy proper. The "confusion," if that is the word for it, between these discourses, indeed a shuttling back and forth between art, religion, and philosophy, is typical or, one might say, symptomatic of Idealist discourse. "Resolutions" to this confusion or fusion vary from one thinker to the next—from Hegel's positing, in the *Phenomenology* and *Encyclopedia* and elsewhere, of philosophy as the discourse to which the otherwise absolute discourses of art and religion tend, to Schelling's proposal of art as the mediating term in the culminating movement of his *System of Transcendental Idealism*.[44] In practice and often even in principle, these realms are not simply distinct. In the excursus that follows, with an eye ultimately on Hölderlin, whom we leave suspended at the moment of the truth (of suspension), I will highlight what is at stake especially in the rhetoric of religion among his philosophical contemporaries. The reader anxious not to be left hanging here could vault over this excursus and get straight to the (moment of) truth.

Excursus on Revelations, Representation, and Religion in the Age of German Idealism

Here I open an immense parenthesis of sorts, to situate Hölderlin's articulation of appearance, truth, and revelation in relation to the most pertinent thinking of his time. To read Hölderlin's contemporaries on this topic—such as Fichte, Schelling, Hegel, Niethammer, and their prime precursor, Kant—is of considerable intrinsic interest, but it should also help us to understand one key context of Hölderlin's writing and to gauge the specificity of his interventions.

We have just seen how Hölderlin's formulation at the charged "moment of truth" in "Germanien" parallels certain Idealist characterizations of the essence of the aesthetic. In acknowledging the necessity of representation, these formulae might seem also to lend themselves to an articulation with Idealist thought on language. Yet if one turns to the major Idealists looking for extended reflections on the nature or function of language one comes up short. Kant's entire corpus contains only a few pages with any detailed attention to language, sign systems, or rhetoric, such as the appropriate sections—paragraphs, really—of the *Anthropology* and *The Critique of Judgment*. Even for Kant's sometimes admiring contemporaries, Herder and Hamann, the absence of a philosophy of language was seen as a major lacuna in the critical philosophy, a charge still alive in Walter Benjamin's early engagement with the neo-Kantian movement of the early twentieth century.[45] Fichte wrote only a single essay on language; Schelling made only scattered remarks on the subject; and even Hegel, despite occasional far-reaching reflections such as that on the "speculative proposition" in the "Preface" of the *Phenomenology*, considers language in any systematic way only in a few brief sections of the *Encyclopedia*, as a circumscribed subsection in the psychology of subjective spirit.[46] Grand claims are made by Hegel for language, that it is "the most perfect expression of spirit," and so forth, but there is no analysis of language commensurate with those claims, almost as if the claims got Hegel off the hook of confronting the matter of language in any detail.

Yet, in another way, the question of language and representation is ubiquitous in idealism, from writings on logic to philosophy of religion. Indeed, nowhere is the matter of representation and, more specifically, textuality engaged in more sustained fashion than in texts about religion and revelation. Hegel, for one, took *Vorstellung*, or representation, as the primary category through which to think religion—indeed, all religion was an affair of representation. Kant's critical philosophy had created a crisis for the thinking of religion in the Germany of his time. By positing the subjective character of knowledge, however transcendentally structured, Kant sent shock waves through the institutions that fostered or had fostered religious and theological discourse. The *Critique of Pure Reason* may have been perfectly respectful about God in the abstract and have left "room" for faith, as the phrase went, but that room seemed to many to have had the ground taken out from under it. Moreover, clarifying what was to fill that room was not the highest priority on Kant's agenda. When Hölderlin, Hegel, and Schelling were theology students at the Tübingen Stift, their intellectual world could fairly be said to have been waiting for Kant's explicit and extended meditation on religion. It was not immediately forthcoming.

It was in this charged atmosphere that an extraordinary text appeared, the *Versuch einer Kritik aller Offenbarung* (*Attempt at a Critique of All Revelation*), published in 1792 without any author's name affixed.[47] The Kantian vocabulary and the dry, exacting style of the text, and the fact that it issued from Kant's publisher, prompted any number of intellectuals, including some steeped in Kant's critical philosophy, to pronounce it the work of the master. After all, censorship considerations—which would plague Kant, Fichte, and others throughout the 1790s—might well have prompted the "sage of Königsberg" to refrain from publishing under his own name. Yet the author was soon revealed as none other than the young Fichte, who had received even something of Kant's "blessing" on the latter's at least partial reading of the manuscript, after which he recommended the younger (unpublished) philosopher's text to be brought out with Kant's own publisher.[48]

What did Fichte argue there? The basic project was to enquire, in Kantian critical fashion, into the conditions of possibility of revelation. Fichte claims at the outset to not be concerned with the content of any given revelation, in keeping with his purely critical project. Much as Kant would proceed in his *Religion Within the Limits of Pure Reason Alone*, published only a year or so after Fichte's text, morality, the domain of what Kant calls practical reason, is the starting point (and indeed the end point) of the reflection. Morality, for Fichte, must begin in and with the self. If the primal moral attitude is respect, its principal modality is self-respect, which entails submission to "the necessary primacy of the law" (49). Although Fichte here anticipates somewhat his later, signature thematization of the absolute I as the ground for the empirical I, the deference to a law "outside" the self is remarkable. Yet this will be thought, rather as Kant did of judgments of the beautiful in his contemporaneous *Critique of Judgment*, in terms of a universally subjective validity. It is reason, with a voice of its own, that "dictates" the law, freely and spontaneously. Although subjective, insofar as exercised by any individual, reason is universally valid insofar as it accords exactly with God's law. Where does one turn to discover this divine law? Not to the Bible, *the* text of revealed religion for so many of Fichte's (overwhelmingly Christian) contemporaries, but to the self-generated discourse of practical reason, which posits a maxim such as this regarding the sacrifice of life for duty: "He who, on the contrary, did not sacrifice his life when required of him by the law is unworthy of life and must lose it as appearance, if the moral law is to be valid also for the world of appearances, in accordance with the causality of the law" (57). To this Fichte adds, tellingly, in a *footnote*: "What a strange coincidence! He who loves his life will lose it, but he who loses it will keep it for eternal life, said Jesus, which says precisely as much as the above." That is to say, the Biblical text, graphically subordinated, is noteworthy for its coincidence (*Zusammentreffen*) with the law derived independently from reason. The Bible is not the source of our moral reason, not even its necessary codification: It *happens* to coincide with it. And by no means all of what is written in the Bible will accord so harmoniously with the dictates of practical reason.

Fichte proclaims: "In God *only* the moral law prevails" (60), a notion that will help sustain the circularity of the relation between morality and divinity on which Fichte's criteria for revelation are based. If Fichte starts to sound heretical here, he does hasten to assure us that the practical reason of the self is itself given by God: We "recognize the law of reason as the law of God" (70). And yet Fichte will acknowledge that "the idea of God, as lawgiver, through the moral law in us, is . . . based on an alienation of what is ours, on translating something subjective into a being outside us; and thus this alienation is the real *principle of religion*, insofar as it is to be used in determining the will" (73). This is, in effect, an etiological version of the primacy of the self's practical reason, its principles of morality, over the text of the Bible or of any other actual or possible revealed religion. One can see why Fichte—picturing God the lawgiver as a translation of something proper to the self—encountered opposition from ordinary educated believers, to say nothing of the censors. Yet somehow or other he and his publisher eventually managed to evade the censure of the censors on the text's anonymous publication.

Fichte's project seems animated by the dream of a pure language of practical reason, of morality operating by the sheer force of reason. Like a good deal of philosophy in the Western tradition, the need to have thought represented in a concrete form, in a given language, a given syntax, proves something of an embarrassment or a scandal in the sense of *scandalon*, an obstacle on what Kant imagined at the outset of *The Critique of Pure Reason* as "the sure path of science" ("der sichere Weg der Wissenschaft"). In the devaluation of the sensible from Plato onward, the realm of representation—as the concretization of thought—is something to be transcended or overcome, left behind without remainder. But no religion, says Fichte, is completely free "from sensibility *in concreto*" (80), clearly indicating that sensibility is something from which one would want to be free. Sensibility emerges as something of a necessary evil for religion, especially (as in Plato) regarding the education of children. Even if all revelation must be revelation "of the infinite spirit" (85) that revelation is bound to something decidedly less than infinite, to representation *in concreto*. The cruder the sensibility, the greater the need for representation. Education is substantially an education beyond representation. All this is the consequence of our "fallen" condition, such that religion—whose goal is to teach or to inculcate morality—must indulge in images and figures, stories and fables, where we unfortunately risk getting "carried away by sensuous attraction" (116). It is good, Fichte states categorically, "to suppress sensibility" (138) in the interests of our freedom.

In keeping with his commitment to the primacy of morality, Fichte argues that revelation is not substantially a matter of the revelation of God's essence as the content of any knowledge, nor is it a matter of political lawgiving, as one might conceive the Mosaic dispensation to be (although Fichte gives no examples of what he has in mind here). Here Fichte strikingly echoes and anticipates the argument that so many Jewish thinkers from Moses Mendelssohn to Levinas have maintained is characteristic of the Judaic religion: that it is a question of law not truth—not revelation in the sense of a true account of divine or historical states of affairs. Thus, anything like Biblical accounts of threatened punishment, promises, and rewards could not possibly be of the order of divine revelation. (125). Almost needless to say, that would exclude a good deal of what counts as Hebraic prophecy.[49]

To summarize a long argument somewhat brutally, Fichte contends that since the end of religion is morality, a pure morality of reason proclaimed through self-consciousness, then revelation is, strictly speaking, superfluous. The only way to justify it is for the purposes of educating people of insufficiently developed sensibilities in order that they might transcend, precisely, sensibility. Revelation is not necessary, and in any event it cannot be proven to be of necessarily divine origin, neither a priori nor a posteriori. It is a discourse of inspiration and imagination, of the concrete and the sensible, that has to be kept in its (im)proper place.

The spectre of imagination and representation haunts not only Fichte's thinking on religion. But before turning to Kant, we might glance at one striking passage from Fichte's *The Vocation of Man*:

There is nothing abiding, neither outside me, nor in me, rather only a ceaseless change. I know of no being, not even of my own. There is no being.—*I myself* know absolutely nothing, and am not.—*Images* exist; they are the only things which exist and they know of them themselves according to the way of images—images which sway past us; which through images depend on images, images without anything reflected in them, without meaning and purpose. I myself am one of these images; indeed, I am myself not this, rather only a confused image of images.—All reality transforms itself into a wonderful dream, without a life, of which is dreamt, and without a spirit who dreams it; . . . [50]

This passage hardly represents the only official position of Fichte's philosophy. It is only one moment in a dialogue between the "I" (who is speaking here) and "the spirit" ("Der Geist") toward the end of an extended conversation, although "Spirit" comments after this passage that the "I" has understood things well. Yet it is telling as a heightened version of the concern about figuration, of a figuration divorced from a stable notion of being—indeed a suspension or even erasure of being—that permeates a good deal of Idealist philosophy and that surfaces in the deep suspicion of texts and inscriptions as repositories of truth. [51]

~

When Kant finally published in book form his long-awaited major statement on religion, *Religion Within the Limits of Reason Alone*, his focus was rather different from Fichte's. His principal concern was the nature of good and evil, especially "radical evil." Yet in the course of his exposition he encounters many of the same issues as Fichte and addresses them in much the same spirit. For Kant, too, morality is the starting point and the end point of religion. "Religion" is not coterminous with much that is usually considered religion: The great "religions" of world history are, in Kant's strict terms, "faiths." Moreover, they are historical faiths to the extent that the content of those faiths is specific to a given culture, language, or race—whatever their understandable and sometimes admirable claims to universality might be. (Yet Kant, for one reason or another, will say that "of all the public religions which have ever existed the Christian alone is moral."[52] Religion is a matter of morality, pure and simple, a morality dictated by reason and reason alone. Much of what counts as the stuff of religion—works of grace, miracles, mysteries—is really only *parerga*, matters bordering on religion but not properly belonging to it. It is not as if reason categorically dismisses these supplements, these *parerga*, but they cannot contribute to the substance of its maxims. Kant has a somewhat less dim view of these supplements to reason than does Fichte, but for him, too, they must be kept in their proper place, the realm of the improper.

What then is the status of Scripture for Kant, the sacred text of the only moral "religion"? Kant's way had been prepared by Eichhorn, Herder, and company, such that he readily thought of the Bible in terms of stories and allegories rather than as the text of a religion in a language commensurate with reason and morality. Speaking of the Bible's way of presenting the conflict between good and evil, Kant writes:

Once this vivid mode of representation, which was in its time the only *popular* one, is divested of its mystical veil, it is easy to see that, for practical purposes, its spirit and rational meaning have been valid and binding for the whole world and for all time, since to each man it lies so near at hand that he knows his duty towards it. (78)

Not only is Scripture seen here as having encoded an utterly universal principle of morality, it is incumbent on us to search the Scriptures:

An attempt such as the present, moreover, to discover in Scripture that sense which harmonizes with the *most holy* teachings of reason is not only allowable but must be deemed a duty. And we can remind ourselves of what the *wise* Teacher said to His disciples regarding someone who went his own way, by which, however, he was bound eventually to arrive at the same goal: "Forbid him not; for he that is not against us is for us."

Note that Jesus is quoted here, from the Gospel of Mark, not as Jesus, much less Christ, but as "the wise teacher." He is quoted in the course of an argument underscoring the recognition of a duty to read Scripture. But how exactly should one read? Kant confronts, more directly than Fichte, the status of the text in religion and in faith(s) in a passage worth quoting at length:

A holy book arouses the greatest respect even among those (indeed, most of all among those) who do not read it, or at least those who can form no coherent religious concept therefrom; and the most sophistical reasoning avails nothing in the face of the decisive assertion, which beats down every objection: *Thus it is written.* It is for this reason that passages in it which are to lay down an article of faith are called simply *texts.* The appointed expositors of such a scripture are themselves, by virtue of their occupation, like unto consecrated persons; and history proves that it has never been possible to destroy a faith grounded in scripture. Even with the most devastating revolutions in the state, whereas the faith established upon tradition and ancient public observances has promptly met its downfall when the state was overthrown. How fortunate, when such a book, fallen into men's hands, contains, along with its statutes, or laws of faith, the purest moral doctrine of religion in its completeness—a doctrine which can be brought into perfect harmony with such statutes ([which serve] as vehicles for its introduction). In this event, both because of the end thereby to be attained and because of the difficulty of rendering intelligible according to natural laws the origin of such enlightenment of the human race as it proceeds from it, such a book can command an esteem like that accorded to revelation. (98)

It should be clear from this rich and complex passage that, quite apart from the perspicacity of the historical argument about the survival of scripture-based faiths, Kant is suspicious of the authority ascribed to scripture by virtue of its textual character, its "writtenness." The simple claim "it is written" is so often taken as if it were proof of divinity. This would be to "fetishize"—as Werner Hamacher has analyzed the problematic in Hegel, Kant, and their contemporaries—the text proper over its content, which ideally, as the religion of pure morality dictated by reason, need not be encoded in anything like scripture or indeed in a text of any kind.[53] When Kant comments on how "fortunate" it is that such a book, such a scripture, should contain the "purest moral doctrine of religion," mainstream Christian theology can take only small comfort in the coincidence, since priority is granted to the self-generated discourse of morality rather than to divine revelation, if it be that. This is the theoretical correlative of Fichte's notation of the "strange coincidence" between a dictate of reason and a Biblical passage as cited above.

Thus the hermeneutics of Scripture proceeds with the dictates of practical reason, of morality, in mind and reads everything accordingly. As Kant says:

. . . the theoretical part of ecclesiastical faith cannot interest us morally if it does not conduce to the performance of all human duties as divine commands (that which constitutes the essence of all religion). Frequently this interpretation may, in the light of the text (of the revelation) appear forced—it may often really be forced; and yet if the text can possibly support it, it must be preferred to a literal interpretation which either contains nothing at all [helpful] to morality or else actually works counter to moral incentives. (100–01)

Kant goes on to explain in a note that the principles guiding interpretation, even admitted and sanctioned interpretative violence, are those of his own self-subsisting moral principles. His insistence on the performance of morality, of active obedience to the law, reiterates Fichte's concern. Earlier I suggested a somewhat unexpected coincidence between Fichte's insistence and a certain strain in Judaic thought, from Mendelssohn to Levinas, on the centrality of law and obedience in Judaism, as opposed to a principle of truth or revelation more characteristic of Christianity (even if the emphasis varies from one strain to the next). This same "neo-Judaic" spirit informs Kant, and yet Kant "must," partly in keeping with the almost official anti-Semitism of the high German Christianity of the 1790s, go out of his way to distance his proposed morality and obedience to the law from that of Judaism.[54] Thus he has recourse to the *canard* that the Jews' obedience to divine law is thoroughly "external," mere "outer observance" (116), even if he might plausibly argue that divine commands take precedence over self-generated moral principles in Judaic religious law. Yet the fact that Kant authorizes a sometimes violent, nonliteral reading of Scripture aligns him with Jesus himself (a Christian but also a Jew), or with Paul (a Christian but also a "radical Jew"), even if from another vantage point he is arguably quoting scripture against scripture, perhaps as Satan famously did.

In all this Kant wants to resist religion's being bound to the text, to textuality, to what might be a sheer supplement to reason. Reason should need no supplement whatsoever. So if there is to be writing, it should be what is "written in the heart," as the Biblical notion goes (Christian *and* Judaic): a writing without writing. This only returns us to the question of language at a different and even more inscrutable level. It is not a problem that has simply been left behind in Kant's day. As Derrida has written:

Now if, today, the "question of religion" actually appears in a new and different light, if there is an unprecedented resurgence, both global and planetary, of this ageless thing, then what is at stake is language, certainly—and more precisely the idiom, literality, writing, that forms the element of all revelation and of all *belief*, an element that is ultimately irreducible and untranslatable—but an idiom that above all is inseparable from the social nexus, from the political, familial, ethnic, communitarian nexus, from the nation and from the people: from autocthony, blood and soil, and from the ever more problematic relation to citizenship and to the state.[55]

Derrida succinctly stresses both the centrality of language and its inextricable position in an institutional nexus. Language is never just a matter of language. Much of what Derrida diagnoses as pertinent to the question of religion "now" was already the case in the vexed political situation of Immanuel Kant in relation to the German and Prussian authorities of the 1790s. Far from being an ivory-tower affair of the armchair philosopher or the theologian, Kant's religious writings were subject to state censorship and taken so seriously that Friedrich Wilhelm II personally wrote to Kant to reprimand him for the affront to what the ruler understood as Christian and Biblical orthodoxy. He singled out Kant's *Religion Within the Limits of Pure Reason Alone* as the prime offender. (Fichte would face even more dogged institutional and governmental opposition in the long drawn out "Atheismus-Streit," although atheism was arguably one of the farthest things from Fichte's mind.) Kant would return, however, to many of the same issues and in exactly the same spirit in his later series of essays finally collected under the title *The Conflict of the Faculties* (*Der Streit der Facultäten*).

Kant's later text moves within and between the faculties of the university, rather as his thought had previously operated with the faculties of the mind. The prime concern is the relation of the faculty of philosophy to those of theology, law, and medicine, the most vexed being the relation to theology. As a question of jurisdiction, it is clearly related to the constraints of censorship under which he labored. Kant returns to the status of the Bible and separates categorically the domains of the Biblical theologian and the philosophical theologian, radically circumscribing the domain of the former. The Biblical theologian has, for example, no authority to ascribe a nonliteral meaning to any Biblical passage, which effectively suspends the whole immense realm of spiritual or allegorical interpretation that should, from Kant's vantage point, be directed to practical morality.[56] (Nonliteral reading is arguably a hermeneutic imperative espoused vigorously by the Bible itself, most emphatically in the letters of Paul.) The demands of what Kant values as "inner rational religion" require jettisoning a good deal of what is contained in the Bible. It turns out, predictably, that the domain of the philosophical theologian encompasses what should be the province of all religion, namely moral reason.[57]

Although Kant makes some grand concessions about Christianity—calling it "the idea of religion" and, to that extent, "natural" (77)—he seems to take away with one hand what he gave with the other, at least if

Christianity is conceived as a religion of the book, as a scripture-based faith. The key passage reads:

The Bible contains within itself a credential of its (moral) divinity that is sufficient for practical purposes—the influence that, as the text of a systematic doctrine of faith, it has always exercised on the hearts of men, both in catechetical instruction and in preaching. This is sufficient reason for preserving it, not only as the organ of universal inner rational religion but also as the legacy (new testament) of a statutory doctrine of faith which will serve us indefinitely as a guiding line. It matters little that scholars who investigate its origin theoretically and historically and study its historical content critically may find it more or less wanting in proofs from a theoretical point of view. The *divinity* of its moral content adequately compensates reason for the *humanity* of its historical narrative which, like an old parchment that is illegible in places, has to be made intelligible by adjustment and conjectures consistent with the whole. And the divinity of its moral content justifies this statement: that the Bible deserves to be kept, put to moral use, and assigned to religion as its guide *just as if it is a divine revelation.* (117–19).

The final phrase, emphasized typographically in the original, could hardly be reassuring to the Prussian censors. *As if*? The Bible *as if* it were a divine revelation? (One recalls that Kant had already staked out, in the *Critique of Judgment*, the realm of the "as if" as that of the aesthetic.) For purposes of moral religion, one should proceed as if the Bible were a divine revelation, which is to say, it may well not be. There is a gap between the humanity of the text and the divinity of its content—and the gap must be filled by reason operating independently. We are to be guided in our interpretation by our sense of the Bible as a whole, but that whole is not even whole. It is an old parchment, illegible in places. And parchment, after all.

Moral reason, of itself, requires no parchment, no text, no human story, however divine the content might be. The worth of the Bible turns out to be "practical" but in an almost banally empirical way. Historically, one can show—Kant maintains—that Christianity has proven its effectiveness in inculcating moral religion. So rather like sensibility in general—the whole realm of what we "learn through the senses"—Christianity may aid in our education. None of it, however, is necessary for morality to function as it should. "The God Who speaks through our own (morally practical) reason," Kant insists, "is an infallible interpreter of His words in the Scriptures, Whom everyone can understand" (123). It is clear in any number of formulations that in assessing the divinity of revelation, reason is the judge and the criterion, which again makes one wonder about the necessity for revelation, if reason is just encountering what it in some sense already knows of its own accord.[58] When it comes to a conflict between the sensible and the supersensible (the telos of education), the sensible, Kant says baldly, "is *nothing*" (105). And yet this nothing, stubbornly, remains.

~

When the young Schelling, a *Wunderkind* if there ever was one, studied at the Tübingen *Stift* during the early years of the French Revolution, with his friends Hegel and Hölderlin, the intellectual agenda was determined in large measure by the thought of Immanuel Kant. Like a number of his adventurous colleagues, he bristled at many of the institution's constraints, although he stopped short of calling it, as one of his classmates did, a "prison."[59] But the years at the *Stift* were very formative and allowed him some occasion to work out his emergent position in relation to the intellectual orthodoxies of the day and to the compelling agenda of how to think after the critical program of Kant was now complete and now that the French Revolution had thrown so very many things into question. The most immediate task at hand within the parameters of the institution was to puzzle through issues of theology and Biblical criticism. Schelling's main written products were his two dissertations, one on of the origins of evil (*de malorum origine*), substantially a reading of Genesis 3, and another on the letters of Paul and the Marcion heresy. For our purposes it is noteworthy how frequently in the dissertations he invokes the texts of Herder and Eichhorn: He was steeped in and sympathetic to those works where his predecessors worked out the hermeneutics of myth, applied to the Bible and to ancient texts especially.[60] In his reading of Genesis he returns to the crucial instance of the myth of the Fall and to the Kantian problematic of radical evil that would preoccupy him at various moments in his intellectual itinerary, such as the "Freedom" essay of 1809. In his major paper on Paul he came to terms with the difficulties negotiating the vagaries of a textual tradition, where so much is at stake in determining what is genuine, what is original, and what is not.[61] Yet it is probably in his first major essay not written for the *Stift*, "On Myths," that Schelling lays out his ideas most freely. There he treats myths as "philosophemes," as inscriptions and encryptions of philosophical truths (155), although not in the form of philosophy. The philosophemes are presented or represented historically (*his-*

torisch dargestellt), which is to say, among other things, as stories. The earliest myths, indeed myths proper, proceed from an ancient *oral* culture, and their "darks signs" ("dunkle Zeichen") (202) have to be read with an awareness of their prehistoric formation: It calls for nothing less than a gift of "divination" to be able to interpret their dark signs appropriately (219). The most ancient cultures we know of derive from the "childhood" of humanity when the faculty of imagination dominated. Like Vico, Warburton, and others before him, Schelling maintains that the available terms of discourse were "figurative" or "improper" ("uneigentlich"). (We should recall, however, and Schelling underscores this, that because discourse is essentially and thoroughly figurative, it cannot yet be poetic "in the strictest sense" [205]). Poetry would depend on the play between figure and nonfigure and so is not yet possible. Nonetheless this originary discourse of pure figure points the way to, indeed already contains, philosophical truth. But it needs to be deciphered, to be translated into the language of philosophy, even if Schelling will sometimes and elsewhere posit the superiority of art or myth to philosophy itself.[62]

With the advent of writing, the introduction of "the dead, cold language of script," everything changes (201). Myth gives way to history proper and to something like philosophy, although not necessarily in the most fortuitous way. The sea change to writing marks a great advance, as it would to Hegel's mind, but brings with it a problem that persists up to and indeed is exacerbated in Schelling's time: the fetishization of the letter. "Fetishization" is not Schelling's word, but he echoes Moses Mendelssohn's contempt for *Buchstabenmenschen*, "letter-men" (not necessarily to be confused with men of letters!), those who grant an undue attention to the letter at the expense of spirit. Schelling implies that this mentality of letters gets in the way of our understanding the ancient oral culture of myth:

Oral philosophy is more fiery, richer, more vital, whereas by contrast already the use of writing accustoms man to a colder, more unwavering, more forcible scrutiny, the former talks one into things more, the latter persuades more, the former is more amusing, the latter more didactic, the former is calculated more in terms of the imagination, the latter in terms of the understanding. (219)

Thus the philosophical method that attempts to do justice to myth and to history has to mediate between these divided domains, although in his early writings Schelling tends to stop short of the radical solution he will later suggest: the work of art. Yet Schelling already demonstrates a capacious understanding of what constitutes truth and in what form truth may come.

From this period, too, emerges a text whose authorship remains obscure to this day but that is often attributed to Schelling. So up for grabs is the authorship of the so-called "oldest System-Program of German Idealism" that it appears in each of the complete works of Hegel, Hölderlin, and Schelling.[63] The text, which survives only as a fragment, is nonetheless staggeringly comprehensive: Ethics, physics, political science, a history of mankind, aesthetics, poetry, religion, and mythology are all addressed schematically in the compass of a few pages. Not only is there an insistence on the totality of all these discourses, in the view of the author these domains tend to bleed into one another. To take only one, albeit privileged, example:

Last of all the Idea that unites all the rest, the Idea of *beauty* taking the word in its higher Platonic sense. I am now convinced that the highest act of Reason, the one through which it encompasses all Ideas, is an aesthetic act, and that *truth and goodness only become sisters in beauty*—the philosopher must possess just as much aesthetic power as the poet. Men without aesthetic sense is what the philosophers-of-the-letter of our times [*unsre Buchstabenphilosophen*] are. The philosophy of spirit is an aesthetic philosophy.[64]

The old trinity of beauty, truth, and goodness is resurrected here but with a preeminence granted, at least momentarily, to the aesthetic. Significantly, the aesthetic is not reduced here to the order of the letter but of the letter articulated with the spirit. Remarkable, too, in this fragment is the attempt to synthesize or unify these not so disparate domains, most palpable in the call for "a new mythology," a discourse that does not yet exist. Mythology, especially as in Schelling's thought (in the wake of Herder and Eichhorn), was a category that already could embrace the religious, the poetic, the historical, and even the philosophical. This "new mythology" is perhaps the discursive correlative of "intellectual intuition" ("intellektuale Anschauung"), the category of the mind that unites the sensible with the intelligible and balances the two.[65]

Schelling's early thinking of myth in the light of philosophy points toward what will become two cornerstones of his philosophical method (to the extent that one can generalize about a very complex career): a will to system and an attention to history. Anyone committed to what is now and then called *historicism* would be hard-pressed to find a kindred spirit in Schelling:

The texture of his work is utterly different from works produced under a banner of historicism. Yet there is an insistence in Schelling's treatment of any number of issues on parting company with what had come down as the notoriously static and transcendental modalities of Kant's system of critical philosophy.[66] One way that Schelling responded to the demands of post-Kantian philosophy came via a turn to what he calls "history."

In his first great systematic work, the *System of Transcendental Idealism* of 1800, Schelling comes to terms with the dilemmas posed by Kantian critical philosophy in part by telling a story. Kant's famously static system organized around the categories (and soon to be criticized by Hegel for being undialectical) gives way in Schelling to what he calls "a history of self-consciousness in epochs." More particularly, that history is conceived as one of revelation: "History as a whole is the ongoing, gradually self-disclosing revelation [*Offenbarung*] of the absolute"(211).[67] Schelling continues:

Hence one can never point out in history the particular places where the mark of providence, or God Himself, is as it were visible. For God never *exists*, if the existent *is* that which presents itself in the objective world; if *He existed* thus, then *we* should not; but He continually reveals Himself. Man, through his history, provides a continuous demonstration of God's presence, a demonstration, however, which only the whole of history can render complete. (211)

The presence, or *Da-sein*, of God is strangely not even of the order of being, of *Sein*. It is only "present" in the fullness of history, which is by definition neither complete nor present.[68] That history includes the future, which *is* not, even more transparently than the present or the past. Thus, any "present" moment of revelation is not fully present until the end of time. The nonbeing of the present, partial moment of revelation may well point forward to the future and to the end, which would signal the belated arrival of being. But it "is" not yet, and, more radically, it "is" not, period.

Schelling posits three periods in the grand story of revelation, in a schema that anticipated the later vision of *The Ages of the World* (*Die Weltalter*). The first is called tragic (when the blind power of fate prevails); the second is that of nature or natural law (or at least of a mechanical lawlike character); the final of the three periods of history does not yet exist. Yet Schelling can name it, in anticipation, the period of providence (*Vorsehung*). One tends to forget the metaphorical (or is it the literal?) sense of the Latinate word providence or its German equivalent *Vorsehung* as a "seeing before." Schelling looks forward to the nonexistent third of the three periods of history to find it an epoch of "looking forward" by and in the divinity of the absolute.

The narrative argument of Schelling's own text moves to its culmination in advocating the work of art as the resolution of the various polarities encountered in thinking his system: subject/object, freedom/necessity, conscious/unconscious, and so forth.[69] In his *Biographia Literaria* Coleridge in effect gives a cogent, schematic summary of what is at stake for Schelling in this period of his philosophical career, and he rightly sees that the main task for Schelling is to overcome somehow the inherited dualisms of post-Cartesian thought, together with the tendency of any given body of thinking to privilege unduly the subjective or the objective, or what Schelling earlier had termed the dogmatic (object-oriented) and the critical (subject-oriented) à la Kant. The work of art comes to the rescue in this philosophical romance (Schelling sometimes speaks of an "odyssey" of self-consciousness, or alternately of such a history as an "epic"[70]) insofar as it putatively unites the poles of subject and object. If philosophy, as it now seems it must, takes as its point of departure, in the wake of Kant, the subjective, or nonobjective, then the task is to determine how that subjective force is balanced by an objective one. Schelling summarizes the dialectic in the final section of the *System of Transcendental Idealism*:

Philosophy sets out from an infinite dichotomy of opposed activities; but the same dichotomy is also the basis of every aesthetic production, and by each individual manifestation of art it is wholly resolved. Now what is this wonderful power whereby, in productive intuition (so the philosopher claims), an infinite opposition is removed? . . . This productive power is the same whereby art also achieves the impossible, namely to resolve an infinite opposition in a finite product. It is the poetic gift, which in its primary potentiality constitutes the primordial intuition, and conversely, what we speak of as the poetic gift is merely productive intuition, reiterated to its highest power. It is one and the same capacity that is active in both, the only one whereby we are able to think and to couple together even what is contradictory—and its name is imagination.[71]

No wonder that Schelling calls it a miracle. The work of art, thus conceived, is *ein Wunder*. No other discourse, to take Schelling at his word here, accomplishes this marvelous, this impossible synthesis.[72]

Schelling returns again to the question of revelation in systematic fashion in the important lectures given in 1802 and published the following year. In his *Lectures on the Method of Academic Study* (*Vorlesungen über die*

Methode des akademischen Studiums) Schelling reflected on how the impulse toward knowledge and even absolute knowledge should unfold in the institutional setting of the university.[73] The two lectures most germane to the present study are "The Historical Construction of Christianity" and "On the Study of Theology." With respect to our main concern, the idea and actuality of revelation, Schelling reprises a notion already familiar from his *System of Transcendental Idealism*: "Every moment of time is a revelation of a particular aspect of God, in each of which He is absolute" (85). Here Schelling is already speaking about (and within) the orbit of Christianity. Although he was trained to be a professional Christian, so to speak, Schelling by no means displays a knee-jerk allegiance to Christianity. He is genuinely interested in and sympathetic to the claims of any number of world religions, and he exhibits a downright fascination with the certain historical formations of the divine, as with the gods of Samothrace, to which he later devoted a major essay. For Schelling, as later for Hegel, the relative privileging of Christianity is in part for philosophical reasons, although one would have to acknowledge a certain circularity here. What Schelling and Hegel come to value in philosophy (and even its methods of storytelling) is informed by the Christianity in which they were steeped and that they studied formally in great depth. Moreover, the quasiphilosophical language of the (Greek) New Testament lends itself more readily than some other religions to the speculative agendas of what comes to be known as German Idealism. If theology is, as Schelling claims, "the highest synthesis of philosophical and historical knowledge," then Christianity, with its emphasis on the peculiar historical character of its God (who is one of three but also simply *one*), is apparently more philosophically rigorous than all the other religions of the world. Christ, for Schelling,

stands as the boundary between two worlds, decreed from all eternity and yet transitory in time. He Himself returns to the invisible realm and promises the coming of the Spirit—not the principle which becomes finite to stay finite but the ideal principle which leads the finite back to the infinite and, as such, is the light of the modern world. (89)

One can glimpse two key things here: first, the mediating position of Christ as a kind of analogue to the straddling and transitional but unifying work of art at the end of the *System of Transcendental Idealism*; second, Christ points to or promises the Spirit to come, displaying the now familiar historical schema that informed Schelling's most systematic work—because the posited third epoch of the world is just that: posited. Short of the end of history, no conjunction of finite and infinite, ideal and temporary, is achieved. Thus revelation is somewhat at odds with its referent: "No idea," Schelling affirms, "can come into being in a temporal manner; it is an expression of the absolute—that is, God himself reveals the idea, and this is why the concept of Revelation is absolutely necessary in Christianity" (89). Revelation is necessary and insufficient. The absolute must be revealed, as Hegel, too, will claim, but any given revelation of it disfigures the absolute to the extent that it is partial, finite, figurative.

Along the lines of the insistence on Christianity being open-ended, with Christ as the inaugural figure of "the modern world" at the same time as he points to an epoch beyond the modern, Schelling sees something strangely utopian in the Catholic Church's proposal that "the people should not be allowed to read the Biblical literature" (97). This seems in line—even though this was not exactly the intent of the Church—with the notion of Christianity as a living, breathing, unfinished religion, "not a thing of the past but an everlasting present" (97).[74] But the present, as he makes clear elsewhere, is not simply present but rather a transitional moment to the future of the spirit, a spirit more promised than actual. It is no accident that in these lectures Schelling invokes Lessing's seminal text, *The Education of the Human Race* (*Die Erziehung des Menschengeschlechts*), which articulated a not-so-secular version of Biblical salvation history, with a triadic rhythm of history, whose third period, the epoch of the spirit, was yet to come.[75]

Turning from the historical construction of Christianity to theology proper, Schelling takes his distance from the Kantian project of thinking religion in purely moral terms. Schelling's interest in religion here is more purely speculative or philosophical. His focus is theology as religious knowledge. He opines: "The essential thing in the study of theology is to combine the speculative with the historical construction of Christianity and its principal doctrines" (101). Indeed, Christianity comes to be the historical idea of what Schelling calls "the modern world" and in such a way that theology is aligned with poetry and philosophy:

[The modern world] has no less clearly demonstrated that it wills Christianity not as an individual empirical phenomenon but as the eternal Idea itself. The lineaments of Christianity, not confined to the past but extending over an immeasurable time, can be clearly recognized in poetry and philosophy. (102)

All this unfolds in the light of Schelling's opening argument in his lectures, which addresses the concept of absolute knowledge. Here Schelling identifies the absolute, as he often does, with God, such that all knowledge properly conceived must be referred to absolute knowledge, which is also knowledge of the absolute: "The absolute is the supreme presupposition of all knowledge, the first knowledge"(10). Schelling also conjures the model of Pythagoras to promote the notion that "all knowledge is a striving for communion with the divine essence, for participation in the primordial knowledge of which the visible universe is the image and whose source is the fountainhead of eternal power" (11–12). This is one reason why Derrida frames his discussion of Schelling and the university in terms of the "theology of translation." If God is, as Schelling maintains, "the Idea of Ideas" (14), then every idea of the order of knowledge is ultimately referred to God.

At the virtual end of his philosophical career Schelling comes full circle and returns to the topics of myth and revelation in a new key.[76] His lectures on the philosophy of revelation in 1841 in Berlin were an intellectual event of the first order—with Kierkegaard and Engels among the (at first) eager auditors.[77] In stark contrast to Hegel's philosophy and the Hegelian legacy, Schelling virtually revels in revelation, not as a discourse that permanently falls short of philosophy's ultimately absolute reason, but as one that exceeds reason and is to be accepted, more or less, on its own terms. Schelling's auditors were perhaps disappointed, however sympathetic to Christianity many of them were, to find that the huge topic of revelation was reduced, in its essence, to a thinking of the appearance of Christ. Moreover, this thinking of revelation was presented as the culmination of the long tangled history of German Idealism, as Schelling traces the complicated trajectory that winds through the work of Kant and Fichte (whom he calls his "teachers"), that of his old friend and then rival Hegel, and not without figuring in his own earlier work. So the topic that was arguably one among others, Christ's appearance, was presented as if it were *the* subject of subjects and its thinking as the culmination of philosophy's labor.

But anyone expecting the equivalent of Hegel's absolute knowledge would find something rather different. Schelling rather perversely insists on a mode of reading that takes revelation literally (*eigentlich*), which, in the case of the Book of Revelation, entails a reading of what is often considered the most highly figurative text in the Biblical canon.[78] As Michael Theunissen has shown in fine detail, Schelling's singular divinity is as much a god of concealment as of revelation, indeed sometimes of revelation as concealment (*Verbergung*).[79] The Old Testament has revealed "the true God" only through the "false" one. For Schelling, the hallmark of Old Testament revelation is its character of suspension (*Spannung*).[80] In particular, he says of the prophets: "Aus den Propheten spricht schon die Potenz der Zukunft . . . " ("In the prophets there speaks already the potential of the future . . . ").[81] Whereas an earlier Schelling might have welcomed this anticipatory mode—and this is a trait that would one day attract an Ernst Bloch to Schelling—this merely anticipatory, suspended relation to the true God leaves, for the Schelling of 1840s, something to be desired. We saw how the younger Schelling recognized the nonpresence of the divine, or the not-yet presence of the divine, as not only what is always the case but also as a positive source of incitement in the never-ending odyssey of the subject. But the late Schelling renders everything inferior to the appearance of Christ, who is at once always present and yet also in some other important way, absent, concealed. For Christ is to come not once but twice, and all of what could be called modern history unfolds in the gap between these two comings. Even so, the conceptual and structural function of Christ's appearance is, as it were, absolute: "*The actual appearance of Christ is more than revelation,* for it is the presupposition of revelation and thereby it sublates itself." ("*Die wirkliche Erscheinung Christi ist mehr denn Offenbarung,* weil sie die Voraussetzung der Offenbarung und damit diese selbst aufhebe").[82] Revelation and more than revelation, the appearance of Christ is both the origin and the goal of the system, although much uncertainty and suspension occurs between origin and goal. Unlike Hegel, Schelling does not stress so much the identity of Christ as Logos, as the principle of reason in divine form. Schelling's Christ is a Logos beyond human reason. Indeed, he comes closer to his friend Hölderlin, who in the late poems of his lucidity saw, as in "Patmos" and "Der Einzige" ("The Unique One"), the necessity of reading the revelation of Christ as the revelation that was at once a disclosure and, for the meanwhile at least, a concealment.

~

Ever since the discovery and publication of Hegel's so-called "early theological writings," their precise status has been contested, both in themselves and in their relation to the later work, whose first great embodiment is the *Phenomenology of Spirit.* For some critics, the very designation of Hegel's early essays on Judaism or on the "spirit" or "positivity" of the

Christian religion as theological is a mistake. Lukács, for one, sees the young Hegel as an "enemy of theology."[83] Certainly Hegel has no fondness for the orthodoxies he encountered at the Tübingen *Stift*, despite the *Stift* being in some ways about as up-to-date as could be, grappling communally and directly with the issues posed by Kant's critical project. He laments in a number of letters to Schelling in the mid-1790s the rigid strictures of Tübingen conservatism ("nowhere is the old system so faithfully propagated as there").[84] Hegel recounts to Schelling how he has been studying Kant's philosophy and comments on the state of affairs of state with regard to how philosophy and theology are taught in Tübingen:

What you tell me about the theological-Kantian—if it should please the gods [*si diis placet*]—course taken by philosophy in Tübingen is not surprising. Orthodoxy is not to be shaken as long as the profession of it is bound up with worldly advantage and interwoven with the totality of a state. This interest is too strong for orthodoxy to be given up so soon. As long as this condition prevails, orthodoxy will have on its side the entire and ever-preponderant herd of blind followers or scribblers devoid of higher interests or thoughts.[85]

Hegel clearly sees that Tübingen's institutional framing of philosophy sets narrow parameters for thought. The theological powers that be, when faced with contrary arguments, simply mutter: "'Yes, it is no doubt true,' go to sleep, and the next morning make coffee and pass it around to others as if nothing had happened."[86] The blame for what we might term this "dogmatic slumber," even if countered by strong doses of coffee, is partly laid at Fichte's door:

However, to the mischief of which you write and whose mode of argumentation I can thus imagine for myself [e.g., Storr], Fichte has indisputably opened the door through his *Critique of All Revelation*. Fichte himself has made moderate use of it, but once his principles are firmly adopted there is no longer any limit to be set to the theological logic.[87]

Hegel charges that Fichte in effect retreats from the purely critical thinking in the mode of Kant to a not-so-surreptitious dogmatism, which is then exacerbated in the hands of Fichte's followers. By contrast, in a number of the early writings on religion, Hegel sees himself more resolutely in the Kantian line that espoused the dictates of practical reason, pure practical reason, as it were.[88]

One of the most striking of Hegel's early works is the so-called "Life of Jesus"(c. 1795), a work considered by many to be marginal, evidenced by its not even being included in the quasistandard, twenty-volume version of his complete works.[89] It stands as an early example of what would soon be codified as a genre in the nineteenth century: "the life of Jesus," as elaborated variously by Renan, David Friedrich Strauss, et al. It also resembles what would later be termed a "harmony" of the Gospels to the extent that it weaves together a single sustained text, in contrast to the four not entirely consistent Gospels of the New Testament.[90]

The "Life of Jesus" is a many-textured document, featuring direct quotation from the Gospels, "free" translation, commentary, and speculation. The dividing line among these last three categories is not always clear. The striking opening of Hegel's text sounds a note that will be sustained throughout:

Pure reason, transcending all limits, is divinity itself—whereby and in accordance with which the very plan of the world is ordered (John 1). Through reason man learns of his destiny, the unconditional purpose of his life. And although at times reason is obscured, it continues to glimmer faintly even in the darkest age for it is never totally extinguished.[91]

In the text's subsequent insistence on practical reason, a religion of morality (and love), as well in the very terms of its articulation, it presents itself as something of a "Gospel according to Kant." (Hegel deliberately casts the opening of his text as a parallel to the opening of the Gospel of John.) Indeed, the Kantian problematic of the primacy of practical reason becomes paramount for Hegel. Yet the confluence of terms between Kant and Hegel is perhaps somewhat misleading.[92] "Pure reason" sounds like pure Kant, and yet Kant never simply identifies reason with divinity the way Hegel does. The organizing principle of Hegel's text is that the Logos (Jesus) is the Logos (reason).

This identification allows Hegel to rewrite the Gospels in radical fashion, literally putting any number of words in Jesus's mouth, that is, within quotation marks. Who ever heard Jesus say the following?

When you regard your ecclesiastical statutes and positive precepts as the highest law given to mankind, you fail to recognize man's dignity and his capacity to derive from his own self the concept of divinity and the comprehension of the divine will. Whoever does not honor this capacity within himself does not revere the Deity. That which a human being is able to call his self, that which transcends death and destruction and will determine its own just deserts, is capable of governing itself. It makes itself known as reason; when it legislates, it does not depend on anything beyond itself; nor can it delegate a different standard of judgment to any other authority in heaven or on earth.

I do not pass off what I teach as some notion of my own, as something that belongs to me. I do not demand that anyone should accept it on my authority, for I am not seeking glory. I submit it only to the judgment of universal reason, that it might determine each individual belief or nonbelief.[93]

It would be one thing if Hegel simply offered this as a gloss of what Jesus really meant. It is quite another that he presents these words as Jesus' own. In the chapter on Blake I attended to the way the New Testament, with its Pauline positing of the superiority of the spirit over the letter that was indeed inimical to it ("the letter killeth, the spirit giveth life"), "authorized" violent interpretation. The spirit does not present itself as such: It is the collective letter of the spirit that remains in and as the New Testament. Yet the letter demands to be read in the spirit of the spirit. As soon as one departs from the letter, however (assuming that we know what a letter is!), it remains an open question as to what would or would not be within the spirit of the letter's spirit.

Hegel makes clear, as early as the so-called "Tübingen Essay" of 1793, that religion, in its history and in principle, has to overcome or transcend whatever is tied to the sensible or the sensual. Only childlike religions dwell in the realm of the sensible.[94] Religion, much as Jesus did, has to leave childish things behind. Thus the letter, poised as it is between sense and spirit, has to transcend the mere letter, has to leave its literality behind and move in the higher, more ethereal realm of the spirit.

Within the two poles of letter and spirit, there are discriminations to be made. With respect to prophecy, the young Hegel sees it as a kind of "vague hovering between letter and spirit" (298). No doubt, the prophets, in their inspired state, are closer to the realm of the spirit than is the ordinary human. Yet Hegel sees the prophets' visions as too caught up in the particularity of their immediate world to be "objective," and so the Jewish prophets consign themselves, against all odds, to the past (298–99). It is left to the visionary writers of the Gospels to render prophecy properly spiritual *après la lettre*.[95] Judaism, Hegel makes clear, is not simply a childlike religion, but its language inhibits the sort of education, or *Bildung*, adequate to a comprehension of the divine:

The state of Jewish culture cannot be called the state of childhood, not can its phraseology be called an undeveloped, childlike phraseology. There are a few deep, childlike tones retained in it, or rather introduced into it, but the remainder, with its forced and difficult mode of expression, is rather a consequence of the supreme miseducation of the people. A purer being has to fight against this mode of speaking, and he suffers under it when he has to reveal himself in forms of that kind; and he cannot dispense with them, since he himself belongs to this people.

The beginning of John's Gospel contains a series of propositional sentences which speak of God and the divine in more appropriate [more literal?] phraseology [*in eigentlicherer Sprache*].[96]

Hegel imagines the language of John—the author of the Gospel but still then thought to be the author of Revelation as well—as "eigentlicher," as more proper, more appropriate to the spirit of the spirit. Language should arguably be proper or not, *eigentlich* or *uneigentlich*. But Hegel employs the odd, perhaps impossible, comparative form here. The language of John's Greek is "more proper" than that of his (Judaic) predecessors but not yet fully proper, hovering somewhere in the improbable space between figurative and literal.

This early unpublished project of Hegel's to write a "Life of Jesus" and to think through the categories of religion as a prolegomenon to his emergent philosophy is striking in the way it points to numerous traits that will become central to the mature Hegel. The Gospel story especially comes to be *the* privileged model for Hegelian story-telling.[97] The death of Christ will turn out to be the paradigm for the central Hegelian category of negation, and similarly, the Resurrection will count as the ultimate instance of "the negation of the negation"—to say nothing of the Son of God being the externalization and sign of the self-division of the absolute, temporarily consigned to finitude only to return, in the end, to the infinitude of the absolute. Had Jesus not been explicitly named the *Logos* (Word and Reason), Hegel would have to have christened him so retroactively.

In the years between the mid-1790s and the composition of the *Phenomenology*, religion and theology gradually began to take a back seat to more purely epistemological matters, as well as, in the Berne period, the most concrete political affairs. But during the first years of the Jena period, as he began to formulate the grand outlines of what would become his "system," Hegel had to articulate in more thoroughgoing fashion the situation of religion in relation to philosophy and now to art as well. With the turn to the emergent system, Hegel for the first time attempted to do justice to the double and not easily harmonized demands of history and theory. In marked contrast to Kant, Hegel (although the way had been paved somewhat by Herder and even the young Schelling), hit on narrating a phenomenology of *Geist* ("spirit," "mind") that would include—in principle—all of cultural history in one grand sweeping story to culminate in spirit's self-conscious recognition of itself in absolute knowledge. The story is (by and large) a progressive one, whose main narrative mechanism is what Jean-Luc Nancy calls the bon mot of *Aufhebung*, the sublation that comprises simultaneously the negation or cancellation of any given "moment" and a transformation to a higher level.[98] The past is past, but not simply so. Nonetheless some cultural moments—to say nothing of whole continents (as in the *Lectures on the Philosophy of History*)—get left more radically behind than others, and the long march of spirit issues, in the end, in something resembling a philosophical transposition of the Biblical narrative from Eden to Revelation, of which the Gospel story of Jesus' incarnation, death, and resurrection would be still another, internal version. That Hegel can speak, at the end of *Faith and Knowledge*, of a "speculative Good Friday" is just one index of how the Gospel narrative and the grand dialectical story of spirit mirror each other.[99]

The *Phenomenology of Spirit*—conceived as a prolegomenon to the "system" but itself already a partial version of it—labors toward its culmination in a trinity of discourses—art, religion, and philosophy—whose common ground and goal are the rendering of the absolute. In the philosophical determination of the three different domains of discourse, one can witness a certain narrative pressure brought to bear on their analysis, whereby the posited need for thought to culminate in absolute knowledge, in thinking in a form fully commensurate with thinking itself, conspires to present art and religion as not only not philosophy but *not yet* philosophy. This is not self-evident, insofar as we know that art, religion, and philosophy can coexist at any given time. Although Hegel does to some extent consider each domain in itself, the sequence of religion, art, and philosophy (complicated somewhat by Hegel considering what he calls "Kunstreligion," or "art-religion") entails that anything other than philosophy will be determined as falling short of it. Philosophy—or, more simply, thought—as pure thinking is the ultimate rendering of the Logos. That Hegel's analysis also takes the form of a story results, once again, in the curious situation of the *not-yet* of art and religion: In some sense they demand, and have to wait for, their translation into the higher realm of philosophy.

Religion is considered primarily under the rubric of representation, or *Vorstellung*, most commonly translated as "picture-thinking." Hegel glosses the term "picture-thinking" as "the synthetic combination of sensuous immediacy and its universality or Thought."[100] He goes on to say:

This *form of picture-thinking* constitutes the specific mode in which Spirit, in this community, becomes aware of itself. This form is not yet Spirit's self-consciousness that has advanced to its Notion *qua* Notion: The mediation is still incomplete. This combination of Being and Thought is, therefore, defective in that spiritual being is still burdened with an unreconciled split into a Here and a Beyond. The *content* is the true content, but all its moments, when placed in the medium of picture-thinking, have the character of being uncomprehended [in terms of the Notion], of appearing as completely independent sides which are externally connected with each other. Before the true form for consciousness, a higher formative development of consciousness is necessary; it must raise its intuition of absolute Substance into the Notion, and equate its consciousness with its self-consciousness *for itself*, just as this has happened for us, or *in itself*. (463)

Throughout the section on "revealed religion" in the *Phenomenology* Hegel is describing primarily what is recognizable as the Christian religion, with no-so-veiled reference to its doctrines and its stories. Yet there is no explicit reference to "Christ," say, or to his "resurrection." Rather, Hegel will speak of the incarnation of the divine being, opting for a translation of the Christian story stripped of a good deal of its "surface" content. This tendency is itself arguably in keeping with the New Testament injunction to interpret in the mode of the spirit or Spirit. In any event, Hegel has found in Christianity the religion that embodies the speculative dialectic that is at once the presupposition and the goal of his analysis. This account of the word or the Word, the Logos that is also Reason, sets forth the whole grand story of the spiraling dialectic, although it does so still in the mode of picture-thinking. Whereas terms such as "the son" and "the father" or "the fall" can, especially to Christians raised on the Bible, seem like perfectly appropriate designations of absolute truths, Hegel reminds us of their resolutely figural character, their being enveloped in "picture-thinking." These words are pictures, however telling, however truthful, however divinely inspired.

On the one hand, the picture-thinking of religion is something of a scandal for philosophy, which demands to think in the mode of thought adequate to the absolute, in the mode of the concept or notion as concept, the *Begriff* as *Begriff*. But, as so often in Hegel, the matter is double-edged;

Hegel has to some extent already made a virtue of the necessity of representation—the necessity of externalization, figuration, and representation—by maintaining, as enunciated in his later *Aesthetics* and *Logic*, that "appearance is essential to essence."[101] Jesus must appear, and it is all the more resonant for Hegel's system, that Jesus, the Logos, is already both Word and Reason. Jesus is indeed the exemplary figure, embodying reason and its intricate history: He is, in Feuerbach's compelling phrase, the "Bild der Bilder," the "image of images." But Jesus is also a figure who points to his own disappearance as figure and toward the spirit to come (rather like Schelling's notion of Christ invoked above). Jesus, as the figure of Reason, points the way to philosophy and its ultimate expression, absolute knowledge; he points the way to the absolute and infinite beyond his finite self. Here, at the penultimate stage of the *Phenomenology*, we are not far in spirit from the young graduate of the Tübingen *Stift*, who had made reason the final criterion for religious truth.

In terms of the centrality of the category of representation, nothing much changes in Hegel's last extended project addressing religion, namely the series of lecture courses he gave on the philosophy of revelation.[102] *Vorstellung* continues to operate in a dual register, as one among many other topics that Hegel takes up in regard to all the religions he considers, as well as being the determining category that identifies the permanent subordination of religion to philosophy, even if philosophy comes to be, in its turn, even more resolutely occupied with rendering the divine. Christianity remains as the most philosophical of religions, the one religion that embodied and presented the dialectic in its intricacies and speculative depth, without, however, quite taking the form of philosophy, without presenting the Logos in a form adequate to the conceptual demands of absolute knowledge, in the form wherein spirit can recognize itself, at long last, fully as spirit.

~

In closing this long parenthesis on Hölderlin's philosophical contemporaries in the matter of religion and revelation I turn to a key figure in this constellation, the largely forgotten Friedrich Immanuel Niethammer. Although hardly a philosopher of Hegel or Schelling's genius, he was an important interlocutor, editor, and writer for the generation struggling with what to do in the aftermath of Kant's critical philosophy. Somewhat older than Hegel and Hölderlin, he was crucial in helping both along in intellectual and professional ways, "tutoring" Hölderlin and coediting with Fichte the *Philosophisches Journal* and then later the *Kritisches Journal der Philosophie* with Hegel.[103] Hölderlin writes to Niethammer in February of 1796 proclaiming gratefully that his addressee is still his "philosophical mentor."[104] This same letter features a dictum often quoted, particularly by those arguing for attending to the specificity of Hölderlin's poetry as poetry, namely: "philosophy is a tyrant." Yet Hölderlin in the same letter is effusive about his plans for reading and writing philosophy, and he outlines to Niethammer his coming projects:

In the philosophical letters I want to discover the principle which explains to me the divisions in which we think and exist, yet which is also capable of dispelling the conflict between subject and object, between our self and the world, yes, also between *reason and revelation,*—theoretically, in intellectual intuition.[105]

The categories Hölderlin invokes are those of Niethammer's own thinking, especially in his writings about reason and revelation. Niethammer had published a long response to and commentary on Fichte's *Attempt at a Critique of All Revelation* within months of his predecessor's publication, and he continued to devote himself to the topic throughout the decade, publishing in 1797 *Doctrinae de revelatione modo rationis praeceptis consentaneo stabiliende periculum,* which appeared the following year in German as *Versuch einer Begründung des Vernunftmäßigen Offenbarungsglaubens* (*Attempt at a Founding of Rational Belief in Revelation*).

It is highly likely that Hölderlin (to say nothing of many in this whole intellectual scene) was familiar with these texts, given Niethammer's importance to him and given, particularly, his immense enthusiasm for Fichte.[106] It was in the early 1790s that Hölderlin was almost giddy with excitement about Fichte's philosophy, so it is hard to imagine he would not have paid attention to his mentor's book-length essay on Fichte's inaugural work.[107] Moreover, Niethammer records in his diary an evening in the summer of 1795 when Fichte, Hölderlin, and Novalis gathered at Niethammer's home, noting that "much was said about religion and about revelation and that for philosophy many questions remained open in this regard."[108] Not just matters for their "day jobs," these philosophico-religious questions were as burning as any for this circle of thinkers. Although this group of thinkers mainly wrote in a somewhat rarified mode of technical philosophy, they often had at least one eye on the people and their education, their *Bildung.*

Niethammer, more than Fichte, Hegel, or Schelling, tried to write somtimes in a somewhat more user-friendly mode.[109] His response to Fichte not only engages the *Critique of All Revelation* on the latter's own terms, it also attempts to frame the issues, at least initially, in a way more intelligible to the generally educated reader.[110] Niethammer's text also, I think, happens to provide an account close to what someone like Hölderlin might have thought about revelation—not in all its details, of course, but in terms of what the parameters were, the issues, the possibilities.

Niethammer's *Über den Versuch einer Kritik aller Offenbarung* (*On the Attempt at a Critique of All Revelation*) engages Fichte's pathbreaking text, one which Neithammer considers "among the most remarkable events (*Erscheinungen*) of our age."[111] Niethammer welcomes the text for its having raised the discussion to a higher level, beyond anything the defenders or attackers of revelation had hitherto achieved. Partly to highlight the distinctiveness of Fichte's achievement, Niethammer offers a review of the genesis of the concept of revelation, and it is here we might be able to glimpse what an enlightened, educated German of the decade might have thought when pondering such a topic. Revelation, as an idea, goes back, undoubtedly, to the "earliest times in the development of the human spirit" (9). Like Herder and company, Niethammer imagines the earliest times to have been an era of ignorance, when men (and women?—they are not mentioned) were prone to conceiving of every unusual phenomenon of nature as a divine revelation: "When it thunders, then the lord is speaking, and when there is lightning, then he is revealing his majesty; a commanding torrent of water announces the punishing Jehovah; and the rainbow becomes the promissory sign of a father reconciled with his earthly sons" (11). Revelation was always a revelation of the supernatural, even if manifest in nature. But this earliest understanding of revelation and its experience (which has its echoes in any number of motifs throughout Hölderlin's poetry) tended to be the product of a "false conclusion," a simple misunderstanding of nature and its parameters. It would take an advance in knowledge and reason before revelation could secure a firmer footing.

Revelation in general is "making known or annunciation" ("Bekanntmachung oder Ankündigung") (16). But this is only its most general determination. "Revelation in the more narrow sense is a making known which occurs through God" (17). Here too, however, the concept risks being too broad, since God, as creator of the world and humanity, is the creator too

of our human faculties of knowledge and so is indirectly the cause of everything we know. The defining characteristic of revelation, then, is really its
"immediacy" ("des unmittelbaren"): Thus, revelation is "what is immediately made known by the divinity" ("unmittelbare Bekanntmachung durch
die Gottheit") (18). The truth revealed must have hitherto been unknown,
so Niethammer stresses the event-character of the teaching that *happens*
through God ("eine von Gott unmittelbare geschehene Belehrung") (18).
Whether a revelation is a revelation or not is a matter of fact (22); it either
is or is not a revelation. But there is a great difficulty in determining with
any certainty the status of a revelation. For revelation is revelation of the supersensible and indeed of the infinite, but in the finite mode of the sensible.
And what do we know of the infinite? Nothing. Thus "one can never come
to certainty about an external appearance [*Erscheinung*] as an immediate
revelation of God" (37). Still, the fact that one can never know does not imply, for Niethammer, that one throws up one's hands and dismisses the possibility of revelation altogether. Our human uncertainty about revelation
has little to do with the ontological status of revelation. The fact that our
being persuaded of the divinity of a revelation always stops short of certainty is no reason to dismiss the idea or possibility of revelation. Moreover,
practical reason can benefit from "revelation," even if our understanding of
it as revelation is not absolute. There is much to be gained by imagining
God *in concreto*, as Nietahammer says, following Fichte, imagining God as
the creator and the executor of the law (51 and 58).

It is no accident that Niethammer invokes in all of this the sublimity
of God, with his exalted, infinite, and unknowable character. But what fails
at the level of absolute knowledge, or knowledge of the absolute, nonetheless triggers a dynamic, rather as in Kant's critical system, whereby practical
reason comes in to fill up the void of knowing. Morality takes the upper
hand to religion proper, and revelation's claims are subordinated to how one
acts in accordance with the laws of reason. The outer sublimity of God is
supplemented by the "inner sublimity and sacredness" of the moral law (62).

Yet the giving way of revelation to the discourse of practical reason
and inner moral law, which is, in effect, always already there, does not
cause Niethammer to jettison the concept or the "fact" of revelation. Niethammer wants to subscribe to the permanent possibility of revelation,
whether or not one can be certain of its truth—and one cannot be certain.
Although in the main Niethammer is faithful to Fichte's project in the *At-*

tempt at a Critique of All Revelation, he is more concerned to underscore the possibility of revelation, whereas Fichte had emphasized more its superfluity and the impossibility of proving it. In this Niethammer seems closer to Hölderlin in his willingness to dwell in the possibility of revelation, even if that means a kind of permanent uncertainty in reading appearances, *Erscheinungen.*

Niethammer returned—after several essays, including a major one on "Über Religion als Wissenschaft zur Bestimmung des Inhalts der Religionen unter der Behandlungsart ihrer Urkunden" ("On Religion as a Science for the Determination of the Content of Religions and the Treatment of Their Documents")[112]—to the vexed question of revelation and reason in even more thoroughgoing fashion in 1797, publishing his lengthy treatise, *Doctrinae de revelatione modo rationis praeceptis consentaneo stabiliendae periculum.* He brought out the same text in a German version a year later, together with a substantial supplement dilating on some of his claims.[113] With this new text on revelation Niethammer broke away from the terms dictated by Fichte, although still faithful to the Kantian project that was also Fichte's point of departure.[114]

Niethammer simply takes as given the need for contemporary philosophy of religion and of revelation to be in line with the Kantian system. He distinguishes sharply between the dogmatic and the idealist(ic). With respect to revelation, the former is object-oriented and concerned with the theological truth of revelation, the latter is subject-oriented (although not to the exclusion of the object). Niethammer associates the merely dogmatic with an early stage, even the earliest, of mankind. At this stage, which also seems to be reproduced in the early phase of a human life, the gaze is turned outward, and one registers (or not) the truth of a state of affairs. But then, as in Kant's philosophy, the (group but also individual) subject turns inward to find reason there and the possibility of developing, in a self-sufficient way, what is necessary for leading a life of morality. For morality is the goal, the highest goal (71). Hence, Niethammer opts to ground his thinking more on the subjectively based belief in revelation, because for him morality is more crucial than truth. That Niethammer prizes the idealistic over the dogmatic virtually necessitates what he in fact undertakes: a rewriting of the term "revelation." Indeed, revelation is virtually distilled to mean the *idea* of god or divinity (*Gottheit*). Almost of the same import is the idea of duty, of *Pflicht.*[115] These are both objects of reason (*Vernunft*) rather than understanding (*Verstand*). Niethammer follows Kant's distinction between theoretical and practical reason, stressing the essential gulf between the two. Similarly, the truth and the necessity of revelations are two different issues, and never the twain shall meet (14). Truth is a theoretical question of knowledge, of *Wissen*; the necessity of revelation is a practical matter. But, as in Kant's *Critique of Judgment*, there is something of a bridge over the gulf between the two, and the bridge is constructed with the materials of imagination and sensibility. If the highest goal is morality, that goal is not immediately available: The highest realm is, in Kantian terms, the domain of the idea, that is to say of the order of reason. Here Niethammer means "ideas" in the Kantian sense of the so-called regulative "ideas" such as God or freedom, which can be thought but not known, and certainly not directly. One characteristic of these "ideas" is that they cannot be represented as such, but they are figured through the mechanism of schematism. Thus ideas are brought down, after a fashion, to the level of the concrete. One thinks not the law as such, say, but one imagines God as the executor of the law. Neithammer does not doubt the efficacy of such imaginings: Indeed, he encourages them. They correspond to an early stage of humanity and an early stage of a human's life, but they can strengthen, heighten, and elevate one's sense of law and duty and so aid in the grand cause of morality. In one important sense, humanity and the individual human never leave such imaginings absolutely behind, because the task of man reaching moral self-sufficiency or self-activity (*Selbsttätigkeit*) is unending. The goal can be approached only asymptotically (37ff.). Thus, short of that goal one can rationalize and even partly embrace anything that aids in morality, religion foremost of all. For example, Niethammer claims it helps to have the "idea of duty presented as an explicit enunciated will of God" (55). Rather as in Fichte and Kant, the text of Scripture has little status as the absolute, historically referential account of the word of God. What appears to be the enunciated will of God is valued for its helpful but inadequate representation of something that cannot be reduced to representation. Even the idea of God is valued as a provocation to reason (73), rather than for its content proper! Revelation, always of the order of representation, is to lead to morality and as such it is, ideally, to be left behind. But so lofty and impossible is the goal of pure morality that Niethammer has to recognize that representation remains. It persists in the rendering of the idea figured and disfigured *in concreto*.

Although Niethammer is explicit in claiming Christianity as the religion that most conforms to the idea of God and of duty that reason will propose for itself—something that is confirmed, to Niethammer's mind, by the spectacular success of Christianity's dissemination worldwide—he says next to nothing about the content of Christian revelation, much less of the Judeo-Christian tradition more generally (109). That is partly because Niethammer has, from the outset, tried to pry the term revelation (*Offenbarung*) loose from its time-honored usage. For Niethammer, revelation becomes an almost thoroughly conceptual entity, nothing on the order of the nitty-gritty details of individual prophecies, laws, or miracles. Revelation becomes reduced essentially to the idea of the divinity and the idea of duty, better to prepare the way for the transition from religion and revelation to morality proper. Thus it is also not hard to glimpse in Niethammer the resolute primacy of practical reason: The ultimate goal of morality seems to inform, retroactively, the account of religion and revelation that leads up to the pure self-activity and self-sufficiency of morality. But until that impossible goal is reached, one is left struggling with the capacity of reason to make sense of what may or may not be revelation.

~   ~   ~

The reading of Hölderlin was suspended at the moment of truth, the moment when truth, or at least *ein Wahres*, was prophesied to appear "between day and night." I argued that this moment bore a considerable relevance to more purely philosophical determinations of truth's appearance, especially when the object of philosophy was either art or religion. In general, one might say that Hölderlin shared with his philosophical colleagues a concern with the centrality, even the vicissitudes, of representation in the rendering of the absolute or the divine.[116] Although ultimately a poet by vocation, he embraced philosophy with the utmost seriousness, such that even a scholar of German Idealism such as Dieter Henrich can see him as a crucial figure in the development of Idealist philosophy proper.[117] Like Niethammer, Hölderlin sees no necessary conflict between reason and revelation. But more than Niethammer, he seems to recognize the necessarily uncertain character of revelation, even as he tends to assume its possibility. He shares Niethammer's interest in religion in its mode of practical reason and is concerned, far more than Schelling, with how religion functions for his people and peoples generally. Like Hegel, Hölderlin sees the language of religion as essentially figurative, but he makes of the figure something different and more radical than Hegel does, and that difference requires further reading. And so we turn back, in closing, to take up again the suspended moment of truth in "Germanien."

The priestess Germania may well be encouraged by the eagle's prophecy of truth's necessary appearance, but what is entailed in the odd specification of the mode of truth's appearance, namely, that it will appear between day and night, "zwischen Tag und Nacht"? The metaphor marks its difference from all those general philosophical formulations about the appearance of art and religion that we invoked. Surely Hölderlin's pregnant phrase cannot be taken literally, as if to mean that on one given day at dusk or dawn truth—or one truth, or the one truth—will appear. One of Hölderlin's most knowledgeable commentators has argued that the phrase "between day and night" should be understood as "morning," contrary to the sense suggested by the order of the words. Jochen Schmidt relies in part on the reference to "morning airs" ("Morgenlüfte") at the opening of the stanza, but he does not take account of the possible shift indicated by the characteristic Hölderlinian word "aber" ("but") in the passage in question.[118] Moreover, the presence of gold could just as well be a sign of sunset as sunrise. Further still, the sequence in the phrase "zwischen Tag und Nacht" more readily suggests evening as the "Zwischenzeit," the transitional time between day and night. Not only is evening more appropriate as the literal referent of the phrase, the poem also powerfully invokes Hölderlin's myth of the "Abendland" ("evening-land," "Hesperia") elaborated in its fullest form in "Brod und Wein." The flight of the divine eagle traced in the third stanza of "Germanien" follows the solar trajectory from the Orient ("Morgenland," or "morning-land") to Germany and the evening-land, a path that figures a certain vision of the trajectory of world history that will find its (dubious) philosophical codification in the thinking of Hegel.[119]

Evening—whatever it means—is emphatically the time of the Hesperian poet and also the time of truth's appearance in "Germanien." But perhaps more important than the determination of the time between day and night as either morning or evening is the recognition that it is a time of transition, of *Übergang*. As it happens, the concept and structure of *Übergang* plays a crucial role throughout Hölderlin's poetic and theoretical work, most pointedly in the brief, enigmatic essay, "Das Werden im Vergehen." There Hölderlin has frequent recourse to the concept of transition or *Übergang*, which he identifies repeatedly in the "Verfahrungsweise" essay as the "form" of metaphor. Hölderlin's identification of the two is hardly accidental, since "metaphor" (from the Greek *meta-pherein*) is a virtual translation of *Übergang*, as well as a translation of "translation" itself. If one reads from the "Verfahrungsweise" essay back to the passage from "Germanien" in question, understanding "evening" as a time of transition, which is to say as metaphor, that would mean that the eagle's oracular utterance is a metaphorical statement that truth must appear as metaphor, a figural pronouncement of truth's appearance *as* figure. This far-reaching notion may well be in keeping with Hölderlin's persistent attempt to reconcile the dualities of thought and existence in a single bridging category, like that of "intellectual intuition," as outlined in the letter to Niethammer. The one truth—or the one thing that is true—has to appear, but appears as figure. Thus a lot turns on what it means to be a figure, on what a figure is, and what this figure figures. "What," as Hölderlin might say, "is this?" "Was ist dies?"

It may be no coincidence that when Hölderlin focuses his attention on the moment of *Übergang*, or transition, it is in the context of a discourse on the fatherland. "Becoming in dissolution" is thought primarily through the category or the example of the fatherland, not unlike the way the *patrie* sometimes forms the horizon of meaning and history for Hölderlin's much-admired "Rousseau." Hölderlin opens the essay entitled "Becoming in Dissolution" abruptly, with this dense reflection:

The declining fatherland, nature and man, insofar as they bear a particular relation of reciprocity, insofar as they constitute a special world which has become ideal and [constitute] a union of things and insofar as they dissolve, so that from the world and from the remaining ancestry and forces of nature, which are the other real principle, there emerges a new world, a new yet also particular reciprocal relation just as the decline emerged from a pure yet particular world. For the world of all worlds, the all in all which always *is*, always *presents* itself in all time—or in the decline, the instant or, more genetically in the becoming of the instant and in the beginning of time and world, and this decline and beginning is—like language—expression, sign, presentation of a living yet particular whole. . . . In the living existence there prevails a mode of relation and of *thematics*, even though all others can be intuited within it; the possibility of all relations is predominant in the transition [*Übergang*], yet the particular ones need to be taken, to be derived from it so that through it there emerges infinity, the finite effect. (IV.1, 282)

The moment of decline or transition is, paradoxically, the moment when totality presents itself, and presents itself in a way that is linguistic, or at the very least is structured like language.[120] Hence the relative ease with which Hölderlin can move between the fatherland, as a historical formation, and a unit of language, like the figure in general or metaphor in particular, the figure that is for so many theorists, from Aristotle onward, the figure par excellence. That elsewhere Hölderlin specifies transition as the "form of metaphor" suggests, from one more vantage point, that language is radically figural, to the extent that one would have to rethink what language is.[121] That the preeminent figure in Hölderlin's essay is the fatherland, which synecdochally stands for or as a world, testifies both to its exemplary character but also to its uncertain status, as a moment always in transition.

An appeal to the doctrines of Hölderlin's "Verfahrungsweise" essay and "Becoming in Dissolution" for such a reading of "Germanien," and especially the lines on the appearance of truth, may seem to come out of the blue, so to speak, but there is further evidence in the poem itself to justify the invocation of that theoretical text. The passage immediately following the prophecy of truth's appearance contains this forbidding injunction of the eagle to Germania:

> Dreifach umschreibe du es,
> Doch ungesprochen auch, wie es da ist,
> Unschuldige, muß es bleiben.

> Threefold circumscribe it,
> Yet unuttered also, just as it is there,
> Innocent one, it must remain.

The one truth, it seems, must not be written or spoken, only "circumscribed," literally "written around." The demand to circumscribe the truth at the same time that it must remain unspoken is a characteristically paradoxical recognition in Hölderlin of the task and the limitation of poetry, its necessity and impossibility. But more puzzling even than the enigma of the eagle's command to circumscribe what must be unspoken is the strange specification that the circumscription be threefold ("dreifach"). Why *threefold*? The Christian trinity might be considered a "threefold" circumscription of the one true God, but the tonality at the end of the poem is more recognizably Greek, with its mythology of "Vater Aether" and "Mutter

Erde."[122] The word "dreifach" also occurs in Hölderlin's "Am Quell der Donau," a poem similar to "Germanien" in its mythology and imagery:

> Zwar gehn wir fast, wie die Waisen;
> Wohl ists, wie sonst, nur jene Pflege nicht wieder;
> Doch Jünglinge, der Kindheit gedenk,
> Im Hauße sind auch diese nicht fremde,
> Sie leben dreifach, eben wie auch
> Die ersten Söhne des Himmels.

> True, like orphans almost we walk;
> Though much is what it was, that tutelage now is lacking;
> But youths who are mindful of childhood,
> These are not strangers now in the house.
> Threefold they live, as did
> The very firstborn of Heaven.

Most commentators agree that the "dreifach" here refers to the three temporal dimensions of past, present, and future, such that "dreifach leben" would be a mode of behavior that takes account of the totality of time in its three dimensions.[123] A reading of the "threefold" in "Germanien" in this light would consider the passage of truth's circumscription as one instance of the rhetorical totalization of time or history prominent in the poem. The eagle's flight, as noted above, traverses the whole of cultural history from its "dawn" in the Orient to its "evening" in the *Abendland* of modern Germany. A more striking instance of such totalization occurs in the eagle's ecstatic vision in the final stanza:

> Es rauschen die Wasser am Fels
> Und Wetter im Wald und bei dem Nahmen derselben
> Tönt auf aus alter Zeit Vergangengöttliches wieder.
> Wie anders ists! und rechthin glänzt und spricht
> Zukünftiges auch erfreulich aus den Fernen.

> The waters roar on the rock
> And thunderstorms in the wood, and at their name
> Divine things past ring out from time immemorial.
> How all is changed! And to the right there gleam
> And speak things yet to come, joy-giving, from the distance.

Here, then, is a present vision that seems to encompass both past and future, "Vergangengöttliches" and "Zukünftiges." The return of the divine is recognized as different from the former presence, signaled by the word "anders" ("different") at the same time as the copulative "ists" marks an identity that overarches that difference. The tension between otherness and identity is maintained here: One can recognize both harmony and opposition (to use the terms of the "Verfahrungsweise" essay) in the uneasily irenic vision of the poem's closing. A reading of the "dreifach" in temporal or historical terms, however, by no means exhausts the possibilities of the "moment of truth" and its subsequent textual elaboration.

The word "dreifach," rare in Hölderlin's poetic corpus, occurs repeatedly and conspicuously in the "Verfahrungsweise" essay, where the context is more epistemological and poetological than temporal or historical.[124] The subject of the section in question is the comprehension of the poetic "I" ("das poetische Ich aufzufassen"), a task described as "the hyperbole of all hyperboles, the boldest and ultimate attempt of the poetic spirit" ("die Hyperbel aller Hyperbeln, der kühnste und letzte Versuch des poetischen Geistes).[125] By hyperbole, Hölderlin may well intend the mathematical sense rather than the rhetorical, but in either case the implication is that the comprehension of the poetic "I" is an impossible, yet imperative, task.[126] In outlining this task Hölderlin formulates, in some of the most tortuous prose in the Idealist corpus, his theory of the threefold nature of the poetic "I":

Within the subjective nature the "I" can form knowledge only as an opposing or relating one; however, within the subjective nature it cannot recognize itself as poetic "I" in a *threefold* quality, for given the way in which [it?] appears within the subjective nature and is differentiated from itself and by and through itself, that which is cognized must always constitute that *threefold* nature of the poetic "I" together with the cognizing and the cognition of both, and must be grasped neither as cognized by the cognizing ["I"], nor as cognizing by the cognizing [itself], nor as the cognized and cognizing by cognition, nor as cognition by the cognizing; in none of these three distinctly considered qualities is it conceived of as pure poetic "I" in its threefold nature: as opposing the harmoniously opposed, as (formally) uniting the harmoniously opposed, as comprehending in one the harmonious opposed, the opposition, and unification; on the contrary, it remains in real contradiction with and for itself. (IV.1, 252–53)

[Innerhalb der subjectiven Natur kann das Ich nur als Entgegensezendes, oder als Beziehendes, innerhalb der subjektiven Natur kann es sich aber nicht als poetisches Ich in *dreifacher* Eigenschaft erkennen, dennso wie es innerhalb der subjek-

tiven Natur erscheint,und von sich selber unterscheiden wird, und an und durch
sich selber unterschieden, so muß das Erkannte immer nur mit dem Erkennenden
und der Erkenntnis beeder zusammengenommen jene *dreifache* Natur des poetischen Ich ausmachen, und weder als Erkanntes aufgefaßt von Erkennenden, noch
als Erkennendes augefaßt vom Erkennenden, in keiner dieser drei abgesondert
gedachten Qualitäten, wird es als reines poetisches Ich in seiner dreifachen Natur,
als entgegengesezend das harmonischentgegengesetzte, als (formal) vereinigend
das harmonischentgegengesezte, als in Einem begreiffend das harmonischentgegengesezte, die Entgegensezung und Vereinigung, erfunden, im Gegentheile
bleibt es mit und für sich selbst im realen Widersprüche.][127]

At least one thing should be clear from this convoluted, if rigorous, prose
about the limitations of the purely subjective "I": The dilemma, or literally
"trilemma," for the poetic mind is to integrate the three "moments" (in the
Hegelian sense) of knower, known, and the act of knowing that relates
them. The objectifying of the "I" is not a sufficient solution to the problem
of mere subjectivity: For Hölderlin, reflection on the very activity of poetic
knowing is equally requisite. Hölderlin's intense admiration for Fichte in
the early and mid-1790s gave way when he sought an epistemological system less resolutely centered on the "I" as the point of departure and the
goal of thinking. The "Verfahrungsweise" essay comes closer to the texture
of Schelling's thought, with its relays back and forth between subject and
object, together with its sometimes seeing in art (and its mental correlative
"intellectual intuition") the principle of resolution and balance.

And yet the very category sometimes called on to mediate those op-
positions is itself highly moveable. Hölderlin's notion of transition bears a
close resemblance to his perhaps more celebrated use of the concept of
caesura in his reading of Sophocles' tragedies. Indeed, the caesura has been
taken as something of a key or a cipher for understanding a good deal of
Hölderlin's work. In the notes on Sophocles' *Oedipus* Hölderlin claims
that poets of his day had to be judged according to what he calls a "lawful
calculation." He goes on to say:

The law, the calculation, the way in which a sensuous system, man in his entirety
develops as if under the influence of the element, and how representation, sensa-
tion, and reason appear in different successions yet always according to a certain
law, exists in tragedy more as a state of balance than as mere succession.

For indeed, the tragic *transport* is actually and the least restrained.

Thereby, in the rhythmic sequence of the representations wherein *transport* presents itself, there becomes necessary *what in poetic meter is called caesura*, the pure word, the counterrhythmic rupture; namely, in order to meet the onrushing change of representations at its highest point in such a manner that very soon there does not appear the change of representations but the representation itself.[128]

As the dramatic equivalent of the break in a poetic line, this caesura constitutes a moment of transition, and a curious one at that. What appears is not nothing (as arguably is the case with the caesura of a poetic line) but "the pure word" ("das reine Wort"), language as sheer language. No longer do we encounter the sequence or the alternation of representations but representation itself, representation as nothing but representation. In both of Sophocles' dramas translated by Hölderlin, *Oedipus* and *Antigone*, the moment of caesura is a decidedly prophetic one. In both plays, the pure word belongs to Tiresias, the blind, oracular prophet who knows the truth but often speaks in riddles. These textual forces combine to align prophecy with transition, metaphor, caesura, and the appearance of representation itself, when representation appears as representation. Rather as we have seen in moments in Benjamin and in Blake, the prophetic word, the pure word, seems to disrupt history, to rupture any simple linear progression or sequence and in such a way as to foreground language itself, especially the prophetic word, which speaks of or orients one to the future in the absence of it.

It is in these same notes to Sophocles that Hölderlin invokes the notion of the turn to the fatherland ("vaterländische Umkehr"). The context is Sophocles' Greece, but the resonances with Hölderlin's Germany are unmistakeable. It can scarcely escape one's notice that a good deal of Hölderlin's high metaphysical poetry (although it is also importantly antimetaphysical—hence its appeal to Heidegger) unfolds within the parameters of this phantom nation of Germany or Germania. In the late poetry especially Hölderlin makes a deliberate turn to the fatherland. In a famous letter to the publisher of his Sophocles translations Hölderlin refers to a group of poems that has to do with "the fatherland or time" ("das Vaterland oder die Zeit").[129] The commonsensical reading of this phrase would tend to understand Hölderlin as referring to two different domains, the fatherland and time. Yet the essay "Becoming in Dissolution" already points to something like the coincidence or overlapping of the two. Indeed, the "or" of "the fatherland or time" can go either way. The second possibility, that the fatherland and time are versions of each other is difficult to grasp but does correspond to the way that for Hölderlin the fatherland is a privileged horizon for thinking human time, at least in the modern world. In "Becoming in Dissolution" Hölderlin had said:

The decline or transition of the fatherland... is felt in the parts of the existing world so that at precisely that moment and to precisely that extent that existence dissolves, the newly-entering, the youthful, the potential is also felt. (IV.1, 282)

This moment, once again, is the one between "being and nonbeing," the transitional moment par excellence. This moment, exemplified in the history of the fatherland, is poised between the finite determination of a past and the—in principle—infinite possibilities of the future toward which it is moving. This is consistent with Hölderlin's conception of poetry as such, since Hölderlin—and here we see one way in which he seems to think outside the received dichotomies of the metaphysical tradition—associates the meaning and the truth of poems with the transition, and its form, namely, metaphor:

Dieser Grund des Gedichts, seine Bedeutung, soll den Übergang bilden zwischen dem Ausdruck, dem Dargestellten, dem sinnlichen Stoffe, dem eigentlich Ausgesprochenen im Gedichte, und zwischen dem Geiste, der idealischen Bedeutung. (IV.1, 244)[130]

[This ground of the poem, its meaning, should form the transition between the expression, the presentation, the sensuous material, what is actually enunciated in the poem, and between the spirit, the idealistic treatment.]

The main lines of the metaphysical tradition, from Aristotle onward, are aligned in determining the place of metaphor as not immediately of the order of truth, as a kind of deviation from or displacement of truth proper. But here truth is or is like metaphor, and vice versa. It is difficult to think the consequences of such an insight or claim, but there is no question that the argument for the figurality of truth counts as a radical departure from the mainstream of Western thought. Thought itself remains in transition in trying to think language as metaphor.

Up until the end of "Germanien," the poem, aside from its invocation of the ancient Greek and perhaps Biblical worlds, focuses on Germany. Then comes a marked turn in the end to "peoples" ("Völker") in the plural. Germania is told to offer, without defense (*wehrlos*), counsel to the "peoples." It is the last word of the poem. Not much is said about these peoples, but the moment seems consistent with Hölderlin's sometime insistence that Germany must turn to the outside, to the rest of the world, to the cosmos of the cosmopolitans. In a letter to his brother, dated the first of the year, 1799, Hölderlin's subject is what he somewhat enigmatically calls "political reading" ("politische Lektüre"). This political reading, which by no means seems confined to "reading" in the literal sense, is thought of in conjunction with speculative philosophy and poetry, the time being ripe for the combined forces of all three.[131] Hölderlin sees the principal German trait as "a fairly narrow domesticity" ("eine ziemlich bornierte Häuslichkeit"). This narrowness must be a countered by a turn outward, which can proceed, through political reading, through speculative philosophy, through poetry. But the future is hardly given. Hölderlin's moment of truth, the appearance of truth between day and night, its appearance as figure, is a moment on the way to an unknown future.

It is hard to say whether this crucial moment of transition is to be construed as historical or allegorical. Certainly it is historical in that it is said to happen, and happen necessarily, and it does so in the course of the becoming and dissolution of the fatherland. In one respect, there is nothing more historical than the fatherland, even its emergence in its disappearance. Indeed, the fatherland is the very paradigm within which history unfolds. And yet the Germany or Germania invoked by Hölderlin is in salient ways imaginary, a powerful idea that partly unites the disparate small states, principalities, and lands of mostly German-speaking peoples. This Germany does not, strictly speaking, exist, and so it is all the more appropriate that Hölderlin imagines this fatherland as metaphorical, as language in transition, as poetry in motion. The bridge from the finite particularities of the past lead to a potentially infinite future whose contours are unknown but intimated through the (highly figural) language of revelation, to say nothing of the revelations figured in the natural world, the lightning bolts and the great storms that Hölderlin persists, poetically, in believing in and reading as divine revelations.

In a neglected essay, "The Riddle of Hölderlin," Paul de Man criticizes the tendency to read as historical prophecy what can at most only appear as such, what should rather be understood as allegory.[132] This is a salutary corrective to any number of reductive readings, but it may be that in "Germanien" it is impossible to decide between history and allegory, because "history" in the form of the fatherland especially is itself allegorical. Although Heidegger could dare to claim, in his commentary on "Germanien," that "the fatherland is Being itself" ("das Vaterland ist das Seyn selbst"), it would be more accurate to say that for Hölderlin the fatherland is always "something else," always in the process of not just becoming but becoming in dissolution. The nation is always other, always becoming other. This is perhaps the case for every country, but it is so in a particular way for Hölderlin's Germany. After all, this is a poet who, as is testified in the letters to Böhlendorff, discovered the real character of the Greeks by traveling to the south of France.[133] Moreover, what he discovered about the Greeks was that their characteristic trait was to assume a foreign character.[134] Not only did the Germans in part imitate the Greeks as a divided people (and so appropriate the "foreign" trait of adopting a foreign character), the Germans are in a more radical sense divided from themselves. Hölderlin claims, famously, that the hardest thing for the Germans to learn is "the free use of one's own" ("das freie Gebrauch des Eigenen" (VI.1, 246). It is no wonder that Hölderlin's poetic thinking of the nation entails a projection into an uncertain future. Poetry, as the art of the figure, is equally the art of the nation; both require a prophetic language of transition, of pure transition to the unknown future to come.

8

Allegories of the Symbol: Rhetoric, Politics, and Prophecy in Coleridge's *The Statesman's Manual*

> And it had clearly escaped everyone's notice that I had already been
> bull-whipped through the Psalms of David and The Book of Job,
> to say nothing of the arrogant and loving Isaiah, the doomed Ezekial,
> and the Helplessly paranoiac Saint Paul: Such a forced march, designed
> to prepare the mind for conciliation and safety, can also prepare it
> for subversion and danger.
>
> —James Baldwin, *The Devil Finds Work*

I

The writings of Coleridge are riddled with a certain ventriloquism of the divine. Many of his poems and prose works perform and reflect on this ventriloquism, from an extensive mobilization of the rhetoric of Biblical prophecy to the founding of an ontology and an aesthetics on the principle of the human repetition of the divine "I AM." The aura of Coleridge as a visionary writer has been evoked largely from his poems and texts auxiliary to them, such as the notorious account of delirious inspiration in the drafting of "Kubla Khan."[1] The previous chapters have argued that a revisionary understanding of Biblical prophecy *as* poetry, elaborated throughout the eighteenth century, prepared the way for a Romantic mythology of the poet as prophet: A good deal of Coleridge's poetry takes its place, and self-consciously so, within this tradition. Yet the language of Coleridge's prose is just as strongly marked by a rhetoric of prophecy, especially in his journalism and political writings. Judaic prophecy was, as Max Weber has shown, a prototypical form of political pamphlet literature.[2] And it is political occasions that most often elicit from Coleridge a sustained prophetic discourse.

A pervasive prophetic strain can be read off from Coleridge's early *Lectures on Revealed Religion* through *The Watchman* (which takes its title from the Biblical epithet for Isaiah and Ezekiel) to the posthumous *Confessions of an Inquiring Spirit,* an extended study of the senses of Biblical inspiration. The text that most resolutely adopts a prophetic stance is one that is both marginal and central in Coleridge's corpus: *The Statesman's Manual.* Scarcely read and barely understood in its own time, this first of the Lay Sermons contains what would emerge as one of Coleridge's most influential pronouncements: the celebrated distinction between symbol and allegory. This circumstance accounts for the odd status of *The Statesman's Manual* as one of the most often cited and least read of Coleridge's works. The passage on symbol and allegory, familiar to many readers as a quotation from an absent text, has become lodged in the critical unconscious even of many who have never read it.[3] The full version of *The Statesman's Manual* is read today almost exclusively by Coleridge scholars, who slightly outnumber the handful of statesmen who actually took up the text addressed to them. A wider and a fuller reading is called for.[4]

The Statesman's Manual was written in 1816 as the first of a projected series of three Lay Sermons. It bears the remarkable subtitle "The Bible, The Best Guide to Political Skill and Foresight." An arcane and unwieldy text that prompted Dorothy Wordsworth to complain of its prodigious obscurity, it lends itself to quotation and anthologization in some of its parts, partly because it is hardly a model of organic form that is so often Coleridge's ideal. Most bodies have one appendix; *The Statesman's Manual* has five. Together the appendices exceed in length the "body" of the text. In its range of topics, the manual reads like a miniature version of Coleridge's envisioned *Opus Maximum,* moving vertiginously as it does from the most topical of current events to ancient philosophical problems, from the Napoleonic Wars to the labyrinthine distinctions of Kantian critical philosophy.

That the daunting text of *The Statesman's Manual* is rarely read has not deterred critics from making pronouncements about it. The first review, in fact, appeared, preposterously, before the work itself. Hazlitt's foresight about this work on foresight enabled him to review the text for *The Examiner* well before reading it, content to judge a book by its advertised cover. Hazlitt doubted Coleridge would get much further, or that it would matter if he did. Of Coleridge's *The Friend*, Hazlitt could ask: "What is it but an immense title-page?"[5] When to Hazlitt's surprise, *The Statesman's Manual* actually appeared, he wrote two sharply critical reviews, remarking of the prophetic Coleridge that he "considers it the safest way to keep up the importance of his oracular communications, by letting them remain a profound secret both to himself and the world."[6] Perhaps in response to Hazlitt, Coleridge arranged to write for *The Courier* his own review of his second Lay Sermon, a singular act of ventriloquism.[7] But even that did not much help the difficult cause of finding an appropriate audience for Coleridge's first sermon. Henry Crabb Robinson expressed a guarded sympathy for the project but thought the attempt a failure owing to Coleridge's miscalculations about his audience, even the announced, restricted one of Higher Classes or the clerisy.[8] The Lay Sermons eventually found one audience waiting to be persuaded, but hardly an ideal one. James Russell Lowell, poet and Professor of English at Harvard, tried the experiment of having the Lay Sermons read aloud to his Rhode Island hens on rainy days when they were "backward with their eggs" and testified that "the effect was magical."[9] Lowell was perhaps banking on the ambiguity of the word "lay" in Coleridge's title.

But if the Lay Sermons were not well received, much less comprehended, they nonetheless remain crucial to an understanding of Coleridge's thought, well beyond the influential distinction between symbol and allegory. In reading *The Statesman's Manual*, however, one must be careful not to take it as a cipher—to say nothing of a synecdoche—for the whole of Coleridge's thought. The text itself makes grand synthesizing gestures and presents a theory of the symbol as synecdoche, valuing it over the detached and fragmentary discourse of allegory. The present reading addresses primarily the first Lay Sermon within a broad range of Coleridge's work, without assuming the viability of the part-for-whole rhetoric that informs Coleridge's own theory and practice of persuasion.

Yet the question of totality imposes itself in the very project of the Lay Sermons. The envisioned trinity of texts was to address the whole of the English people in their various economic divisions. *The Statesman's Manual* was directed on its title page to "the Higher Classes of Society," the second Lay Sermon to "the Higher and Middle Classes of Society," and a third was to address "the Lower and Laboring Classes" but in fact was never written.

(I return later to speculate on why this third sermon to the lower classes never materialized.) The totalizing gesture of address, even if it never succeeded, parallels similar gestures in a period of Coleridge's work when he was preoccupied with summing and summoning up the totality of his life and work. In 1817 Coleridge published both the *Biographia Literaria* and the *Sibylline Leaves*, the first being the "seminarrative" of his literary life and opinions and the second a collection of his verse to make up for "the fragmentary and widely scattered state" of his poems.[10] It contains, Coleridge underlines, "the whole of the author's compositions, from 1793 to the present date, with the exception of a few works not yet finished, and those publications in the first edition of his juvenile poems, over which he had no control," in other words, all the poems that were whole or wholly his. If the *Biographia* stands as the narrative and critical program of his whole literary life, and *Sibylline Leaves* represents the whole of his poetic production, the Lay Sermons constitute addresses to the entirety of the English nation on the pressing social issues of the day. They are the politico-theological correlative to the more popular and readable *Biographia* and *Sibylline Leaves*.[11] Even in their abbreviated and awkward form, the Lay Sermons stand as one version of the elusive encyclopedic text of which Coleridge so often dreamed.

The bold address of *The Statesman's Manual* to "the Higher Classes of Society" seems at first simply a divisive gesture, excluding from the outset all readers from the middle and lower classes, perhaps even pitting one class against another. And indeed the content of the sermons will partially bear out that thesis. But perhaps Coleridge's problematic address takes a realistic account of the divided economic character of English society and corresponding differences in education and interest. Does his gesture not acknowledge the impossibility of a homogenous readership, recognizing that an address should be class specific, if it is to be understood at all?[12] A similar strategy of circumscribed address was common to a principal nemesis of Coleridge in these years of the Napoleonic Wars and their aftermath: William Cobbett. Cobbett's *Weekly Political Register* was addressed to "Journeymen and Laborers," and the full title of his later *Advice to Young Men* spells out its target audience in advance: *And (incidentally) to Young Women, in the Middle and Higher Ranks of Life*. In their strategies of addressing class-specific audiences, Coleridge and Cobbett, despite their overt political differences, agree in principle to forego the false universalism of texts that seem to address all people from all walks of life, as if class society had already withered away. But this is only one way to understand Coleridge's practice in the Lay Sermons; a more complicated rhetorical scenario may emerge in the course of its reading.

From his earliest literary endeavors, Coleridge had been acutely aware of the politics of address. In a 1795 article "On The Present War," he wrote:

In the disclosal of Opinion, it is our duty to consider the character of those, to whom we address ourselves, their situations, and probable degree of knowledge. We should be bold in the avowal of *political* Truth among those only whose minds are susceptible of reasoning: and never to the multitude, who ignorant and needy must necessarily act from the impulse of inflamed Passions." (I, 43)

Even in the most radical stage of Coleridge's itinerary, the era of his dream of pantisocracy, the whole is not quite the whole. If the multitude here is not expressly "swinish," as famously on occasion in Burke, that large segment of the population is nonetheless judged incapable even of reasoning and thus not ready for what Coleridge calls, echoing Godwin, "political truth." The very concept of political truth transforms traditional notions of "truth" as that which is objectively constituted and independent of any discourse.[13] The idea of *political* truth, by contrast, requires that it not be "universal": neither universally propounded nor universally perceived. Against the myth of truth as unified and indivisible, the Coleridgean concept posits truth as divisible and, in effect, divisive. In part, it is precisely the notion that politics is a matter of truth (rather than of power or justice) that separates Coleridge from the phantasmatic multitude he sets himself against. The multitude Coleridge opposes tends in an odd way to be more Burkean than he (Burkean, that is, insofar as that implies that a certain political pragmatism takes priority over truth).[14] One of the striking and constant features of Coleridge's writing, throughout all phases of his career, is the explicit co-implication of politics and metaphysics. Coleridge never ceases to ground his political programs in an ontology, a theology, or both, and thus the criteria for political judgment are never given simply as political. The politics of any text in such a program will be informed by a concomitant metaphysics, especially in those of Coleridge's texts where the totality of the "system" is at stake. Yet tracing this problematic will show that the very rhetoric of totality will turn out to be itself exclusionary in consequential ways.

The concern for totality announced in the program of the Lay Sermons finds its textual correlative in what is at once the sermons' object of study and their principal authority: the Bible. The opening argument of

The Statesman's Manual rests on a claim for the all-encompassing character of Biblical principles: "If our whole knowledge and information concerning the Bible had been confined to the one fact of its immediate derivation from God, we should still presume that it contained rules and assistances for all conditions of men under all circumstances; and therefore for communities no less than for individuals" (5). The force of Coleridge's rhetoric lies in its seeming concession and circumscription ("*confined* to the *one* fact"), which nonetheless still permit the extraordinary claim that the Bible provides rules for *all* men under *all* circumstances. Almost lost in the middle of Coleridge's sentence is the content of the one "fact," namely, that the Bible is immediately derived from God. Biblical criticism from the late seventeenth century onward, and especially in the late eighteenth century, had been quietly questioning precisely that "fact." And Coleridge was well aware from his reading of Eichhorn, Herder, and others, that historical evidence suggested the all-too-human character of the Bible's composition. Hence, the strategic importance of prophetic discourse, for, as Coleridge argued in his 1795 lectures on religion: "A prophet among the Jews was one who had received communication from the Deity. These communications consisted sometimes of Admonitions and moral Precepts, but more frequently contained annunciations of future Events."[15] The prophet, then, is the intermediary figure of immediacy. And to make matters more complex, there are degrees of mediation within this general economy of prophetic immediacy. As Coleridge noted in a reading of Jeremiah 33, a chapter predicting the joyful reestablishment of Judah, and one in which most of the words are delivered as if verbatim from God: "It is important to distinguish carefully the Word of God which came to the Prophets from the inferences, which they as unaided Men drew from the divine declarations. Thus: Jeremiah probably supposed that this splendid promise was to be fulfilled at the close of 70 years: but this is neither expressed or implied in the prophetic words themselves dictated by the Lord."[16] Coleridge's distinction can be made only in this way, however, if one has already accepted that the Hebrew Scriptures are themselves accurate accounts of the precise words of God and the precise words of the prophet. Despite his profound respect for the textual criticism of Eichhorn, Coleridge refuses the latter's vocabulary of "fiction" and "invention" to characterize the language of the prophets. Prophetic discourse seems to be "its own evidence," as Coleridge will say repeatedly of reason and religion in general.

The Statesman's Manual is, above all, a plea for the conduct and understanding of political life in the light of Biblical principles. The Bible, Coleridge had contended, provides rules and assistance for all men under all conditions. But his text, as we have noted, is by no means addressed to all men under all conditions: Rather, it speaks to the higher classes and to the clerisy. They are charged with studying the revealed will and word of God, because it affords "important truths"—and here Coleridge cites Isaiah in a telling phrase—"for a thousand generations" (7). These truths, the manual's subtitle suggests, have especially to do with foresight, with the language of prophecy in the strict sense. Coleridge apostrophizes the imaginary statesmen of the text whom he assumes are conversant with the Gospels: "And should you not feel a deeper interest in predictions which are permanent prophecies, because they are at the same time eternal truths? Predictions which in containing the grounds of fulfillment involve the principles of foresight" (7–8). Prophecies are not only eternal truths, as opposed to temporary insights or circumscribed predictions, they are equally the grounds and principles for all foresight—and not just foresight. Coleridge's juxtaposition of prophecy and principle here is consistent with his extravagant praise of Burke in the *Biographia Literaria*:

How are we to explain the notorious fact, that the speeches and writings of EDMUND BURKE are more interesting at the present day, than they were found at the time of their first publication; while those of his illustrious confederates are either forgotten, or exist only to furnish proofs, that the same conclusion, which one man had deduced scientifically, *may* be brought out by another in consequence of errors that luckily chanced to neutralize each other. . . . The satisfactory solution is, that Edmund Burke possessed and had sedulously sharpened that eye, which sees all things, actions, and events, in relation to the *laws* that determine their existence and circumscribe their possibility. He referred habitually to *principles*. He was a *scientific* statesman; and therefore a *seer*. For every principle contains within it the germ of a prophecy; and the prophetic power is the essential privilege of science, so the fulfillment of its oracles supplies the outward and (to men in general) the *only* test of its claim to the title. (VII, 191–92).

Rather like Wordsworth in his apostrophe to the genius of Burke in the late drafts of *The Prelude*, Coleridge praises Burke as the opponent of theory—"upstart theory" Wordsworth called it—and the champion of "principle."[17] Burke's *Reflections on the Revolution in France* had negotiated a difficult argument against abstract *theory* and metaphysics—of which the

French revolutionaries were massively guilty—and in favor of *principles*, distinguished from mere theories or speculations by their time-honored historical elaborations. Yet despite his emphasis on the pragmatism of political thinking, his rhetoric of principle and natural law implies a regularity and homogeneity of history such that one can *know* it, and even know it in advance.[18] (Indeed, a constant embarrassment for the opponents of Burke in the 1790s was that he had been largely correct in his predictions for the future of the revolution.) Coleridge recasts the Burkean pragmatist in relation to the Biblical prophet, such that the former will seem more inspired and the latter more scientific than they otherwise might: Statesman and seer virtually blend into one and the same figure. That is one reason why, in Coleridge's discourse on the current distresses in England through the optic of political economy, the ancient Biblical prophet emerges once again from the shadowy past.

From the outset of *The Statesman's Manual*, the extraordinary status accorded prophetic discourse is evident, as is the corresponding burden placed on it. Coleridge is well aware that Hebrew prophecy in its own time was of the utmost topicality and urgency, yet he assigns it a permanent place in the canon of political wisdom, and even of political theory. The prophetic is, in De Quincey's terms, literature of knowledge *and* literature of power: It has the ephemerality of a topical discourse of persuasion and, ideally, the timelessness of the most fundamental truths. This tension can be ascribed in part to its mixed discursive mode, both performative and constative: The promise, threat, or warning so characteristic of Biblical prophecy, is performative and "instantaneous," and the content of those speech-acts is supposedly constative or descriptive of a future state of affairs. In *How to Do Things with Words*, J. L. Austin begins with a seemingly strict opposition between performative and constative, only to undo the stability of that distinction in the long run through the rigor of his analysis.[19] Coleridge seems perfectly aware of the uncertain or mixed mode of prophetic speech-acts and is quick to seize on some of the possibilities afforded by it.[20] The dual character of topicality and permanence—which Coleridge prizes in the Bible as well as in Burke—is precisely what he tries to achieve in his own text, which grounds its attempt to remedy the distresses of the nation in an enlightened understanding of principles of theology and metaphysics. Hence the strategic value of Coleridge's joining his voice to the voices of the prophets.

In his *Lectures on the Sacred Poetry of the Hebrews*, Lowth had re-marked on the odd temporality of prophetic grammar, whereby a past event could be rendered in a present or future tense, and a future event in a past tense. A related reversibility of temporal reference informs Cole-ridge's understanding of the Hebrew Scriptures. He writes that, according to our relative position on the banks of the stream of time, "the Sacred His-tory becomes prophetic, the Sacred Prophecies historical, while the power and substance of both inhere in its Laws, its Promises, and its Commina-tions" (29–30).[21] Once again, Coleridge's formulation implicitly under-scores the mixed locutionary mode of prophecy as both performative and constative. The constative reference to an event, past or future, coexists with the law and the promise, which are in their structure performative. But the temporality of the performative is not fixed to the moment of its utterance, and all the more so when written down or quoted. The perfor-mative can, in principle, be repeated or reiterated infinitely, and thus its in-stantaneity—a promise is a promise as soon as it is uttered—is complicated by the possibility of its future repetition. A promise is something like a bro-ken record, forever repeating itself, whether or not it is actually enunciated again and again. Similarly, the constative reference to an historical event can always be interpreted or reinscribed, such that its temporal character is also by no means fixed. Thus the language of Biblical prophecy can be taken up in Coleridge's text alternately as the equivalent of timeless law and "wisdom" literature *or* as political commentary of the greatest urgency. (And the "or" does not signal a division of alternatives between which one has to choose.) But there is still a further complication to the language of prophecy that in part accounts for its ambiguous power. The prophetic promise is typically a promise of an event, but the character of the promise *as* event can take precedence over the content of whatever is promised. Such was the case in the Book of Jonah, discussed above in relation to Blake, where God's interest was not so much in the literal fulfillment of his threat as in the power of the threat to change the hearts and minds of Jonah's people. And certainly before the predicted event occurs, the prom-ise *is* the event. But it is difficult to confront the performative without in-scribing it into a narrative of a constative order.[22] If the performative sus-pends the question of truth—it makes no sense to ask whether a promise, as such, is true or false—the inscription of a performative within the frame of the constative tends in the opposite direction. What then of the truth,

the "political truth" at stake in Coleridge's text? It is precisely by resolv-
ing—or dissolving—the performative of the promise and the law into a
constative order of history that the question of truth can be restored or appear to be, a movement that parallels Coleridge's larger program of grounding politics in a metaphysics and a theology. It is no accident that for Coleridge, no less than for most Christian readers of prophecy in the eighteenth
century, prediction—rather than the more typical threat, promise, or
warning—becomes the paradigm for prophetic discourse. The performative comes to be effaced in the necessity to construct a prophetic history, a
story of—among other things—political truth.

The predictions of the Bible have, for Coleridge, two spheres of influence, corresponding to the two Testaments. He imagines that the statesman will have directed his primary attention to "the promises and information conveyed in the records of the evangelists and apostles" (8). Of
these promises Coleridge writes that they "need only a lively trust in them,
on our own part, to be the means and pledges of our *eternal* welfare! information that opens up to our knowledge a kingdom that is not of this
world, thrones that cannot be shaken, and sceptres that can neither be bro-
ken or transferred" (8). The knowledge afforded by the Bible is not simply
"given": It requires trust and "only" trust to acquire the status of knowledge, although a knowledge that is not empirically verifiable, because it is
not "of this world."[23] To the New Testament concern for our welfare that
is eternal and otherworldly (with its implication of a theocratic kingdom
that cannot be challenged), Coleridge opposes an interest in "the temporal
destinies of men and nations, sorted up for our instruction in the archives
of the Old Testament" (8). The Old Testament is temporarily cast as the
archive of the temporal, but even as an archive it presents the possibility of
retrieval and reinterpretation, the possibility of "permanent prophecy."

The opposition between the temporal character of the Old Testament and the spiritual character of the New is a foundational commonplace of Christian thought. Even so, it is odd that Coleridge should make
so categoric a distinction between the two, as if the New Testament had
nothing directly to do with the temporal destinies of men and nations.
Coleridge cites the Gospel's own phrase—a "kingdom not of this world"—
to authorize the separation, but a whole range of alternative strategies was
available to the Protestant poets and politicians of his day. The Pauline
doctrine that "the letter killeth, but the spirit giveth life," opposes the lit-

eral law of the Jews to the spiritual love of the Christians, yet the New Testament is no less an archive than the Old: Its doctrine of the spirit is inscribed in "dead" letters of its own. The same sorts of interpretive practices, allegorical or otherwise, govern its reading, and a "spiritual" rereading of the New Testament might well be applied to the "temporal destinies of men and nations," thus undoing Coleridge's too clear-cut distinction between the temporal and the otherworldly, the Old and the New. Blake's work, to take only one instance, was just such an allegorical reading of the New Testament. Yet, in a stunning gesture, atypical for a Christian thinker of his day, Coleridge holds up the Old Testament rather than the New as "the code of true political economy."

The Bible as a whole, but especially the Old Testament, is of such moment that Coleridge can claim "it would be a wise method of sympathizing with the tone and spirit of the Times, if we elevated even our daily newspapers and political journals into COMMENTS ON THE BIBLE" (35). Thus Coleridge not only calls for journalism to apply wisdom from the Bible to the analysis of current events, he also states that the Bible is to be the very medium of politics on which journalism will comment. The Bible *is* the text of history, written in advance of its occurrence as events. From the perspective of the contemporary moment, the Word is the beginning and the end of history. Even though Coleridge rarely has recourse in this text to the mechanics of typology, to the discourse of type and antitype, it is almost as if contemporary history in general were here reduced to having a typological relation especially to the Old Testament, the great code of political economy.

In a revisionary political program grounded in the Old Testament, the prophets will necessarily loom large. Quotations and allusions to the prophets pervade *The Statesman's Manual* as they do the second Lay Sermon, which takes as its text Isaiah's saying "Blessed are ye that sow beside all waters." In the two Lay Sermons, there are more citations from and allusions to the prophets than there are paragraphs of text: The language of prophecy informs the principles and details of argument and exposition, prompting its author at virtually every turn.[24] If prophecy is history, and history prophecy, then any attempt to understand the present historical conjuncture will have much to learn from the Biblical prophets, the most authoritative—because divinely inspired—of historians. In the Old Testament, the prophets are among the most conspicuously political figures, and although their politics are not of a piece, Northrop Frye can rightly summarize the ethos of prophecy as "the individualizing of the revolutionary impulse."[25] Unlike the king and the priest, the prophet is often called on to challenge the behavior of established authorities as well as of ordinary people. In rejecting the politics and the prose of Coleridge's Lay Sermons, Hazlitt was not discounting the possibility of a "prophetic" politics: Indeed, he recalls with favor the prophets of the Old Testament who "cashiered kings," a phrase that still resonates from its quite different context in Burke's *Reflections on the Revolution in France.* Yet Coleridge, in Hazlitt's view, not only betrays the antinomian ethos of the prophets so he can legitimate anachronistically a theory of divine right, he also fails to offer an illustration of how "the Jewish history" pertained to the situation of England in the post-Napoleonic period. There is no denying that Coleridge hedges and defers on this point, in a stylistic and argumentative gesture that is virtually his signature. But, in the end, Coleridge does provide a single example of the kind of interpretation he envisions. It draws on what is arguably *the* exemplary historical event of modernity, and as the only example Coleridge offers of the hermeneutic he advocates, it bears scrutiny in some detail.

In writing of the revolutionary government of France, Coleridge claims, citing Isaiah, that it "shewed no mercy, and very heavily laid its yoke." He exhorts his audience of statesmen to:

Turn then to the chapter from which the last words were cited, and read the following seven verses; and I am deceived if you will not be compelled to admit, that the Prophet Isaiah revealed the true philosophy of the French revolution more than two thousand years before it became a sad irrevocable truth of history. (34)

The key verses from Isaiah, as quoted by Coleridge, read as follows:

And thou saidst, I shall be a lady for ever: so that thou didst not lay these things to thy heart, neither didst remember the latter end of it. Therefore, hear now this, thou that art given to pleasures, that dwellest carelessly, that sayest in thine heart, I am, and none else besides me! I shall not sit as a widow, neither shall I know the loss of children. But these two things shall come to thee in a moment, in one day; the loss of children, and widowhood; they shall come upon thee in their perfection, for the multitude of thy sorceries, and for the abundance of thine enchantments. For thou hast trusted in thy wickedness, thou hast said, there is no overseer. Thy wisdom and thy knowledge, it hath perverted thee; and thou hast said in thine heart, I am, and none else besides me. Therefore shall evil come upon thee, thou shalt not know* from whence it riseth: and mischief shall fall upon thee, thou shalt not be able to put it off; and desolation shall come upon thee suddenly, which thou shalt not know. Stand now with thine enchantments, and with the multitude of thy sorceries, wherein thou hast labored from thy youth; if so be thou shalt be able to profit, if so be thou mayest prevail. Thou art wearied in the multitude of thy counsels: let now the astrologers, the stargazers, the monthly prognosticators stand up, and save thee from these things that shall come upon thee. (34)

The asterisk inserted within the citation from Isaiah is Coleridge's own. He interrupts the text, designed to elucidate the philosophy of the French Revolution, to note the correspondence between Isaiah's prophecy and a turning point in the Napoleonic Wars. Coleridge glosses the phrase "thou shalt not know from whence it riseth" in this way:

The Reader will scarcely fail to find in this verse a remembrancer of the sudden setting-in of the frost, a fortnight before the usual time (in a country too, where the commencement of its two seasons is in general scarcely less regular than that of the wet and dry seasons between the tropics) which caused, and the desolation which accompanied, the flight from Moscow. The Russians baffled the *physical* forces of the imperial Jacobin, because they were inaccessible to his *imaginary* forces. The faith in St. Nicholas kept off at safe distance the more pernicious superstition of the Destinies of Napoleon the Great. The English in the Peninsula overcame the real, because they *set at defiance*, and had heard only to despise, the imaginary powers of the irresistible Emperor. Thank heaven, the heart of the country was sound at the *core*. (34–35n)

Coleridge's application of the prophecy from Isaiah is inserted within the Biblical passage, almost as if in parentheses, and in such a way as to suggest it was not a matter of interpretation but a recognition as universal as a rudimentary perception: "The Reader will scarcely fail to find. . . . " When Coleridge descends from generalities to the minute particulars of application—to the sudden oncoming of frost in Russia in the winter of 1812—his reading is highly implausible, if not absurd.[26] The passage Coleridge cites from Isaiah predicts a sudden calamity, whose origin is obscure to those who experience it. (And this at a moment when Coleridge is speaking of interpretation as if it were a simple matter of experience.) Isaiah's verses do not offer the slightest outline of a specific event, understood in phenomenal terms, and yet Coleridge claims that no reader will fail to recognize the correspondence. Even granting the elasticity of reference occasioned by prophetic figuration, as we have seen outlined by Lowth, Hurd, and others, Coleridge's reading appears forced, at best. His more abstract notion of the French Revolution's philosophy (itself fatally "abstract," as Burke insinuated repeatedly in his *Reflections*) is more plausible and potentially persuasive. Coleridge's underscoring the denial of an "overseer" in Isaiah could resonate with a similar denial in the atheistic program of the French revolutionaries. And surely this link would have found much sympathy in any anti-Jacobin or anti-Napoleonic audience.

What seems to make the verses from Isaiah particularly sinister for Coleridge is the repeated pronouncement "I am," a demonic parody of "the divine I AM," that Coleridge takes as the foundation of his theology, ontology, psychology, and aesthetics.[27] Precisely the formula that is the most encompassing for Coleridge, applicable to the most private and individual of statements as well as to the divine pronouncement of being, is (mis)quoted by the evil pseudodeity conjured by Isaiah as a principle of exclusion: "I am and none else besides me!" Whatever historical and personal force this passage from Isaiah may have for readers other than the author of the Lay Sermons, the model that Coleridge holds up is meant to be of universal import: a model for reading contemporary history in the light of Biblical prophecy.

Why does so much turn in *The Statesman's Manual* on the interpretation of passages such as the one from Isaiah? The citations from the prophets are not simply more "poetic" or elegant formulations than those Coleridge might have invented. The point of such citation is to suggest ultimately that Coleridge's analysis of contemporary politics and matters of philosophy coincides with God's own. The prophetic quotations—unlike, say, the application of Biblical dicta of wisdom literature or laws of conduct—bear the kind of temporality able to provide the links between history and theology, politics and philosophy. The language of the prophet is understood as an intervention in history but as one whose relevance recurs at specific moments. The prophet is eminently citable, in Walter Benjamin's full sense of the term, and citable as authority. Like the Biblical prophet, Coleridge presents himself as a vehicle for divine vision, and the foresight he affords the statesman corresponds to and consists in the hindsight of correctly reading the prophets whose truths, he insists, are for a thousand generations.

The specific failures of Coleridge's interpretations in the *Lay Sermons* need not undermine the validity of his principle of Biblical authority, although one may begin to doubt Coleridge's claim at the outset that the Bible provided rules and assistance for *all* men under *all* circumstances. Coleridge's formulation of the goal of prophetic reading forces a reconsideration of the topic of political divisiveness raised in the earlier discussion of audience and the rhetoric of address. He promises the imagined statesmen and clerisy that a reading of the Bible along the lines he suggests "will raise you above the mass of mankind, and therefore will best entitle and qualify you to guide and control them" (25). *The Statesman's Manual,* then, is a program for the higher classes of society to read the Bible so as to control and guide the lower classes.

Even granted that few texts could successfully address all the divided classes of English society, how might such a program of hermeneutic control be reconciled with the putative universality of the Gospel and the Church posited by Protestantism? At the outset of his sermon, Coleridge remarks:

It is enough for us to know that the land, in which we abide, has like another Goshen *been severed from the plague,* and that we have light in *our* dwellings. The road of salvation for *us* is a high road and the wayfares, though "simple, need not err therein." The Gospel lies open in the marketplace, and on every window seat, so that (*virtually,* at least) the deaf may hear the words of the Book! It is preached at every turning, so that the blind may see them. (Isa.xxix.18) (6)

The Gospel indeed lies open for all, thanks to the Bible societies making it available to virtually anyone who could read, but the high road of salvation seems designated, in this text, for the higher classes. On the one hand, Coleridge rejoices at the prospect of the Gospel being readily available; on the other, he repeatedly laments that his own age has given birth to a hybrid monster called the reading public. The verses from Isaiah cited here anticipate the logic of Coleridge's text, because they describe the inability of the unlearned to understand, figured in the incapacity to read "the words of a book that is sealed" (28.11). Even the prophets and seers are said to have had their eyes covered (28.10). The privileged person in this scenario is not the prophet but the interpreter of the book, the one who can unseal the text closed off to all others. To cite the verses from Isaiah is an implicit claim to have understood them and perhaps further still, a claim to a certain mastery of the text cited.[28] The reader of prophecy, in Coleridge's text, comes to displace even the prophet as the vehicle of knowledge and inspiration. A similar rhetoric informs his late meditation on the inspiration of Scripture, the *Confessions of an Inquiring Spirit*, in which the scene of reading described is virtually indistinguishable from that of prophetic inspiration: "I will retire *up into the mountain*, and hold secret commune with my Bible above the contagious blastments of prejudice, and the fog-blight of selfish superstition."[29] The mountain is a classic site for prophetic enthusiasm, where the figure singled out for divine vision is accorded the singular privilege of knowing God's will: Physical proximity implies spiritual proximity. Long after prophecy is officially silenced, the act of reading recapitulates and transforms it: Reading prophecy can itself attain an aura of the prophetic. The tension between public and private, however cumbersome and anachronistic that distinction is in the realm of Biblical prophecy, surfaces here regarding the act of reading. In *The Statesman's Manual* Coleridge himself is torn between tendencies pulling in opposite directions. He hopes that more texts like his own will be addressed to their "appropriate class of Readers" but regrets:

this cannot be! For among other odd burs and kecksies, the misgrowth of our luxuriant activity, we now have a READING PUBLIC—as strange a phrase, methinks, as ever forced a splenetic smile on the staid countenance of Meditation; and yet no fiction! For our Readers have, in good truth, multiplied exceedingly, and have waxed proud. . . . From a popular philosophy and a philosophic populace, Good Sense deliver us! (36–8)

In the second Lay Sermon, Coleridge would lament the absence of popular philosophy, and in his autoreview he congratulated himself on producing a truly popular work (!), such that one can trace the discrepancies between his positions with regard to the audiences he is addressing. The "READING PUBLIC" seems to be a sheer oxymoron: The two terms don't belong together. But even within the parameters of *The Statesman's Manual*, perhaps the passage just quoted could be construed as another instance of Coleridge recognizing the historically established differences between classes and thus as a savvy if cynical expression of rhetorical *Realpolitik*. Yet his diatribe against the reading public might be accepted more readily if it did not coexist with propositions such as "Reason and Religion are their own Evidence" (10 and 57). In such apodictic pronouncements, reason sounds as if it is a universal principle, but if so, there are severe divisions within the sphere of reason: Reason, no less than truth, is divided within itself. In his early doctrine of "political truth" and the strategies of its dissemination,

Coleridge cautioned against disclosing those truths to minds not "susceptible of reasoning" and "never to the multitude." *The Statesman's Manual* is torn between the universalizing tendency of its rhetoric of reason and the specific character of its intervention against the alarming trends evident in the upstart English populace. It is characteristic of Coleridge, and it is the archideological gesture of his work, to represent as universal what is in fact partisan, strategic, and historically circumscribed. Such gestures are not merely thematic: They inform the very mode of address of his texts as well as their content. Coleridge's *Logic*, for example, insofar as it is the discourse of the Logos—of reason as such—might seem to have a claim to universality like that of the religion and reason in *The Statesman's Manual*. One finds, however, that the *Logic* is written to awaken powers "as the concerns of life and society require, whether for the bar, the pulpit, or the senate."[30] This oscillation between totalization and specification would remain problematic if left unresolved, and Coleridge's principal source of resolution is the authority of the Bible. This is yet another reason why his voice so often gives way to quotation of the divine, the prophetic word.

This ventriloquism operates in another manner consistent with *The Statesman's Manual*'s project of a hermeneutic to control the masses as well as with the lament of the new reading public. Coleridge puts words in the mouths of the very classes he has excluded from his text in advance. Having just compared the principles of "our" religion and the sublime ideas of the Bible to the fixed stars, Coleridge writes:

At the annunciation of *principles*, of *ideas*, the soul of man awakes, and starts up, as an exile in a far distant land at the unexpected sounds of his native language, when after long years of absence, and almost of oblivion, he is suddenly addressed in his own mother tongue. He weeps for joy, and embraces the speaker as his brother. How else can we explain the fact so honorable to Great Britain, that the poorest* amongst us will contend with as much enthusiasm as the richest for the rights of property? These rights are the spheres and necessary conditions of free agency. (24–5)

Coleridge's argument moves from Biblical ideas to principles in general and illustrates their force with the imaginary scenario of an exiled Englishman who suddenly hears the sound of his native language for the first time in years. Language is made to function here as a discourse of universality, precisely at the moment when the very scenario depends on historical and linguistic differences. In an argument pointing also to the putative absence of differences between rich and poor—both will contend for the rights of property—the native English language serves to level all class differences. All the exile hears, the anecdote suggests, is English, not even English inflected or accented in any particular way, certainly nothing like a dialect. And this universalized English is glossed as the mother tongue, further underlining its natural character. Thus the passage from Biblical ideas to principles in general moves a step farther to potential differences of an historical character, only to have those differences obliterated in the very medium that registers them and that is the medium of their institution: language.

The asterisk in the passage glossing "the poorest" points to the proof-text for Coleridge's contention about the lack of difference between rich and poor: an essay by Goldsmith on the distresses of the poor. The anecdote recounts the story of a disabled soldier who goes through numerous transformations from bound laborer to prisoner, to plantation slave, to press-ganged soldier and sailor, and finally to a beggar. Having lost several limbs in battle, in addition to all his other burdens, he is nonetheless said to exclaim: " . . . one man is born with a silver spoon in his mouth, and another with a wooden ladle. However, blessed be God, I enjoy good health, and will forever love liberty and Old England. Liberty, property, and Old England, for ever, huzza."[31] One wonders whether the triad of "Liberty, Property, and Old England" tripped off the tongues of the poor in one country as easily as "Liberty, Equality, and Fraternity" in another. In an acute passage from *The Statesman's Manual* Coleridge argues persuasively against solving "the riddle of the French Revolution by ANECDOTES" (14). Yet that is precisely the tactic Coleridge deploys in his use of the anecdote from Goldsmith. How exemplary of the English poor can Goldsmith's sentinel be, given that he is indefatigably cheerful despite incessant misfortune and a good deal of oppression? Can such a "part" represent the whole of its class? The collapse of class distinctions on issues of property and liberty is one way to unify a text that is always threatening to divide itself. But what Coleridge offers here as the contemporary vox populi bears little resemblance to what historians have reconstructed of it in our own time. Goldsmith's anecdote invoked by Coleridge hardly accords with the evidence of working-class consciousness assembled in E. P. Thompson's magisterial study of the topic.[32] But even in Coleridge's own time, this voice of the poor summoned to chime in with the "higher classes of society" must have sounded too good to be true.[33]

The same Coleridge—or is it the same?—who here ventriloquizes the poor as defenders of the right to property, had once written to John Thelwall in 1796: "The real source of inconstancy, depravity, & prostitution, is *Property*, which mixes with & poisons every thing good—& is beyond doubt the Origin of all Evil."[34] In his *Lectures on Revealed Religion* of the previous year, Coleridge mounted a similar attack on property, grounding his authority on Jesus and the teachings of the Gospel: "I have asserted that Jesus Christ forbids to his disciples all property—and teaches us that accumulation was incompatible with Salvation!"[35] Then, as early as 1802, Coleridge could write for *The Morning Post*: "As far back as the memory reaches, it was an axiom in politics with us, that in every country in which property prevailed, property must be the grand basis of the government; and that that government was the best, in which the power was most exactly proportioned to the property."[36] Coleridge's memory of his own positions on property does not reach back very far.[37] Such "oscillations"—to borrow a word he often used in connection with parliamentary politics—have been well documented, especially in terms of politics.[38] Yet whether one laments or celebrates Coleridge's apostasy, the paramount interest of his strategies here lies in his systematic attempt to represent his changing political views as identical with and authorized by God's own. Hence the frequent citation of the Bible, and especially of the prophets, whose enigmatic, highly figured utterances can be enlisted in virtually any interpretation of the present when a virtuoso interpreter is in control of the text.

It is not an arduous task to demonstrate the political contradictions between one Coleridge text and the next, especially given the immense distance traveled between 1795 and 1815. Of greater moment, however, are the contradictions *within* the very project and execution of the Lay Sermons. As has been established already, *The Statesman's Manual* was to be the first of three sermons that in their totality would address all the divided economic classes of England. Why Coleridge failed in the attempt, and why he never wrote the third sermon to the "Lower and Laboring Classes," may by now be somewhat clearer. It was not, as with "Kubla Khan," because of an ill-timed knock at the door. And not, as with his many encyclopedic projects, because the task set was simply too grandiose. Rather, it was because Coleridge had, this time, nothing to say: nothing to say *to* the working classes on behalf of them.

The failure of Coleridge to carry through with his sermon to the lower and laboring classes cannot quite be accounted for by appealing to Coleridge's long-standing belief that one should plead *for* the oppressed not *to* them:

That general Illumination should precede Revolution, is a truth as obvious, as that the Vessel should be cleansed before we fill it with a pure Liquor. But the mode of diffusing it is not discoverable with equal facility. We certainly should never attempt to make Proselytes by appeals to the *selfish* feelings—and consequently, should plead *for* the Oppressed, not *to* them. (*CW*, I, 43)

David Erdman terms this strategy ultraconservative, yet it is characteristic of Coleridge even in the radical phases of his career. Coleridge proceeds in his *Conciones ad Populum* of 1795 to criticize Godwin's notion of the "gradual descent" of truth, contending that society as presently constituted does not resemble "a chain that ascends in a continuity of Links" (I, 43). He concludes: "But alas! between the Parlor and the Kitchen, the Tap and the Coffee-Room there is a gulph that may not be passed" (I, 43). The very title of an address to the people entitled *Conciones ad Populum* hardly helps bridge this gulf, for the use of Latin suggests that, for Coleridge, "the people" had already been circumscribed to something like the clerisy.

This "unbridgeable" gap would be acknowledged again in the project of the Lay Sermons and the necessity for a separate address to each major economic class. That the third sermon never materialized is due only partly to Coleridge's philosophy of political address, which asserted itself again during the composition of the Lay Sermons.[39] No doubt it was also due to the content of the address to the higher classes, almost necessarily at odds with the envisioned address to the lower and laboring classes. Not that Coleridge's politics even in 1816 were simply antithetical to the interest of the working classes: He did valuable work in support of progressive child-labor legislation, for example, and was a staunch advocate of unambiguously progressive causes, such as the abolition of the slave trade. But the Lay Sermons, and especially the unwritten third one, were designed to expose the champions of the lower classes whom Coleridge called "our Incendiaries," meaning Cobbett, Francis Jeffrey, and the Hunt brothers. "Hateful under all names these wretches are most hateful to me as Liberticides," Coleridge exclaimed.[40] Cobbett, as we noted, was an immensely popular author with a large audience of working-class people. But in writing to a publisher geared toward that class, Coleridge expressed his contempt for the way that

Cobbett and Hunt "address you as Beasts who have no future Selves—as if by a natural necessity you must *all* for ever remain poor & slaving."[41] It is true that Cobbett's writing is less driven by an ethos of individualism and voluntarism than Coleridge's. And thus the category of the self has a radically different function in Cobbett's work, permeated as it is by a working-class consciousness. But even Cobbett's work—most of it future-oriented, all of it during this period at least "reformist"—allowed for and urged change for the better, even on a strictly individual basis.[42] Projects as distinct as *A Grammar of the English Language*, *Advice to Young Men*, and *Cottage Economy* as well as the steady stream of advice and analysis in the *Political Register*, would contradict Coleridge's severe assessment of Cobbett on this count.[43] While the working classes were buying Cobbett's *Political Register* by the tens of thousands, it is difficult to imagine Coleridge's third sermon "To the Lower and Laboring Classes" meeting with much success, were he to have proposed anything continuous with the first sermon that had advocated those classes be controlled and guided by the clerisy and the upper classes. The unwritten third sermon was as visionary a project— though for different reasons—as the frenzied writing of "Kubla Khan."

The political and interpretive program of *The Statesman's Manual* elaborated to this point may seem far removed from the theory of symbol and allegory that is the text's principal legacy. Yet a similar rhetoric organizes and authorizes both the political agenda and the theory of figuration, such that each can be read as an allegory of the other. The articulation between the two is enabled by, among other things, the strategic invocation of the language of prophecy common to both. In Coleridge's rhetorical theory as well as in his politics, quotation of the divine word will serve as authority and example.

II

Coleridge's celebrated theory of symbol and allegory seems to present a theory of figuration of universal significance and application, but it has for Coleridge all the urgency of a hot political topic: "It is among the miseries of the present age," Coleridge writes, "that it recognizes no medium between *Literal* and *Metaphorical*. Faith is either to be buried in the dead letter, or its name and honors usurped by a counterfeit product of the mechanical understanding, which in the blindness of self-complacency confounds SYMBOLS with ALLEGORIES" (30).[44] Noting the failure to locate a medium between the literal and the metaphorical might be a prelude to revealing just such a medium. But if Coleridge is uneasy with the simple binary opposition of literal and figurative, he nonetheless proceeds to make a categorical distinction between symbol and allegory, and it is not at all clear that the notion of the symbol is supposed to constitute the medium between the literal and metaphorical. Coleridge continues in a tone that seems, for the moment, to have left all political urgency behind:

Now an Allegory is but a translation of abstract notions into a picture-language which is itself nothing but an abstraction from objects of the senses; the principal being more worthless even than its phantom proxy, both alike unsubstantial, and the former shapeless to boot. On the other hand a Symbol (ὁ ἔστιν ἀει ταυτηγόρικον) is characterized by a translucence of the Special in the Individual or of the General in the Especial or of the Universal in the General. Above all by the translucence of the Eternal through and in the Temporal. It always partakes of the Reality which it renders intelligible; and while it enunciates the whole, abides itself as a living part in that Unity, of which it is the representative. The other are but empty echoes which the fancy arbitrarily associates with apparitions of matter, less beautiful but not less shadowy than the sloping orchard or hillside pasture-field seen in the transparent lake below. (30–1)

It is difficult to imagine a starker opposition than the one Coleridge draws here between symbol and allegory. Who would not choose—if there were a choice—symbol over allegory? Who would not choose reality, unity, representation, and totality over abstraction, translation, and phantom proxies? Indeed, the choice would be tantamount to one between life and death, given the echoes of Milton's Death from *Paradise Lost* in this account of allegory, as well as the rhetoric of death so often aligned by Coleridge with everything mechanical. Yet Coleridge's own representation of the differences between symbol and allegory complicates the very claims he is making. Paul de Man's reading of this passage focuses on the figure of "translucence," on the "shining through" of the symbol, which he claims does not entail the "organic or material richness" one expects from the rest of the passage. De Man argues further that:

The material substantiality dissolves and becomes a mere reflection of a more original unity that does not exist in the material world. It is all the more surprising to see Coleridge, in the final part of the passage, characterize allegory negatively as being *merely* a reflection. In truth, the spiritualization of the symbol has been carried so far that the moment of material existence by which it was originally defined has now become altogether unimportant; symbol and allegory alike now have a common origin beyond the world of matter.[45]

If de Man is correct, Coleridge's distinction is far less categorical than it appears. But what of de Man's own "translation" of the text? The most cogent objection to his reading comes from Jerome Christensen, who calls attention to de Man's substitution of "reflection" for "translucence."[46] The two categories refer to different physical phenomena, so what could justify the substitution of one for the other? A possible answer lies elsewhere in *The Statesman's Manual*, where Coleridge explicitly associates reflection with the idea of the symbol:

O what a mine of undiscovered treasures, what a new world of Power and Truth would the Bible promise to our future meditation, if in some gracious moment one solitary text of all its inspired contents should but dawn upon us in the pure untroubled brightness of an IDEA, that most glorious birth of the God-like within us, which even as the Light, its material symbol, reflects itself from a thousand surfaces (50).

The figural and conceptual system that connects idea, light, truth, reflection, symbol, and the divine pervades the text and makes possible a link between the literal and figurative senses of the term "reflection." Moreover, Coleridge insists here on the representational character of the symbol, thus inscribing it in an essentially mimetic economy.

The circumscribed debate about the structure of translucence proper to the symbol may distract readers from a more fundamental burden of Coleridge's text: to demonstrate the *possibility* of symbols in the strict sense. What kind of symbol is Coleridge speaking of? What is its proper sphere? From the moment Coleridge writes "Now an Allegory . . . ," the passage seems to encompass every sort of symbol and allegory, although the distinction is raised with respect to another one, namely, that between Biblical history and Enlightenment historiography. Of the former history Coleridge claims:

In the Scriptures they are the *educts* of the Imagination; of that reconciling and mediatory power, which incorporating the Reason in Images of Sense, and organizing (as it were) the flux of the Senses by the permanence and self-circling energies of the Reason, gives birth to a system of symbols, harmonious in themselves, and consubstantial with the truths, of which they are the *conductors*. These are the

Wheels which Ezekiel beheld, when the hand of the Lord was upon him, and he saw visions of God as he sate among the captives of the river of Chebar. *Whither-soever the Spirit was to go, the wheels went, and thither was their spirit to go: for the spirit of the living creature was in the wheels also.* The truths and the symbols that represent them move in conjunction and form the living chariot that bears up (for *us*) the throne of the Divine Humanity. Hence by a derivative, indeed, but not a divided influence, and though in a secondary yet in more than a metaphorical sense, the Sacred Book is worthily entitled *the* WORD OF GOD. (28–29)

To this last sentence, Hazlitt retorted, echoing *Tristram Shandy*: "Of all the cants that were ever canted in this canting world, this is the worst." Through the maze of Coleridge's tortured syntax, one can glimpse his struggle with an immense and genuine problem: In what sense is the Bible the word of God?[47] The question of mediation is crucial here, as it is in Coleridge's early and late reflections on the prophet as the human figure who most immediately transmitted the word of God. It is also related to Coleridge's lament that there is no *medium* between the literal and the metaphorical, because the Bible in his analysis is composed of the word of God, literally and otherwise.[48] In the passage on light as the material symbol of the idea, I pointed to the chain of concepts and figures related to the symbol. Here one sees an extension of that same chain to include imagination, incorporation, truth, and spirit, all of which together with the symbol are enlisted to characterize the Biblical histories as vehicles of the divine word. The prophetic pre-text for Coleridge here is the first chapter of Ezekiel, with its sublime vision of the divine chariot or *merkabah*.[49] Coleridge places the emphasis on the consubstantiality of spirit and wheel, of the divine and its material vehicle. But the context in Ezekiel is a difficult one to invoke as exemplary of the coincidence of tenor and vehicle. Here is the spectacular opening "vision" of Ezekiel from which Coleridge quotes:

And I looked, and behold, a whirlwind came out of the north, a great cloud, and a fire infolding itself, and a brightness *was* about it, and out of the midst thereof as the color of amber, out of the midst of the fire./Also out of the midst thereof *came* the likeness of four living creatures. And this *was* their appearance; they had the likeness of a man./And every one had four faces, and every one had four wings./ And their feet *were* straight feet; and the sole of their feet *was* like the sole of a calf's foot: and they sparkled like the color of burnishing brass./And *they had* the hands of a man under the wings on their four sides and they four had their faces and their wings./Their wings *were* joined one to another; they turned not when they went;

they went every one straight forward./As for the likeness of their faces, they four had the face of a man, and the face of a lion, on the right side: and they four had the face of an ox on the left side; they four also had the face of an eagle. (1.4–10)

Just before the passage cited by Coleridge on the identity of wheel and spirit, Ezekiel records: "The appearance of the wheels and their work *was* like unto the color of a beryl: and they four had one likeness: and their appearance and their work *was* as it were a wheel in the middle of a wheel." By this point, it is exceedingly difficult to tell whether we are to understand Ezekiel's vision of the chariot literally or figuratively. The problem pertains to virtually all the vision's elements. The passage begins with what appears to be a literal chariot, only to have it transformed into a seemingly figurative one. Is the chariot that is to be exemplary of the symbol really "symbolic," or is it rather a translation, a phantom proxy? To gloss the symbol and illuminate the system of symbols, Coleridge has recourse to one of the most sublime prophetic visions, but a vision that is scarcely visualizable, a vision that can be only "represented" in words, and one whose figural character is repeatedly underscored by Ezekiel, in the phrases "as it were" (כַּאֲשֶׁר) and "a likeness" (כְּעֵין)."[50] In his *Guide for the Perplexed* Maimonides singled out this passage as an example of the sublime, that is, as a negative index rather than a faithful representation of God's glory.[51] The hallmark of the sublime is the incommensurability of the representation and referent, and Ezekiel's summarizing phrase "This was the appearance of the likeness of the glory of God" marks precisely the distance between the two, rather than their identity.

Is it any accident that Coleridge chooses a vehicle as the exemplary symbol of the symbolic? Coleridge's theologicopolitical program presents the chariot of the divine as consubstantial with the truth it represents, and this vehicle functions as a figure for language, not least because it appears at the moment preceding the definitions of symbol and allegory and serves to exemplify the symbolic. But can one transfer so easily from the divine vehicle to the human, translating from one mode to the other? The "vehicles" of ordinary language are not at all consubstantial with the truths they represent: They are, at best, arbitrary signs of them. Coleridge had often argued against the Lockean heritage of the arbitrariness of the sign, as in his letters to Godwin around the turn of the nineteenth century.[52] And so his attempt at once to naturalize and to sacralize language must go some way toward collapsing the difference between the human and the divine.

An appropriate "vehicle" for this is the chariot, because the vehicle is, as in Aristotle, the oldest of metaphors for metaphor, enabling the transfer of sense from one locus to another. But the structure of metaphor raises the specter of translation—a concept inextricable from that of metaphor—that Coleridge specifies as the characteristic of allegory, not symbol.[53] In citing Ezekiel, Coleridge tried to point to the consubstantiality of the symbol and what it represents, but had to efface the figural character of Ezekiel's description in order to do so. Something gets lost in the translation, namely, the very structure of translation. In offering the chariot as the symbol of the symbol, Coleridge fails to take account of the allegorical moment of figuration and translation (translation, again, being the hallmark of allegory rather than symbol).[54] Which is to say, that in *The Statesman's Manual* he presents the symbol in the mode of allegory that is antithetical to it. What Coleridge posits as the symbol of the symbol turns out instead to be its allegory.

But perhaps Coleridge is ultimately not so concerned with the translation from the divine to the human as some passages of his text and many commentators suggest. Indeed, the greater the number of examples that Coleridge offers for the symbol, the clearer it becomes that the symbol, in the strict sense, has nothing to do with human language. How can this be so? In pleading for a distinction between superstitions and truths worthy of belief, Coleridge writes of the enabling distinction: "It is found in the study of the Old and New Testament, if only it be combined with a spiritual partaking of the Redeemer's Blood, of which, mysterious as the symbol may be, the sacramental Wine is no mere or arbitrary memento" (88). Coleridge seems to pass effortlessly here from the textual scenario of reading the Bible to the sacramental model of internalization of the divine, by way of the symbol.[55] This coincides with the passage from Isaiah cited immediately after the distinction between symbol and allegory: "It shall be even as when the hungry dreameth, and behold! he eateth; but he waketh and his soul is empty: or as when the thirsty dreameth, and behold he drinketh; but he awaketh and is faint!" (Isaiah xxix.8) (31). Allegory is empty, the symbol is full, and this plenitude can be thoroughly internalized or incorporated (taken into the body), fulfilling the requirement of "partaking" definitive of the symbol. (The figuration here is continuous with the many passages from both testaments of the Bible showing prophets and seers literally eating God's words, all of which can be related to the scene of the word becoming flesh.) As in the general statement on symbol and allegory, the emphasis on the Redeemer's blood underscores the nonarbitrary character of the relation. The wine is not a symbol merely by virtue of the resemblance between wine and blood: It becomes a symbol through Jesus' pronouncement of the identity of blood and wine. Yet, through that divine act of language the relation between blood and wine becomes, paradoxically, nonlinguistic: It becomes real in every sense of the word. It is crucial that Coleridge's example of the symbol is drawn from the absolute instance of presence, the very basis of the doctrine of the real presence.[56] The question, however, remains: Once one invokes the absolute instance of presence as a model for the symbol, can any instance of human language live up to that model and function as a symbol?

Still another passage on the symbolic presents not just a vehicle or a "symbol" for the Lord but the Lord himself. In commenting on Jakob Böhme's analogy between the sun and the Son of God—the verbal parallel between the two is similar in English and German—Coleridge writes: "The immanent Energy of the divine Consciousness is, and is the cause of, the coeternal Filiation of the Logos, the essential Symbol of the Deity, the substantial infinite, sole adequate Idea, in God, of God; in and by whom the Father *necessarily* self-manifested, doth *freely* in the ineffable overflowing of Goodness create, and, in proportion to the containing power, manifest himself to, all Creatures" (XII, 1, 564). Here not only is the son as privileged symbol of the Logos "symbolic" in the full sense, the Logos itself is a symbol. It has both a static timelessness, as coeternal and continuous with God, and a changing temporality, as the filial manifestation and realization of the deity. This symbol, then, is much like the wheels of Ezekiel's chariot that are constantly on the move yet at one with the spirit of the Lord. The former example of the symbolic—the blood of the Eucharist—may seem to allow for the transition from the divine to the human through the act of internalization or incorporation (itself often understood as a figure for reading, in the prophetic books and elsewhere).[57] But does not the character of the examples Coleridge provides restrict the sense of the symbolic, such that it can hardly apply to language that is all too human? Can any poetic symbol—no matter how seductive, powerful or seemingly natural—allow the "Eternal" to shine in and through the temporal? Some of Coleridge's apologists have emphasized that the force of the distinction between symbol and allegory depends on the insistence on literal *partaking*.[58] But compared to the Logos and to the blood of the Eucharist as symbols of the symbolic, any human language and any poetry must be allegorical, if the choice has to be made between the senses of symbol and allegory set out by Coleridge. Circumscribed to the word of God, Coleridge's theory of the symbol may or may not be tenable: That question is more a matter of faith than of literary interpretation. Yet no understanding of literature can base a general theory of poetic symbolism on the permanently miraculous relation between the blood of Christ and sacramental wine, much less on the Logos as such.

But what if we expand the range of Coleridge's symbols of the symbolic? Can the radical separation of the divine and the human still be maintained, as I have been arguing against the grain of a good deal of Coleridgean criticism? Another possible sphere of the symbolic is nature, arguably the proper domain of the symbol, as outlined in an appendix to *The Statesman's Manual*:

True natural philosophy is comprised in the study of the science and language of *symbols*. The power delegated to nature is all in every part; and by a symbol I mean, not a metaphor or allegory or any other figure of speech or form of fancy, but an actual and essential part of that, the whole of which it represents. Thus our Lord speaks symbolically when he says that "the eye is the light of the body."[59] (79)

There is no doubt that Coleridge refers to nature here, but only to a point: the point at which Coleridge *cites* God's word. Here the divine word functions as a gloss to the natural symbol, implying a continuity between the two. But the actual rhetoric of the passage is at odds with its explicit claims. In arguing for a nonlinguistic symbol—having nothing to do with any figure of speech—Coleridge cites a Biblical text as authority, and the authority invoked is thoroughly linguistic *and* figural.[60] If one looks to the two versions of these verses in the Gospels describing the eye as the light of the body, one finds that Christ's saying does not name a natural relation at all, as if perhaps to say that the eye is the source of light for the body. On the contrary, the relation posited in the Gospels is an ethical one. The verses from Luke read: "The light of the body is the eye; therefore when thine eye is single, thy whole body is also full of light; but when thine eye is evil, thy body is full of darkness" (11.34-35). Even the light named here is not natural, because the word for "light" (*luknon*) denotes a lamp rather than a natural source. Coleridge may well intend to speak of a nonlinguistic "language" of natural symbols, a language without tropes or figures, but the rhetoric of the example belies his theoretical claim. Once again, an allegory of the symbol emerges just where we were led to expect a symbol of the symbolic.

When Coleridge claims to be speaking not of "a metaphor or allegory or any other figure of speech or form of fancy, but an actual and essential part of that, the whole of which it represents," he invokes the categories definitive of the symbol and putatively exemplified by the chariot of Ezekiel. Coleridge wants to speak of a language of nature before language but offers a linguistic example of the symbol as illustration. Precisely where Coleridge renounces the rhetoric of figure, he exemplifies the natural structure by a synecdoche, that which allows the substitution of part for whole. The link between the symbolic and the synecdochal is made explicit in a notebook entry: "The Symbolical . . . cannot perhaps be better defined, in distinction from the Allegorical, than that it is always itself a *part* of that of the whole of which it is representative—Here comes a *Sail*—that is, A ship, is a symbolical Expression—Behold our Lion, when we speak of some gallant Soldier, is allegorical. . . . "[61] The recourse to synecdoche in Coleridge, whether acknowledged or not, parallels the various gestures of totalization rehearsed at the outset of the chapter. The strategic value of such synecdochic rhetoric is unquestionable: What better figure for the encyclopedic burden of Coleridge's texts than a part that stands for a whole not represented or representable as such? At times, the persuasive use of synecdoche is relatively harmless, but its enlistment in certain political agendas is far less so. In March of 1817, a few months after the publication of *The Statesman's Manual*, Coleridge writes to his publisher T. J. Street: "Alas! dear Sir! what is mankind but the Few in all ages? Take them away, and how long, think you, would the rest differ from the Negroes and the New Zealanders . . . ?"[62] Coleridge began the Lay Sermons with the intention of addressing the whole of English society in its class divisions but ended without a sermon for the lower and laboring classes. In the Lay Sermons and in the less public forum of his correspondence, he does away with those classes—as well as a race and a nation—in silence or in the violence of a figure of speech.

One could trace a similar problematic within the second Lay Sermon, with its similar reliance on prophetic rhetoric and its language tailored now not only for the higher classes but the middle classes as well.[63] But the closing analysis will be confined primarily to what is overtly different in that sermon from *The Statesman's Manual*, namely its avowedly allegorical vision. It could come as a shock to the reader of the first Lay

Sermon familiar with the denigration of allegory to find that the second of the series is introduced by what Coleridge terms an "Allegoric Vision." But the second sermon may turn out to be continuous with the first, after all.

In grasping for a resolution to "existing Distresses and Discontents," as the subtitle phrases it, Coleridge begins with the axiom that all extremes meet, and his allegoric vision will narrate one version of that meeting. The vision is granted to a pilgrim traveling through an abstractly allegorical landscape, caught between melancholy and hope, autumn and spring. The visionary he happens on transports him into a dreamworld setting that the pilgrim recognizes as "the Valley of Life." The pilgrim soon enters a fantastical building, with every window portraying "some horrible tale, or preternatural incident, so that not a ray of light could enter, untinged by the medium through which it passed" (134). Once in the building, which appears to be the temple of "the only true Religion," the pilgrim finds it hard to comprehend what he sees, because he is constantly being presented with "MYSTERIES." Soon those inside the temple seem to recognize it for what it is: the Temple of Superstition, thus prompting a hasty exit by the narrator. He and his newfound companions now encounter another figure, a woman with a "divine unity of expression," whose name is revealed as RELIGION. This figure offers the pilgrim a vision, and it is at this moment that the text begins to sound like an allegory of the symbolic: "She led us to an eminence in the midst of the valley, from the top of which we could command the whole plain, and observe the relation of different parts, of each to the other, and of each to the whole, and of all to each." This holistic vision of the interrelation of parts draws heavily on the rhetoric of the symbol set out in the first Lay Sermon. And it comes strategically as the mediating moment between the preceding vision of SUPERSTITION and the subsequent vision of NATURE, itself described in terms of reflection, surface, and the blind functioning of mechanisms reminiscent of the language of allegory. Thus the true religion mediates between the twin extremes of superstition and nature: nature, that is, as envisioned through the atheistic dogmatism of Enlightenment thinkers.[64] How can Coleridge in the first Lay Sermon denounce allegory altogether only to have recourse to it in the second and, more than that, to enlist allegory to tell the truth about religion? Is Coleridge now acknowledging the necessity of writing about the symbolic in an allegorical mode? Or is he just performing a contradiction virtually built into the impossible project of the Lay Sermons?

When the "allegoric vision" appears in the second Lay Sermon, it is not for the first or the last time in Coleridge's works. Coleridge wrote at least four versions of essentially the "same" vision, first in 1795 for his Lectures, then a revised version for *The Courier* of July 31, 1811, followed by the instance just discussed, and finally a version for an edition of his works in 1829. The phrasing, imagery, and some of the plot change from one instance to the next, although the basic structure of religion as mediator between superstition and nature remains constant. The most crucial difference is the changing referent of the false religion, identified, implicitly or explicitly, in 1795 as the Church of England and in later decades as the Church of Rome. Thus the vision of the true religion is indeed allegorical, in that it is eminently detachable, translatable from one context and referent to another. The representation cannot, in either instance, *partake* of the reality it renders intelligible, cannot be a symbolic rendering of the true religion as symbolic. As such, the vision introducing the second Lay Sermon is an allegory of allegory, an allegory of the necessity of allegorizing the symbolic. The symbolic, even confined in its proper sphere to the language of the Bible and the language of nature, can be rendered only allegorically, and so the representation is always of another order from its referent. The notorious denigration of allegory in *The Statesman's Manual* seems excessive, even within the corpus of Coleridge's works. He often designated poems of his own composition as allegories, spoke in admiring tones of allegorical writers like Spenser, and found the "allegoric vision" just rehearsed congenial enough to use it again and again throughout his work.

If it is correct to say that there is in human language no such thing as a symbol in the strict sense, that is not necessarily to argue against Coleridge, but it certainly is to go against the grain of a good many Coleridgeans. It is a common strategy among critics to transpose the concept of the symbol outlined in *The Statesman's Manual* to disparate realms of experience, especially to the aesthetic and the poetic. Coleridge is perhaps the first of Coleridgeans to do so, in part by systematically associating the symbol with the imagination. The set piece on allegory and symbol in *The Statesman's Manual* explicitly links allegory with fancy, the debased opposite of imagination as set out famously in chapter XIII of the *Biographia*. If the symbol is invoked via the language of prophecy, the imagination relies no less on a ventriloquism of the divine:

The IMAGINATION then I consider either as primary or secondary. The primary IMAGINATION I hold to be the living Power and prime Agent of all human Perception, and as a repetition in the finite mind of the eternal act of creation in the infinite I AM. The secondary I consider as an echo of the former, coexisting with the conscious will, yet still identical with the primary in the *kind* of its agency, and differing only in *degree*, and the *mode* of its operation. It dissolves, diffuses, dissipates, in order to re-create; or where this process is rendered impossible, yet still at all events it struggles to idealize and to unify. It is essentially *vital*, even as all objects (*as* objects) are essentially fixed and dead. (VII,1,304)

In the readings of the passage offered to date, critics have tended to underscore the creativity and the vitality of the imagination and even to see this passage as the culmination of a long tradition working toward the enunciation of "the creative imagination."[65] But what if one emphasizes different terms of the passage?

Most critics agree that the secondary imagination is the faculty responsible for the production of poetry in the broad and the narrow senses of the term (the primary being a universal faculty of perception, as Kant's transcendental imagination), and the secondary imagination is determined as the *echo* of the primary. The primary imagination is itself structured as something of an echo, or, more precisely, a *repetition* of the divine I AM. Poetry is, in a word, the echo of the repetition of the divine I AM. But that formula is an abbreviation of its longer Biblical version, usually translated: "I AM that I AM." Thus if one considers these relations simultaneously as determining the model for poetry, the language of the poetic imagination is structured as the echo of a repetition of a tautology. The echo of a repetition of a tautology. To read the definition of imagination in this way is already to align it more closely with fancy, the faculty of mind supposed to be the opposite or contrary of imagination, and associated by Coleridge with memory, the law of association, and all the arbitrariness that entails. Fancy seems to inhabit the imagination from which it is supposed to be excluded, much as allegory inhabits the Coleridgean symbol.

When the "I am" surfaces here in the *Biographia*'s definition of imagination, it does so as a version of a finite "I" already present in a number of guises: the empirical autobiographical "I" of Coleridge's narrative of his life and opinions, the epistemological "I" of a transposed German idealism, as well as the ultimate divine "I." In its final version, in the chapter on imagination, it appears as what may be called the aesthetic "I." Much of the burden of the text is to negotiate a smooth passage from one order to the other. But how does Coleridge arrive at the final "I" of the poetic or the aesthetic? The advantage of the "I am" formula for the other categories lay in its universality, "I am" being in grammatical terms the lowest common denominator. Who cannot say "I am"? Yet it is precisely the universality of the "I am" that renders it so problematic when enlisted as a principle of aesthetic judgment.[66] Coleridge, in effect, demands that the reader distinguish between poems that say "I am" and poems that do not. Yet the discriminations of aesthetic judgment require something other and less than such a totalizing and universalizing discourse.

If the model of imagination as a principle of aesthetic practice and judgment is already problematic as staged in the *Biographia*, the symbol, as conceptualized in *The Statesman's Manual*, is all the more so when enlisted in an aesthetic program. In a related context, Walter Benjamin provided a telling critique of appeals to the symbol in literary contexts when it is really more properly a theological concept. In the *Origin of German Tragic Drama* he wrote:

But it is precisely this illegitimate talk of the symbolic which permits the examination of every artistic form "in depth," and has an immeasurably comforting effect on the practice of investigation into the arts. The most remarkable thing about the popular use of the term is that a concept which, as it were categorically, insists on the indivisible unity of form and content, should nevertheless serve the philosophical extenuation of that impotence which, because of the absence of dialectical rigor, fails to do justice to content in formal analysis and to form in the aesthetics of content. For this abuse occurs wherever in the work of art the "manifestation" of an "idea" is declared a symbol. The unity of the material and transcendental object, which constitutes the paradox of the theological symbol, is distorted into a relationship between appearance and essence. The introduction of this distorted conception of the symbol into aesthetics was a romantic and destructive extravagance that preceded the desolation of modern art criticism.[67]

Benjamin ascribes serious, deleterious effects to the mistranslation of the theological symbol into the realm of the aesthetic. I have been suggesting that Coleridge's doctrine of the symbol cannot suffer such a translation, cannot be transposed from the theological or natural models to the realm of language, whether poetic or not. And yet this is precisely what a good many Coleridgeans do. Thomas McFarland, for example, begins a defense of the symbol and an attack on de Man's reading of Coleridge by making the plausible argument that Coleridge's definition of the symbol marks it as theological. McFarland even enlists Benjamin's critique of the aesthetic use of the properly theological concept of the symbol. Yet McFarland soon forgets Benjamin's (and Coleridge's?) lesson by claiming that there are no more "palpably symbolic poems than 'Kubla Khan' and 'The Ancient Mariner.'[68] McFarland and others are partly following Coleridge's lead, to the extent that in *The Statesman's Manual* he had aligned the symbol with the imagination and allegory with the fancy, as if the symbol were a viable aesthetic category. But the reading of the theoretical pronouncement on the symbol and especially its exemplifications shows that its religious and sacramental character—modeled on nothing less than the incarnation of Christ and the sacrament of the Eucharist—is precisely what prevents it from being translatable into the domain of the aesthetic and of poetry in particular.

In attempting to formulate a theory of the symbol in superiority and opposition to allegory, Coleridge in *The Statesman's Manual* presents and exemplifies that very theory in an allegorical mode. A similar problem plagues his political program and its attendant rhetoric: The plan to address in the Lay Sermons the whole, living unity of English society passes over the lower and laboring classes in silence or in the violence of certain synecdoches. A "symbolic" politics of representation and unity gives way to an allegorical one of partial translation and division. Coleridge's politics, rhetoric, and theory of language are all grounded in a theological metaphysics authorized by a certain ventriloquism of the divine word, whose prime vehicle is prophecy. The political program as well as the rhetorical theory and practice rely on a system of tropes privileging the synecdoche that, while making a claim to universality and totality, enforces a regime of hierarchy and exclusion. Perhaps there is no politics or rhetoric without some version of hierarchy and exclusion. But the performance of *The Statesman's Manual* stages this contradiction in a spectacular and problematic way, and one with consequences for thinking about rhetoric and politics in Coleridge's wake. In the first of the *Lay Sermons*, Coleridge made an ambitious attempt to establish the Bible as *the* model of rhetorical and political strategy, only to have his own strategies lose a good deal in their allegorical translation.

REFERENCE MATTER

Notes

1. I am thinking primarily of William Lisle Bowles's poetic drama, *St. John in Patmos*. Bowles is little read now except occasionally as a major early influence on Coleridge—and then really only for his sonnets. It is also well known that Milton thought of the Book of Revelation as a kind of drama, as his contemporary Joseph Mede contended. Prophecy and oracles are often very central to dramatic plot (*Oedipus Rex, Macbeth*, etc.). For one good study of the phenomenon, see Rebecca Bushnell, *Prophesying Tragedy* (Ithaca and London: Cornell University Press, 1986).

2. The prophet is understood as male here, because prophecy is almost invariably a male (and masculine) phenomenon. Deborah is one of the few prominent prophetesses in the Bible (there are at most seven, according to a rabbinic calculation), and the sibyls of classical literature are shadowy figures of legend rather than authors whose writings one can now read. The most exceptional woman prophet of the Romantic period, Joanna Southcott, has been well studied in the monograph by James K. Hopkins, *A Woman to Deliver Her People: Joanna Southcott and English Millenariansim in an Era of Revolution* (Austin: University of Texas Press, 1982). By and large, women poets of the eighteenth century in Britain and in Germany were unlikely to adopt what Milton called "the prophetic strain," even when, as Germaine Greer argues in *Slip-Shod Sibyls*, women's poetry tended to be highly self-conscious. Recent scholarship, however, has begun to uncover a culture of women prophets in the seventeenth century. See Phyllis Mack, "Women as Prophets During the English Civil War," in *The Origins of Anglo-American Radicalism*, ed. Margaret C. Jacob and James R. Jacob (New Jersey and London: Humanities Press, 1991), 72–88. The writings of Lady Eleanor Davies (1590–1652) constitute an important body of prophetic work, but no real tradition of women writing prophecy continued through to the Romantic period. Thus a copious and representative anthology such as Paula Feldman's *British Woman Poets of the Romantic Era* (Baltimore and London: Johns Hopkins University Press, 1997) contains very little that could be considered prophetic. One semiexception is Anna Letitia Barbauld's "Eighteen Hundred and Eleven." Another would be Mary

Robinson's reply to Coleridge's "Kubla Khan." Joanna Southcott, once again, has the greatest claim of any British woman of the period to the mantle of prophecy, although her writing is of quite a different character from that of the writers considered here. My own view is that she is most interesting for a sociological study of prophecy in the period. One can look forward to the forthcoming work on Southcott by Sonia Hofkosh and Kim Ian Michasiw. In the meantime, the reader is invited to consult the informative account by James Hopkins cited above.

One might also note that the contrast drawn here between prophet and psalmist is only a generalization. A good many of the psalms have a prophetic element and some commentators, such as Augustine in the *City of God*, emphasize precisely that aspect of the psalms.

3. Moreover, the energies that typically went into the production of poetic and philosophical texts in Germany and England were in France channelled more directly into practical politics. There is, nonetheless, a recognizably "prophetic" tradition in French writing of the time, on which one can consult the two authoritative books by Paul Bénichou: *Le sacre de l'écrivain: 1750–1830* (Paris: J. Corti, 1973) and *Le temps des prophètes: doctrines de l'age romantique* (Paris: Gallimard, 1977). The fullest study of the phenomenon of prophecy in the late eighteenth and early nineteenth century in Britain is Murray Roston's *Prophet and Poet: The Bible and the Growth of Romanticism* (Evanston, Ill.: Northwestern University Press, 1965). For the best of the many brief studies of the relations between poetry and prophecy, see Geoffrey Hartman, "The Poetics of Prophecy," in *High Romantic Argument*, ed. Lawrence Lipking (Ithaca and London: Cornell University Press, 1981), 15–40.

4. For a probing reflection on what it means to "date" a poem and how a poem "dates," see Jacques Derrida, *Shibboleth* (Paris: Gallilée, 1986).

5. Max Weber, *Economy and Society*, ed. Günther Roth and Claus Wittich, trans. by various hands (Berkeley: University of California Press, 1968), 439.

6. Ibid., 440.

7. Maurice Blanchot, "La parole prophétique," in *Le livre à venir* (Paris: Gallimard, 1959), 122–23. My translation. The internal quotation comes from the book Blanchot is discussing: Andre Néher's brilliant study *L'essence du prophétisme* (Paris: P.U.F., 1955). Also of considerable interest is Neher's *Amos: Contribution à l'etude du prophétisme* (Paris: J. Vrin, 1955). Néher's work was influential for several generations of French intellectuals, such as Paul Ricoeur.

8. Gerhard von Rad, *The Message of the Prophets*, trans. D. M. G. Stalker (London: SCM Press, 1968), 30.

9. Blanchot, *Le livre à venir*, 117.

10. Claus Westermann, *Grundformen prophetischer Rede* (Munich: Chr. Kaiser Verlag, 1960), esp. 64ff. The text is available in English as *Basic Forms of Prophetic Speech*, trans. H. C. White (Philadelphia: Fortress Press, 1967). The corresponding passages in the translation are found on 90 ff.

11. On this point, see J. Lindblom, *Prophecy in Ancient Israel* (Philadelphia: Fortress Press, 1962), 26.

12. Samuel Johnson, *A Dictionary of the English Language*, 2nd. ed. (London, 1755–56). See also Hobbes's definition: "The name of PROPHET, signifieth in Scripture sometimes *Prolocutor*; that is, he that speaketh from God to Man, or from man to God: And sometime *Praedictor*, or a foreteller of things to come: And sometimes one that speaketh incoherently, as men that are distracted. It is most frequently used in the sense of speaking of God to the People." *Leviathan*, ed. C. B. Macpherson (Harmondsworth: Penguin, 1968), 456. Thus Hobbes, typical of seventeenth-century thinkers, tends to be less reductive than his eighteenth-century counterparts.

13. Joseph Butler, *The Analogy of Religion* (1736; reprint, New York: Frederick Ungar, 1961), 226.

14. Walter Benjamin, *Briefe*, ed. Gershom Scholem and Theodor W. Adorno (Frankfurt am Main: Suhrkamp, 1978), I, 126. Further references to this letter will be given by page number in the text. I have consulted *The Correspondence of Walter Benjamin 1910–1940*, trans. Manfred R. Jacobson and Evelyn M. Jacobson (Chicago and London: University of Chicago Press, 1994) and made slight modifications.

15. The study most attentive to this aspect of Benjamin's thought is Winfried Menninghaus, *Walter Benjamins Theorie der Sprachmagie* (Frankfurt am Main: Suhrkamp, 1980). Menninghaus's is partly a demystifying reading, offering helpful parallels from the linguistic speculations of Herder and Humboldt.

16. Walter Benjamin, *Reflections*, ed. Peter Demetz, trans. Edmund Jephcott (New York and London: Harcourt Brace, 1979), 316–17. Translation slightly modified.

17. A powerful account of the prophet as a mediator can be found in the opening chapters of Spinoza's *Theologico-Political Treatise* (1670). Spinoza was massively influential for German thinkers of the late eighteenth and early nineteenth centuries and was not unimportant for English thinkers. Still worth reading is Matthew Arnold's essay, "Spinoza and the Bible," in his *Essays in Criticism: First Series*, ed. Sister Thomas Marion Hoctor (Chicago and London: University of Chicago Press, 1964), 183–203.

18. But only one emblem: Another, in Benjamin, is the interlinear version of the Bible, which graphically demonstrates the simultaneous necessity and difficulty of translation. See "The Task of the Translator," in *Illuminations*, trans. Harry Zohn (New York: Schocken, 1969), 82. Strictly speaking, the interlinear version of the Bible is a model for translation. But one could show that for Benjamin, as I will indicate briefly later, translation is built in language(s), not just some process that makes up for the accidental differences in given languages.

19. *Briefe* I, 126.

20. Ibid., 127.

21. Compare the famous final proposition of Wittgenstein's *Tractatus logico-*

philosophicus: "Wovon man nicht sprechen kann, darüber muß man schweigen." ("Whereof one cannot speak, thereof one must be silent.")

22. On this see the provocative study by Phillipe Lacoue-Labarthe and Jean-Luc Nancy, *L'absolu littéraire* (Paris: Seuil, 1978).

23. But only potentially. Not every actual instance of prose would be "prose" in the sense that Schlegel—the most particular subject of Benjamin's dissertation —ascribes to it.

24. This claim seems not unrelated to Shelley's argument in the "Defense of Poetry" that the only morally legitimate poetry would be that which suspended any given moral design.

25. "Horizon" here may suggest a limit that provides intelligibility, but typically in Benjamin the divine is also the unknowable, even if its effects are realized in the most concrete ways in history and in daily life.

26. Benjamin works this out most pointedly in his "Critique of Violence," to be discussed momentarily. For a provocative analysis of the politicolinguistic stakes involved in that essay, see Werner Hamacher, "Afformative, Strike," in *Walter Benjamin's Philosophy: Destruction and Experience*, ed. Andrew Benjamin and John Osborne (London and New York: Routledge, 1993), 110–38.

27. As is clear from even this bald summary, Benjamin is more interested in the similarities between the two Creation stories than in the huge differences in their sequences and hierarchies.

28. Much of Benjamin's thinking along these lines seems informed by Hebraic discourse, for which the word *davar* means equally "word" and "action" (as well as "matter" or "thing").

29. On the nonspecificity of translation as the structure of language, see Jacques Derrida's reading of (primarily) Benjamin in "Les tours de Babel" ("The Towers of Babel"), in *Difference in Translation*, ed. Joseph Graham (Ithaca and London: Cornell University Press, 1985), French version 209–48, English version 165–207.

30. See especially Paul de Man, "Phenomenality and Materiality in Kant," in *Hermeneutics: Questions and Prospects*, ed. Gary Shapiro and Alan Sica (Amherst: University of Massachusetts Press, 1984), 121–44. On the system of the faculties of the mind in the three critiques, see the excellent analysis by Gilles Deleuze, *Kant's Faculties of the Mind* (Minneapolis and London: University of Minnesota Press, 1986). For a searching analysis of the transcendental imagination in Kant, see Martin Heidegger, *Kant und das Problem der Metaphysik*, 4th ed. (Frankfurt am Main: Klostermann, 1973). See also Slavoj Žižek, "The Deadlock of the Transcendental Imagination: Martin Heidegger as a Reader of Kant," the opening chapter of his *The Ticklish Subject: The Absent Centre of Political Ontology* (London and New York: Verso, 1999).

31. See "On the Program of the Coming Philosophy," in *Gesammelte Schriften*. The English version is contained in *Benjamin: Philosophy, Aesthetic, History*, ed.

Gary Smith (Chicago and London: University of Chicago Press, 1989), 1–12. Benjamin's charge repeats the prescient contemporary critique of Kant by Hamann.

32. Walter Benjamin, *Der Begriff der Kunstkritik in der deutschen Romantik* (Frankfurt am Main: Suhrkamp, 1973), p. 102. The German reads " . . . die Aufgabe der Kritik [ist] die Vollendung des Werkes."

33. For an excellent reading of the problematic of critique in this (Romantic) phase of Benjamin's work, see Samuel Weber, "Criticism Underway: Walter Benjamin's *Romantic Concept of Criticism*," in *Romantic Revolutions*, ed. Kenneth Johnston et al. (Bloomington and Indianapolis: Indiana University Press, 1990), 302–19. Weber points out that *Vollendung* also means, for Benjamin, consummation and dissolution and so stands as a rather double-edged concept and not simply as a version of some unequivocally upbeat Messianism.

34. The note of Messianism is sounded in the opening pages of Benjamin's dissertation, but it is not often discussed as such. However, the emphasis on completion, fulfilment, etc. is pervasive.

35. For a powerful reading and critique of Benjamin's essay and especially the obscure concept of divine violence, see Jacques Derrida, "'Force de loi': le 'fondement mystique de l'autorité,'"/"'Force of Law'": The 'Mystical Foundation of Authority,'" *Cardozo Law Review* 2 (July/Aug. 1990): 919–1046.

36. Benjamin opposes divine violence to mythical violence along the lines, as Derrida suggests, of an opposition the Judaic and the Greek, a rather dubious distinction in this case. For the moment, we are more concerned with describing a matrix of motifs and structures in Benjamin's work than with evaluating their truth.

37. I have dealt at greater length with this and other material from the "Theses on the Philosophy of History," in "Reversal, Quotation (Benjamin's History)," *MLN* 106 (1991): 622–47.

38. Walter Benjamin, *Gesammelte Schriften*, I.3, 1236. Hereafter *G. S.*

39. On the tendency of historiography to side with the victors, Benjamin follows the critique sketched out in various places by Nietzsche ("Wir Philologen" ["We Philologists"], among others). Benjamin was rather ruthless and relentless in his condemnation of the turn of mind that displaced the present for the future, scorning even his beloved Hölderlin's remark, "I love the children of future generations," (*G. S.*, V.1, 599). Benjamin was very much preoccupied with various formulations of the "infinite task," as in Kant's philosophy of history and, presumably, in Schleiermacher's hermeneutics (although Benjamin is sketchy on this latter).

40. Ibid.

41. *G. S.*, I.3, 1233.

42. Ibid., I.3, 1238.

43. *G. S.*, I.2, 701. Translation modified from Harry Zohn's version in *Illuminations*.

44. Ibid., 702.

45. Indeed, the Messianic might be the name for the sheerly figural, or at least, that which can only be figured.

46. See the fragment that begins "Die aktuell messianischen Momente im Kunstwerk . . . ," in *G. S.*, VI, 126.

47. Benjamin summarizes his thinking on this point in the "Historico-Political Fragment." He thinks there of the Messianic precisely in terms of an end, not a goal.

CHAPTER 2

1. Since writing the first version of this chapter, two germane studies have appeared. David Riede offers a thoroughgoing demystification of the Wordsworthian claim to inspiration in his *Oracles and Hierophants: Constructions of Romantic Authority* (Ithaca and London: Cornell University Press, 1991). He by and large focuses on different passages than I do, providing many instances of the phenomenon I am sketching here. Thomas McFarland emphasizes the futurity of "The Prophetic Stance" in the chapter of that name in his *William Wordsworth: Intensity and Achievement* (Oxford: Clarendon Press, 1992).

2. William Wordsworth, *The Prelude*, ed. Jonathan Wordsworth et al. (New York: Norton, 1978), Book I, lines 46–58. All further references to *The Prelude* will be given in the body of the text.

3. For a fine reading of Wordsworth's sense of vocation that approaches the text from a different vantage point, see Guinn Batten, *The Orphaned Imagination: Melancholy and Commodity Culture in English Romanticism* (Durham and London: Duke University Press, 1998), for the chapter on Wordsworth.

4. "Preface to the Edition of 1815." In *The Prose Works of William Wordsworth*, vol. 3, ed. W. J. B. Owen and Jane Worthington Smyser (Oxford: Clarendon Press, 1974), 34.

5. The literature on this episode is particularly rich. Among the most provocative and insightful readings are Mary Jacobus, "Wordsworth and the Language of the Dream," in her *Romanticism, Writing, and Sexual Differences: Essays on 'The Prelude'* (Oxford: Clarendon Press, 1989), 97–125; Geoffrey H. Hartman, *Wordsworth's Poetry 1787–1814*, 2nd ed. (New Haven: 1971); Forest Pyle, *The Ideology of Imagination* (Stanford: Stanford University Press, 1995); Timothy Bahti, *Ends of the Lyric* (Baltimore and London: 1996); and J. Hillis Miller, *The Disappearance of God: Five Nineteenth Century Writers* (New York: University of Illinois Press, 1965).

6. See Jane Worthington Smyser, "Wordsworth's Dream of Poetry and Science," *PMLA* 71, no. 1 (Mar. 1956): 269–75. The dream also has other literary and even philosophical precedents, if one can call Descartes's dreams philosophical.

7. Although harmony sometimes sounds like an odd word to use with respect to prophetic rhetoric, Josephine Miles does precisely that in a compelling discussion on the sublime style in Blake. See her *Eras and Modes in English Poetry* (Berkeley and Los Angeles: University of California Press, 1964), 84.

8. For an excellent reading of the Dream of the Arab sequence as a poetry of enshrinement, see Forest Pyle, *The Ideology of Imagination: Subject and Society in the Discourse of Romanticism* (Stanford: Stanford University Press, 1995), chapter 2. Pyle is also very attentive to the texture of (historical) otherness, mainly Hispanic and Arab, inscribed in this section of *The Prelude*.

9. One could also emphasize here the destruction of the "*children* of the earth."

10. See, for example, M. H. Abrams, *Natural Supernaturalism* (New York: Norton, 1971), esp. 21–28.

11. *The Poetical Works of William Wordsworth*, ed. Thomas Hutchinson, rev. Ernest de Selincourt (London: Oxford University Press, 1950), 590.

12. *The Poems of Thomas Gray, William Collins, and Oliver Goldsmith*, ed. Roger Lonsdale (London: Longman, 1969), 427–29. Coleridge found that Collins's poem about inspiration recreated in him the very sort of experience described in the poem: "Now Collins' Ode on the poetical character . . . has inspired & whirled *me* along with greater agitations of enthusiasm than any of the most *impassioned* Scene in Schiller or Shakespeare . . . " *Collected Letters of Samuel Taylor Coleridge*, ed. E. L. Griggs, vol. 1 (Oxford: Oxford University Press, 1956), 279.

13. For a good reading of the sexual problematic of the poem, see Thomas Weiskel, *The Romantic Sublime* (Baltimore and London: Johns Hopkins University Press, 1976), 124f. For an important general commentary on the poem in the context of Collins's entire poetic production, see A. S. P. Woodhouse, "The Poetry of Collins Reconsidered," in *From Sensibility to Romanticism*, ed. F. W. Hilles and Harold Bloom (New York: Oxford University Press, 1965), 93–137.

14. For a valuable study of Collins's poetic relation to Milton, see Paul S. Sherwin, *Precious Bane: Collins and the Miltonic Legacy* (Austin and London: University of Texas Press, 1977).

15. Collins was only twenty-five when he wrote this, although the closing line sounds like the swan song of a poetic career. Hazlitt found the last line appropriate for the end of his life as an essayist, as he (mis)quoted it at the very end of his "A Farewell to Essay-Writing," in *The Complete Works of William Hazlitt*, ed. P. P. Howe, vol. 17 (London and Toronto: J. M. Dent and Sons, 1930–34), 320.

16. *The Poems of Thomas Gray, William Collins, and Oliver Goldsmith*, 170–72.

17. Ibid., 185–86.

18. For a fuller reading of the importance of Gray's poem for Blake, see David V. Erdman, *Prophet Against Empire*, 3rd ed. (Princeton: Princeton University Press, 1977), 47 ff.

19. See Suvir Kaul, *Thomas Gray and Literary Authority: A Study in Ideology and Poetics* (Stanford: Stanford University Press, 1992).

20. The foremost proponent of this line of criticism is Marshall Brown in his *Preromanticism* (Stanford: Stanford University Press, 1991). See esp. the beginning chapters for stimulating and wide-ranging readings of Collins and Gray. For the most suggestive recent reading of Young, especially of the *Night Thoughts*, see

Shaun Irlam, *Elations: The Poetics of Enthusiasm in Eighteenth-century Britain* (Stanford: Stanford University Press, 1999).

21. *The Works of Edward Young, D. D.* II (London, 1813), 9.

22. Ibid., 2.

23. Ibid., 8.

24. Ibid., 28.

25. Immanuel Kant, *Kritik der Urteilskraft.* Werkausgabe, vol. 10 (Frankfurt am Main: Suhrkamp, 1977), 165.

26. Ibid., 27.

27. *Conjectures on Original Composition* (1759), in *Literary Criticism in England,* ed. G. W. Chapman (New York: Knopf, 1966), 370.

28. *The Poetical Works of Christopher Smart,* vol. 1: *Jubilate Agno,* ed. Karina Williamson (Oxford: Clarendon Press, 1980), 15.

29. Smart went so far as to align himself with Christ on the charge on madness: "For I am under the same accusation with my Saviour—for they said, he is besides himself." Ibid., 36.

30. Ibid., 44.

31. Ibid., 63.

32. Ibid., 15. Jesus, too, was to come "with a sword" in his mouth.

33. Clement Hawes, *Mania and Literary Style: The Rhetoric of Enthusiasm from the Ranters to Christopher Smart* (Cambridge: Cambridge University Press, 1996), 168. In general, Hawes's is the most helpful extended reading of *Jubilate Agno.*

34. Howard Weinbrot offers a substantial discussion of Smart as one of the chief examples of "philosemitism" in his *Britannia's Issue: The Rise of British Literature from Dryden to Osssian* (Cambridge: Cambridge University Press, 1993). See esp. Part IV, "Expanding the Borders: Jews and Jesus: This Israel, This England."

35. *The Poetical Works of Christopher Smart,* 75.

36. See Clement Hawes, *Mania and Literary Style,* 168.

37. *The Poetical Works of Christopher Smart,* I, 15. In a less flippant mode, Smart asserts: "For Christ being A and O[mega] is all the intermediate letters without doubt." It is much to Smart's advantage to make Christ as the Logos (word and reason), the guarantor of all possible letters.

38. Ibid., 14.

39. For an incisive and boldly speculative account of the problematic of translation in Smart, see Alan Liu, "Christopher Smart's 'uncommunicated letters': Translation and the Ethics of Literary History," *Boundary 2* 14: 1/2 (1985–86): 115–46.

40. See Julia Kristeva, "Reading the Bible," in her *New Maladies of the Soul,* trans. Ross Guberman (New York: Columbia University Press, 1995), 116.

41. For probing of this and related matters, see Clement Hawes, "The Utopian Public Sphere: Intersubjectivity in *Jubilate Agno,*" in *Christopher Smart and the Enlightenment,* ed. Clement Hawes (New York: St. Martin's, 1999), 195–212.

42. *The Poetical Works of Christopher Smart,* vol. 1, 97.

43. Ibid., 94.

44. Milton Wilson, *Shelley's Later Poetry* (New York: Columbia University Press, 1959), 11–12.

45. Harold Bloom, *The Visionary Company,* rev. ed. (Ithaca and London: Cornell University Press, 1971), 282.

46. Percy Bysshe Shelley, *Poetical Works,* ed. Thomas Hutchinson, rev. by G. M. Matthews (London: Oxford University Press, 1970), 338. All further references to Shelley's poetry will be to this edition.

47. Ibid., 344.

48. These examples could be multiplied. I would point to Shelley's neglected "Ode to Liberty," whose opening testifies to the poet being enveloped in a fury of wind and voice, a voice that he claims merely to "record." But Milton Wilson is correct to say that the poem as a whole "is about the poet's inability to sustain his prophetic imagination." *Shelley's Later Poetry,* 201.

49. *Shelley's Prose,* ed. David Lee Clark (Albuquerque: University of New Mexico Press, 1966), 279.

50. Ibid., 297.

51. Friedrich Schlegel, *Literary Notebooks 1797–1801,* ed. Hans Eichner (Toronto: University of Toronto Press, 1957), 187.

52. Ibid., 138.

53. Friedrich Schlegel, *Kritische Schriften,* ed. Wolfdietrich Rasch (Munich: Hanser, 1970), 55.

54. *Literary Notebooks,* 48.

55. Ibid., 344.

56. One should acknowledge that not every instance of the prophet in Schlegel's lexicon is so positively marked. Schlegel once described himself in relation to Novalis in this way: "He's a magician, I'm only a prophet." ("Er Zauberer, ich nur Prophet.") In *Kritische Friedrich Schlegel Ausgabe,* vol. 18 (Munich: Ferdinand Schöningh, 1963), 142. Schlegel's tone is sometimes hard to read, but it is perhaps not all that self-deprecating if Schlegel casts himself as the prophet as opposed to the putatively superior magician.

57. For an account of Coleridge's disappointment with the person and even the "countenance" of Klopstock, see *Collected Letters of Samuel Taylor Coleridge,* ed. E. L. Griggs, vol. 2 (London and New York: Oxford University Press, 1956), 441–45.

58. For the text of "An Young" see Friedrich Gottlob Klopstock, *Ausgewählte Werke,* ed. K. A. Schleiden (Munich: Hanser, 1962), 66.

59. Ibid., 999.

60. Novalis, *Die Christenheit oder Europa,* ed. Otto Heuschle (Stuttgart: Reclam, 1973), 62.

61. Klopstock, *Ausgewählte Werke*, 1008.

62. Ibid., 1001.

63. *Die Werke Friedrich von Hardenbergs*, ed. Paul Kluckhohn and Richard Samuel, 2nd ed. (Stuttgart: Kohlhammer, 1960 ff.), 3:685–86.

64. Various insightful readings of this text can be consulted. The most persuasive recent one is William Arctander O'Brien's in his *Novalis: Signs of Revolution* (Durham: Duke University Press, 1995). O'Brien situates this work and many others in a rich context of contemporary philosophy (especially philosophy of language and epistemology). Heidegger invokes a saying from this text of Novalis as a kind of touchstone for his essay "The Way to Language" ("Der Weg zur Sprache") but does not provide a reading of it.

65. *Werke*, II, 672.

66. This is very close to Wordsworth's remarks on geometry in *The Prelude*.

67. Max Weber, *Ancient Judaism*, trans. Hans H. Genth and Don Martindale (New York: Free Press, 1967), 272.

68. *The Message of the Prophets* (New York: Harper and Row, 1967), 32.

69. On the conservative strain of religiopolitical thought and literature in German Romanticism, the classic analysis is the conservative one by Carl Schmitt, *Political Romanticism*, trans. Guy Oakes (Cambridge, Mass.: MIT Press, 1986). For the English tradition, the study most attentive to the nonradical strain of prophetic and especially apocalyptic writing is Steven Goldsmith's *Unbuilding Jerusalem* (Ithaca and London: Cornell University Press, 1993). I take up some of Goldsmith's arguments in the section on Hurd and Warburton.

70. For a superb reading of the politics and philosophical stakes of Fichte's *Addresses*, see Etienne Balibar, "Fichte and the Internal Border: On *Addresses to the German Nation*," in his *Masses, Classes, Ideas: Studies in Politics and Philosophy Before and After Marx*, trans. James Swenson (New York: Routledge, 1994), 61–84. See also the excellent essay by Marc Redfield, "Imagi-Nation: The Imagined Community and the Aesthetics of Mourning," *diacritics* 29:4 (1999), a special issue, "Grounds for Comparison: Around the Work of Benedict Anderson," ed. Jonathan Culler and Pheng Cheah. I take up the problematic of the nation in Fichte in a chapter on "The Sublime of the Nation" in a work in progress, *The Language of the Sublime*.

71. *Fichtes Werke*, ed. I. H. Fichte, 8 vols. (Berlin: 1845–46), 7:306. The English translation follows the edition of *Addresses to the German Nation* by George A. Kelly (New York: Harper & Row, 1968), 40.

72. But one problem Fichte raises is this: Who exactly is a German? Just being born a German or speaking the language is not enough to guarantee that one is German. Moreover, because Fichte ties nationality to language, rather than to blood or soil, anyone can in principle become a German, even if, in practice, that proves difficult to do.

CHAPTER 3

1. In his lengthy and laudatory essay on Lowth's lectures Moses Mendelssohn begins by noting that for as much intellectual labor as had been devoted to Scripture in terms of translation, commentary, and theological or philosophical explanation, a correspondingly small effort had been expended on displaying the *beauty* of the text—of the sort routinely mustered for Homer and Virgil. At long last, Lowth was stepping in to fill the void. See Moses Mendelssohn, "Robert Lowth, De sacra poesi Hebraeorum," in *Gesammelte Schriften*, vol. 4 (Stuttgart–Bad Canstatt: Friedrich Frommann, 1977), 20. I believe David Norton overstates the case in his well-informed *A History of the Bible as Literature*, vol. 2 (From 1700 to the present day), when he describes Lowth as an "aesthete" (62).

2. Some other predecessors in Lowth's undertaking are Robert Boyle, *Some Considerations Touching the Style of the Holy Scriptures* (London: 1661); and Anthony Blackwall, *The Sacred Classics Defended and Illustrated* (London: 1725). Neither work proved particularly influential. Joseph Trapp was the first Professor of Poetry at Oxford, lecturing from 1708 to 1718. His *Praelectiones Poeticae* were published in 1711, 1715, and 1719. The English version, *Lectures on Poetry*, appeared in 1742. For a strong statement of Lowth's originality and importance, see the chapter "Robert Lowth, Unacknowledged Legislator," in James Engell's *The Committed Word: Literature and Public Values* (University Park, Pa.: Penn State Press, 1999). Although I am sympathetic to arguments in favor of Lowth's importance I think Engell overstates the case considerably when he says: " . . . Lowth changes profoundly all definitions of poetry and alters its practice permanently" (191).

3. Roberth Lowth, *Lectures on the Sacred Poetry of the Hebrews*, Trans. G. Gregory, 2 vols. (London: 1787), 53. The text is a translation of Lowth's *De sacra poesie hebraeorum*, 2 vols. (Göttingen: 1758 and 1761), which includes the important annotations of J. D. Michaelis to the first Latin edition of 1753. Gregory's translation is also supplemented by notes of his own. Further references to Lowth will be given in the body of the text: The first number indicates the volume (both Latin and English), the second gives the pages of the English translation, and the third gives the chapter of the English text, since most libraries do not possess copies of the Göttingen edition.

4. For an illuminating account of the parameters of the defense of poetry as a genre, see Margaret Ferguson, *Trials of Desire: Renaissance Defences of Poetry* (New Haven: Yale University Press, 1983), esp. chapter 1.

5. See St. Augustine, *De doctrina christiana*, book 2, section 7; and D. W. Robertson's introduction to his own translation, *On Christian Doctrine* (Indianapolis and New York: Bobbs-Merrill, 1958), xiv–xvii.

6. This does not prevent Lowth from praising a good many "secular" poets, but it still matters that Lowth's general formulations about the calling of poetry exclude its merely secular versions.

7. On the ineffable sublimity of the Hebrew poets, Lowth is echoing his predecessor, Joseph Trapp, from the opening pages of his *Lectures on Poetry*.

8. The category of the sublime in Lowth is not opposed to the beautiful, as, say, in Burke or Kant. Lowth follows the Longinian tradition in not sharply distinguishing the two.

9. See the authoritative account by Wilbur S. Howell, *Eighteenth-Century British Logic and Rhetoric* (Princeton: Princeton University Press, 1971).

10. Friedrich Meinecke singles out Lowth as an important figure in the development of historicism. He writes: "Lowth's book was perhaps the most significant intellectual achievement of the entire pre-Romantic movement in England. Without intending to do so, he nevertheless contributed to the liberation of historical research from the bonds of theology, in that it brought the purely human and historical content and value of the Bible into view." *Die Enstehung des Historismus* (Munich and Berlin: 1936), 27. I borrow here Elinor Shaffer's translation of the passage in her *"Kubla Khan" and "The Fall of Jerusalem": The Mythological School in Biblical Criticism and Secular Literature, 1770–1880* (Cambridge: Cambridge University Press, 1975), 20.

11. The most authoritative recent inquiry is James Kugel's *The Idea of Biblical Poetry.* The concept of parallelism is also operative in major works on non-Biblical poetics, as in Roman Jakobson, "Linguistics and Poetics," in *Style and Language,* ed. Thomas Sebeok (Cambridge, Mass.: MIT Press, 1960), esp. 69; and in Michael Riffaterre, "Describing Poetic Structures," in *Structuralism,* ed. Jacques Ehrmann (New York: Doubleday, 1970), esp. 189.

12. The case for Lowth's originality is made throughout the informative study by Brian Hepworth, *Robert Lowth* (Boston: Twayne, 1978). Kugel's *The Idea of Biblical Poetry: Parallelism and Its History* (New Haven: Yale University Press, 1981) demonstrates that many of Lowth's insights had been anticipated by a variety of predecessors but acknowledges his originality as an assimilator of material that had never been treated in so systematic or extensive a fashion. David Norton makes a similar point in his *A History of the Bible As Literature,* vol. 2 (Cambridge: Cambridge University Press, 1993). See the section on "Robert Lowth's *De sacra poesi hebraeorum.*"

13. See *The Idea of Biblical Poetry,* 149 ff.

14. *Elizabethan Critical Essays,* ed. G. Gregory Smith, 2 vols. (London: Oxford University Press, 1904), 1:154.

15. Ibid., 155.   16. Ibid.

17. Ibid., II, 6.   18. Ibid., 7.

19. In his early prose works and journals, Gerard Manley Hopkins reflected more than once on the informing character of parallelism for poetry in general, and he does so in terms sometimes very close to Lowth. He writes: "The artificial part of poetry, perhaps we shall be right to say all artifice, reduces itself to the principle of parallelism. The structure of poetry is that of continuous parallelism, ranging from the technical so-called Parallelism of Hebrew poetry and the antiphons

of Church music up to the intricacy of Greek or Italian or English verse. . . . Now the force of this recurrence is to beget a recurrence or parallelism answering to it in the words or thought and, speaking roughly and rather for the tendency than for the invariable result, the more marked parallelism in structure whether of elaboration or of emphasis begets more marked parallelism in the words and sense." *The Note-Books and Papers of Gerard Manley Hopkins*, ed. Humphrey House (London and New York: Oxford University Press, 1937), 92–93.

20. That parallelism is a matter of clauses and phrases rather than metre, say, may be one reason why Moses Mendelssohn, in his review of Lowth's lectures, claimed that one could recognize the spirit of Hebrew poetry in translation much better than in translations of Greek or Roman poetry. See *Gesammmelte Schriften*, vol. 4, 25.

21. For a persuasive critique of Lowth's scheme, see Kugel, *The Idea of Biblical Poetry*, esp. 12ff. Lowth himself saw no need to revise his system; he repeats it almost verbatim in the "Preliminary Dissertation" to his important translation of *Isaiah* (London, 1787).

22. Translations from the Bible will be given to the King James version in English or the Luther version in German, except where a passage is being cited already as a citation from one of the authors under consideration.

23. See Kugel, *The Idea of Biblical Poetry*, 49 ff.

24. Ibid., 155.

25. Ibid., 227.

26. See, for example, Roman Jakobson, "Two Types of Language and Two Types of Aphasic Development," in his *Language in Literature* (Cambridge, Mass. and London: Harvard University Press, 1987), 95–114.

27. See the entry on prosopopoeia in Heinrich Lausberg, *Handbuch der literarischen Rhetorik: Die Grundlegung der Literaturwissenschaft*, 2nd. ed. revised and expanded (Munich: Hueber, 1973). The whole of Lowth's thirteenth lecture is devoted to prosopopoeia, and it figures prominently in systematic treatises on rhetoric in this period. For a more speculative, metacritical analysis of prosopopoeia, see Paul de Man, "Hypogram and Inscription: Michael Riffaterre's Poetics of Reading," *diacritics* 11.4 (1981), 17–35. For a nuanced elaboration of the same problematic, see Cynthia Chase, "Giving a Face to a Name: De Man's Figures," in *Decomposing Figures: Rhetorical Readings in the Romantic Tradition* (Baltimore and London: Johns Hopkins University Press, 1986), 82–112.

28. Alexander Geddes would later stress that "the Jewish historians . . . put in the mouth of the Lord words which he had never spoke and assigned to him views which he never had" (cited in Fuller, Reginald C., *Alexander Geddes 1737––1802: A Pioneer of Biblical Criticism* [Sheffield: Almond, 1984], 40). Similar observations are now almost commonplace: Even a not-so-secular critic like Northrop Frye can write of Isaiah that "praising the tolerant policy of Cyrus, [he] has God say to him: 'I will give thee the treasures of darkness, and the hoards of

secret places' (45.3)." In *Words with Power* (New York: Harcourt, Brace and World, 1990), 237.

29. David Hume, *The Natural History of Religion* (1757), reprint, ed. H. F. Kent (Stanford: Stanford University Press, 1957), 29.

30. This confessional gesture does not escape the problematic character of philosophical discourses that attempt to contain the aberrations of metaphorical discourse by putting metaphor in its place. For a magisterial analysis of this persistent issue, see Jacques Derrida, "White Mythology," in *Margins of Philosophy*, trans. Alan Bass (Chicago: University of Chicago Press, 1982), 207–71.

31. Hume, *Natural History*, 29–30. It is worth noting here that one "cause" of prosopopoeia, in Hume's analysis, is anxiety about the future, as if were necessary to have the future speak to us to resolve our uncertainty.

32. For Hume's concept of the "intelligent author," see ibid., 21.

33. Hugh Blair, *Lectures on Rhetoric and Belles Lettres* (1783), reprint (Carbondale: Southern Illinois University Press, 1965), 325.

34. On the positional power of language, as distinct but not entirely divorced from its representational function, I am indebted to the work of Paul de Man and Jacques Derrida, and to J. L. Austin's theory of speech-acts.

35. For a detailed study of this topic, not limited to the prophetic books, see James Ballantine, *The Hidden God* (Oxford: Oxford University Press, 1982). For a trenchant analysis of the problematic of God's face in Levinas and beyond, see Jill Robbins, *Altered Reading: Levinas and Literature* (Chicago and London: University of Chicago Press, 1999), esp. 32 ff.

36. J. L. Austin, *How to Do Things with Words*, ed. J. O.Urmson (London: Oxford University Press, 1962), 86. Thus the content of the prophecy can be termed constative, whereas the prophecy itself is often implicitly or explicitly performative, and the conjunction of the two partly accounts for both the power of prophecy and the difficulty in assessing its claims. This problem will be taken up again in the chapter on Coleridge.

37. For an excellent treatment of this topic in the eighteenth century, see Hans Frei, *The Eclipse of Biblical Narrative: A Study in Eighteenth and Ninteenth Century Hermeneutics* (New Haven: Yale University Press, 1974), esp. chapters 2 and 3.

38. For a defense of the "vitality" of prophetic discourse in part made possible by figurative language, see Peter Ackroyd, "The Vitality of the Word of God in the Old Testament," *Annual of the Swedish Theological Institute in Jerusalem* 1 (1962), 7–23.

39. See the fifth and sixth sermons by Richard Hurd, *Twelve Sermons Introductory to the Study of the Prophecies*, in *The Works of Richard Hurd*, vol. 5 (London: 1811).

40. *The Collected Works of Samuel Taylor Coleridge*, vol. 6., *Lay Sermons* (Princeton: Princeton University Press, and London: Routledge & Kegan Paul, 1972), 29–30.

41. E. S. Shaffer, *"Kubla Khan" and "The Fall of Jerusalem": The Mythological School in Biblical Criticism and Secular Literature* (Cambridge: Cambridge University Press, 1975), 45.

42. Stephen Prickett, "The Religious Context," in *The Romantics*, ed. Stephen Prickett (London: Methuen, 1981), 144. David Norton also claims that Lowth's translation of Isaiah was the first text to introduce free verse in English. See his informative study, *A History of the Bible As Literature*, vol. 2., 72.

43. *Gibbon's Autobiography*, ed. M. M. Reese (London: Routledge & Kegan Paul, 1970), 32.

44. On the distinction between and the interdependence of poetics and hermeneutics, see Paul de Man, "Introduction" to Hans Robert Jauss, *Toward an Aesthetic of Reception*, trans. Timothy Bahti (Minneapolis: University of Minnesota Press, 1982), ix–x.

45. See Stephen Prickett, "The Religious Context," 150.

46. Lowth has often been considered a major force in the European intellectual movement now known as Orientalism. See, for example, Edward Said, *Orientalism* (New York: Pantheon, 1978), 17; and Hans Aarsleff, *The Study of Language in England 1770–1860* (Princeton: Princeton University Press, 1967), 14n. The best study of the importance of Orientalism for Biblical study is E. S. Shaffer's *"Kubla Khan" and "The Fall of Jerusalem,"* esp. chapter 3.

47. This point is made by Brian Hepworth, *Robert Lowth*, 147.

48. *The Complete Poetry and Prose of William Blake*, ed. David Erdman, rev. (Berkeley and Los Angeles: University of California Press, 1982), 34. All subsequent citations from this edition will be given in the text and abbreviated as "E" plus the page number.

CHAPTER 4

1. *Twelve Sermons Introductory to the Study of the Prophecies*, in *The Works of Richard Hurd* (London, 1811), V, xiv. All further references to Hurd as well as Gibbon are to this text and will be given by page number in the body of the chapter.

2. On the place of Hurd in the history of literary criticism, see René Wellek, *The Rise of Literary History* (New York: McGraw-Hill, 1966). Geoffrey Hartman situates Hurd in the genealogy of structuralism in his *Beyond Formalism* (New Haven: Yale University Press, 1970), 5. On Hurd as a reader of Spenserian romance, see Patricia Parker, *Inescapable Romance* (Princeton: Princeton University Press, 1979). For an assessment of the hermeneutical project of Hurd's literary criticism, together with a brief discussion of his sermons on prophecy, see Donald Marshall, "The History of Eighteenth-Century Criticism and Modern Hermeneutical Philosophy: The Example of Richard Hurd," *The Eighteenth Century: Theory and Interpretation*, 21 (Autumn 1980), 199–211. For an overview of Hurd's literary criticism with an emphasis on genre, see Hoyt Trowbridge, "Bishop Hurd: A Rein-

terpretation," *PMLA* 58:2 (June 1943): 450–64. The range and depth of Hurd's "secular" activity was not uncommon for bishops of his day. On the institution of the bishop during the period, see Norman Sykes, *Church and State in England in the XVIIIth Century* (Cambridge: Cambridge University Press, 1935).

3. Leslie Stephen, *Essays on Freethinking and Plainspeaking* (New York and London: G. P. Putnam's Sons, 1905), 323. For a more generous account of Hurd and his place in the Warburton circle, see A. W. Evans, *Warburton and the War-burtonians: A Study in Some Eighteenth-Century Controversies* (London: Oxford University Press, 1932).

4. For a reading of Hurd that concentrates on his ideological positioning, see Steven Goldsmith, *Unbuilding Jerusalem* (Ithaca and London: Cornell University Press, 1993), for the section of chapter 2 entitled "Richard Hurd: Apocalypse and the Eighteenth-Century Anglican State." Goldsmith makes the salutary argument that the discourse surrounding apocalypse in the late eighteenth century was not confined to radical and republican circles, not limited, as he says, "to an opposi-tional politics" (109). Nonetheless, Goldsmith must rely on what he calls the "gen-eral contours" of "circumstance" more than the direct testimony of the text. He is certainly right to accuse Hurd of a certain aesthetization of prophecy. The ques-tion is whether there is a huge difference between any aesthetic mobilization of prophecy and what Goldsmith calls aestheticization. My suspicion is that the dif-ferences between a Hurd and a Geddes, or even a Blake, are political and that they cannot be located at the level of form.

5. Modern hermeneutic theory, notably in Heidegger and Hans-Georg Gada-mer, has argued that "prejudice" and "preconception" are constitutive of inter-pretation, by virtue of the very structure of linguistic understanding. On Heideg-ger's concepts of *Vorgriff, Vorsicht,* and *Vorhabe,* see *Sein und Zeit* (Tübingen: Max Niemeyer, 1977), 14th ed., esp. paragraph 32. On *Vorurteil,* see Hans-Georg Gada-mer, *Wahrheit und Methode* (Tübingen: Max Niemeyer, 1960), esp. 250 ff. The understanding of the relations between prejudice as a structural constitutive of in-terpretation and as a given historical bias remains a desideratum for hermeneutic theory. On the importance of German philosophical hermeneutics, especially Gadamerian, for literary criticism, see Cyrus Hamlin, *Hermeneutics of Form: Ro-mantic Poetics in Theory & Practice* (New Haven: Henry R. Schwab, 1998), esp. chapter 1, "The Limits of Interpretation."

6. Gibbon, in reviewing Hurd's commentary on Horace, complained of the author's style being "clouded with obscure metaphors." This is not quite to say that Hurd's style was itself prophetic. For Gibbon's comments see *The English Essays of Edward Gibbon,* ed. Patricia C. Craddock (Oxford: Oxford University Press, 1972), 27.

7. My emphasis.

8. Paul Ricoeur, *Freud and Philosophy: An Essay on Interpretation,* trans. Denis Savage (New Haven and London: Yale University Press, 1970), 32 ff.

9. "Toward a Hermeneutic of the Idea of Revelation," in *Essays on Biblical Interpretation*, ed. Lewis M. Mudge (Philadelphia: Fortress Press, 1980), 93.

10. For an excellent discussion of this problematic in the New Testament, see C. H. Dodd, *The Parables of the Kingdom*, rev. ed. (1961; reprint, London: Collins, 1978), esp. chapter 2.

11. Noted in Maurice Pope, *The Story of Decipherment* (London: Thames & Hudson, 1975), 119.

12. *Gibbon's Autobiography*, 91.

13. For a incisive reading of the Warburton essay, see Jacques Derrida, "SCRIBBLE (pouvoir/écrire)," written as a preface to a reissue of the French translation of Warburton's essay, in William Warburton, *Essai sur les hieroglyphes des egyptiens*, trans. Leonard Des Malpeines, ed. Patrick Tort (Paris: Aubier Flammarion, 1977), 7–43. An almost complete translation of the Derrida text appeared as "Scribble (writing-power)," trans. Cary Plotkin, *Yale French Studies* 58 (1979), 117–47. Derrida notes the exemplary status of prophetic speech only in passing, since he is concerned strategically more with the figure of the priest than the prophet.

14. Leslie Stephen, *Essays on Freethinking and Plainspeaking* (New York: Putnam's, 1905), 333.

15. William Warburton, *The Divine Legation of Moses Demonstrated*, 4 vols. (London, 1736). Reprint, ed. René Wellek (New York: Garland, 1978). Further references to this work will be indicated by page number in the body of the text; all refer to vol. 2, which contains Book IV, the essay on hieroglyphs.

16. Warburton uses the word "betray" here to mean "reveal," but the Egyptian hieroglyphs will soon be acknowledged to "betray" their original in another sense.

17. Warburton himself published in 1736 a treatise entitled *Alliance Between Church and State*, two years before he realized a personal alliance of that sort by becoming tutor to the Prince of Wales's family. Warburton's treatise was one of the influential models for Coleridge's *On the Constitution of the Church and State*. For a still authoritative account of the life, see Mark Pattison, "Life of Bishop Warburton," in his *Essays*, ed. Henry Nettleship (Oxford, 1889), vol. 2, 119–76.

18. This termed was coined by Paul de Man, with reference to a similar structure in Condillac, in a seminar at Yale University in the spring of 1983.

19. Warburton and Hurd are by no means alone in this regard. Joseph Butler, for example, also speaks of the "hieroglyphical and figurative language" of the Scriptures. See his *The Analogy of Religion* (1736). Reprint, ed. Ernest C. Mossner (New York: Ungar, 1961), 150.

20. Pascal, *Oeuvres Complètes*, ed. Louis Lafuna (Paris: Seuil), 624.

21. Hurd quotes with approval the opinion of "the learned Bishop Andrews,"who thought there was hardly a phrase in the Book of Revelation that was "not taken out of Daniel or some other prophet" (265n–66n). The implications of the citational character of prophetic tradition are taken up in the chapter on Blake.

22. A discourse of duration that refers to a single topic that is itself not neces-

sarily temporal is one definition of allegory. See the opening pages of Paul de Man's "Pascal's Allegory of Persuasion," in *Allegory and Representation*, ed. Stephen J. Greenblatt (Baltimore: Johns Hopkins University Press, 1981), 1–25.

23. Aside from such textual "authority," Hurd would also be relying on well-established traditions in Protestant commentary and even historiography.

CHAPTER 5

1. Karl Barth, *Die protestantische Theologie im 19. Jahrhundert*, 3rd. ed. 2 vols. (Hamburg: Siebenstern Verlag, 1969), 1:263.

2. Rudolf Haym, *Herder nach seinem Leben und seinen Werken*, 2 vols. (Berlin: 1958), 1:297.

3. Emmanuel Hirsch, *Geschichte der neuern evangelischen Theologie*, vol. 4 (Gütersloh: C. Bertelsmann, 1952), 208.

4. For a valuable assessment of Herder's place in the history of Biblical hermeneutics and in the wider context of European intellectual history, see Hans Frei, *The Eclipse of Biblical Narrative: A Study of Eighteenth and Nineteenth Century Hermeneutics* (New Haven and London: Yale University Press, 1974), esp. chapter 10.

5. Herder's work takes in place in what has come to be known as Orientalism. Indeed, when the first volume of *Vom Geiste der Ebräischen Poesie* appeared in English, it was translated as *Oriental Dialogues*. On the literary-historical importance of Herder's Orientalism, see the informed discussion by E. S. Shaffer, *"Kubla Khan" and "The Fall of Jerusalem"* (Cambridge: Cambridge University Press, 1975), esp. chapter 3, "The Oriental idyll."

6. J. G. Herder, *Sämtliche Werke*, ed. Bernhard Suphan (Berlin: Weidemann, 1877–1913), X, 7. Further references to this edition will be given by volume and page number in the body of the text.

7. *The Collected Works of Samuel Taylor Coleridge*, XII.2, 1051.

8. Lowth's lectures were read more widely in Germany than in most European countries, in part because they appeared in 1768 with copious annotations from J. D. Michaelis, the prominent Göttingen philologist.

9. Elaine Scarry, *The Body in Pain* (New York: Oxford University Press, 1985), 193.

10. Herder's emphasis here on the primacy of the deed parallels his proposal, in his *Essay on the Origin of Language*, of the *verb* as the original linguistic unit. In doing so, Herder goes against the grain of most eighteenth-century thought on the subject, which tended to promote the noun as the originary part of speech.

11. See Hirsch, *Geschichte*, IV, 232 ff.

12. Johann Gottfried Herder, *Briefe zür Beförderung der Humanität*, ed. Hans Dietrich Irmscher (Frankfurt am Main: Deutscher Klassiker Verlag, 1991). References to this text will be given by page number in the body of the work.

13. One reason Herder valued Hebrew poetry was that he thought the very

structure of the Hebrew language was conducive to a direct appeal to the ear, which in his *Essay on the Origin of Languages* and elsewhere is considered the most immediate sense organ.

14. Herder's promotion of the Hebrews as the singular yet universal nation finds many echoes in subsequent decades, as, for example, in Schiller's "The Mission of Moses" ("Die Sendung Moses"), an essay that formed part of a series on "universal history." Schiller notes how the two largest religions of the world— Christianity and "Islamism"—both have their roots in the religion of the Jews. He credits Judaism with communicating the precious truth of the doctrine of one God. "Viewed in this light," Schiller observes, "the Hebrews must appear to us as a nation invested with the highest importance as a subject of universal history, and the evil which has been imputed to them or the efforts of shallow wits to degrade them in public appreciation, should not prevent us from doing them justice. The low and depraved character of the nation cannot efface the sublime merit of its lawgiver, nor can it do away with the great influence which this nation has acquired in history." *Schiller's Complete Works*, trans. and ed. Charles J. Hempel (Philadelphia: I. Kohler, 1861), II, 358. On the tangled history of German anti-Semitism and philo-Hebraism in the eighteenth century, see Frank Manuel, *The Broken Staff: Judaism Through Christian Eyes* (Cambridge, Mass. and London: Harvard University Press, 1992), esp. chapter 10, "The German Janus." Manuel is attentive, among other things, to the discrepancies between the way Jewish history and culture, especially Biblical culture, was handled in "polite" discourse and how Jews were actually treated in terms of social and public policy.

15. On this matter, see W. H. Bruford, *Germany in the Eighteenth Century: The Social Background of the Literary Revival* (Cambridge: Cambridge University Press, 1968), esp. part 2, chapters 1 and 2 ("The Nobility in General" and "Courts and Courtiers").

16. Eichhorn is mentioned in passing as an important figure in Orientalism in Edward Said's pioneering study *Orientalism* (New York: Random House, 1978), 17.

17. For a brief sketch of Michaelis's career and ideas, see J. C. Flaherty, "J. D. Michaelis: Rational Biblicist," *Journal of English and Germanic Philology* 49 (1950), 172–81. See also the helpful essay by Anna-Ruth Löwenbrück, "Johann David Michaelis' Verdienst um die philologisch-historische Bibelkritik," in *Historische Kritik und biblischer Kanon in der deutschen Aufklärung*, ed. Henning Graf Reventlow, Walter Soarn, and John Woodbridge (Wiesbaden: Otto Harrassowitz, 1988), 157–70.

18. The best study of their interrelations, as well as the most thorough exposition and analysis of Eichhorn's study of prophecy, is by Eberhard Sehmsdorf, *Die Prophetenauslegung bei J. G. Eichhorn* (Göttingen: Vanderhoeck & Ruprecht, 1971).

19. *Collected Letters of Samuel Taylor Coleridge*, IV, 929.

20. See, for example, Robert Barth, *Coleridge and Christian Doctrine* (Cambridge, Mass.: Harvard University Press, 1969), 56n.

21. But even in the great Eichhorn, the wheat must be separated from the chaff. As Kathleen Coburn notes: "Coleridge wrote, regarding Eichhorn in particular and the *Neologic Divines* in general, that he would 'regard it as a service of no mean value to the English student' if he should do what he proposed to do in his own work, 'i.e., extract the numerous medicinal herbs for us, from the hemlock & other noxious weeds' (ms. note in Eichhorn's *Neue Testament* II 161—Green's copy). See *The Notebooks of Samuel Taylor Coleridge*, ed. Kathleen Coburn (New York: Bollingen Foundation, and London: Routledge and Kegan Paul, 1957), vol. 3, notes to entry 4401. For the full version of Coleridge's annotations to Eichhorn, see *Collected Works of Samuel Taylor Coleridge* (Princeton: Princeton University Press, and London: RKP, 1984), XII, 2.

22. See Brevard S. Childs, *Introduction to the Old Testament As Scripture* (Philadelphia: Fortress Press, 1979), 113. Childs also credits Eichhorn as the pioneer in the critical genre of introductions to Biblical texts.

23. For a good analysis of the situation of classical philology in Germany in the middle and late eighteenth century, see the "Introduction" to F. A. Wolf, *Prolegomena to Homer*, translated and introduced by Anthony Grafton, Glenn W. Most, and James E. G. Zetzel (Princeton: Princeton University Press, 1985). The authors pay some explicit attention to Eichhorn and the relations between classical and Biblical/Orientalist philology. They do, however, somewhat misleadingly characterize Eichhorn's work as "theology" when really it is only philology applied to sacred texts.

24. Sehmsdorf argues that Eichhorn stresses the poetic character of the Hebrew prophets more than Herder does, although I find that misleading. For Sehmsdorf, Herder's appeal to "spirit" seems to exclude the poetic, but my sense of Herder's use of "spirit" suggests that it includes it and is virtually its condition of possibility.

25. J. G. Eichhorn, *Urgeschichte* (Altdorf and Nuremberg: Monath und Kussler, 1793). All further references will be given by page number in the body of the text. There is no English translation of this work.

26. It is perhaps not a matter of indifference that Eichhorn uses the word "created" ("schöpfte") for the text of Genesis, a rather loaded term when the text is about God's creation.

27. This issue is still rather hotly contested. Criticism sensitive to feminist concerns has drawn attention to the radical differences in the presentation and hierarchy of gender in the two Creation stories (before Genesis 2.4 and after). See Patricia Parker, "Coming Second: Woman's Place," in *Literary Fat Ladies: Rhetoric, Gender, Property* (London and New York: Methuen, 1987), 178–233.

28. The young Hegelian David Friedrich Strauss discusses Eichhorn as a forerunner in the new discipline of myth criticism in his *The Life of Jesus Critically Examined*, trans. George Eliot (Philadelphia: Fortress Press, 1972), 46–60. See also the informative study by Christian Hartlich and Walter Sachs, *Der Ursprung des Mythosbegriffs in der modernen Bibelwissenschaft* (Tübingen: J. C .B. Mohr, 1952), 20–38.

29. We shall return to the importance and pervasiveness of this Hegelian trajectory in the chapter on Hölderlin.

30. For Lessing's historico-rationalist position, see his "New Hypothesis Concerning the Evangelists Considered as Merely Human Historians," in *Lessing's Theological Writings*, ed. Henry Chadwick (Stanford: Stanford University Press, 1957), 65–81.

31. We tend to associate critical Biblical scholarship with the "traditions" of Dissent circles; thus Geddes as a (Scottish) Catholic is rather singular in this regard. On this context of Biblical scholarship, see Albert Goodwin, *The Friends of Liberty: The English Democratic Movement in the Age of the French Revolution* (Cambridge, Mass. and London: Harvard University Press, 1979), 68.

32. In the chapter on Blake I take up Jerome McGann's thesis that Geddes's analysis of the composition of the Bible, especially the arbitrary character of its ordering, may have informed Blake's not-so-narrative mode in his brief epics.

33. Alexander Geddes, *Critical Remarks on the Hebrew Scriptures corresponding with a new translation of the Bible*, vol. 1 (London, 1800), 25. I am grateful to Leslie Brisman for drawing my attention long ago in a seminar on Romanticism and Protestantism to the importance of Geddes.

34. Ibid., vi.

CHAPTER 6

1. For a sensible discussion of Blake's madness (as well as a neglected general appreciation), see Georges Bataille, *Le littérature et le mal* (Paris: Gallimard, 1957), for the chapter on Blake.

2. William Butler Yeats, "William Blake and the Imagination," in *Ideas of Good and Evil* (London: Macmillan, 1961), 111.

3. E. P. Thompson, *The Making of the English Working Class* (Harmondsworth: Penguin, 1968), 56. Thompson followed up this lead in his later study *Witness Against the Beast: William Blake and the Moral Law* (New York: New Press, 1993). Jon Mee has situated Blake in a resonant context of radical culture in his *Dangerous Enthusiasm: William Blake and the Culture of Radicalism in the 1790s* (Oxford: Clarendon Press, 1992). Also of interest in this connection is Clarke Garrett's study, *Respectable Folly: Millenarians & the French Revolution in France & England* (Baltimore: Johns Hopkins University Press, 1975), especially for its analysis of the popular works of Richard Brothers and Joanna Southcott, compared to whom Blake looks more plausibly sane.

4. For a helpful discussion of Blake's heterodox notions of originality—to which I return later—see John Barrell, *The Political Theory of Painting* (New Haven: Yale University Press, 1986), chapter 3: "A Blake Dictionary."

5. *The Complete Poetry and Prose of William Blake*, ed. David Erdman, rev. ed. (Berkeley: University of California Press, 1982), 617. Hereafter cited in the body of the text as E. References to poems will be given by page and plate number, ex-

cept for those to *Milton*, which will be indicated by M plus the plate number. Readers should also consult the visual splendour of the Princeton/Blake Trust edition of the poems.

6. This may be the place to recall that words underlined or in bold in the King James Version do not indicate emphasis but words that fill in the elliptical sense of the Hebrew, Aramaic, or Greek.

7. For an amusing, if somewhat flippant, take on the Book of Jonah in the light of speech-act theory, see Terry Eagleton, "J. L. Austin and the Book of Jonah," in *The Book and the Text: The Bible and Literary Theory*, ed. Regina Schwartz (Cambridge, Mass. and Oxford: Basil Blackwell, 1990), 231–36. Eagleton comments pertinently, if hyperbolically: "The only successful prophet is an ineffectual one, one whose warnings fail to materialize. All good prophets are false prophets, undoing their own utterances in the very act of producing them" (233). One could say that the dream of prophetic discourse involves such a coincidence of the performative and the perlocutionary. But it is not given in advance, and it does not function in this way in the Book of Jonah. The Book of Jonah demonstrates how the perlocutionary and/or performative coexists uneasily with the Deuteronomist's insistence on the truth—on what comes true—of the prophetic word.

8. Jonah's case is rather different from most of the other prophets, in that his "book" is the closest thing to a book, in the sense of a sustained narrative. Most of the other "books" of the prophets are decidedly discontinuous collections of sayings.

9. William Hazlitt, *Lectures on the English Poets & The Spirit of the Age* (London: J. M. Dent & Sons, 1910), 9.

10. For one of Blake's many statements on the need for definition, that is, for definite lines and outlines in art, see the "Descriptive Catalogue" of 1809, esp. E, 550.

11. In this reading centered on *Milton* the visual text plays a relatively minor role, although even here there is some sense that the visual—not just a series of "illustrations"—lends an aura of concreteness to the content. For one of the best considerations of the visual dimension of Blake's work in relation to language, see David L. Clark, "How to Do Things with Shakespeare: Illustrative Theory and Practice in Blake's Pity," in *The Mind in Creation: Essays on English Romantic Literature in Honour of Ross Woodman* (Montreal: McGill-Queens, 1992), 106–33. See also, on the more general problematic of the "visible": David L. Clark, "'Visibility Should Not Be Visible': Blake's Borders and the Regimes of Sight," *The Wordsworth Circle* 24 (winter 1994): 29–36.

12. Taylor's usage is not at all uncommon for his time. This sense is not quite identical with that of "to preach," which Samuel Johnson lists in his *Dictionary* as the second sense of "to prophesy."

13. *The Complete Writings of Thomas Paine* (New York: Citadel Press, 1969), I, 475. In this paragraph all the subsequent phrases cited are from the same section of *The Age of Reason*.

14. Ibid., 505.

15. This is partly a false problem for Blake, since it is based on the spurious division of the divine and the human to begin with. But Blake nonetheless inherits a discursive framework with many tenets to which he cannot fully subscribe.

16. It is no accident that the prophets as ventriloquized through Blake are already revising themselves to speak a language of the spirit rather than the letter, as when Isaiah says he saw not God "in any finite organical perception."

17. John Locke, *An Essay concerning Human Understanding,* ed. Peter H. Nidditch (Oxford: Oxford University Press, 1979), 698. For excellent synthetic accounts of Locke's positions on "Reason," "Revelation," "The Bible," and so on, see John Yolton, *A Locke Dictionary* (Oxford: Blackwell, 1993).

18. Ibid., 699 (my emphasis). Locke's criticism of enthusiasm, vigorous as it is, sounds mild compared to Hume's. The latter blamed enthusiasm for "the most cruel disorders in human society." See David Hume, "Of Superstition and Enthusiasm," in *On the Standard of Taste and Other Essays,*" ed. John W. Lenz (Indianapolis: Bobbs-Merrill, 1965), 149. On the discourse of enthusiasm, see the still authoritative study by R. A. Knox, *Enthusiasm* (Oxford: Clarendon Press, 1957). For the peculiarities of the history of the term in the eighteenth century, see Susie L. Tucker, *Enthusiasm: A Study in Semantic Change* (Cambridge: Cambridge University Press, 1972).

19. Ibid., 703.

20. Locke is famously critical in his *Essay concerning Human Understanding* of figurative language as inimical to truth and understanding. And yet figurative language is not something one can simply do without, and Locke certainly does not himself. The opening propositions of the *Essay* and indeed the central argument of the text depend on the inaugural analogy in which Locke contends that the understanding is "like the eye," thus guaranteeing the link between perception and cognition. For a brief probing analysis of figurative language in Locke and epistemology generally, see Paul de Man, "The Epistemology of Metaphor," in *Critical Inquiry* 5:1 (autumn 1978), 113–30. For a more extended treatment of the same problematic in Locke, see Geoff Bennington, "The Perfect Cheat: Locke and Empiricism's Rhetoric," in *The Figural and the Literal: Problems of Language in the History of Science and Philosophy 1630–1800,* ed. A. Benjamin, G. Cantor, and J. Christie (Manchester: Manchester University Press, 1987), 103–23. On the general question of the rhetoric of empiricism (including Locke), see the thoroughgoing account in Jules David Law, *The Rhetoric of Empiricism* (Ithaca and London: Cornell University Press, 1993). For an excellent analysis on the relation of language and experience in Locke (and beyond), see Cathy Caruth, *Empirical Truths and Critical Fictions* (Baltimore and London: Johns Hopkins University Press, 1991).

21. Ibid., 705.

22. Of course, in Blake, where the "text" is often as visual as it is verbal, this notion does not pertain in the same way.

23. Ibid., 691.

24. Ibid., 704. Locke makes a similar claim in the closing pages of *The Reasonableness of Christianity, as delivered in the Scriptures.*

25. Yet for someone who was, in Blake's view, pseudo-Christian, Locke paid a good deal of attention to Christian theology. See Richard Ashcraft, "John Locke's Library: Portrait of an Intellectual," in *A Locke Miscellany,* ed. Jean S. Yolton (Bristol: Thoemmes, 1990), 226–45.

26. More heterodox—and seemingly not in the spirit of the Biblical text—is Ezekiel's (that is, Blake's Ezekiel) claim that the gods originate in the Poetic Genius.

27. Milton had somewhat contradictory positions on the universality of prophecy and prophesying (which are not always the same thing), even in one and the same work, such as his *Christian Doctrine.* On the one hand, he maintained that "All believers have not the gift of prophecy but the Holy Spirit in them is an equivalent for prophecy, dreams, and visions" (*The Works of John Milton* [New York: Columbia University Press, 1933], *Christian Doctrine* 1.27, XVI, 119). And yet he also thought that each believer was "authorized to prophesy" (*Christian Doctrine,* 1.32, XVII, 325). He perhaps comes closest to Blake when he says that "men acting according to the will of God, outspoken or implanted, are prophets" (I D2, VII, p. 83).

28. It is also characteristic of a good many of Blake's poems not called prophecies, such as the "Book of Los" or the "Book of Urizen," even if the gestures of invocation, calling, or dictation are less extended.

29. Indeed, it is something like the opposite of a fall, insofar as it is a sacrifice to achieve a higher end. This economy of sacrifice, also figured in a descent, will be featured prominently in *Milton.*

30. The classic explication of this peculiarity of Blake's thought is by Northrop Frye in his *Fearful Symmetry,* 2nd. ed. (Princeton: Princeton University Press, 1969).

31. But the two revolutions were often thought analogous in Blake's time. The letter from Burke's French correspondent De Pont that prompted the *Reflections on the Revolution in France* presupposed that Burke would be a supporter of the French Revolution because he had been remarkably supportive of the American Revolution.

32. It is remarkable that England's "Glorious" Revolution plays no significant role in Blake's historicomythical thinking.

33. G.W.F. Hegel, *Vorlesungen über die Philosophie der Geschichte* (Theorie Werkausabe), vol. 12, 114 (Frankfurt am Main: Suhrkamp, 1970), 197.

34. Breaking the cycle of the "dull round" was, in Blake's earliest work, the function of "the Poetic or Prophetic character" (E, 3).

35. On this point see Harold Bloom, "Blake's *Jerusalem*: The Bard of Sensibility and the Form of Prophecy," in *The Ringers in the Tower* (Chicago and London: University of Chicago Press, 1971), 65–79; and, more generally, Vincent Arthur De Luca, *Words of Eternity* (Princeton: Princeton University Press, 1991), esp. chapter 3.

36. See Robert M. Maniquis, "Holy Savagery and Wild Justice: English Romanticism and the Terror," *Studies in Romanticism* 28 (1989): 365–95.

37. For a valuable discussion of the satiric mode in Blake, see Martin Price, *To the Palace of Wisdom* (Carbondale: Southern Illinois University Press, 1964), 390–445. See also the neglected chapters on Blake in Josephine Miles, *Eras & Modes in English Poetry* (Berkeley and Los Angeles: University of California Press, 1964). She comments pertinently: "The low language of satire accorded with the threatening language of prophecy" (88).

38. *Sir Isaac Newton's Daniel and the Apocalypse*, ed. Sir William Whitla (London: John Murray, 1922), 149.

39. This is the first in a series of reversals. Tilottama Rajan sees reversal as the key hermeneutic principle in Blake's brief epics. See her valuable account in *The Supplement of Reading* (Ithaca and London: Cornell University Press, 1990), chapter 9.

40. Gerald Bruns, emphasizing prophecy's address to the immediate situation, goes so far as to suggest that the "prophetic word has something unwritable about it." See his "Canon and Power in the Hebrew Scriptures," in *Canons*, ed. Robert von Hallberg (Chicago: University of Chicago Press, 1983), 73. The paradox, however, is that virtually the only prophetic utterances we know about are the ones written down.

41. This is a not-so-common strategy in texts about the origins of language in the eighteenth century, which tend, as Derrida has shown, to promote voice over writing. But there are exceptions. One notable English case that privileges writing precisely by tracing it to its divine origin on Mount Sinai is Daniel Defoe's *Essay Upon Literature* of 1726. One might also note here that not everyone agreed that Hebrew writing originated with Moses and the dispensation of the tablets. Augustine, for example, in his massively influential *City of God*, argues that Hebrew was recorded as a written language in the succession of fathers from Abraham onward. Augustine states this position as a prelude to disputing some of the claims for the primacy of Egyptian learning and letters over the Hebrew counterparts. See *City of God*, book 18, chapter 39.

42. W. J. T. Mitchell has explored at length the issue of writing in Blake, and he records the curious comment made by Paul de Man in conversation that Blake did not need to be deconstructed because he was fully aware of the "primacy" of writing over speech. That surely cannot mean that there is nothing in Blake that calls for or performs "deconstruction." See W. J. T. Mitchell, "Visible Language: Blake's Wond'rous Art of Writing," in *Romanticism and Contemporary Criticism*, ed. Morris Eaves and Michael Fischer (Ithaca and London: Cornell University Press, 1986), 46–86.

43. For other examples of the directives to record the prophetic word in "books," see Jeremiah 30.2 and 36.4, the latter for its mention of Baruch the scribe who records all the words of the Lord transmitted to Jeremiah. In addition to the

Biblical tradition proper, Blake is likely to have been familiar with the legitimation of writing in Swedenborg's *HEAVEN and its Wonders, and HELL: From Things Heard & Seen.* See especially the section on "Writing in Heaven," in which Swedenborg testifies to receiving texts from God, and not only spoken words. Swedenborg likens himself to Ezekiel and St. John the Divine, who likewise were presented with scrolls and books from God. *HEAVEN and its Wonders, and HELL: From Things Heard & Seen* (London: J. M. Dent & Co., 1909), 112 ff.

44. But in his excellent *Blake and the Idea of the Book* (Princeton: Princeton University Press, 1993) Joseph Viscomi shows, among other things, that Blake's modes of production did not *in principle* prevent him publishing and selling widely. It was in part a matter of the "invisible hand" of the market.

45. I do not suggest that calling the poem an example of this genre or that clears up all that many problems, nor is it certain that the poem would not evade or exceed any generic classification. Benjamin says that the significant work of art "will either establish the genre or abolish it [*hebt sie auf*]; and the perfect work will do both." In *Origin of German Tragic Drama,* trans. John Osborne (London: New Left Books, 1977), 44.

46. See Blake's "On Virgil" (E, 270) and "The Laocoon" (E, 274).

47. Moreover, the hero of the epic is technically Jesus, who is, ultimately, the Prince of Peace, even if he sometimes appears with a sword in his mouth.

48. See also the very end of *Paradise Regained:* " . . . he unobserved / Home to his Mother's house private return'd." One could argue that the focus on the domestic and the individual was one way for Milton to write political allegory rather than political commentary, which would have been exceedingly dangerous during the composition of *Paradise Lost* undertaken in the first years after the Restoration.

49. For the fullest reading of Milton along these lines, see Christopher Hill, *Milton and the English Revolution* (Harmondsworth: Penguin, 1979). For an illuminating reading of Milton's politics anchored in questions of the epic genre, see David Quint, *Epic and Empire* (Princeton: Princeton University Press, 1993), esp. chapter 7. See also the interesting polemical essay by Fredric Jameson, "Religion and Ideology: A Reading of *Paradise Lost,*" in *Literature, Politics, and Theory,* ed. Francis Barker et al. (London and New York: Methuen, 1986), 35–54. For an authoritative, straightforward account see Mary Ann Radzinowicz, "The Politics of *Paradise Lost,*" in *Politics of Discourse: The Literature and History of Seventeenth-Century England,* ed. Kevin Sharpe and Steven N. Zwicker (Berkeley and Los Angeles: University of California Press, 1987), 204–29.

50. On the counterpoint of Biblical and Classical discourse in Milton, see Northrop Frye, *One Foot in Eden* (Toronto: University of Toronto Press, 1967).

51. The epyllion comes across as a less "classical" genre even if there were some examples and even if English examples, such as Marlowe's *Hero and Leander,* adopt classical subject matter or themes.

52. For a very good account of the prehistory of *Paradise Regained* see Barbara Lewalski, *Milton's Brief Epic* (Providence: Brown University Press, 1966).

53. But it should be noted that *Milton*, especially after the Bard's song, has the texture of a narrative only in fits and starts and in this regard is not so typical of epic, brief or otherwise.

54. In *William Blake: A Critical Essay* (1868). Reprint, ed. Hugh J. Luke (Lincoln: University of Nebraska Press, 1970), 265.

55. It is worth noting that Blake's denunciation is followed immediately by a critique of Plato making "Socrates say that Poets & Prophets do not Know or Understand what they write or Utter" (E, 554). This, Blake snorts, "is a most pernicious Falsehood."

56. This passage is no haphaxlogomenon in Blake. He elsewhere speaks favorably of "sublime allegory," and the word "sublime" always has a positive valence in Blake (as in "the sublime of the Bible").

57. John Mee, for example, who is committed to establishing Blake's place in the community of London's radical semiunderground, invokes only the dismissal of allegory. See his *Dangerous Enthusiasm*, 12–13. This gesture is fairly typical of historicizing projects, although David Erdman, for one, has no problem working with a concept of historical allegory or even allegory, period. Northrop Frye's strategy was to distinguish essentially between "good" and "bad" allegory—not his terms—aligning Blake's practice with the former. For a probing analysis of different ways of conceiving allegory, see J. Hillis Miller, "The Two Allegories," in *Allegory, Myth, and Symbol* (Harvard Studies in English 9), ed. Morton Bloomfield (Cambridge: Harvard University Press, 1981), 355–70. For a brilliant series of reflections on the historical and theoretical status of allegory, centered in the Renaissance but extended much further, see Gordon Teskey, *Allegory and Violence* (Ithaca and London: Cornell University Press, 1997).

58. Walter Benjamin, *Origin of German Tragic Drama*, trans. John Osborne (London: New Left Books, 1977), 175.

59. Northrop Frye has remarked on the resistance to allegory in literary study residing in the critic's reluctance to deal with texts that seem to prescribe their allegorical meanings in advance, thus inhibiting the freedom of the interpreter. On the history of the resistance to allegory and its occasional rehabilitation, see the classic essay by Paul de Man, "The Rhetoric of Temporality," in *Blindness and Insight*, 2nd ed. rev. (Minneapolis: University of Minnesota Press, 1983), 187–228.

60. Los is not one among other figures in Blake's allegorical universe. This figure of "Time" is equated with the Spirit of Prophecy and is arguably the presiding "deity" of the poem, even if he is not a providential force controlling all its action.

61. See Paul de Man, "Pascal's Allegory of Persuasion," in *Allegory and Representation*, ed. Stephen Greenblatt (Baltimore and London: Johns Hopkins University Press, 1981), 1–25.

62. In this, the "style" of prophetic discourse accords well with its typically discontinuous vision of history.

63. On the importance of Howes's argument, see especially Leslie Tannenbaum's discussion in his *Biblical Tradition in Blake's Early Prophecies: The Great Code of Art* (Princeton: Princeton University Press, 1982), 28–35.

64. For an authoritative discussion of the redaction of the prophetic books and their canonical coherence, see Brevard S. Childs, *Introduction to the Old Testament As Scripture* (Philadelphia: Fortress Press, 1979).

65. Jerome McGann argues that a possible source for this aspect of Blake's work, exemplified in the *Book of Urizen*, is Alexander Geddes's account of Biblical redaction, where the model for the text is one of units that can be shuffled from one place to the next. See his "The Idea of the Indeterminate Text: Blake's Bible of Hell and Dr. Alexander Geddes," *Studies in Romanticism* 25 (fall 1986): 303–24. And yet one could hardly claim that the sequences are sheerly arbitrary, as if they were somehow harbingers of the cut-up texts of a William Burroughs.

66. In this account I am leaving aside the prose "Preface" and the hymn "And did those feet in ancient time?" featured in two copies of *Milton*. Each of the prefatory pieces—the Preface, the invocation of the Muses, the Bard's song—is about inspiration and the poetic act of imagination.

67. Jerome McGann notes Blake's "refusal to employ either single or double quotation marks to distinguish the speaking voices in his texts." See the chapter "William Blake Illuminates the Truth," which bears a good deal on *Milton*, in his *Towards a Literature of Knowledge* (Chicago: University of Chicago Press, 1989), 28.

68. See Neil Hertz, *The End of the Line: Essays on Psychoanalysis and the Sublime* (New York and London: Columbia University Press, 1985), esp. chapter 1.

69. In his *Milton's Poetry of Choice and Its Romantic Heirs* (Ithaca and London: Cornell University Press, 1973) Leslie Brisman charts the omnipresence of this structure in Milton and its history of influence in Romantic poetry.

70. Or is it so pedestrian? Blake records his place of abode as South Molton Street, and it's perhaps not only coincidental that "Molton" is so close to "Milton." Blake also puns on the street name by putting it in proximity with the word "molten" (Plate 4).

71. For a very suggestive analysis of the problematic of friendship (which cites Blake's dictum), see Jacques Derrida, *Politiques de l'amitié* (Paris: Galilée, 1994).

72. It should go without saying that it is important that it is Milton who is returning as a redeemer, not, say, Shakespeare or Spenser. Blake seems closest to Milton in his heterodox and vigorous readings of the Bible, in his identification of poetry and prophecy, and perhaps in their both being caught up in a tumultuous, revolutionary moment of British history and in their taking a stance of resistance.

73. Howard Weinbrot, however, has shown how problematic the term "Augustan" is; the terms used here are really just shorthand rather than accurate des-

ignations. See his *Augustus Caesar in "Augustan" England: The Decline of a Classical Norm* (Princeton: Princeton University Press, 1978).

74. John Milton, *Complete Poetry and Major Prose*, 671. But see Hazlitt's comment: "Milton has borrowed more than any other writer, and exhausted every source of imitation, sacred or profane," quoted in *The Romantics on Milton*, ed. Joseph Anthony Wittreich Jr. (Cleveland: Case Western University Press, 1970), 381. Thus Blake is quoting an exemplary quoter.

75. *The Poems of Alexander Pope*, ed. John Butt (London: Methuen, 1968), 189. The fact that Virgil's Fourth Eclogue was often read by Christians as a Messianic allegory hardly softens Pope's blow, from Blake's point of view.

76. The fullest study of this aspect of Milton's work is by William Kerrigan, *The Prophetic Milton* (Charlottesville: University of Virginia Press, 1974). See also Marshall Grossman, "Milton and the Rhetoric of Prophecy," in *The Cambridge Companion to Milton* (Cambridge: Cambridge University Press, 1989), 167–81.

77. This is to avoid the complicated historical and hermeneutic question about the precise (and possibly changing) views of Milton on the status of Christ as God and man. Here I simply want to stress the rather different emphasis in Blake.

78. For a spirited and suspicious modern account of Milton's God, somewhat in the tradition of Blake, see William Empson's classic *Milton's God*, rev. ed. (Cambridge: Cambridge University Press, 1981).

79. *The Anxiety of Influence* (London and New York: Oxford University Press, 1973), 14

80. For the moment I am proceeding as if the opposition between (Christian) spirit and (Judaic) letter were a plausible and stable one. This is, however, not the case. One could show, as I attempt to do elsewhere, that there is already a complicated dialectic of letter and spirit within the Hebrew Scriptures, which is subsequently flattened out in its Christian reception so as to promote the specificity of the Christian *pneuma*, or spirit.

81. Throughout this chapter I often stress the preliminary matter of the poem (title page, preface, and epigraphs) because it seems unusually crucial to this programmatic and metapoetic poem. For a provocative and informed analysis of the various "thresholds" to the literary work, see Gerard Genette, *Seuils* (Paris: Seuil, 1987). Also in English as *Paratexts: The Thresholds of Texuality*, trans. Jane E. Lewin (Cambridge: Cambridge University Press, 1997).

82. *Complete Poems and Major Prose*, 744.

83. Christopher Hill, *The World Turned Upside Down* (Harmondsworth: Penguin, 1975), 91. The passage from Hill occurs in a chapter entitled "A Nation of Prophets," itself a phrase taken from *Areopagitica*. For a change, the "all" in "all the Lord's people" included women. For the new phenomenon of woman as prophet (somewhat distinct from the more familiar figure of the woman as mystic), see the informative essay by Phyllis Mack, "Women as Prophets during the

English Civil War," in *The Origins of Anglo-American Radicalism*, ed. Margaret C. Jacob and James R. Jacob (New Jersey and London: Humanities Press International, 1991),72–89. These women were precursors of Joanna Southcott, even if Southcott, as far as I know, does not appeal to them as such.

84. Joseph Anthony Wittreich Jr., *Angel of Apocalypse: Blake's Idea of Milton* (Madison: University of Wisconsin Press, 1975), 250. But Bloom's sense of the dialectic of influence is more subtle. It involves gain as well as loss, and the debilitating effect on the ephebe's imagination by no means brings the process of poetic production to a halt.

85. E. P. Thompson remarks of Blake: "He took each author (even the Old Testament prophets) as his equal, or as something less." See *Witness Against the Beast*, xvi.

86. For a provocative reflection of the difficulty of referring to "falling," see the excellent essay by Cathy Caruth, "The Falling Body and the Impact of Reference," in her *Unclaimed Experience: Trauma, Narrative, and History* (Baltimore and London: Johns Hopkins University Press, 1996), 73–90.

87. See Alexander Pope's *Peri Bathous or The Art of Sinking in Poetry*, his parody of Longinus. One might say that to imitate Milton is always to risk parodying him.

88. On the terrifying (rather than the cute) character of the Cherubim in the Hebrew Bible, see the helpful essay by Leslie Brisman, "Blake's Comme-bined Cherubim: A Note on *Milton*, Plate 32," in *Blake: An Illustrated Quarterly* 21 (1987–88): 95–98.

89. The English terms "past" and "future" have no exact correlative in the system of Hebrew tenses. The distinction is closer to one between "perfect" and "imperfect" tenses. The fact that past and future could both fall in the category of "perfect" is one reason that they can be used interchangeably in prophetic discourse.

90. For an exemplary reading of the two versions of the sower parable, see Frank Kermode, *The Genesis of Secrecy* (Cambridge, Mass. and London: Harvard University Press, 1979).

91. When Satan comes on Uriel for the first time, Milton writes that the former soon "Saw with in ken a glorious Angel stand,/The same whom *John* saw also in the Sun" (*Paradise Lost*, III, 621–23).

92. *Fearful Symmetry*, 317. (Frye's inspired pun on Moses continues the tradition still further.) For an informed study of the citational character of prophetic discourse, see John Day, "Prophecy," in *It Is Written: Scripture Citing Scripture*, ed. D. A. Carson and H. G. M. Wilson (Cambridge: Cambridge University Press, 1988), 39–55. See also, in the same volume, the essay on "Revelation" by G. K. Beale, 318–336.

93. This verse from Revelation echoes Isaiah 9.5, the verse immediately preceding the prophecy of the Prince of Peace.

94. For an illuminating essay on this topic, see Morton D. Paley, "The Figure of the Garment in *The Four Zoas, Milton*, and *Jerusalem*," in *Blake's Sublime Alle-*

gory, ed. S. C. Curran and J. A. Wittreich Jr. (Madison: University of Wisconsin Press, 1973), 119–39. Paley also shows how the "garment" is implicated in the tropological network of weaving and the making of the texts that so preoccupies Blake in his later work.

CHAPTER 7

1. *"Sämtliche Werke,"* ed. Friedrich Beissner and Adolf Beck. 8 vols. (Stuttgart: Cotta/Kohlhammer, 1943–85), VI.1, 116. All further references in the body of the text to the *Grosse Stuttgarter Ausgabe* (*GSA*) will be given by volume and page number. All citations from Hölderlin's poetry come from the first part ("Text") of volume II.

2. One notable contemporary exception is Bettina Von Arnim's effusion: "To me his sayings are the sayings of an oracle, which he, as the God's priest proclaims in madness, for certainly all worldly life is mad in relation to him . . . " ("Mir sind seine Sprüche wie Orakelsprüche, die er als der Priester des Gottes im Wahnsinn ausruft, und gewiß ist alles Weltleben ihn gegenüber wahnsinnig . . . "). Not only does she speak of Hölderlin as oracular, but also she employs Hölderlin's terms (like caesura, rhythm) to characterize poetic revelation in general: "Thus the poetic God reveals himself." ("So offenbare sich der dichtende Gott.") See *Die Günderode,* prefaced by Christa Wolf (Frankfurt am Main: Insel, 1982), 248.

3. "Hölderlin," in *Hölderlin: Beiträge zu seinem Verständnis in unserm Jahrhundert,* ed. Alfred Kelletat (Tübingen: J. C. B. Mohr, 1961), 2. The text appeared originally in *Blätter für die Kunst,* Folie 11 and 12 (1919), 11–13. George's prose poem, of which I have cited the first sentence, follows a series of quotations from Hölderlin's poems strung together as if to form a single poem.

4. Hans-Georg Gadamer, "Hölderlin und das Zukünftige," in *Kleine Schriften* 2 (Tübingen: J. C. B. Mohr, 1967), 47.

5. But who exactly are "we"? Heidegger takes up the question of the "we" in his reading of "Germanien," to be discussed later on.

6. Theodor Wiesengrund Adorno, "Parataxis," in *Gesammelte Schriften* 11 (Frankfurt am Main: Suhrkamp, 1974), 259. ("Das 'Was bleibet' . . . deutet, der puren grammatischen Form nach, auf Seiendes und das Gedächtnis daran, wie das der Propheten; keineswegs auf das Sein, das nicht sowohl in der Zeit bliebe, als Zeitlichem transzendent wäre.")

7. For an informative study of the Nazi reception of Hölderlin, see Claudia Albert, "Dient Kulturarbeit dem Sieg?—Hölderlin-Rezeption von 1933–45," in *Hölderlin und die Moderne: Eine Bestandsaufnahme,* ed. Gerhard Kurz, Valérie Lawitschka, Jürgen Wertheimer (Tübingen: Attempo, 1995), 153–73.

8. Jochen Schmidt points out that even so scrupulous a critic as Peter Szondi saw signs of resistance in Beißner's work and activities, such that Beißner could by no means be condemned in blanket fashion. It is not out of the question that Beißner would have that publishing Hölderlin would have counted as an affront to

Nazi ideology, even if party functionaries would have had trouble seeing it as so. For an account of Szondi's understanding of Beißner, as well as a wide-ranging history of reception and editing, see Jochen Schmidt, "Hölderlin in 20.Jahrhundert. Rezeption und Edition," in *Hölderlin und die Moderne*, ed. Gerhard Kurz et al. (Tübingen: Attempo, 1995), 105–25. See also Jochen Schmidt, "Deutschland und Frankreich als Gegnmodelle in Hölderlins Geschichtsdenken: Evolution statt Revolution," in *Dichter und ihre Nation*, ed. Helmut Scheuer (Frankfurt am Main: Suhrkamp, 1993), 176–99. Schmidt reproduces the passages from Hölderlin's letters cited by Beißner, many of which speak of resistance and imagine a "revolution" beyond the present moment that would bring about a better world.

9. On the identification of the fatherland as Swabia, see *GSA*, VI, 117.

10. Martin Heidegger, *Hölderlins Hymnen "Germanien" und "Der Rhein,"* Gesamtausgabe, vol. 39 (Frankfurt am Main: Vittorio Klostermann, 1980), 4. For one reading of the relation of aesthetics and politics in Heidegger, see the nuanced and provocative study by Phillipe Lacoue-Labarthe, *Heidegger, Art and Politics*, trans. Chris Turner (Oxford: Blackwell, 1990).

11. ("Wir müssen mit der Tatsache fertig werden, daß die Deutschen volle hundert Jahre Zeit brauchten, bis überhaupt das Werk Hölderlins in jener Gestalt vor uns kam, die uns zwingt einzugestehen, daß wir seiner Größe und zukünftigen Macht heute noch in keiner Weise gewachsen sind") 23.

12. ("Hölderlins Dichtungen werden von Jahr zu Jahr unerschöpflicher, größer, fremder—in einem letztgültigen Sinne nirgends einzureihen. Es fehlt ihnen noch der wirkliche geschichtlich-geistige Raum. Er kommt ihnen nicht von außen, sondern sie selbst werden ihn sich schaffen müssen. Wenn wir nicht gesonnen sind, künftig in den Wettern dieser Dichtung auszuharren, dann bleibt dieser Versuch in der Tat nur ein neugieriges Spiel") 23.

13. ("Die Dichter sind, wenn sie in ihrem Wesen sind, *prophetisch*. Sie sind aber keine 'Propheten' nach der jüdisch-christlichen Bedeutung dieses Namens. Die 'Propheten' dieser Religionen sagen nicht erst nur voraus das voraufgründende Wort des Heiligen. Sie sagen sogleich vorher den Gott, auf den die Sicherheit der Rettung in die überirdische Seligkeit rechnet. Man verunstalte Hölderlins Dichtung nicht durch 'das Religiöse der Religion,' die eine Sache der römischen Dichtung des Verhältnisses zwischen Menschen und Göttern bleibt. Man überbürde nicht das Wesen dieses Dichtertums, indem man den Dichter zu seinem 'Seher' im Sinne des Wahrsagers macht. Das dichterisch zum voraus gesagte Heilige öffnet nur den Zeit-Raum eines Erscheinens der Götter und weist in die Ortschaft des Wohnens des geschichtlichen Menschen auf dieser Erde. Das Wesen dieser Dichters darf nicht in der Entsprechung zu jenen 'Propheten' gedacht, sondern das 'Prophetische' dieser Dichtung muß aus dem Wesen des dichtenden Voraussagens begriffen werden.") Martin Heidegger, *Erläuteungen zu Hölderlins Dichtung*, 4th ed. (Frankfurt am Main: Vittorio Klostermann, 1971), 114. It is not

only when Heidegger is speaking directly of Hölderlin that the latter's work serves as the paradigm for the future. In the posthumously published *Beiträge zur Philosophie (Vom Ereignis)*, when Heidegger speaks of "the future ones" ("die Zukünftigen") he singles out Hölderlin as their "most future" poet: "Hölderlin ist der Zukünftigste, weil er am weitestem herkommt und in dieser Weite das Größte *durchmißt* und verwandelt." ("Hölderlin is the most future one, because he comes from farthest away and to this extent permeates and the transforms the greatest.") *Beiträge zur Philosophie (Vom Ereignis)*, Gesamtausgabe vol. 65 (Frankfurt am Main: Vittorio Klostermann, 1989), 401. I am grateful to Geoff Waite for drawing my attention to this work by Heidegger.

14. See the provocative study by Marlene Zarader, *La dette impensé: Heidegger et l'héritage hebraique* (Paris: Seuil, 1990), esp. 56–69. Zarader shows how the presence of the Judaic exceeds Heidegger's acknowledgment of it. My thanks to Jill Robbins for pointing me to this text.

15. For this history, see Helen Fehervary, *Hölderlin and the Left* (Heidelberg: C. H. Winter, 1977). The politics of Left and Right also inform the editing of Hölderlin's work; the Roter Stern's Frankfurter edition is a politically charged response to the Stuttgart edition begun under the auspices of the Nazi regime.

16. In political terms, Hölderlin's prose (especially in the letters) is much more clear-cut.

17. For a fuller, attentive reading of "Wie Wenn am Feiertage," one that pays attention to the complicated question of mediation, see Timothy Bahti, *Ends of the Lyric* (Baltimore and London: Johns Hopkins University Press, 1996), chapter 5.

18. In modern German *Ahnung* often means something no less exalted than "hunch," but in Hölderlin's time, it could denote a much more positive state of consciousness, as, for example, in the opening propositions of Schelling's *Die Weltalter (The Ages of the World)*: "Das Vergangene wird gewußt, das Gewußte wird erkannt, das Zukünftige wird geahndet. Das Gewußte wird erzählt, das Erkannte word dargestellt, das geahndete word geweissagt." F. W. J. Schelling, *Schriften 1813–1830* (Darmstadt: Wissenschaftliche Buchgesellschaft, 1969), 5. Schelling's treatise was to be divided between sections on the past, present, and future, but only the first part, on the past, was completed. On the importance of *Ahnung* as a modality of language in Hölderlin, see Rainer Nägele, *Literatur und Utopie: Versuche zu Hölderlin* (Heidelberg: Lothar Stein Verlag, 1968).

19. Benjamin, a little snidely, takes Hölderlin to task for expressing his love for "the children of coming generations" (*G. S.*, V.1, 599). This is consistent with Benjamin's critique of the disabling effects on the present of an excessive preoccupation with the future.

20. For a fine discussion of this passage and the problems with Heidegger's reading of it, see Hans-Jost Frey, *Studies in Poetic Discourse*, trans. William Whobrey (Stanford: Stanford University Press, 1996).

21. On the topic of closure, thematic and otherwise, in Hölderlin, see the very helpful study by Alice Kuzniar, *Delayed Endings* (Athens: University of Georgia, 1987).

22. See also the chilling end of "Dichterberuf" where Hölderlin changes the final line, which first posits a benign and predictable relation between God and man—"as long as God is not absent" ("solange der Gott nicht fehlet") to anticipating the moment when "Gottes Fehl hilft." Giorgio Agamben singles this out as the inaugural moment of "poetic atheology." See his *The End of the Poem: Studies in Poetics*, trans. Daniel Heller-Roazen (Stanford: Stanford University Press, 1999), 90–91. These same lines, including their different versions, are discussed trenchantly by Fritz Lang in Jean-Luc Godard's *Contempt*.

23. This phrase is explicitly invoked in the famous fragment called "das älteste Systemprogram" ("the oldest program of a system"), which has been ascribed alternately to Hölderlin, Hegel, and Schelling. I discuss the text briefly later on in the chapter.

24. See E. M. Butler, *The Tyranny of Greece over Germany* (Cambridge: Cambridge University Press, 1935).

25. *Hegel's Aesthetics*, trans. T. M. Knox (Oxford: Clarendon Press, 1974 and 1975), 2 vols., vol. 1, 457. Further references will be given by volume and page number in the body of the text.

26. But all symbolic art—in the schema that divides art according to categories of symbolic, classical, and romantic—is termed by Hegel "pre-art" ("Vorkunst"), not yet at the level of classical art, which is paradigmatic for art in general. For Hegel, all art is "symbolic" in another sense, namely, in that it is characterized by the "interpenetration" ("Ineinandersein") of form and meaning.

27. To rehearse Hegel's conception of the oracle is not to give a historically accurate account of it. Modern scholarship, exemplified particularly in the authoritative, demystifying study by Joseph Fontenrose, *The Delphic Oracle* (Berkeley and Los Angeles: University of California Press, 1978), demonstrates that such notions are reductive and romanticized. Hegel, typically, seems to be thinking mainly about the oracles celebrated in literary works and thus is addressing "legendary" rather than actual, run-of-the-mill oracles. The ambiguous, gnomic utterance is by no means the paradigm for oracular discourse. Of the major Romantics, Thomas De Quincey, a considerable scholar of Greek culture, is one of the few to approach the more modern, historical view. In one version of his essay entitled "The Pagan Oracles" De Quincey added a lengthy appendix that compared the oracles as a center for commercial and political exchange to the modern institution closest to it: the Bank of England. See Thomas De Quincey, *Collected Writings*, Vol. VII (Edinburgh: Adam and Charles Black, 1890). In our own time, Gregory Nagy has summarized the politics of the oracle in this way: "The essence of oracular poetry is that it serves to uphold the existing order; it derives its authority from such ultimate sources of authorization as Apollo's Oracle at Delphi." In *Pindar's Homer*

(Baltimore and London: Johns Hopkins University Press, 1990), 167. Nonetheless, this is not how the oracle tends to resonate in Hölderlin.

28. Plutarch, *Moralia*, V., trans. Frank Cole Babbit (London and Cambridge, Mass.: Heinemann and Harvard University Press, 1957), 333–35. For Herodotus's account of the poetic character of oracles, see his *Histories*, 7.6.3–5.

29. Heraclitus, Fragment 18, reads: "The lord whose oracle is at Delphi neither speaks nor conceals, but gives signs." (ὁ ἄναξ οὗ τὸ μαντεῖόν ἐστι τὸ ἐν Δελφοῖς οὔτε λέγει οὔτε κρύπτει ἀλλὰ σημαίνει). Phillip Wheelright, *Heraclitus* (New York: Athenaeum, 1974), 20 (English) and 137 (Greek), for Fragment 18.

30. Hegel makes this point about poetry and art at the end of the *Phenomenology of Spirit* and again in the *Aesthetics*.

31. Max Kommerell, "Hölderlins Hymnen in freien Rhythmen," in *Gedanken über Gedichte* (Frankfurt am Main: Vittorio Klostermann, 1956), 461.

32. On Wieland, and for an analysis of his not atypical conjunction of patriotism/nationalism and cosmopolitanism, see Irmtraut Sahmland, "Ein Weltbürger und seine Nation: Christoph Martin Wieland," in *Dichter und ihre Nation*, ed. Helmut Scheuer (Frankurt am Main: Suhrkamp, 1993), 88–102.

33. On this issue, see W. H. Bruford, *Germany in the Eighteenth Century: The Social Background to the Literary Revival* (Cambridge: Cambridge University Press, 1965); and James H. Sheehan, *German History 1770–1866* (Oxford: Clarendon Press, 1989), esp. chapter 1. Yet if there is anything to unite Germany in this period, it is language. This is not the case with every nation. See the probing analysis of the different formations of nations by Eric Hobsbawm, *Nations and Nationalisms Since 1780: Programme, Myth, Reality* (Cambridge: Cambridge University Press, 1992).

34. This is recognizably a sublime situation. I explore the problematic of what I call "The Sublime of the Nation" in a book-length work in progress on the sublime.

35. The list could be lengthened to include George's tribute to Hölderlin in *Blätter für die Kunst* and the prominent literary history by H. A. Korff, *Geist der Goethezeit*, 4 vols., 2nd ed. (Leipzig: S. Hirzel Verlag, 1940–50). Korff treats much of Hölderlin's work under the rubric of prophecy and devotes more space to "Germanien" than to many other poems now generally considered superior. See especially vol. 3., chapter 1, part 3, "Die Gesichte des Sehers."

36. Jean-Pierre Vernant stresses the nonurban character of the Greek oracle, always located outside the sphere of the *polis*. Hence the relatively easy identification of the oracular word as "natural." See Jean-Pierre Vernant, "Speech and Mute Signs," in *Mortals and Immortals*, ed. Froma T. Zeitlin (Princeton: Princeton University Press, 1991), 303–17.

37. Vincent Scully, *The Earth, The Temple, The Gods* (New Haven: Yale University Press, 1979), 45.

38. See my brief reading of the Dream of the Arab passage in chapter 2.

39. The word "scheint" most likely means "seems" rather than the more literal "shines," but the juxtaposition *scheint* and *umschattet* constitutes nonetheless a strikingly chiaroscuro vision.

40. G. W. F. Hegel, *TWA*, 12, 392.

41. *Werke*, XII, 392. The word *erscheinen* is emphasized in the original. Compare Schelling's formulation in his late lectures on revelation, where the topic is Christ becoming man: "Now we have arrived at the time of the real appearance. This time was predetermined: as the time was fulfilled; for everything had to have occurred that could happen in external fashion." ("Nun sind wir auf den Zeitpunkt der wirklichen Erscheinung gekommen. Diese Zeit war eine vorausbestimmte: als die Zeit erfüllt war; denn es mußte alles geschehen sein, was äußerlich geschehen konnte.")In *Philosophie der Offenbarung 1841/42*, ed. Manfred Frank (Frankfurt an Main: Suhrkamp, 1977), 285.

42. Ibid., 393.

43. I do not engage at length here the tangled question of how to read Hölderlin's poetry in relation to philosophy. There is a rich tradition of readings of Hölderlin by philosophers or philosophically oriented critics: Dilthey, Nietzsche, Benjamin, Heidegger, Gadamer, Adorno, Peter Szondi, Paul de Man, et al. There is even a strong contingent of philosophically oriented critics, such as Cyrus Hamlin and Glenn Most, who, at least strategically, sometimes resist reading the poetry in relation to Idealist philosophy. The fact that Hölderlin wrote essays and fragments that are recognizably philosophical by any account does not of itself mean that one can import this or that passage of his own or his contemporaries' philosophy as an authorized explication of his poetry. Still, it is remarkable—and it conforms to a poetological principle of Hölderlin's own—that a "prosaic" and possibly philosophical passage can have its proper place even in the most poetic of discourses.

44. Hölderlin's speculations on intellectual intuition (*intellektuale Anschauung*) take their place here. A number of the thinkers and poets of the period were fascinated by this hypothetical notion of a faculty, if that's what it is, that would combine and bridge the sensible and the supersensible.

45. See his essay "On the Program of the Coming Philosophy." *G. S.*, II.1, 157–71.

46. For a comprehensive and lucid account of the often overlooked matter of language in Hegel, see Josef Simon, *Das Problem der Sprache bei Hegel* (Stuttgart, 1966).

47. For the German text of the *Versuch*, I am using the text from *Fichtes Werke*, ed. Immanuel Hermann Fichte, vol. 1., 1845. Reprint. (Berlin: De Gruyter, 1971). The English translation is *Attempt at a Critique of All Revelation*, trans. Garret Green (Cambridge: Cambridge University Press, 1978). All quotations will be from this text and will be given by page number in the body of the text.

48. For a still authoritative account of Fichte's religious philosophy, including

details on the later scandal about Fichte's "atheism," see Emanuel Hirsch, *Fichtes Religionsphilosophie im Rahmen der philosophischen Gesamtentwicklung Fichtes* (Göttingen: Vandenhoeck & Ruprecht, 1914). See also the shorter account in a different frame in Hirsch's *Geschichte der neuern evangelischen Theologie, im Zusammenhang mit den allgemeinen Bewegungen des europäischen Denkens*, vol. 4 (Gütersloh: C. Bertelsmann, 1951). The fullest reading of the *Offenbarung* text is by Michael Kessler, *Kritik aller Offenbarung: Untersuchungen zu einem Forschungsprogramm Johann Gottlieb Fichtes und zur Entstehung und Wirkung seines "Versuchs" von 1792* (Mainz: Matthias Grünewald, 1986).

49. Elsewhere Fichte calls attention to the "childish representations of the prophets" (142), one more obstacle to get beyond if one is to have a religion of pure morality.

50. Fichte, *Werke*, II, 245. The passage is from "Die Bestimmung des Menschen." For an alternate English translation of the passage, see Johann Gottlieb Fichte, *The Vocation of Man*, trans. William Smith (La Salle, Ill.: Open Court, 1965), 89.

51. One can also trace Kant's embarrassment about inscription, imagination, and figuration in the two prefaces to the *Critique of Pure Reason* (1781 and 1787). I attempt a reading of this problematic in my book in progress on *The Language of the Sublime*.

52. Immanuel Kant, *Religion Within the Limits of Reason Alone*, trans. Theodore M. Green and Hoyt H. Hudson (New York: Harper, 1960), 47. Further quotations will be given by page number in the body of the text.

53. Especially in the first section of his *Pleroma-Reading in Hegel* (Stanford: Stanford University Press, 1998).

54. For the unseemly side of Kant's view of the Jews in general, see the section on them in his *Anthropology*.

55. Jacques Derrida, "Faith and Knowledge: The Two Sources of 'Religion Within the Limits of Reason Alone'," in *Religion*, ed. Jacques Derrida and Gianni Vattimo (Stanford: Stanford University Press, 1998), 4.

56. See Immanuel Kant, *The Conflict of the Faculties* (*Der Streit der Fakultäten*), trans. Mary J. Gregor (Lincoln and London: University of Nebraska Press, 1979), 37.

57. To say nothing of the matter of the truth of the Bible, about which the Biblical theologian has nothing to say. That, according to Kant, is the province of the philosopher.

58. For example, Kant claims of any given revelation: "The mark of its divinity (at least as the *conditio sine qua non*) is its harmony with what reason pronounces worthy of God" (81).

59. See the comment by Georg Kerner, quoted in Manfred Frank, *Eine Einführung in Schellings Philosophie* (Frankfurt am Main: Suhrkamp, 1985), 16.

60. For an excellent study of the intellectual atmosphere and the protocols of study in Schelling's years at the *Stift*, see Wilhelm G. Jacobs, *Zwischen Revolution*

und Orthodoxie? Schelling und seine Freunde im Stift und an der Universität Tübingen: Texte und Untersuchungen (Stuttgart-Bad Cannstatt: Frommann, 1989). Jacobs assembles much valuable information on precisely who taught and wrote on what. One sees, for example, how the spirit of Eichhorn and Herder informed a good deal of the undertakings at the Stift, in its "Orientalism" (in the—at least partially —good sense!), its comparative understanding of cultures, its probing into the status of the Bible as a text. Some of the interesting projects, close to Hölderlin and Schelling, include Christian Ludwig Nueffer's dissertation *Specimen hoc de poesi Ebreorum* (*Specimens of Hebrew Poetry*), which attends to the poetic achievement of the prophets. Similarly close is Magenau's thesis *On the Figures of the Orientals in their Poems* (*Über die Bilder der Orentaler in ihren Gedichten*), which construes prophecy as a sublime, figurative art of a people (*Volk*).

61. In Schelling's unpublished essays of the time one of the dominant modes is that of reading the Gospels in the light of Kant's thinking on the primacy of practical reason. See Dieter Henrich, "Some Historical Presuppositions of Hegel's System," in *Hegel and the Philosophy of Religion*, ed. Darrel E. Christensen (The Hague: Nijhoff, 1970), 24–44.

62. For a helpful analysis of the relations between Schelling and Hölderlin on this and other points, see Guido Schmidlin, "Hölderlin und Schellings Philosophie der Mythologie und Offenbarung," *Hölderlin-Jahrbuch* 17 (1971–72): 43–55.

63. I tend to agree with the verdict that the likeliest author is Schelling. For an early and still compelling argument for Schelling's authorshhip, see the important study by Franz Rosenzweig (whose dissertation was on *Hegel and the State*), "Das älteste Systemprogramm des deutschen Idealismus" ("The Oldest System Programme of German Idealism"), now reprinted in Franz Rosenzweig, *Zweistromland: Kleinere Schriften zur Religion und Philosophie*, ed. Gesine Palmer (Berlin and Vienna: Philo, 2000), 109–56. For Manfred Frank's similar view on this, see his *Der kommenede Gott: Vorlesungen über die Neue Mythologie* (Frankurt am Main: Suhrkamp, 1982), 154 ff.

64. Quoted from H. S. Harris, *Hegel's Development: Toward the Sunlight 1770–1801* (Oxford: Clarendon, 1972), 511. Harris translates the entire text, along with other early unpublished works, as an appendix.

65. Sometimes, however, Schelling takes pains to distinguish between intellectual and aesthetic intuition.

66. This does not hold for the "noncritical" texts by Kant that are more or less contemporaneous with the three Critiques, such as the *Anthropology* or any number of the shorter essays, such as those on the perpetual peace or the putative beginnings of mankind.

67. F. W. J. Schelling, *System of Transcendental Idealism*, trans. Michael Vater and Stephen Heath (Charlottesville: University of Virginia Press, 1978), 230. The German text used here is *System des Transzendentalen Idealismus*, Ed. Ruth-Eva Schulz (Hamburg: Felix Meiner, 1957).

68. It is no wonder that Schelling has of late emerged as a crucial figure in the antimetaphysical line of thinking that runs through Heidegger, Derrida, and others. This is visible in recent works such as Slavoj Žižek's *The Indivisible Remainder: An Essay on Schelling and Related Matters* (London: Verso, 1996); and in the work in progress of David Clark that will culminate in a book to be titled *Mourning Schelling: On the Remains of Idealism.* In the meantime one can consult the following essays by Clark: "Otherwise Than God: Marion, Schelling," in *Trajectories of Mysticism in Theory and Literature,* ed. Phillip Leonard (London: Macmillan, 2000), 133–76; "Mourning Becomes Theory: Schelling and the Absent Body of Philosophy," in "Schelling and Romanticism," *Romantic Circles Praxis Series,* ed. David Ferris (June 2000): 16 pars. http://www.rc.umd.edu/praxis/schelling/clark/clark.html; "Heidegger's Craving: Being-on-Schelling," *diacritics* 27.3 (1997): 8–33; "The Necessary Heritage of Darkness: Tropics of Negativity in Schelling, Derrida, and de Man," *Intersections: Nineteenth-Century Philosophy and Contemporary Theory,* ed. Tilottama Rajan and David L. Clark (Albany: SUNY Press, 1995), 79–146. Especially the first essay by Clark noted above addresses the problematic of thinking God outside the traditional metaphysical category of being.

69. On the place of art in Schelling's philosophy, see the excellent and thorough account by Dieter Jähnig, *Schelling.* Not the least virtue of Jähnig's study derives from his profound knowledge of Hölderlin's writings, especially the texts about poetry.

70. See Friedrich Wilhelm Joseph Schelling, *Schriften 1804–1812* (Berlin: Union Verlag, 1982), p. 80. The last phrase is cited from "Religion und Philosophie," a lengthy, major (and to my knowledge, untranslated) essay from 1804.

71. *System of Transcendental Idealism,* p. 230.

72. Schelling sometimes spoke of language as a miraculous medium for passing from the inside to the out and back. See the version of *The Ages of the World* (1946), 56–57. F. W. J. Schelling, *Die Weltalter. In den Urfassungen von 1811 und 1813,* ed. Manfred Schröter, C. H. Beck, 1946, 56–7.

73. For a searching analysis of the problematic of philosophy in the university, see Jacques Derrida, "Language and Institutions of Philosophy," *Recherches Semiotiques/Semiotic Inquiry* (June 1985): 91–154. The fourth and final segment of the essay is about Schelling and is entitled "Theology of Translation." For the English version of the Schelling text under consideration I am using F. W. J. Schelling, *On University Studies,* trans. E. S. Morgan, ed. Norbert Guterman (Athens, Ohio: Ohio University Press, 1966). The German text is F. W. J. Schelling, *Vorlesungen über die Methode des akademischen Studiums,* ed. Walter E. Ehrhardt (Hamburg: Felix Meiner, 1974).

74. This corresponds with Novalis's notion of Christianity, although he conceives of it in terms of *The Bible* being open ended, not just the religion based in the Bible.

75. Lessing's text was seminal for the entire generation of thinkers under con-

sideration, Hegel perhaps foremost of all. On the Biblical triadic rhythm of history, transposed to literary and philosophical texts of the Romantic period (mainly British and German), see the comprehensive study by M. H. Abrams, *Natural Supernaturalism.*

76. On the late phase of Schelling's work in relation to the itineraries of German Idealism, see the magisterial work by Walter Schulz, *Die Vollendung des deutschen Idealismus in der Spätphilosophie Schellings* (Pfullingen: Neske, 1975). I was fortunate to be able to hear Schulz's last lectures on Hegel at the University of Tübingen in the fall of 1977, when he continued to read Schelling as a foil to the not-so-absolute Hegel. For Schulz and others, the "late" phase of the career begins long before the end, and indeed often with the "Freedom" essay of 1809 or with *The Ages of the World,* whose first version comes from 1813.

77. For a good account of the intellectual scene at the historic juncture of Schelling's lectures see Manfred Frank's introduction to his edition of F. W. J. Schelling, *Philosophie der Offenbarung 1841/42* (Frankfurt am Main: Suhrkamp, 1977). For an informed overview of Schelling's philosophy of religion, which takes the 1841 lectures as the point of departure, see Emil Fackenheim, "Schelling's Philosophy of Religion," in his *The God Within: Kant, Schelling, and Historicity,* ed. John Burbidge (Toronto, Buffalo, and London: University of Toronto Press, 1996), 92–108.

78. On the strange need to read Revelation literally, see Victor C. Hayes, *Schelling's Philosophy of Mythology and Revelation,* Australian Association for the Study of Religions, University of Western Sydney, 1995.

79. See the helpful essay by Michael Theunissen, "Die Dialektik der Offenbarung: Zur Auseinandestezung Schellings und Kierkegaards mit der Religionsphilosophie Hegels," in *Philosophisches Jahrbuch* 72 (1964/65): 134–60.

80. *Philosophie der Offenbarung,* 279. For a still valuable account of the framework surrounding this issue, see Paul Tillich, *The Construction of the History of Religion in Schelling's Positive Philosophy,* trans. and ed. Victor Nuovo (Lewisburg: Bucknell University Press, 1975).

81. Ibid., 281.

82. Ibid., 279.

83. Georg Lukács, *Der Junge Hegel,* vol. 1 (Frankfurt am Main: Suhrkamp, 1973), 43. Walter Kaufmann characterizes the same early writings as "antitheological." See his "Hegel's Early Antitheological Phase," *Philosophical Review* 63 (1954): 3–18.

84. *Hegel: The Letters,* trans. Clark Butler and Christiane Seiler (Bloomington: Indiana University Press, 1984), 28.

85. Ibid., 31.

86. Ibid.

87. Ibid.

88. For an adventurous reading of the institutional and conceptual/rhetoric

problematics of the early theological writings, see Hermann Timm, *Fallhöhe des Geistes: Das religiöse Denken des jungen Hegel* (Frankfurt am Main: Syndikat, 1979).

89. That is, in the twenty-volume edition of the *Werke* published by Suhrkamp (*TWA*), the "Life of Jesus" is nowhere to be found. And this is despite the fact that it is just about the only text of the period that has come down to us in completed form.

90. For one of the few good accounts of this text, see the superbly contextualized reading by H. S. Harris in his *Hegel's Development: Toward the Sunlight* (Oxford: Clarendon, 1972), esp. 194–207.

91. "The Life of Jesus," in Hegel, *Three Essays 1793–1795*, ed. and trans. Peter Fuss and John Dobbins (Notre Dame: University of Notre Dame Press, 1984), 104. The German text is found in *Hegels Theologische Jugendschriften*, ed. Hermann Nohl (Tübingen: J. C. B. Mohr, 1907).

92. Ibid., 118.

93. Ibid., 118.

94. Ibid., 37.

95. The later Hegel has very little to say about prophecy even in his extensive lectures on Christianity and Judaism in the late 1810s and throughout the 1820s. It seems that, in general, prophecy was something of an embarrassment for Hegel, a kind of discursive indignity beneath the absolute. Hegel seems to have shared an Enlightenment disdain for both prophecy and miracles, almost along the lines of an unbeliever like Hume. The young Hegel had a rather dim view of the Biblical prophets, seeing them as "national poets" who "harangue" their people (*Three Essays*, 60). In "The Spirit of Christianity" he sees the prophets caught in a noble but vain attempt to capture some of the former glory of the spirit of Judaism: "Inspired men had from time to time tried to cleave to the old genius of their nation and to revivify it in its death throes. But when the genius of the nation has fled, inspiration cannot conjure it back; inspiration cannot enchant away a people's fate, although if it be pure and living, it can call a new spirit forth out of the depths of its life. But the Jewish prophets kindled their flame from the torch of a languishing genius to which they tried to restore its old vigor and, by destroying the many-sided interests of the time, its old dread sublime unity" (*Early Theological Writings*, 203).

96. From "The Spirit of Christianity," in G. W. F. Hegel, *Early Theological Writings*, trans. T. M. Knox (Philadelphia: University of Pennsylvania Press, 1971), 256. For the German text, "Jesus trat night lange . . . ," see G. W. F. Hegel, *Der Geist des Christentums: Schriften 1796–1800*, ed. Werner Hamacher (Frankfurt am Main: Ullstein, 1978), 473.

97. For a thorough study of Hegel focusing on the Gospel story, see Stephen Crites, *Dialectic and Gospel in the Development of Hegel's Thinking* (University Park, Pa.: Penn State University Press, 1998).

98. See Jean-Luc Nancy, *La remarque spéculative: sur un bon mot de Hegel*

(Paris: Galilée, 1975). Translated by Celine Surprenant, *The Speculative Remark: (One of Hegel's Bons Mots)* (Stanford: Stanford University Press, 2001).

99. For the relevant passage from the very ending of the text, see G. W. F. Hegel, *Faith and Knowledge*, trans. Walter Cerf, ed. H. S. Harris (Binghamton: SUNY Press, 1977), 191. The parallel to the end of the *Phenomenology* with its vision of the Golgotha of the spirit is clear. For an inspired reading of what is at stake in the closing moments of the *Phenomenology* for the enterprise as a whole, see Rebecca Comay, "'Famous Last Words': Mourning and Melancholia at the End of Hegel's *Phenomenology*," forthcoming in a book entitled *Mourning Sickness: Hegel and the Impossibility of Memory*.

100. *Hegel's Phenomenology of Spirit*, trans. A. V. Miller (Oxford and New York: Oxford University Press, 1977), 463.

101. *TWA*, vol. 13, 21. *Hegel's Aesthetics*, vol. 1, 8.

102. The same is true for religion and its systemic place in Hegel's *Encyclopedia*.

103. The fullest study of Niethammer's career is by Michael Schwarzmeier, *Friedrich Immanuel Niethammer, ein bayerischer Schulreformer*. Schriften der bayerischen Landesgeschichte (München: C. H. Beck, 1937). Schwarzmeier necessarily focuses on the later work.

104. *GSA*, VI, 1. 206.

105. *GSA*, VI, 1. 203. My emphasis.

106. Niethammer has been conspicuously neglected in the literature on German Idealism. Two important exceptions to this tendency are Dieter Henrich, esp. *Der Grund im Bewußtsein: Untersuchungen zu Hölderlins Denken (1794–1795)* (Stuttgart: Klett-Cotta, 1992); and Manfred Frank, esp. in his *Unendliche Annäherung: Die Anfänge der philosophischen Frühromantik* (Frankfurt am Main: Suhrkamp, 1997).

107. For some time, though, as noted above, the identity of the author of the *Critique of All Revelation* was not known. Niethammer's commentary never mentions Fichte's name, nor Kant's.

108. *GSA* VI, 2, 705.

109. In his role as education administrator, in the early years of the nineteenth century, Niethammer was worried about the declining status of the Bible as a pedagogical text and meditated on the idea of a new poetic Bible that would serve as a "national book" to unify the German nation. For a brief, insightful discussion of this, see Friedrich Kittler, *Discourse Networks 1800/1900*, trans. Michael Metterer with Chris Cullen (Stanford: Stanford University Press, 1990), esp. 148–49. See also the discussion of Niethammer's project in relation to Goethe in the trenchant study by Aleida Assman, *Arbeit am nationalen Gedächtnis: Eine kurze Geschichte der deutschen Bildungsidee* (Frankfurt am Main/New York: Campus, 1993), 34 ff.

110. Soon, however, Niethammer's penchant for logical distinctions takes over, and the text becomes more demanding to follow.

111. Friedrich Immanuel Niethammer, *Uber den Versuch einer Kritik aller Of-*

fenbarung (Jena, 1972), 5. All further quotations will be given by page number in the body of the text. Translations are mine.

112. Published as a separate book. Neustrelitz, 1795.

113. Friedrich Immanuel Niethammer, *Versuch einer Begründung des Verninft-mäßigen OffenbarungsGlaubens* (*Attempt at a Foundation for Rational Belief in Revelation*) (Leipzig and Jena, 1798.) (The supplement was first published by Niethammer as an autoreview.) All quotations will be given by page number in the body of the text. Translations are mine.

114. For Schelling's brief, enthusiastic review of Niethammer's text, see his "Über Offenbarung und Volksunterricht," in *Historische-kritische Ausgabe im Auftrag der bayerischen Akademie der Wissenschaften*, vol. 4, ed. Wilhelm G. Jacobs and Walter Schieche (Stuttgart: Frohmann-Holzboog, 1988), 249–56.

115. Here we glimpse the side of Niethammer aligned with Pietism, a powerful force for Hölderlin, too.

116. For a good general account of how the poetry of Hölderlin engages issues in a way that is, if not theological, then in a certain strong relation to theology, see Wolfgang Binder, "Hölderlin: Theologie und Kunstwerk," *Hölderlin Jahrbuch* 17 (1971–72): 1–29.

117. See, among many relevant publications, Henrich's most extensive work, *Der Grund im Bewußtsein. Untersuchungen zu Hölderlins Denken (1794–1795)* (Stuttgart: Klett-Cotta, 1992).

118. Schmidt's fuller argument runs as follows: "Three images point to the revelation, to the becoming-'true' of the divine: the oncoming of the twilight and the morning ('between day and night,' 'morning airs,' 'the increase of the gold'—in Hölderlin always the symbol of the holy—until it overflows more than pure springs, until finally the storm brews in heaven, when the 'anger' becomes 'serious')." ("Drei Bilder deuten auf die Offenbarung, auf das 'Wahr' werden des Göttlichen: das Heraufkommen der Dämmerung und des Morgens ('zwischen Tag und Nacht,' 'Morgenlüfte,' 'das Anwachsen des Goldes'—bei Hölderlin immer das Symbol des Heiligen—bis es überflüßiger, denn lautere Quellen ist, schließlich das Gewitter, das sich am Himmel zusammenbraut, bis der 'Zorn' 'ernst' wird.") In "Der Begriff der Zorn in Hölderlins Spätwerk," *Hölderlin-Jahrbuch* (1967–68): 136.

119. Hölderlin here parallels the eagle-eyed viewpoint of Hegel in a famous passage from his lectures on the philosophy of history: "In general the movement of world history is given in the geographical overview. The sun, the light rises in the east ("morning-land"). Light is, however, relation to itself; the general light in itself is at the same time the subject in the sun. . . . World history moves from east to west, since Europe is absolutely the end of world history and Asia the beginning." ["In der geographischen Übersicht ist im allgemeinen der Zug der Weltgeschichte angegeben worden. Die Sonne, das Licht geht im Morgenlande auf. Das Licht ist aber Beziehung auf sich; das in sich selbst allgemeine Licht ist

zugleich als Subjekt in der Sonne. . . . Die Weltgeschichte geht von Osten nach Westen, denn Europa ist schlechtin das Ende der Weltgeschichte, Asien der Anfang."] *TWA*, 12, 133–34. In Hölderlin's poetry, numerous parallel trajectories riddle his poetic worldscapes, most notably in "Am Quell der Donau" and "Dichterberuf."

120. On this point see the helpful essay by Christoph Prignitz, "Der Gedanke des Vaterlands im Werk Hölderlins," *Jahrbuch des freien deutschen Hochstifts*, 1976, 88–113.

121. One could say that such a thinking is part of the grand project of Heidegger and of Derrida.

122. Hölderlin, however, is often disposed to harmonize the two rival mythologies, as we have noted above.

123. Hölderlin was almost undoubtedly familiar with Schiller's poem of the mid-1790s, "Spruche des Konfuzius," which begins "Dreifach ist der Schritt der Zeit;/Zögernd kommt die Zukunft hergezogen,/Pfeilschnell ist das Jetzt entflogen,/Ewig still steht die Vergangenheit." ("Threefold is the step of time;/the future comes hesitantly, pulled here, the past stands still eternally.") In *Werke in drei Bänden* (Munich: Hanser, 1966), II, 712. On the general problem of temporality in Hölderlin's poetry, which as lyric is often considered apart from questions of narrative, see the helpful study by Eric Santner, *Friedrich Hölderlin: Narrative Vigilance and the Poetic Imagination* (New Brunswick, N.J.: Rutgers University Press, 1986).

124. It so happens that Maurice Blanchot, who, unique among critics, pays particular attention to the "moment of truth" in "Germanien," cites the passage in question *three* times throughout his works. In *L'éspace littéraire* he characterizes the passage as possessing a "splendide rigeur"(Paris: Gallimard, 1955), 378. It is cited again as the epigraph for *La part du feu* (Paris: Gallimard, 1949), and in "La parole sacrée," in *La part du feu*, 129–30. Each of the translations is somewhat different.

125. *GSA* IV.1, 252.

126. For an instance of Hölderlin's use of "hyperbole" in the mathematical sense, see the end of the fragment "Hermokrates an Cephalus," *GSA* IV.1, 253.

127. *GSA* IV.1, 252–54. My emphasis.

128. V, 196.

129. IV, 244.

130. Hölderlin also writes: "Between the expression (the presentation) and the free idealistic treatment lies the foundation and meaning of the poem. This is what lends the poem its seriousness, its fixity, its truth." ("Zwischen dem Ausdrucke (der Darstellung) und der freien idealischen Behandlung liegt die Begründung und Bedeutung des Gedichte. Sie ist's, die dem Gedichte seiner Ernst, seine Festigkeit, seine Wahrheit gibt") (*GSA* IV.1, 245). The only critic, to my knowledge, who points to the importance of this alignment of meaning, truth, and transition is Annette Hornbacher, in her *Die Blume des Mundes: Zu Hölderlins poetol-*

ogisch-poetischem Sprachdenken (Würzburg: Königshausen & Neumann, 1995). See esp. chapter 3.

131. *GSA*, VI, 1, 303.

132. Paul de Man, "The Riddle of Hölderlin," *New York Review of Books* (Nov. 19, 1970), 52. The essay is reprinted in Paul de Man, *Critical Writings 1957–1978*, ed. Lindsay Waters (Minneapolis: University of Minnesota Press, 1983), 198–213.

133. For the two letters to Böhlendorff, see *GSA*, VI, 425–28 and 432–33. For the two most substantial readings of the letters, see Peter Szondi, "Hölderlins Überwindung des Klassizismus," in his *Hölderlin-Studien* (Frankfurt am Main: Suhrkamp, 197); and Andzej Warminski, "Hölderlin in France," *Studies in Romanticism* 22, no. 2 (summer 1983), 173–98.

134. For readings that detail the "internal foreignness" of Germany and the Germans, see Antoine Berman, *L'épreuve de l'étranger: culture et traduction dans l'Allemagne romantique* (Paris: Gallimard, 1984), esp. chapter 2: "le national et l'étranger," 250–78.

CHAPTER 8

1. For a still valuable general account of Coleridge's poetry, see Reeve Parker, *Coleridge's Art of Meditation* (Ithaca and London: Cornell University Press, 1977). On the more particular topic of inspiration and the sense that the voice is possessed by some other or something else, see Susan Eilenberg, *Strange Power of Speech: Wordsworth, Coleridge, and Literary Possession* (New York: Oxford University Press, 1992).

2. *Economy and Society*, trans. various hands (Berkeley and Los Angeles: University of California Press, 1978), 138.

3. It should be acknowledged that Coleridge's distinction between symbol and allegory has numerous parallels in Continental, especially German thought, as in Schelling and, to a lesser extent, Goethe.

4. Among the important readings that go beyond the set piece on symbol and allegory are Frances Ferguson, "Coleridge on Language and Delusion," *Genre* 2 (summer 1978), 191–207; Jean-Pierre Mileur, "Biblical History and the Author's Share: *The Statesman's Manual*," in *Vision and Revision: Coleridge's Art of Immanence* (Berkeley: University of California Press, 1981), chapter 4; John A. Hodgson, "Transcendental Tropes: Coleridge's Rhetoric of Allegory and Symbol," in *Allegory, Myth, and Symbol*, ed. Morton W. Bloomfield, Harvard University English Studies 9 (Cambridge: Harvard University Press, 1981), 273–92; Steven Knapp, *Personification and the Sublime* (Cambridge: Harvard University Press, 1985), chapter 1. Even when these critics deal suggestively with issues of history and violence, they still leave the question of Coleridge's politics largely unexamined.

5. *The Complete Works of William Hazlitt*, ed. P. P. Howe (London: J. M. Dent, 1930–34), VII, 115.

6. Ibid., VII, 115.

7. On Coleridge's review of his own work, see David V. Erdman, "Coleridge on Coleridge," in *Studies in Romanticism* I (1961): 47–64.

8. Coleridge contends at some points that *The Statesman's Manual* was addressed not so much to the Higher Classes in general as to the clerisy or "the Learned and Reflecting of all Ranks and Profession, especially among the Higher Class." See *Collected Letters of Samuel Taylor Coleridge* (Oxford: Clarendon Press, 1956–71), IV, 695. On the clerisy, see Stephen Prickett, "Coleridge and the Idea of the Clerisy," *Reading Coleridge*, ed. Walter B. Crawford (Ithaca and London: Cornell University Press, 1979), 252–73. For a briefer, more critical treatment, see Jerome McGann, *The Romantic Ideology* (Chicago: University of Chicago Press, 1983), chapter 9. On the social configurations of readership in the period and in relation to Coleridge, see the excellent study by Jon Klancher, *The Making of English Reading Audiences, 1790–1832* (Madison: University of Wisconsin Press, 1987).

9. *The Collected Works of Samuel Taylor Coleridge*, vol. 6, xxxiv. All further references to volume 6 (*Lay Sermons*) will be given by page number in the body of the text. References to other volumes of the *Collected Works* will be given by volume and page number in the text.

10. "Preface" to *Sibylline Leaves* (London, 1817).

11. "Popular" is a relative term here. The *Biographia Literaria* was neither well received nor much requested in Coleridge's lifetime. Its canonization as a central text of Romanticism was a long time in coming.

12. Hazlitt, for one, thought that texts tended to find their most appropriate class.

13. I discuss Godwin's theory of language and (briefly) the status of truth in relation to the political in my "Promises, Promises: Social and Other Contracts in the English Jacobins (Godwin/Inchbald)," in *New Romanticisms*, ed. David L. Clark and Donald C. Goellnicht (Toronto: University of Toronto Press, 1994), 225–50. For an impressively wide-ranging account of the performative in the period, see Angela Esterhammer, *The Romantic Performative: Language and Action in British and German Romanticism* (Stanford: Stanford University Press, 2000).

14. This can be only a generalization, however. Appeals to absolute truth, often accompanied by citations of divine authority, span the political spectrum in Coleridge's day and our own.

15. *CW*, I, 149–50.

16. *Marginalia* I, in *CW*, III, 438.

17. For a sustained and acute reading of the Wordsworth-Burke relation, including a discussion of the question of "theory," see James Chandler, *Wordsworth's Second Nature* (Chicago: University of Chicago Press, 1984).

18. I cannot take up here the tangled question of natural law in Burke. In short, he both does and does not appeal to nature (and its laws or lawlike order) in his analyses of history and politics.

19. Austin shows how there can be no reliable grammatical test of a statement's performative or constative character. Hence the need to consider the totality of the speech situation or its rhetorical scene, broadly understood.

20. In the second Lay Sermon, Coleridge notes, on a related matter, the "promise" from Isaiah that is the text of his sermon—the saying "Blessed are ye that sow beside all waters"—is a "Command in the form of a Promise" (140), thus acknowledging that what appears to be one kind of speech-act can function in a mode different from its apparent one.

21. Elinor Shaffer notes the importance of this passage and the way it has been made possible by the work of the Higher Criticism of the Bible. See *"Kubla Khan" and "The Fall of Jerusalem,"* 45.

22. For an elaborate demonstration of this tendency, see Paul de Man, "Shelley Disfigured," *The Rhetoric of Romanticism*, 93–125.

23. On the importance of faith in Coleridge's program, see Wayne C. Anderson, "The Prince of Preparatory Authors: The Problem of Conveying Belief in Coleridge's *The Statesman's Manual*," in *The Wordsworth Circle* 14 (1978), 28–32. Anderson shows how in Coleridge's argument understanding is dependent on faith.

24. Part of the text's power lies in its mobilization of citations. As Emerson said: "We value Coleridge for his quotations." See his essay "Quotation and Originality," in *Ralph Waldo Emerson*, Oxford Authors Series (Oxford: Oxford University Press, 1990).

25. Northrop Frye, *The Great Code* (New York and London: Harcourt Brace Jovanovich, 1982), 125.

26. There is even, as R. J. White notes in his edition of the *Lay Sermons*, considerable doubt as to whether the frost was premature or not. See the first editor's footnote on 35.

27. For a detailed analysis of the centrality of the "I am" in Coleridge's work, see Thomas McFarland, *Coleridge and the Pantheist Tradition* (Oxford: Oxford University Press, 1969). I will return later to address this problematic in the *Biographia Literaria*.

28. For an illuminating treatment of this problematic, geared somewhat more to allusion than quotation, see David Bromwich, *Hazlitt: The Mind of a Critic* (New York and Oxford: Oxford University Press, 1983), chapter 9.

29. *Confessions of an Inquiring Spirit.*, 41–42. I cite this from the most readily available edition for in the more exact redition from the new Collected Works the passage reads: "I will retire from the Multitude 'up into the Mountain,' and hold secret commune with the Bible . . . " (*Shorter Works and Fragments II*, ed. H. J. Jackson and J. R. de J. Jackson (Princeton: Princeton University Press, 1995), 1120. The editors indicate that the phrase "Up into the Mountain" points to something like the Mosaic theophany in Exodus 24.15–18.

30. *CW*, XIII, 23.

31. *The Citizen of the World*, in *Works* (Oxford: Oxford University Press, 1966),

II, 465. Not all editions of Goldsmith (Masson's, for example) recount the anecdote in the same form, but the outlines and moral are essentially the same in all the versions of which I am aware.

32. One could add, however, in Coleridge's defense that there was a certain pervasive myth of English—especially Protestant—liberty such that nationalism did, in some respects, tend to override class differences. See, for example, Linda Colley, *Britons: Forging the Nation 1707–1837* (New Haven and London: Yale University Press, 1992), esp. chapter 2, "Protestants."

33. For an insightful general account of the anecdote as a genre in historiography and literary history, see Joel Fineman, "The History of the Anecdote: Fiction and Friction," in *The New Historicism*, ed. H. Aram Veeser (New York and London: Routledge, 1989), 49–76.

34. *Collected Letters*, Vol. 1, 214.

35. *CW*, I, 226

36. *CW*, III, 1, 372–73. One should not imply, however, that to be antiproperty was a guarantee of radicalism or, even more, that to be proproperty was conservative. The most radical politicophilosophical work of the 1790s, Godwin's *An Enquiry Concerning Political Justice*, repeatedly speaks of property as "sacred."

37. For a useful full-scale study of the topic of property in its historical and philosophical context, see John Morrow, *Coleridge's Political Thought: Property, Morality, and the Limits of Traditional Discourse* (New York: St. Martin's Press, 1990). The most germane section is chapter 4, "Politics, Property, and Political Economy, 1810–19."

38. See, for example, Jerome Christensen, "'Like a Guilty Thing Surprised': Deconstruction, Coleridge, and the Apostasy of Criticism," *Critical Inquiry* 12 (summer 1986), 769–87, as well as his short statement "Once an Apostate Always an Apostate," *Studies in Romanticism*, vol. 21, no. 3 (fall 1982), 461–74. See also Norman Fruman, *The Damaged Archangel* (New York: Braziller, 1971). For a classic, although contested, statement on Coleridge's apostasy, see E. P. Thompson, "Disenchantment or Default? A Lay Sermon," in *Power and Consciousness*, ed. Conor Cruise O'Brien and William Dean Vanech (New York: NYU Press, 1969), 149–81. There is no need to measure all Coleridge's pronouncements by the hobgoblin of "foolish consistency." But it is important to recognize the similarity of rhetorical strategy involved in arguing radically different positions.

39. In polemicizing against Cobbett, Hunt, Francis Jeffrey, and company, Coleridge exclaims: "On all occasions, but most of all and with a more bustling malignity, whenever any public distress inclines the lower classes to turbulence, and renders them more apt to be alienated from the government of their country—in all places and at every opportunity pleading *to* the Poor and Ignorant, no where and at no time are they found actually pleading *for* them" (148).

40. *Collected Letters*, IV, 714. In the passage of the second Lay Sermon that

deals with just these incendiaries, Coleridge accuses them of hating the very people they think of as their constituencies and raises the stakes by quoting the Gospel of John: "He that hateth his brother is a murderer" (145).

41. Ibid., 679.

42. For an excellent survey of Cobbett's life and work as well as the Cobbett phenomenon, see Raymond Williams, *Cobbett* (Oxford and New York: Oxford University Press, 1983).

43. For a good account of the reformist impulse in Cobbett, see David Bromwich, *A Choice of Inheritance* (Cambridge, Mass.: Harvard University Press, 1989), chapter 2.

44. In *On the Constitution of Church and State* Coleridge writes in a similar vein that "the mistaking of symbols and analogies for metaphors . . . has been a main occasion and support of the worst of errors in Protestantism." See *On the Constitution of Church and State*, ed. John Colmer (Princeton and London: Princeton University Press and Routledge & Kegan Paul, 1976), 120n.

45. Paul de Man, *Blindness and Insight*, rev. ed. (Minneapolis: University of Minnesota Press, 1983), 192.

46. See Jerome Christensen, "The Symbol's Errant Allegory: Coleridge and his Critics," *ELH* (1978): 640–42. Christensen's point about translucence is well taken, but one aspect of his argument is less telling, if intended as a criticism of de Man's reading. He writes: "It is an error for the deconstructor to privilege theory and practice as either discrete, inviolable regions of discourse or as polemical counters: Those modes must be figured as allegorical signs within the general text we know as 'Coleridge.' As we shall see, in Coleridge the undeniable and pervasive wish for a metaphysical continuity that is involved in his promotion of the symbol is typically breached by a discourse that divulges the obdurate discontinuities of signification. Coleridge's metaphysical symbolism is transgressed by a discursive allegory." Christensen is exactly right, but the same point could be derived from de Man's reading, especially in the larger context of "The Rhetoric of Temporality." Steven Knapp also criticizes de Man's insistence on the materiality of the symbol, noting that "what is at issue in the promotion of the symbol is not the metaphysical status of representation but the practical consequences of action and belief" (*Personification and the Sublime*, 16). Knapp is correct to underline practical consequences in this highly political text, but the metaphysical and the political cannot be disentangled in this text or in Coleridge generally. Coleridge goes out of his way—often in cumbersome fashion—to ground political action and interpretation in a principled metaphysics and a theology. That is to say, Coleridge cannot easily be enlisted in a pragmatist argument "against theory."

47. For a full discussion of this problem in Coleridge, see Anthony John Harding's informative study, *Coleridge and the Inspired Word* (Kingston and Montreal: McGill-Queen's University Press, 1985).

48. One might summarize Coleridge's position by saying that the Bible contains the word of God without always literally reproducing it. Again, for the fullest study of this topic, see Harding's *Coleridge and the Inspired Word.*

49. Ezekiel's vision of the chariot was a crucial text for several of the Romantics, especially Shelley. See Harold Bloom, "Shelley and His Precursors," in *Poetry and Repression* (New Haven and London: Yale University Press, 1976), 83–111.

50. This effacement of figurality seems related to the distinctly un-Kantian notion that ideas of reason can be incorporated in sense. The *Critique of Pure Reason* makes it clear that ideas of reason cannot, strictly speaking, even be represented, much less incorporated in the media available to the senses. Coleridge's passage thus marks a sharp divergence from Kant in a text otherwise massively indebted to him.

51. For Maimonides' rich reading of this passage, see his *Guide for the Perplexed,* 2 vols., trans. Shlomo Pines (Chicago and London: University of Chicago Press, 1963).

52. The fullest study of this and related issues in Coleridge is by James McCusick, *Coleridge's Philosophy of Language* (New Haven and London: Yale University Press, 1986). In general McCusick's commentary and analysis are lucid and accurate, although I would part company with his discussion of the "arbitrariness" of the sign in Locke, which he takes to be negatively marked. Although that arbitrariness is partly problematic for Locke, it also, as later in Hegel, serves as a test, a vehicle for, and a proof of the active powers of the mind.

53. On the metaphorical character of Aristotle's definition of metaphor, see Jacques Derrida's magisterial essay "White Mythology: Metaphor in the Text of Philosophy," in *Margins,* trans. Alan Bass (Chicago: University of Chicago Press, 1982), 207–73; as well as, for a more extended discussion of the "vehicular" character of metaphor, Derrida's "Le retrait de la métaphore," in *Psyché* (Paris: Galilée, 1987), 63–94.

54. Herbert Marks eloquently sums up what is at stake in the chariot passage by saying: "The *merkabah,* or divine chariot, is a paradoxical icon of mobility, a literal and figurative vehicle whose only goal is to evade by constant transference all recuperative translations." See his "On Prophetic Stammering," *Yale Journal of Criticism,* vol. 1, no. 1 (fall 1987), 8.

55. Robert Barth, S. J., has rightly called attention to the sacramental character of the symbol. See esp. the first chapter of his study *The Symbolic Imagination* (Princeton: Princeton University Press, 1977). For a more general account of Coleridge's theology, see Barth's *Coleridge and Christian Doctrine* (Cambridge, Mass.: Harvard University Press, 1969).

56. On the complicated issue of the real presence in Reformation and post-Reformation thinking, see Jaroslav Pelikan, *The Christian Tradition: A History of the Development of Doctrine,* vol. 4 (*Reformation of Church and Dogma (1300–1700)*) (Chicago and London: University of Chicago Press, 1984).

57. For an extended and rigorous analysis of this issue (reading—incorpora-

tion—the Eucharist) primarily in Hegel but also in European thought from the Enlightenment to Lacan and Derrida, see Werner Hamacher, *Pleroma—zu Genesis und Struktur einer dialektischen Hermeneutik bei Hegel,* which is a book-length introduction to his edition of G. W. F. Hegel, *Der Geist des Christentums: Schriften 1796–1800* (Berlin: Ullstein, 1978). Wordsworth proposes a model of language as incarnation or incorporation in his *Essays Upon Epitaphs*: "Words are too awful an instrument for good and evil to be trifled with: They hold above all other external powers a dominion over thoughts. If words be not . . . an incarnation of the thought but only a clothing of it, then surely will they prove an ill gift; such a one as those poisoned vestments, read of in the stories of superstitious times, which had power to consume and to alienate from his right mind the victim who had put them on." In *Wordsworth's Literary Criticism,* ed. J. B. Owen (London: Routledge & Kegan Paul, 1974), 154.

58. See J. Robert Barth, S. J.: "It is far from a matter of taking Coleridge too literally; on the contrary, the problem comes from not taking him literally enough. Coleridge means what he says: The symbol truly partakes of the reality it represents." In *The Symbolic Imagination,* 115.

59. M. H. Abrams makes the helpful point that the symbol, for Coleridge, is "a specialized term that applies only to objects in the Book of Scripture and the Book of Nature, as he is at pains to point out in *The Statesman's Manual,* in passages which present-day critics unwarily cite as though they applied to any literary use of 'symbols' in the broad modern sense." See "Coleridge and the Romantic Vision of the World," in *The Correspondent Breeze* (New York: Norton, 1984), 221. Abrams's cautionary remark has not had as decisive an effect on Coleridge scholarship as it should have. The restriction of the symbol to the language of the Bible and the language of Nature, however, does not dissipate all its conceptual and rhetorical problems as presented in *The Statesman's Manual.*

60. I am assuming, following Nietzsche, that there is no such a thing as a human language without figuration. But even if one posits such a language, the performance of Coleridge's text cannot live up to its claim. For Nietzsche's view of the irreducibly figural character of language, see *Friedrich Nietzsche on Rhetoric and Language,* ed. and trans. Sander L. Gilman, Carole Blair, and David J. Parent (New York and Oxford: Oxford University Press, 1989). Nietzsche's most extreme formulation reads: "What is usually called language is all figuration." ("Eigentlich ist alles Figuration, was man gewöhnlich Rede nennt.") See p. 25 for the English and p. 24 for the German.

61. A draft of the same passage is found in *The Notebooks of Samuel Taylor Coleridge,* vol. 3, ed. Kathleen Coburn (Princeton: Princeton University Press, 1973), entry number 4503. I am grateful to Tony Brinkley for pointing out this passage to me.

62. *Collected Letters,* IV, 714.

63. A rather different political profile emerges in the second sermon, dictated

in part by Coleridge's audience. The text is marked by an anticommercialism and anticapitalism that one could hardly glimpse in the first sermon.

64. As an institution, religion functions as a mediating force, much like the symbol does in linguistic terms and the imagination does in the register of the psyche.

65. See, for example, the discussion of Coleridge in James Engell, *The Creative Imagination* (Cambridge, Mass. and London: Harvard University Press, 1981).

66. The burden of moving from the "I" of subjective experience to the universality of judgment *as if* of a logical judgment is the undertaking of Kant's aesthetics.

67. Walter Benjamin, *The Origin of German Tragic Drama*, trans. John Osborne (London: New Left Books, 1977), 160.

68. Thomas McFarland, "Involute and Symbol in the Romantic Imagination," in *Coleridge, Keats and the Imagination*, ed. J. Robert Barth, S.J. and John L. Mahoney (Columbia and London: University of Missouri Press, 1990), 42.

Index

Adorno, Theodoro, 174–75
allegory, and Benjamin, 148; and Blake, 140, 147–52 passim, 159; and Coleridge, 4, 251–52, 270–83 passim; and Collins, 28; and de Man, 148, 248; and Eichhorn, 118; and Hölderlin, 201, 248; and Lowth, 62–63, 67, 69, 71; and Spenser, 149; and Swinburne, 147; and Wordsworth, 24; Christian, 159
anxiety of influence, 31, 41–42, 156
apocalypse, 2, 30; and Blake, 141, 155, 160, 165, 170–71; and Bloom, 37; and Gibbon, 83; and Hurd, 83–89 passim, 100, 103; and Klopstock, 42; and Shelley, 37; and Smart, 34; and Warburton, 100; and Wordsworth, 25–26; and Young, 32
Aristotle, 274–75
apostrophe, 78–79
Augustine, 56. See also figurative language
Austin, J. L., 11, 70, 97, 130, 257

bard, and Biblical prophet, 30; and Blake, 137, 151–53, 157, 160; and Collins, 27; and Gray, 30–31
Barth, Karl, 106
Bate, Walter Jackson, 31
Benjamin, Walter, 6–18, 148, 155, 208, 263; "Critique of Violence," 14; The Concept of Aesthetic Critique in German Romanticism, 13; letter to Martin

Buber, 7–10; The Origin of German Tragic Drama, 282; "Theses on the Philosophy of History," 15–18. See also allegory; historicism; Messianic; poetry; translation
Bible, and historicism, 37; as literature, 56, 122; and myth, 2, 37, 77, 120; and poetry, 37, 56–81 passim; Daniel, 91, 104, 142; Deuteronomy, 64, 72–75 passim, 80, 85; Ezekiel, 33, 50–51, 56, 93, 97–101 passim, 120, 132–35 passim, 141, 144, 150, 160–61, 165–70 passim, 200, 251, 273–78 passim; Genesis, 11–12, 115–19 passim, 218; Habbakuk, 141, 145; Isaiah, 25, 38, 56, 60, 73–81 passim, 85–86, 91–92, 108–10, 120, 132–36 passim, 140, 145, 150–54 passim, 165, 168, 251, 256, 260–64, 275; Jeremiah, 23, 25, 33, 79, 85, 97–99, 150, 160–61, 255; Job, 38, 64, 147, 234; Jonah, 32, 129–30, 258; John, 104, 111, 136, 145, 170, 200, 228–30; Mark, 168, 213; Matthew, 168–69; New Testament, 42, 73–74, 82, 86, 90–93, 111, 121, 167, 217, 223, 228–32 passim, 259–60, 275; Old Testament, 20, 27, 86, 90–94 passim, 109–115 passim, 170, 226, 259–61; Paul, 104, 131–36 passim, 148, 159, 215–18 passim, 229, 259; Pentateuch, 75, 118; Proverbs, 60, 183; Psalms, 59–60, 78; Revelation, 25–26, 85, 103–4, 142, 145, 160, 169–71 passim, 200, 225, 230–31; Song of

Cultural Memory | *in the Present*

J. Hillis Miller / Manuel Asensi, *Black Holes / J. Hillis Miller; or, Boustrophedonic Reading*

Miryam Sas, *Fault Lines: Cultural Memory and Japanese Surrealism*

Peter Schwenger, *Fantasm and Fiction: On Textual Envisioning*

Didier Maleuvre, *Museum Memories: History, Technology, Art*

Jacques Derrida, *Monolingualism of the Other; or, The Prosthesis of Origin*

Andrew Baruch Wachtel, *Making a Nation, Breaking a Nation: Literature and Cultural Politics in Yugoslavia*

Niklas Luhmann, *Love as Passion: The Codification of Intimacy*

Mieke Bal, ed., *The Practice of Cultural Analysis: Exposing Interdisciplinary Interpretation*

Jacques Derrida and Gianni Vattimo, eds., *Religion*